JOOMLA!® 5:
BOOTS ON THE GROUND
Advance Edition
VOLUME 1

Herb Boeckenhaupt
Author

= = = = = = = = = =

Brandon Batie – Utah, USA
Philip Cave – Leeds, UK
Technical Editors

Sharon Lee Hall
Proofreader & Continuity

= = = = =

September 2022

All about Joomla! 5 by the How To Do It Gurus

HOW TO DO IT?
All about Joomla! 5 by the How To Do It Gurus

JOOMLA!® 5:
BOOTS ON THE GROUND
Advance Edition
VOLUME 1

Herb Boeckenhaupt
Author

Brandon Batie – Utah, USA
Philip Cave – Leeds, UK
Technical Editors

Sharon Lee Hall
Proofreading/Continuity

September 2022

The *"How To Do It GURU"* and *"Boots on the Ground,"* are Publishing projects of the 200mph Media Group, LLC, for the purpose of authoring and distributing books as learning and instruction tutorials about the Open Source program, JOOMLA!® 5, and other software products or Extensions to those products.

Book Registration Information

Paperback ISBN - 9798353320951

Publisher Contact Information

Herb Boeckenhaupt
200mph Media Group, LLC
240 Red Fox Run, Salisbury, NC 28147 USA
Publisher@howtodoit.guru

TABLE OF CONTENTS

Actual contents are subject to change, revisions and corrections based on the final, Stable Release, of the Joomla! 5 program.

x

xii

xviii

JOOMLA!® 5
BOOTS ON THE GROUND
ADVANCE EDITION
VOLUME 1

"Joomla! 5: Boots on the Ground, Advance Edition" is a two-book group that covers all aspects related to the administration of a Joomla! 5 website.

This book, *"Joomla! 5: Boots on the Ground, Advance Edition, Volume 1,"* is the first Joomla! 5 book to be released in the series since the new version was announced. It is possible that some differences might be noted with respect to the content of this book and the final version of the Joomla! 5 release. It is doubtful that the changes will be major ones that would adversely affect the Administrator's ability to create and manage the website. There may be improvements and enhancements and those will, in all probability, be minor in nature. Certainly, they will not reach the level whereby an Administrator could not distinguish differences and alter procedures as outlined in the Chapter Exercises.

References within this Book

There are references in this book at refer to other "Boots on the Ground" Chapters in the companion *Volume 2*. Those references are placed in the text to let you know where more advanced information about the topic is available. This book, *Volume 1*, contains thirty-one (31) Chapters.

Volume 2 will contain more advanced topics relative to Joomla! 5 website administration, beginning with Chapter Thirty-Two (32). See *Appendix A* for a list of the Chapter topics to be covered in the second volume. There will be twenty-eight (28) or more Chapters in the companion edition.

Updates, Corrections to Content

This publication and it's accuracy is subject to change based on the final release version of the Joomla! 5 program. Any deviation between the contents of this book and the final release version is subject to change and/or correction as required.

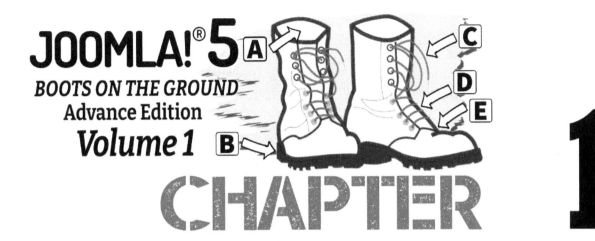

INTRODUCTION:
New Joomla! 5 Edition

Many of today's websites are created using the increasingly popular online services that create websites with pre-written material and nice photos, where all a website administrator needs to do is stick in some of their own text and use the stock photos. Before the advent of online website-tonight services, website administrators had to do a lot of coding for even a basic website. The internet realm was owned by programmers and coders who had the market cornered.

Shortly after the internet and websites came into being, a new way of building websites started being used. It was called a Content Management System ("CMS" for short). A "CMS" operated on a whole different premise than the old code-a-page methods.

This was a major leap forward and made it much easier for people to build websites. In fact, almost overnight, thousands upon thousands of people acquired website building skills. Being a website administrator became a very competitive business. However, the coders still had the competitive for-hire edge because there were not too many good, by today's standards, "CMS" programs available.

Filling the Void
Joomla! was one of the early programs that filled the void between website coders and non-coders. Wordpress also came onto the scene, but it was still code intensive and somewhat difficult to use. It was also limited pretty much to "blog" type of websites,

Joomla! caused the axis of building websites to shift and brought many new website administrators into play that were not actually programmers savvy enough to administer Wordpress websites. Joomla! featured the "model-view-controller" method whereby the program operating code, website content and design were all separate elements.

Since then, Joomla! was to become a different breed of website building tool, and began setting the standard for how high-quality websites are created and administered. Joomla! 5 is an excellent example of how website building tools have advanced in the past few years. Joomla! 5 also allows developers to "layer" their Template and Page-Building Extensions into the platform. More on this subject in later chapters.

At present, Joomla! is used for about 1.5 percent of the worlds websites, which is a pretty significant number. This is more than the online services of Squarespace and Wix combined. However, Wordpress is still the dominant program because it specialized in a particular format (the "blog"). Joomla! websites can be created for any type of website and the "blog" content is but a small part of the possible types of content that can be created.

How Joomla! Arrived on the Scene

Joomla! was created from another open-source program called "Mambo" and offered a highly viable alternative. "Mambo" was created by several programmers in Australia. In 2005, Joomla! was "forked" off from "Mambo" under various open-source rules, thus creating a distinctly new product. Complete information about that event can be found using an internet search, so it will not be repeated here.

By separating content, design and background operating code, Joomla! was able to demonstrate that a decent website could be created by simply placing content and images into a template thus building a website that was different than any others.

That method worked quite well except for one thing. The sophistication of the internet realm and service providers were taking quantum leaps forward and it was hard to keep pace, but a corps of volunteer programmers joined the effort and kept coding away and improving Joomla! By the looks of Version 3 and 4 and the new Version 5, they have succeeded well beyond the expectations of any detractors.

The coders and programmers, along with all the support teams and committees deserve a great deal of recognition and credit for their efforts in bringing the product from conception to implementation and making it one of the most popular "CMS" programs in the world.

Recognizing the Programmers

Here is a "**WELL DONE**" from the 200mph Media Group, LLC., to all of the great programmers involved in bringing Joomla! 5 to life. Your efforts are well-recognized by not only our company, but by all of those that have benefited from the software, and there are hundreds of thousands that have done so. We acknowledge your great work by using the "Boots on the Ground" name for our Joomla! 5 book series

– in recognition of the "army" of volunteer programmers that have made the program a demonstrated success through innovation.

The "drag and drop" Website Services

With online website building services, you can "drag 'n drop" text, images and a bunch of other stuff into a pre-made website layout. That might be fine for individuals or small businesses that only need an internet presence. However, they come up short if you need a more robust website with sophisticated content and interactions between screens and more, especially websites for businesses.

That is not to say that when used to build a website on their platforms, some of the "drag 'n drop" website builders do not provide some advanced features. The major difference is in the approach and the fact that multiple users can participate in content editing in Joomla!, plus it provides many more types of static and dynamic content. This is something which "drag 'n drop" doesn't offer across the board.

They Fill a Niche

Small business owners know "their business" and work hard at making it a success. Their desire for a personalized website has brought about those "drag 'n drop" type of website builders so they can put together an acceptable website without a lot of stress of website-building knowledge.

The problem is that many, many websites tend to begin to be nothing more than clones or "look a likes" as a result. With Joomla! 5 and a knowledgeable Administrator, a highly personalized website can be developed with many, many features not found in the "drag 'n drop" platforms.

There is no intent here to downplay the value or functional quality of the online website building services, or website-tonight website builders. They, and other "CMS" programs all have their place in the website world.

The Goal of this Book

We really do not want to generate an argument about which website service or method is better. Nor do we wish to perform massive comparisons of website building services and Joomla!, Wordpress, Squarespace, Wix and a host of other services all have their place. In fact, there are many new similar services with newer Bootstrap features available, so things are getting very competitive for all of them.

Our goal, through Publishing this book, is to make you a proficient Administrator of the Joomla! 5 Bootstrap 5 Edition so you can create websites that transcend the cookie cutter environment.

Our focus will be on getting an Administrator quickly up to speed on the use of Joomla! 5 so you can install, create and manage a website and its content on one of the world's most robust and highly popular website platforms that is being used on millions of website around the world.

Updating from Version 3 or 4

Joomla! 5 has been released as a "Stable" version, one that can be used for active websites and also meaning it will be possible to upgrade websites from Version 3 to Version 4 and then to Version 5. There may also be a direct upgrade path from Version 3 directly to Version 5 [possibly!].

However, this upgrade only applies to the core-Joomla! platform. Templates and Extensions that have been added to Version 3 may not work with Version 4 nor Version 5. It's a good bet they will not, so prepare for that eventuality.

This subject will be discussed further detail with additional information in Chapter 36, "UPDATING: Joomla! 5 from Joomla! 3 & 4," *Joomla! 5: Boots on the Ground, Advance Edition, Volume 2*.

Get Up to Speed With Joomla! 5

Because Joomla! 5 is the latest generation and will be supported for years to come, Joomla! 3 and 4 will slowly become the "version of the past." Both Versions will also stop being supported at some point, so it is suggested that getting up to speed on Joomla! 5 will be to your advantage. Joomla! 3 and 4 can still be used to create websites and there are thousands of Extensions available that may be added. However, anticipate that "nothing new" will be added to Joomla! 3, and that Joomla! 5 will be the focus of both Template and Extension developers from now on.

Joomla! 5 Announced Early

The joomla.org website indicated in later 2022 that Joomla! 5 is in the works and that it might be ready at some point in the not-too-distant future That is why we did an immediate deep dive to determine if there are any significant differences from the Administrator's functions and possible actions.

We did not find any in the newly improved Joomla! 5 platform. The "Home Dashboard" and the functions are exactly the same as Joomla! 4. To make this book as current as possible, we have upgraded all of the Content and Exercises for Joomla! Version 5. What can be determined is that most of the improvements have all been within the Back-End and the core platform. There were no noticeable changes in the screen layouts and the administrative techniques.

How this Book Works: The *"Boots on the Ground"* Approach

First, Chapters in this book will be technical and direct to the point with as much detailed information presented in an understandable way.

Second, descriptions and explanations will be devoted to "what" you will be doing and then "how to do it." More detailed information about every Joomla! 5 topic can be found in the companion books in the upcoming *"Boots on the Ground"* Series. See the end of this book for the future planned titles.

Third, comprehensive Exercises will be included that will guide you step-by-step through the processes of creating everything regarding Content on the website.

Fourth, if and when known issues or potential problem areas are identified, you will be alerted to them with suggestions on how to avoid any issues. If there are any, work-arounds will also be explained.

Fifth, by following the Exercises from the start of the book onward, you will be progressively building a website where most of the features of Joomla! 5 will be explained through practical participation in performing Administrator's tasks. You will not be building a content-filled website. What you will be building is a website that demonstrates the many "how's" of doing things on the Joomla! 5 platform.

Sixth, Exercises will build Content and features upon the previous Exercises so there will be visible results of the actions taken as you progress through the Chapters of this book. You should start completing Exercises early on, all those that follow will build upon them. Start doing the Exercises in Chapter 7 and continue thereafter.

So, with that, let's lace up and put our *"boots on the ground,"* march forward in the footsteps and start using this new Joomla! 5 Bootstrap 5 Version.

Our Previously Published Joomla Titles:

	**Joomla! 1.6** **Cengage Publishing** **PICTURE YOURSELF SERIES** **Building a Website** **in 20 Minutes!**	Also translated into Spanish Language. Sold worldwide via Amazon.com and in retail bookstores.
	**Joomla! 3 BOOT CAMP** **Cengage Publishing** **30-Minutes Lessons** **to Joomla! 3 Mastery**	Highly acclaimed book. Sold worldwide via Amazon.com and in retail bookstores. This book is still available online and in bookstores.
	**Joomla! 5: BASIC TRAINING – Boots on the Ground** **Published by the 200mph Media Group, LLC.** **and howtodoit.guru Publishing** This book is currently available online at *amazon.com* for the full-printed, paperback.	

JOOMLA!® 5 Ⓐ
BOOTS ON THE GROUND
Advance Edition
Volume 1 Ⓑ

Ⓒ
Ⓓ
Ⓔ

CHAPTER 2

INTRODUCTION:
Joomla! 5 and Bootstrap 5

Joomla! has released a recent version to which we devote this book. Version 5, the latest release, offers an incredible amount of latitude in creating all types of websites.

This updated version of Joomla! has, what can best be jokingly described as having "hair under its arms." It has monster improvements and integrations that are not readily visible to the common user, but be assured, there has been a lot of brilliant work and coding put into this latest version.

The volunteer coders can take credit for these great improvements, although at certain points in the book, we will point out where there might be some short-comings or omissions. None of these are critical issues, and hopefully, by pointing them out, version upgrades can be made in the future to keep improving the software.

A tremendous number of websites have been built on the recent Joomla! 3 and 4 platforms, which is being superseded by the new Version 5. Note we said superseded not replaced. Joomla! 4 is still a highly usable and viable platform with thousands of Extensions available to enhance functionality. While there are a tremendous number of differences between the versions, in this book, we will help both the novice and the experienced Joomla! user thread their way to using the new platform to build high-quality websites.

What's New in this Version?

Looking back, Joomla! Version 3 and 4 utilized Bootstrap Version 2, 3 and 4 for enhanced Templates and Content display. The new Joomla! 5 has taken a bigger step and changed to the new "Bootstrap 5 Framework" with the underlying code that controls how webpages can be displayed. This "Bootstrap 5 Framework" layer is separate from the "Developers Framework" that is discussed in Chapter 3, "INTRODUCTION: How the Joomla! 5 CMS Works" and as shown in Figure 5-1 below.

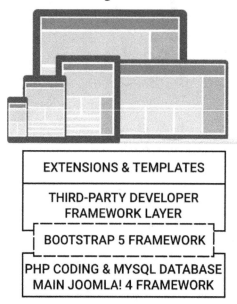

EXTENSIONS & TEMPLATES

THIRD-PARTY DEVELOPER FRAMEWORK LAYER

BOOTSTRAP 5 FRAMEWORK

PHP CODING & MYSQL DATABASE MAIN JOOMLA! 4 FRAMEWORK

Figure 5-1

Just like the Developers "Framework," the Bootstrap 5 "Framework" doesn't need any attention from the Administrator. It is built into the code that operates in the background. However, many of the settings can be changed if desired. Knowing that, you should also know that you do not need to change the programming code itself because, in most instances, there are also Control Areas which allow the Administrator to change some of the Bootstrap 5 parameters. More on that subject below.

Many Faces of Bootstrap

Both Joomla! 5 and the Developer Framework can, and often does, use Bootstrap 5 at the same time, which is entirely possible. Joomla! 5 uses it in one way and Third-Party Developer's Components, Modules and Templates in another. This is what gives this combination such outstanding horsepower and flexibility for building websites.

Bootstrap 5 Defined

There are any number of textbook definitions for Bootstrap, but here it is in a nutshell:

"Bootstrap 5 is a popular and very powerful "Mobile First Framework" for building Front-Ends for responsive websites. It is based on construction of a responsive grid system for laying out a webpage and utilization of pre-defined Elements and Components."

A "responsive website" is one that displays the same Content on devices ranging from the desktop computer down to the mobile devices. However, because of screen sizes, some pages/screens may arrange themselves differently, and Bootstrap 5 is what makes this possible.

Bootstrap 5 makes the User Interface, or the control of the visual and responsive aspects of the website, behave in a certain manner – allowing Developers and designers extremely wide latitudes in creating website displays for all screen sizes.

For the most part, you can ignore most everything about Bootstrap 5 except the Cascading Style Sheets ("CSS"), and the Syntactically Cascading Style Sheet ("SCSS") coding. Both are coding shorthand for the implementation of Cascading Style Sheets (*see:* Chapter 18, "VISUAL: Style Sheets").

As the Administrator, you probably will not be required to make any direct modifications to the Bootstrap 5 coding or the Cascading Style Sheet files directly. Typically, changes you might need to make are accomplished through an interface, or Control Area built into a Component, Module or Template.

It should also be noted that changes can be made but not on/in any of the core or source files. Typically, when modifications are needed, an "override" is created. By doing so, when the core or source files are updated, the modifications do not get written over and remain in play as modified.

If you are interested in more information about these subjects, search the internet for the terms "SCSS" or "Bootstrap 5," where you will find an abundance of useful guides and insights. Books are also readily available, but they are more applicable for use by programmers vs. Joomla! 5 website Administrators.

Origin of Bootstrap

There is an interesting story here. Bootstrap was created in mid-2010 by a Designer and Developer working for Twitter. It has become one of the most popular "Front-End Frameworks" used on websites all over the world.

At present, Bootstrap is maintained by a small team of volunteer Developers who keep working to make improvements to the Framework.

The "Mobile First" Concept

Bootstrap's initial and continuing goal is to design websites and Content on a "Mobile First" objective. In other words, design websites for their optimal display on mobile devices, then on others, such as: tablets, laptops and desktops. This way, websites get the best configuration that can display websites equally good on small screens all the way up to the big screens.

That is what Bootstrap is all about. Making sure there is a method of making display of the same website Content compatible with any size screen being used to access and view the Content. There was/is brilliance in that concept and the developers the had the perfect vision to implement how this all could be accomplished. They succeeded to an incredibly high degree and literally changed the world of website construction.

What Does Bootstrap 5 Actually Do

Bootstrap 5 does several things. Bootstrap 5 is based on the concept of "Mobile First," which means that designs and layouts are created to appear best on mobile devices. Then, the secondary consideration is to make these same layouts appear properly on large screen devices.

Bootstrap 5 helps in building websites that are highly responsive, allowing them to be viewed on display screens of all sizes. This is referred to as "Fluid" or "Responsive" layouts.

Bootstrap 5 provides pre-coded and pre-designed popular Elements and Component layouts that can be used on any website and mobile device with equal visual results.

Bootstrap 5 provides a way to inject a standard set of visual and design codes into a website/mobile device, and through Control Area interfaces, allows a Joomla! 5 Administrator to make changes to customize the look.

Bootstrap 5 refers to "Themes," (as does Wordpress), but in Joomla! 5, they are called "Templates," with the terms being interchangeable. Make a mental note about this. However, a "Template" itself may have different Themes, *re:* color schemes and such.

Also, Bootstrap! 5 Components are also called Elements, or vice versa. Make a mental note about this also.

Bootstrap 5 is based on solid functional principles and provides error-free coding to enhance and optimize content display on a website. What makes it a highly functional tool is the fact that the website Administrator ["Super User"], does not require proficiency in the underlying code, upon which it relies, for webpage layouts and design.

How Bootstrap 5 Works

Before getting into the workings of Bootstrap 5, the big question that needs to be answered is: *"Exactly what does it do?"*

Using Bootstrap 5 ensures that a website, built on any software platform, can be fully responsive, that is: *will display equally well on any screen viewing the website/webpages.*

In the past, websites were designed using "fixed-width" settings, *re:* 1200 pixels, 100% and so on. They were great to look at on desktop monitors, but when mobile devices came down the road, viewing the same website resulted in visual train wrecks. The websites looked like postage stamps and were simply the original website shrunk down to the screen size. The coding used for the website layouts simply did not work well for the smaller screens. Enter Bootstrap, which has evolved into the Front-End Framework of choice for Joomla! 5.

The Grid System

Bootstrap 5 works by providing a flexible "grid system" upon which a webpage is built. It is formally referred to as: "Flexbox Powered Grid." On large monitors, the full width of the grid is displayed. On small screen devices, the grid is automatically narrowed pre-determined "Break Points," to fit the width of the device and, instead of the content displaying horizontally, it begins to automatically stack content vertically for better display. The "stacking" is based on screen-size predetermined "breaks" in the horizontal grid.

The 12-Column FlexGrid

Bootstrap 5 essentially divides the width of the screen into 12 equal columns, whose number expand, or collapse, based on the width of the device viewport (screen). The horizontal grid will collapse, stacking the column vertically, when the screen is small, then expand and stack them horizontally when the screen is larger. Figure 5-2 shows what this 12-column grid looks like and a few of the different ways it can be divided horizontally.

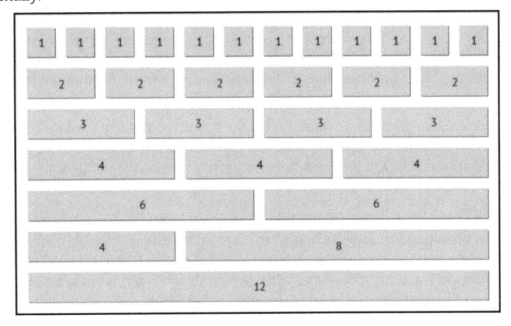

Figure 5-2

Shown in Figure 5-2 are seven possible rows of Content and how they can be divided to create the screen display. For example, if a two-column grid is desired, then the columns would be combined as 6 + 6, side by side. A three column layout would be 3 + 3 + 3, and so on.

The result is that a 1200-pixel wide screen display on a desktop will also display properly on a mobile device without simply shrinking it to fit the screen. The "grid system" rearranges the grid boxes to display vertically on the mobile device, based on screen size width, using what is known as: "CSS-Classes," as indicated in Figure 5-3. The layout of Bootstrap-based pages can include any combination of columns desired to optimize a website layout.

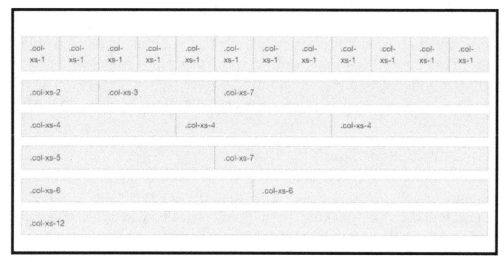

Figure 5-3

At this point, this information may not have much meaning. It will be discussed in greater detail in Chapters 17-19 when Templates, Style Sheets and Template/Page Builders are addressed. There, you will learn that the Template and Page Builders have controls whereby you may drag Content Areas to the exact width desired based on the Bootstrap Grid.

In fact, between Bootstrap, the Joomla! Framework and Third-Party Frameworks, the "CSS class" codes above, will likely never need to be entered manually into any Style Sheets or Templates. The Frameworks have controls whereby the width of the Content Areas are selected by using familiar "drag 'n drop" methods.

Bootstrap Elements/Components

The Elements/Components used by Bootstrap 5 (don't confuse them with Joomla! 5 Components) they have the same name but are *NOT* the same). These items are pre-coded to work well on wide screen and small screen devices, giving them an elastic rubber-band like capability along with "stacking" capabilities..

The fun part of this is that knowledge of the Bootstrap 5 coding is not required. Bootstrap 5 Components often use a Control Panel, or similar feature, to allow for modifications such as colors, fonts and sizing, layout details and more. Its enjoyable to use when customizing a website built on Joomla! 5, particularly when designing a new or modifying, page or website Templates.

The website *getbootstrap.com* has an abundance of examples of Bootstrap 5 Components, and other examples of their use. It also has a great documentation section to examine the different elements in detail. Search the internet for more tutorial-type information about Bootstrap 5 if you wish to delve deeper and learn more about it. However, make note that individual Bootstrap 5 Elements or Components cannot (Yet!), be imported and used in Joomla! 5 as Extensions. They won't work in that manner.

Not Interchangeable

The Bootstrap 5 Components cannot be "dropped into" a Joomla! 5 website and expect to work or display in the same manner. They do not interchange. However, Page and Template Builder Extensions, once installed into a Joomla! 5 website can create similar layouts. In fact, some extensions have the Bootstrap 5 Components as pre-configured, drag 'n drop, pieces that can be added to the Joomla! 5 webpage layout with relative ease.

The Bootstrap Website Epidemic

The opinions here are not stated with the intent to be critical, but rather, observational.

Early on, when Bootstrap came on the scene, many websites began taking on the same format. They all started looking the same. The entire website was on one screen, they had the same Content Areas, and other than a few photos and color choices, they started to look like clones of each other. Another thing that was noticeable was all the motion and animation of the parts of the screen when scrolling or opening Content areas. This was epidemic because websites all started looking and feeling visually the same, and from our vantage point, made one dizzy, or seasick, with all the motion going on while scrolling the screen.

Too Many Similar Page Layouts

Should you browse the internet looking for Bootstrap website layouts, you will find them remarkably similar. They all seem to have the same general layout as to page Content, many of which simply won't work for most websites. But there they are, by the thousands, the same thing over and over and over.

Additionally, the "content areas" on the Bootstrap-based websites were essentially the same, with the same Components, laid out in the same way on the page. There were both monotonous to look at, and in many cases, could not be easily adapted to different website Content needs. This can be called the "Agency Look," as most were designed for "Template Shops" or "Tech Companies" and everyone just copied each other's and plugged in their own information.

This epidemic was dampened somewhat when the "CMS" platforms, like Wordpress, Joomla! and others began to incorporate Bootstrap into their core functions. However, Wordpress websites tended to keep the same format for "Themes" and thousands of them were cranked out that all looked and acted the same, as described above. In fact, it actually led to a rush of websites using Wordpress that used the same, or similar, Themes, over and over and over.

Joomla!, on the other hand, didn't fall into that trap and the many Developer Shops that build Templates, incorporated Bootstrap 5 into their own webpages and Template Builders. The epidemic was cured with the construction of websites that no longer were "cookie cutter" in their look, feel and content layout. It allowed Templates and individual webpages to be created and customized. Thus, the cookie-cutter Bootstrap-only Template/Theme format went out the window when using Joomla!

Bootstrap 5 dramatically expanded the many content areas, and visual displays of Joomla! 5. The combination of the two has resulted in one of the most flexible and useful "CMS" stand-alone software products available.

Online Website Building Services

A rapidly expanding trend is the explosion of website building services that operate online, or are cloud-based. There is no software to download or install. You create an account on the provider's cloud-based platform, select a theme for your website, make a bunch of settings to change color and images. Then, add your own text and images.

These services also host the website for you. Most "require" hosting on their server. You have probably viewed commercials and advertisements on television/cable promoting these services. There are a good number of them. These are in the "website tonight" category that promise personal and business website success in one hour, or overnight, or instantly. Fulfillment of those promises is something else altogether and limited to the eye of the beholder.

Make no mistake about it, these "website tonight" services fill a niche in the realm of websites, but the more sophisticated websites typically use Wordpress or Joomla!, allowing a higher degree of content creation and management. Occasionally, some sites will use another platform, like Drupal, or hosted on different coding bases. However, these require a high degree of website coding knowledge on the part of the Administrator.

How Joomla! 5 Utilizes Bootstrap 5

Generally, Joomla! 5 uses Bootstrap primarily for displaying content on the Front-End. It makes a website more powerful. The Template developers have worked many of the Bootstrap 5 features into their product. The Administrator only need to utilize the features by adding content as needed.

If the Administrators wants to add a nice looking "Contact Us" Form, that can be easily accomplished, a custom Form Extension can be added. This would include the Bootstrap 5 coding behind it, which allows the ability to create a great looking online forms. An example of this will be shown in Chapter 33, "CONTENT: Using Form Extensions in Joomla! 5," found in *Joomla! 5: Boots on the Ground, Advance Edition, Volume 2.*

How Bootstrap 5 Enhances Joomla! 5

As you work with Joomla! 5 and search for Templates, you will see the term: *"This Template is a responsive Joomla Template based on Bootstrap."* Or you might see other similar descriptions.

The point here is that Joomla! 5 Templates are mostly based on the features of Bootstrap 5, and together, they greatly enhance website building capabilities. Fixed and rigid content layouts can be changed to fluid and responsive versions. This is the key to displaying websites equally well on desktop screens and mobile devices.

If you want to see some examples of Joomla! Templates based on Bootstrap, go to: *templatki.com*, and prowl around. Open some of the Joomla! Templates and view the "Live Demo" version. When you open them on the desktop, you see the full-width version. You can select the mobile device view in the upper area of the screen to see how the Template content is displayed on mobile devices.

Remember, only Templates built or converted to Joomla! 5 can be used. Others will not install, or if installed, may not work properly. In fact, and we will be repeating this often:

"Joomla! 3 or 4 Extensions/Templates can break a Joomla! website beyond the point of recovery. It is not a good practice to attempt to use Joomla! 3 or 4 Extensions/Templates on a Joomla! 5 website, period. However, those created for Version 4 may likely function correctly on a Joomla! 5 website."

Note:

The above website reference was not an endorsement of the Templates sold by any Developer website. It is simply named to point out a convenient resource for viewing demonstration Templates. Throughout this book, any referenced to third-parties are for informational purposes and are not recommendations. If a recommendation is made, it will be specifically stated.

Business-Themed Templates

Another trend that is rapidly gaining traction is the business-theme Template. There are Templates for almost any kind or type of business. The whole website is created for you, and all you need to do is plug in your businesses information, select some color, drop in some photos from a library or a few of your own, and *voila!* -- you have a website. Sound familiar?

These are creating the same similar looking, constantly repeating website designs mentioned earlier.

However, there are Template sources that create viable and customizable Joomla! 5 Templates that don't look like they were poured out of a bowl of cookie dough. By the brilliant use of Bootstrap 5 Components/Elements, their website Templates can be dramatically changed to create fantastic looking websites, even when using a "boilerplate" Template. It just takes a little creativity and some knowledge of how Joomla! 5 Templates can be modified.

Bootstrap 5 Components

As a website Administrator and "chief cook & bottle washer," you are going to be working with Template Builders and Page Builders (covered in Chapter 19, "VISUAL: Using Template/Page Builders.")

When doing so, you will be able to design your own Templates or Pages. You will be building them on the Bootstrap 5 Framework, while at the same time, using a specialized Extension that has been created the same way. The actual Bootstrap 5 Framework will be invisible, but you will be using it via the Component, Module and Template Control Areas.

At first, you might be just a little confused about some items, but after using the features of a Bootstrap 5 enabled Component, and some experimentation, you will get the hang of it soon enough.

Bootstrap 5 is a software entity of itself, and because it works "within" Joomla! 5 and requires no direct involvement on the part of the Administrator, it will not be discussed within this book in detail.

There exists an abundance of books devoted entirely to the subject of coding and creating websites using Bootstrap 5 by itself. An internet topical search will result in plenty of reading resources where you can get a quick look at what Bootstrap does and how it works.

JOOMLA!® 5 [A]
BOOTS ON THE GROUND
Advance Edition
Volume 1 [B]
CHAPTER 3

INTRODUCTION:
How the Joomla! 5 "CMS" Works

Among website building software, Joomla! 5 is classified as a "Content Management System," commonly referred to as a "CMS." Knowing that, what is the requirement for a product to be so classified? This is easy to explain, but first, a bit of understanding on the definition of a "CMS."

There are loads of "CMS" programs that can build websites. Joomla! and Wordpress being two of the most popular stand-alone types. Both are "CMS" platforms that separate the operating code from the design and the actual Content of the website.

Joomla! and Wordpress operate on software and databases installed on a website server. The website-tonight versions operate on the internet cloud, that is: you do not load anything onto a server, or even your computer. Instead, you log into a cloud-based server, call up your account or website project, and proceed from there. The "software" to create the website is accessed on their website, along with storing your website files, making it accessible to viewers on their platform.

The abilities to create websites and Content is limited to what is provided using their platform. Some of those online services are fairly good, some are okay, and some simply create junkyard quality cookie-cutter websites. Most are extremely limited as to what type of level of customization that can be applied to their Templates. Yes, "changes" can be made, but higher-level customization are just not possible.

The biggest fault with these services is they have pre-built website Templates, and this leads to many websites all looking the same as each other. In fact, some of the Joomla! Template Builders are beginning to do the same thing by providing Templates for various industries or small businesses. The result could be many websites utilizing the same layouts, Content flow, etc. Whether this ends up as a good or bad thing will need to be determined in the future after more utilization occurs.

Joomla! 5 has many Extensions that can be added to those "look-alikes" which can change the layouts and look. These topics will be explored throughout this book.

What's a CMS?

Basically, a "CMS" is a website software platform that separates the operating core coding, the design and layout from the Content. The idea is to free up the graphic designers from the underlying code that runs the software and also to free up the Content creators from the technical design aspects of the site.

Consider it this way (take any given news-based website): The code that it operates on is created and maintained by programmers. The layout, design, graphics and visual aspects are created and maintained by graphic designers. Then there are loads of Content Editors that simply type their stories into an Article Workspace, and it appears in the proper location on the website. That's it. That's a "CMS" in a nutshell. Three skill sets, working separately but together, to produce the end product.

The Word "Joomla"

It's interesting to know the meaning of the word "Joomla" as it might apply to the "CMS" concept of building websites. The name Joomla is a phonetic spelling for the Swahili word *"Jumla,"* which means **"all together"** or **"as a whole."** Not a bad choice for the name of a "CMS" platform, especially this one. The term "Joomla!" (with an exclamation mark only), is a trademark of Open Source Matters, Inc.

One of the many advantages of using a "CMS" is that technical experts do not need to know how to write Content, nor do Content editors need to know programming or graphic design. Everyone does their own job of creating the product and we, as end users of Joomla! 5, reap the benefits by having a great platform that displays good looking webpages. All we need to do is pour in the Content.

How the Joomla! 5 "CMS" Works

If you are not a programmer, and chances are you aren't, the following information isn't going to make much sense to you, but it is worth providing it for informational purposes.

The Core Program

Joomla! 5 (as were all previous versions), is built using programming code called "PHP," and a database system called "MySQL." Several other databases are also now being used, but "MySQL" is the most prevalent. Together, the programmers create "PHP" code that interacts with database tables. Additionally, the database also stores the Content entered for Front-End display, along with all the other Content. This is what happens when you set up the "Database Configuration," as shown in Figure 3-1. This starts the connection, followed by several other steps that are outlined in Chapter 4, "ADMIN: Installing a Joomla! 5 Instance."

Figure 3-1

How this connection is accomplished isn't important, nor do you need to know any of the details. Suffice to say that the core operating code is written to work with a database, and together both let you get to the next part of the "CMS" – the Visual Management.

Enhanced by Extensions

We need to inject something here about expanding the features of the core code, which is not modified by using Extensions. Extensions typically add more code and more database tables. When Extensions are installed by the Administrator, all of this takes place automatically without additional knowledge needed on your part. When the Extension installation is complete, that's all there is to it. The Extension adds new code files and additional database tables, but does not alter the Joomla! 5 default code. Once an Extension is installed, an easy process that takes no time to accomplish, all you need to do is use the Extension for its intended purpose.

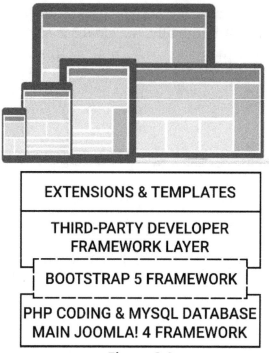

EXTENSIONS & TEMPLATES

THIRD-PARTY DEVELOPER
FRAMEWORK LAYER

BOOTSTRAP 5 FRAMEWORK

PHP CODING & MYSQL DATABASE
MAIN JOOMLA! 4 FRAMEWORK

Figure 3-2

A Developer "Framework" Layer Over the Core

Many Joomla! developer shops, those that create great Extensions and Templates, have come up with different approaches to adding a second code operating layer which is called a "Framework." This "Framework" capability makes Joomla! so much more than a simple "CMS" as it opens vast horizons for developers. Some incredible and fantastic Extensions and Templates have been created that operate within their respective "Frameworks" and function on top of the Joomla! core, as is shown in Figure 3-1.

There are a large number of "Frameworks" that can be included in a Joomla! 5 website. There are too many to list and explain here individually. However, when adding specialized Extensions and some Templates, and especially the Page Building Extensions, the developers are very likely to include their own "Frameworks" into the website structure upon installation.

In our book: *Joomla! 5: Boots on the Ground, Advance Edition, Volume 2*, in Chapter 46, "ADMIN: Joomla! Third-Party Frameworks," discusses these with an overview of how they generally operate. This information may be valuable for selecting which or how many different "Frameworks" to add to your website for expanded capabilities. For now, all you need to know is that third-party "Frameworks" are quite often included as part of Extensions, especially with Template Builders (*see:* Chapter 19, "VISUAL: Using Template/Page Builders."

Many "Framework Layers" Possible

It is possible, if several different Extensions from different developers are installed, each might have its own "Framework" under which it operates. This is OK, because many different "Framework" layer models can function within a Joomla! 5 website at the same time, so that issue is of no real concern to the Administrator. This ability is what makes Joomla! 5 such a powerful website building platform.

Visual Management: Templates

Complimenting the core code and the database is the visual side of a Joomla! 5 website which is based on Templates. There are literally thousands upon thousands of Templates available for use with the Joomla! platform, some are free, others need to be purchased.

Templates come in so many different combinations of layout and color schemes, they simply cannot be fully described in this book. However, there are things you need to know about Templates which will be discussed in Chapter 17.

As mentioned above, there is the possibility of a second level of operating code layered on top of the Joomla! core ("Frameworks"). This is code that generates an operating system that floats above the core programming upon which developers, as Template creators or specialty Extension programmers, use to make their Extension Packages operate uniquely within the program.

Templates are the Extensions that create the website's appearance, present information in a visually appealing way and provide for a method of navigation around the website. How all of this works is discussed in detail in the Chapter mentioned above. Templates are actually Extensions but are managed differently and "thought of" separately from Extensions *per se.*

No Effect on the Core Framework

The default Extensions and Templates will continue to operate properly after a "Framework," or additional Templates, are installed. The two work independently of each other, yet have their use as being interchangeable. The "Framework-based" Extensions do not replace the core features. Both, or several, can be used on the same website simultaneously. Also, screen/page views can be switched from one Template to another which is another power feature in Joomla! 5.

Template/Page Layout Builders

Something that began to show up on the Joomla! scene in later editions of Version 3 were Template Building and Page Layout Builders. These programs operate in the "Framework" Layer concept allowing Administrators to create their own within Joomla! instead of using canned or pre-designed Templates.

The first Template builders were external programs which allowed creation of a Template using a graphic based program. Then, the Template file was exported in a proper format and could be installed in Joomla! via the standard Extension installation procedure.

These "builder" Extensions (they are "mini-programs"), allow Administrators to build beautiful and functional Templates of all types. In addition to website-wide Templates, Page Builders give Administrators the same latitude in building individual pages or screens. And the neat thing about both Template and Page Builders is that the Administrator doesn't need to know code or programming to create them. Again, more about Templates can be found in Chapter 19, "VISUAL: Using Template/Page Builders." Their use can be both fun and challenging.

Templates are Extensions

Templates are Joomla! Extensions. However, they install into a different area of the website compared to Components or Modules. You may find Templates discussed as if they were separate entities in Joomla! and in a way they are, but they are still Extensions. If you find this is the case, keep in mind Templates ARE Extensions, because they are added onto the website, but are simply administered and used in a different manner.

Content Management: Multiple Editor Capability

If you are the only Administrator of a website and responsible for adding and managing all the Content, this topic should not be of much interest. However, if you have a larger more complex website with several Authors or Content Editors, posting Content such as, blog items, product listings, promotional materials and the like, then you need to know this.

Joomla!'s Access Control ("ACL"), allows the Administrator to create many different levels of Authors and Content Managers. It also allows the editing access to be restricted to certain Content, such as only Articles in certain Categories, or even down to individual Articles themselves. For example, an "ACL" can be configured whereby Authors can access only those Content Items which they have individually written or created.

Chapter 24, "USERS: Access, Actions & Permissions," will guide you step-by-step through the process of creating and managing the "ACL" features of Joomla! 5.

Specialized Extensions

There are thousands of specialized Components that can perform a multitude of different tasks in the creation of Content. For example, there are many Components available that help Administrators create various online Forms for website visitors to submit information. There is also an enormous collection of Components that facilitate the addition of all types of Photo Galleries and visual display variables. Online Shopping Carts are also available as Extensions.

These specialized Components, which install as Extensions into the Joomla! 5 platform are available via the *joomla.org* website or are sold by individual developer shops. Visit the Extensions Directory ("JED"), on the Joomla! website and look around. An internet search activity might also be helpful in finding individual developers that provide Extensions and Components that are not listed in the "JED."

Also, it is worth noting that the installation of Extensions is a straight-forward undertaking, with no particular complications – PROVIDED – the Extension is compatible with the version of Joomla! you are using. Before attempting to install them onto your website, make sure the Extension is Joomla! 5 compatible.

Most Joomla! 3 Extensions WILL NOT install into a Joomla! 5 website. Do not attempt to do so. Attempting this may break your website beyond any possibility of recovery. It is possible that many Extensions constructed for Joomla! 5 might work correctly when installed into a Joomla! 5 instance.

Preconfigured Templates with Content

Something new is being introduced for Joomla! 5, which is akin to the "website-tonight" type of system. These are Templates built upon Frameworks that come populated with Content which can be edited and the layouts modified. This saves the Administrators loads of work, so be aware of these new Templates when looking for an enhancement to your website. These are "specialty templates" and are now a going trend with developer shops to provide more products. They typically install into a new website instance, but not into a Joomla! 5 website that has already been created. These new types create a complete Joomla! 5 website from scratch.

How it all Works Together

As the Administrator, you drive the bus. It is up to you to install the correct Extensions and implement, or invoke, certain Templates for the website. Keep in mind, that you can assign different Templates to different sections of the website.

Next, you need to control the Content Editors. If it is a small one-person website, that is likely you. But if a larger website, you will need to set up User Access Control ("ACL"), to manage Editors and their access to Content.

Additionally, if website Visitors are required to Register to access portions of the website, you also need to take care of that function. See Chapter 23, "USERS: Managing Users" for more information.

Ignoring the "Users" part of things for the moment, you need to decide which Modules to use, what kind to display, and where to put them on the Template layout. Modules are interesting and can greatly enhance a website and the information displayed on the individual pages or screens as they are often called.

Next, and the most important, is that Articles need to be created, categorized and accessed through the use of Menu Link Items within Menus. The exception being "Featured Articles," which automatically display on the main website screen and are associated with the "HOME" Menu Link Item in the Main Menu. More on all that later in this book.

Finally, you need to manage updates to the Joomla! core program, along with occasional updates that are issued by the developers of Extensions you have installed on the website. Each are updated occasionally. Joomla! updates itself as needed and Developers update their Extensions periodically as they improve upon them. However, these type of Extensions need to conform to certain rules and be listed in the "JED" to have the updating feature.

While all of this may sound complicated right now, as you go through this book and perform the Exercises, which are designed to teach you how to do things in a step-by-step manner, the entire picture of the Joomla! 5 "CMS" will become clearer.

After you perform the same tasks a few times, you will find that you will have mastered them and can repeat the actions with ease. After all, millions of websites have been built on the Joomla! platform by users all over the world, so how hard can it be?

At some point, the step-by-step instructions will be brief and take you through the processes quickly.

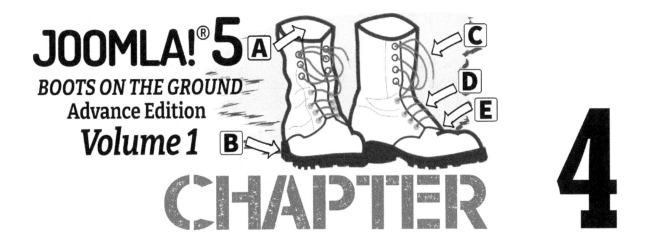

INTRODUCTION:
Installing a Joomla! 5 Instance

At the start, Joomla! 5 seems to be a complex program, and it is! However, once you have jumped the hurdles of preparing a website hosting platform, then installing the actual Joomla! 5 files, the fun really begins. From that point forward, you can experience the enjoyment of unleashing the full power of the program to create almost any type of website by using all the features of Joomla! 5 and the many Extensions available.

There is a learning curve involved with Joomla! 5. The curve is initially somewhat steep. But once you grasp the basics and apply those fundamentals to your website project, you will find that website administration quickly gets very easy.

Joomla! 5 must be manually installed either on a hosted server location, or via an "ISP's" automatic installed process. The choice of "ISP" is yours. Installation is not required on any specific "ISP" service. There are many that provided reliable and consistent server hosting locations.

If your website project is for a single domain only, then using the "ISP's" auto installer is fine. Many have a simple monthly plan that gives you access to the "Admin Back-End" of a Joomla! 5 website (but usually nothing more), they have automatically created for you under the domain name of your choice. Some even provide the domain name free with their hosting packages.

If you are planning to host a lot of websites for your company or clients, having your own webserver onto which many domains can be added and Joomla! installed, can be very advantageous. These type of domain servers give you more options and more control over many parts of the server and the domains via their own respective control panels.

Which Web Hosting Platform?

For simplicity, the hosting platforms and type of Joomla! 5 that will be installed and used throughout this book will be those that host the "MySQL" or "MySQLi" Databases. "My-See-Quill" is an extremely popular database that stores website configurations, operating file information and Content within their database tables..

However, several other types of database databases beyond "MySQL" that can be used with Joomla! 5, but you are not likely to run into any of those on most website hosting services.

Essentially, a website hosting platform is used if you are going to host many websites for your company or clients. For a single, individual, or small business website, using and managing a website hosting platform might be too costly, unless additional advanced features are needed. Use of a "hosting server" and how to prepare them for installing a Joomla! 5 website is going to be explained.

If you are going to host a single website, the hosting providers generally provide a pre-configured website, and no installation or configuration effort is required on your part. The "ISP's" system will have an "auto-installer" that does it all where you typically can by-pass some of the more complex parts of the installation process and simply use the service providers built-in functions to do so. After their installation is complete, they provide you with the Administrator's Username and Password (which you can change after login).

If your intent is to host websites for your own projects, or for clients (such as we do at 200mph Media Group, LLC), leasing a server onto which you can install any number of websites on their own databases, then the following is exactly what you will need to do to set up the server and install Joomla! 5.

There are two types of website hosting platforms widely available, depending upon which hosting "ISP" provider is chosen. In fact, some hosting providers offer a choice of which hosting platform to use.

Parallels Plesk Control Panel	This is probably the most popular insomuch as the domain creation and management is contained in the same environment as the Control Panel for the individual website. Each domain has its own Control Panel that is accessed by the same administrative interface. Both the hosting server control location and the website control is accessed on the same screen.
WHM/cPanel	On this platform, a Web Host Manager ("WHM") is used to set up the domain, then you need to shift to the respective website **cPanel** for the actual administration of it. Each domain has its own **cPanel** that is accessed by it's own interface. However, you may obtain a single

	instance website domain location with only the **cPanel** and no "WHM."
ISP Provided	The hosting platform here is based on what the hosting provider uses. Here you sign up for a domain, select Joomla! 5 as the platform, and the "ISP" sets up everything. They may even have their own customized Control Panel for the website that is different from either of the above.

Each type of website hosting platform does essentially the same thing. They host the program files, have database functions and otherwise allow a website to be installed and accessed. This is true if you install it yourself on a webserver, or if the "ISP" installs it via their auto-installer.

What needs to be done at this point, is determine whether you are hosting a single website, or whether you will be hosting many. This book assumes the latter with regards to installation on the web hosting platform.

This is what should have already been completed:

1. Obtained ownership of one or more domain name(s).

2. Secured a website hosting platform account from a service provider.

3. Created a domain location on the webserver. In Plesk, this is on the accounts page. In cPanel, this is first done on the "WHM," then on the cPanel itself.

4. Created a directory in the domain's control panel to install Joomla! 5, naming the directory under root directory as noted in the Exercise. ("*myfirstsite*").

5. Uploaded the most recent version of the Joomla! 5 package installer file from the joomla.org website. After installation, if it not the most recent, the Administrator's "Home Dashboard" will alert you to update the installation.

6. Extracted the Joomla! 5 installer package file ("unzipped" the file).

7. Created a database for the website.

8. Created a "full-privilege" or "all-privileges" User for the database.

More than One Instance

Joomla! 5 can be installed at both the "root level" of a domain's location on the webserver and also, within any sub-directory within the domain. However, each Joomla! 5 installation must have its own database. In this book, we have chosen to install it initially into the *"myfirstsite"* sub-directory. This means more than one instance of Joomla! 5 can be installed under a single domain, but only if you have acquired a website hosting platform vs. a single website instance.

Clarification of the Installation Location

Normally, so that the website visitors will have access to a website by entering the domain name into the browser location bar, the domain's files are installed at the "root" level of the domain's file structure. In a cPanel Server, it is the "public_html" location. On a Plesk Server, it is the "httpdocs" location.

However, when first creating or developing a website, it isn't a good idea to have the website accessible during that time. Thus, placing the installation initially into a sub-directory within the domain, all the tasks to ready the website can be performed without direct public access.

When all the installation work is done, it can easily be moved to the "root" level and thereby made accessible to website visitors when they enter the domain in the browser location bar mentioned.

Websites installed in a sub-directory within the domain's file structure cannot be directly accessed unless the name of the sub-directory is known. In fact, some websites that are directly accessed at the "root" level, may have sub-sites located within sub-directories that can be accessed via links in the main website.

EXERCISE 4-1: INSTALLING JOOMLA! 5 ON THE WEBSERVER

Objective: After going through the process of setting up a website domain location on a "Parallels Plesk Control Panel," or the "WHM/cPanel," you will find that the actual process of installing of Joomla! 5 is a bit of a breeze. There isn't much to it, so let's get going:

Access the Installed Location

In a browser's location bar, enter your domain name location as such: *"(domainname)/myfirstsite."* The first Joomla! 5 installer screen will open, which is the starting point for the installation process steps, as follows:

Refer to Figure 4-1 for the following:

Step 1	A	Select English ("United Kingdom") as the language. This is the near the same as using "US English." The full language change to "US English: can

		be made later.
Step 2	**B**	Enter "MY FIRST SITE" for the website name (all uppercase, without the quotes).
Step 3	**C**	Execute the Setup Login Data action.

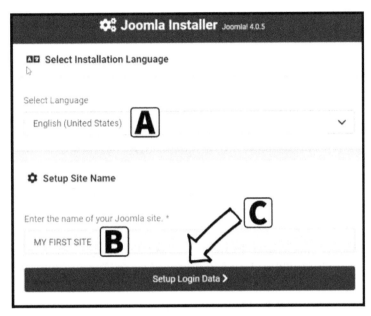

Figure 4-1

Refer to Figure 4-2 for the following:

Step 4	**D**	Enter your name, or the name you wish to use as the Administrator. It does not to be your real name.
Step 5	**E**	Enter your chosen "Administrator Username."
Step 6	**F**	Enter the chosen "Password" for the Administrator.
Step 7	**G**	Enter the official "Administrator's email address."
Step 8	**H**	Execute the Setup Database Connection action as shown in Figure 4-3 below.

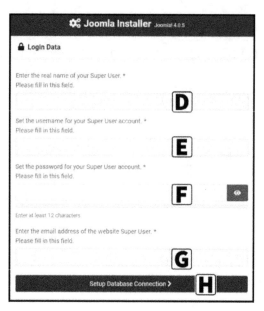

Figure 4-2

Refer to Figure 4-3 for the following:

Step 9	I	Select the type of database to be used, in this case: "MySQLi," which is a version of "MySQL." Leave the "localhost" selection as it is. If the database is hosted on another server, the "IP" address of the server would be entered into this field.
Step 10	J	Enter the database "User's Name" that was designated when the database was created. Be careful here! When you created the database user, the same exact name must be used in this field.
Step 11	K	Enter the password associated with the database username.
Step 12	L	Enter the full name of the database, depending upon which type of website hosting platform being used. The exact name of the database, after being created, must be entered here.
Step 13	M	Enter the prefix for the database, to distinguish it from any others. Make sure that the _"underscore follows the prefix. See the note at the end of this Chapter about database names on the different types of webservers.
Step 14	N	Select the "Default" Connection Encryption.
Step 15	O	Execute the Install Joomla action, which will start by showing the Joomla! logo as a "spinner" as shown in Figure 4-4.

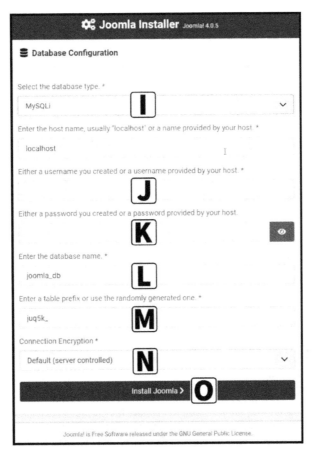

Figure 4-3

While Joomla! 5 is installing, which may take a few minutes, the following screen will display with the Joomla! Logo acting as a "spinner" to indicate it is working.

It only takes a few minutes for the installation activity to complete. Do not close the browser window or leave the screen.

Figure 4-4

Delete the Installation Folder

When the website is installed and the "Open Administrator" action is initiated, the "installation" folder within the Joomla! 5 file structure can, and should be, be deleted. If this folder were to remain, anyone could access the link and perform a re-installation action, over-riding any previous Content creation. The "installation" folder is deleted to: 1) prevent another installation activity, and 2) ensure the Content that was added is not over-written either on purpose or accidentally.

When the installing process is completed, the next screen to be displayed is:

Refer to Figure 4-5 for the following:

Step 19	**P**	Execute the "Open Administrator" action.

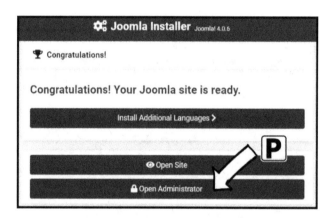

Figure 4-5

At this point, the "Administrator Login" screen will open, so complete the following steps to access the Back-End:

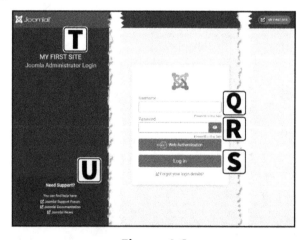

Figure 4-6

Refer to Figure 4-6 for the following:

Step 20	Q	Enter the Administrator's "Username."
Step 21	R	Enter the "Password" for the Administrator.
Step 22	S	Execute the Log in action.
	U	If help is needed, use the links in the left panel at the bottom of the page.
	T	The left panel will identify the name of the website into which you are logging into as the Administrator.

Refer to Figure 4-7 for the following:

When the Joomla! 5 Administrator's Back-End opens, several checks are performed in the background, one of which is to check the version of Joomla! 5 you have installed against the latest release. A previous version of the program could be installed, and in such an instance, the "Notifications" will alert the Administrator that an update is available.

	V	This is the "Notifications" Panel on the Admin Back-End.
	W	This block will indicate that the Joomla! 5 version installed is the latest, or that it requires updating. In such a case, the "Joomla Logo" box will be red in color. Click on the box and follow the prompts that will guide you through the updating process.

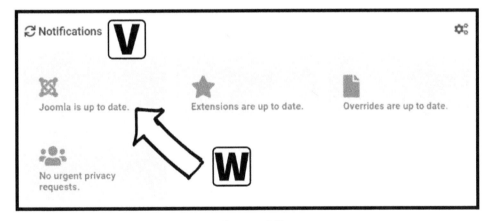

Figure 4-7

Database Names on Webservers

Each type of server has a different requirement for their domain names during the installation of a Joomla! 5 and other types of websites, as follows:

On a Plesk	When a database is given a name on this type of server, the name is literal. When installing Joomla! 5, that name is entered without any prefix. The name is entered exactly as it was specified when the database was

33

Server	created. The username is also entered exactly as created.
On a cPanel Server	On a cPanel Server, databases are automatically assigned a prefix that is the name of the server followed by an underscore, like this: servername_domainname. The username for the database, is entered in a similar manner as: servername_databasename. If any issues with the database names, go to the domains cPanel and open the "Databases," scrolling down to the location where they are listed. The exact name(s) of the database and user can be found at that location. Those are the names which must be entered in the data fields on the installer form screen.

PHP Error Messages After Installing Joomla! 5

There is another program on the webserver that helps run Joomla! 5. It is called "PHP," and it is very possible that a message about the current version being used will be displayed after logging on the Administrator's Back-End, as shown in Figure 4-8.

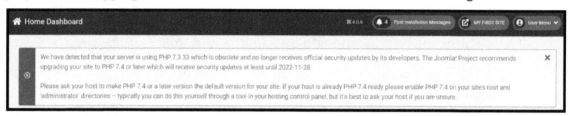

Figure 4-8

This message will appear when there is any issue between the "PHP" versions on the server and the version under which Joomla! 5 has been installed. It can be easily corrected if you have access to the server instance.

If you do not have access to the server controls, contact the "ISP" for support.

JOOMLA!® 5
BOOTS ON THE GROUND
Advance Edition
Volume 1

CHAPTER

5

A

B

C

D

E

ADMIN:
Administrator's "Home Dashboard"

Now that you have successfully installed Joomla! 5 on a hosting location, you can log in and access the Administrator's ["Super User'] area of the website. In Joomla! 5 parlance, this is called the "Administrator's Dashboard," or the "Home Dashboard." The URL to access this area is, where "domainname" is replaced with the actual URL of your website:

http://domainname/administrator

This will open the login page where you enter the Administrator's Username/Password that was designated during the installation process.

About the Home Dashboard

A Joomla! 5 website is managed via the Administrator's ("Super User's") "Home Dashboard," or the "Back-End," as it may be occasionally referred to throughout this book. This is the location where everything on the website is initially managed by the "Super User," who is the only user that can access this area of the website, unless others have been given specific permissions to do so.

At any time and as necessary, additional Users with Back-End login permissions may be created/added, but only by the "Super User" or main administrator.

There are alternate ways to manage content and other elements from the website Front-End, but that will be addressed in a later Chapter. The "Front-End" is the viewer facing part of the website that is accessible to visitors. They cannot see the Back-End without login privileges allowing access to the "Super User's" "Home Dashboard." For now, only the administration via the Back-End will be discussed.

The Back-End is where the details of the website are added and fine-tuned by providing a means of adding features and managing Content. It is also the location where the layout of the website is established and where the Content for each webpage is determined. The overall look and feel of the website is managed by the Template that is applied, which can/may be modified to alter the layout and visual appearance of the Front-End.

The Navigation System, the feature that allows Users to view Content, is also managed in the Back-End. These are the Menus that are created to get you to target destinations on the website.

What Happened During Installation

When you installed Joomla! 5, folders and files were created in the *"myfirstsite"* directory. Also, a database was populated with the MySQL data-tables and some populated content data.

To populate the website with additional content, "Sample Data" should be installed. This "Sample Data" will be used in some of the tutorials and Exercises in the Chapters in this book. Chapter 7, "Fast Track Double Time Start," will guide you through adding the "Sample Data" and performing other fundamental management tasks.

Elements Added During Installation

By default, within the installation actions, Joomla! 5 configured the Back-End and a minimal Front-End. The installation process included these essential elements:

- Created administrative areas in the Back-End to manage the website and the Content.

- Created an Administrator (you), who is designated as the main Manager of the website and at this point, the only User that can access the Back-End via a username/password that was designated during installation.

- When the Sample Data installation option was selected, a collection of Menus, content Categories and Articles were added to the initially installed bare-bones website.

- Some Modules were also installed and placed in default Template's Module Positions on the website screens.

- This also installed and activated a number of default "Components."

- A series of Extensions were activated that provided the ability to add more features.

All of the Back-End management features and their functions are discussed in Chapters dedicated to each individually. This Chapter presents information regarding the Back-End, including where and how to do things with website management, along with content.

"Super User" Defined

In the Joomla! 5 world, the "Super User" is the single User that it is authorized to make changes to the website. The "Super User" may change the Templates, add or remove Components, Modules and Plugins. They may also change the configurations that are applied across the website. They also have the permissions to change the "Options" that might be applied to several types of Content.

More than one "Super User" may exist, and this is done through addition of Users to the "Super User Group," in addition to any other assigned Group. This allows several people to be the "key persons" to administer the website at the highest level of administration.

Throughout the remainder of this book, the "Super User" will be referred to as the "Administrator."

Administrator's ("Super User") Dashboard

The Administrator "Home Dashboard," (Figure 5-1), is the hub of website management activity. Everything is started and managed from this location after a proper "Super User" login credential is entered.

Knowledge and mastery of the Back-End is essential for all aspects of the website's management. It is strongly suggested that the Administrator log-in and spend some time looking over the many "Home Dashboard" screens and get familiar with the location of the different management areas and Content controls. Do this before you dive into Chapter 7, "Fast Track Double Time Start."

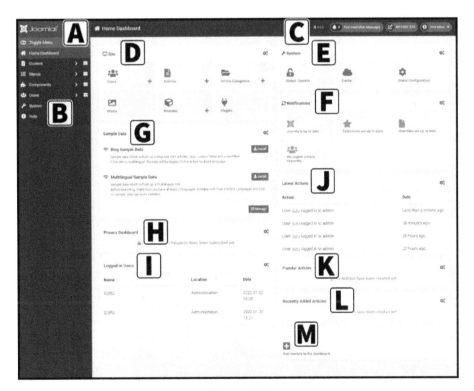

Figure 5-1

Refer to Figure 5-1 for the following:

A	The "Home Dashboard" heading will change depending upon what screen you are viewing. Clicking the Joomla! logo at the top left of will take you back to the Administrator "Home Dashboard" from any other screen at any time. It is possible that some of the blocks on the Back-End Screen may be in different locations based on the viewing screen size and resolution.
B	The left side menu accesses other important administrative areas. Each of these areas are covered in depth in other Chapters of the book, but are briefly explained below.
C	Here you will find the identification of the current Joomla! version that is installed. The Box/arrow icon, when clicked, will open a new browser window showing the website Front-End. The Envelope icon is a messaging feature to send emails to Registered Users. The Bell icon provides access to Alert Messages while the Person icon opens the User Menu, allowing you to edit your profile.

The boxes displayed on the Administrator's "Home Dashboard" , which contains the "Home Dashboard," are individual modules and will be discussed independently below.

D	**Site.** This module provides rapid access to the main Content Management Areas of the website. By default, six rapid access blocks are located here. They are identified by their functions, or the content areas which are controlled by accessing the management screens.
E	**System.** The rapid access here deals with some higher level Administrator functions.
F	**Update Checks.** When the Administrator "Home Dashboard" opens, Joomla! 5 automatically begins checking itself and the Extensions that are installed. The results of the checking are displayed when completed.
G	**Sample Data.** The functions in these panels allow the installation of "Blog Sample Data" or "Multilingual Sample Data." The module can be removed if no longer required.
H	**Privacy Dashboard.** This modules displays requests from Users regarding privacy status.
I	**Logged-in Users.** Shows the most recent logged in Users. This too, can be shut off using the gear icon, unless you have a compelling reason to monitor User logins.
J	**Latest Actions.** When the Administrator, or any User that has editing privileges, performs any tasks, they are recorded here for reference.
K	**Popular Articles.** Based on the number of "views," or "hits," the list of the most popular Articles are shown here. The shut off option is also available.

L	**Recently Added Articles.** When Articles are added to the website, the most recent are listed here.
M	If desired, any Joomla! 5 Module can be added to the "Home Dashboard" view. This function is available at the bottom of the first column of blocks.
N	Every module has a "gear icon." Clicking this icon allows the Administrator to Edit or "Unpublish" the module. If Edit is selected, there are additional configuration settings available. At this point, take a look at the setting "Options" – but do not change any of them – *look but don't touch!*

In Chapter 7, "Fast Track Double Time Start," there are exercises that will guide you through the creation of website Content. After completing the Exercises in that Chapter, you will be able to create and manage Content.

The remaining Chapters in this book address specific parts of Joomla! 5 administration in detail, including the use of each Manager function that affects and controls Content. These Chapters are all dedicated to providing you with a resource and reference to allow effective management of a website based on the new Joomla! 5 Bootstrap 5 version.

The Dashboard Sections/Blocks

By default, the Administrator's login result displays the overall administration area, also referred to as the "Home Dashboard," which has many, many sub-screens for the various Back-End administration activities.

If you are a Joomla! 5 User, much of the "Home Dashboard" will be familiar. All of the same functions are available, the only challenge is determining where everything is located. However, there have been significant changes made that you should be aware of as the Super User.

As a new Administrator, the Exercises throughout this book will guide you through the understanding and use of each section of the Back-End and how it helps create and manage Content, functionality, and website appearance.

The remainder of this Chapter will take you step-by-step through the Back-End Menus and tell you what they do and how to use them. There are no exercises to complete. You should use this Chapter as a reference while learning how to administer the website. The Back-End sections are fully explained on their functionality and use.

Using the Left Side Menu

Generally, this Menu remains visible on nearly all screens in the Back-End, although there are instances where it does not. In any instance, clicking on the Joomla! logo at the top left corner will always take you back to the Administrator "Home Dashboard" .

Toggle Menu	Toggle this switch and the left menu minimizes with only icons showing. The expanded view can be restored by simply clicking the action button again.

Home Dashboard	On any Menu, this button takes you back to the main "Home Dashboard" screen. It doesn't do anything else but provide a back-navigation route to the "Home Dashboard" main screen.
Content	This opens a Menu that contains links to areas of Content on the website. Each link item will be covered in detail in another Chapter of the book.
Menus	Accesses the Menu Management area where all Menu Link Items are managed, and new Menus created and managed. You can also access each additional Menu that has been created on the website. Menus are thoroughly discussed in two latter chapters.
Components	Components that were installed are accessed here, along with any Extensions that have been added to the website as Components. Components are individually discussed in their respective Chapters. Any Component that is added to the website will also be listed here for management access.
Users	This section allows for the management of the website Users, either as one of the "Super Users" or the Registered Users. Entire Chapters are devoted to the management of Users and Access Control ("ACL").
System	When clicked, a new group of informational blocks opens in the main area of the screen. This is an important area and you will likely be accessing this section many times as you manage the website. All of the functions will be presented and discussed in different Chapters that follow.
Help	Don't expect to see ordinary Help screens when you open this. It opens a selection of links to various resources. Some of them make sense as being under a "Help" section, others do not. There is still much work to be done to create a full collection of "helpful" sections of information on the joomla.org website

In the following outlines we have assigned a designation of Control Area to make it easier, later on in the book, to refer back to the locations listed.

Content Control Area

Joomla! 5 has various types of Content or functional features that you will use almost continually as an Administrator of the website. At this point, we are going to define them in general and will explain their actual use in Chapters that follow.

Articles	This accesses the Articles that have been created on the website whether they are "Published" for viewing or not. Article creation is fully explained in Chapter 10, "CONTENT: Articles."

Categories	Articles can be collected into groups, or Categories. You can have as many Categories as desired. Categories may also be nested as Sub-Categories. Category creation is explained in Chapter 9, "CONTENT: Categories."
Featured Articles	Featured Articles are those Articles that automatically appear on the Front Page, or Home Screen, of the website. This designation is made when the Article is created and can be changed at any time. When the designation is removed, it no longer appears on the Front Page, but will remain within its assigned Category. The "Home" Menu Link Item must also be configured to display the Featured Articles.
Workflows	Workflows are methods by which content is handled from creation to Publishing. Workflows are devoted to "Stages" of processing. An example would be that one editor creates an Article, and an Administrator is required to approve it. Thus, a "Workflow" is created.
Fields	Fields can be created that are associated with Categories and Articles. They can be used in many ways to provide specific content and control the way it is displayed. There are many types of fields that may be added and controlled. See Chapter 13, "CONTENT: Content Fields & Field Groups."
Field Groups	In the same way Articles can be assigned to Categories, "Custom Fields" can be assigned to "Field Groups." Field Groups appear as a tab in the configuration area of Articles. The Field Groups are an excellent way to Custom enhance the Content of every part of the website.
Media	This link directly opens the Media Manager, where the Media Content is stored and catalogued into folders, or Categorical groups.
Site Modules	Modules are another form of Content, similar to website Articles, but with many more Content Options. Modules are generally used to display very specific Content often related to Components. One feature of Modules is that they may be placed anywhere on all or only selected screens. Modules are explained in Chapter 12, "CONTENT: Modules. Modules listed are only used on the website and visible on the Front-End, although similar Modules can also be viewed on the Back-End. Do not confuse Modules with Articles, although Modules can contain Article-type content. Articles are the primary means of displaying website Content, Modules do not function in that way.

Administrator Modules	Administrator Modules may also display a variety of Content and information and are typically only shown to Super Users on the Back-End of the website. When Extensions are installed, they may also include Administrator Modules to control or configure their use.

Log Out to Release Content

When one Administrator opens a Content Item in the Back-End, that item cannot be accessed in the Back-End by any other Administrator or Editor at any level. This prevents two "Super Users" or Editors from working on the same Content piece at the same time.

If an Administrator leaves the Back-End without "saving" or "closing" the Content Items he/she checked out, it will remain inaccessible, or "locked" by the system. By formally "exiting" the Content Item when editing is completed, it releases the Content item for access by other Administrators.

Obviously, if you are the only Administrator for the website, this isn't a big deal because when you log back in, it recognizes you as the individual that had the Content Item open in the first place. However, if there are multiple other Super Users or Editors, the checked-out Content needs to be released when you are done. Everyone needs, and should, log out of the Back-End to prevent content from being inaccessible.

In their wisdom, the Joomla! programmers have created a method whereby the primary Administrator can "check-in" the Content globally, thus over-riding any checked-out Content that was locked, returning the Content item to an "available for access" state. This task is covered in a later Chapter.

Menus and Menu Management Control Area

Manage	This is the Control Area where additional Menus can be created, or older ones deleted. Whenever a new Menu is desired, it must first be created here, then a companion Menu Module must be created and positioned on all or selected website pages, depending on the website plan.
All Menu Items	This Control Area serves as a fast access to all Menus and all Menu Link Items. Any Menu Link Item can be changed at this location by deleting, renaming, resetting the Article target, or modifying the Modules that are assigned to that Menu Link Item. More on this in Chapter 12, "CONTENT: Modules, and Chapter 21, "NAVIGATION: Menu Systems."
Bottom Menu (Only with Sample Data)	Use only if "Blog Sample Data" is installed. This accesses an added Menu Module called Bottom Menu.
Author Menu	Use only if "Blog Sample Data" is installed.

(Only with Sample Data)	Accesses an added Menu Module called Author Menu, which is accessible after a Front-End login has been performed.
Main Menu Blog (Only with Sample Data)	Use only if "Blog Sample Data" is installed. Accesses an added Menu Module called Main Menu Blog. More about this kind of Menu will be explained in Chapter 23, "USERS: Managing Users."
Main Menu	Every website must have a Main Menu, or a Menu by another name, which is the "Main Menu". This Menu always displays when the website is accessed. Knowing that, make note that ANY webpage can be designated as the Default Home Page for the "HOME" button, or button with another name, but is designated as the "HOME" button.

Types of Extensions in Joomla!

Before moving forward, a discussion of Extensions is necessary. Extensions expand the operation and functions of Joomla! 5. In a nutshell, Extensions are add-ons that can only be installed by the Administrator to achieve certain Content or display objectives of the website.

Joomla! 5 consists of six types of default Extensions (Figure 5-2). Each Extension has unique characteristics regarding Content and how it is displayed, or accessed by website visitors.

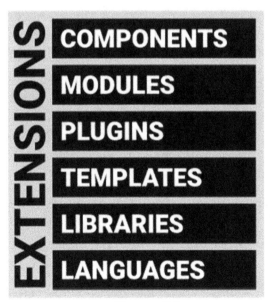

Figure 5-2

Extensions Defined

The Extension types as shown in Figure 5-2 are summarized as follows.

Components	These are "mini-applications" that operate inside the Joomla! 5 Bootstrap Framework. An example of a Component is a photo gallery that displays images in a configurable way and displays it on a webpage from a Menu Link Item. Most of the heavy lifting in Joomla! is performed by Components. Six Chapters in this book have been devoted to the Components that come with the default installation. There are many third-party Components available for use on Joomla! 5 websites. See the Extensions section of the joomla.org website's Extensions Directory for the complete listing.
Modules	Modules are visible areas on the page that contain Extensions that can be associated, or not, with a Component. An example is a Module that might display the latest Article Content, but displayed in a Menu or List Format. Every Template has what are called "Module Positions." These are physical places on the webpage screen into which Modules can be designated to display. This allows for a high degree of customization. See Chapter 12, "CONTENT: Modules," for more information.
Plugins	Plugins are action routines that are generally associated with "triggered events." When a "triggered event" occurs, it executes a function associated with a Plugin. One example is to have a Module displayed within an Article. When the Article is opened for viewing, the Plugin is triggered to display the designated Module. There are all kinds of Plugins within Joomla! and they generally operate unattended. They are pretty much on auto pilot when installed (usually as part of a Component or Module), and require little or no intervention by the Administrator. Because of this, there is no Chapter in this book that is dedicated specifically to Plugins. However, they may be mentions and references throughout the Chapters as to their use and function. In some instances, Plugins might need to be "Enabled" if this is not their default State when installed.
Libraries	Libraries are packages of code that provide a related group of functions to the core Joomla! 5 Bootstrap Framework, or to the Extensions. Routine Administrator functions normally do not require interaction with the code Libraries. They are simply code repositories that the programs core uses for itself. It is possible that Libraries might need to be accessed by Developers that are performing customizations.
Languages	If you want more than one "Language" for your website, you can add specific "Language" Extensions. Joomla! is used worldwide and websites are built on many different languages. Chapter 28, "COMPONENT:

	Multilingual Associations," is devoted to this topic.
Templates	The actual physical structure and visual layout of the website pages are controlled by the Templates being used. A Template displays the website in a certain layout, with Module Positions, Style Sheets, and control over Content and appearance. In fact, Templates now have been designed so they are fluid and highly responsive to display Content on large monitors and small mobile devices without modification of their code or Style Sheets. In addition, more than one Template can be used on a website by associating a different Template with a specific Menu Link Item in a Menu. Chapter 17, "VISUAL: Templates and Chapter 18, "VISUAL: Style Sheets," along with Chapter 19, "VISUAL: Using Template/Page Builders," covers the subject thoroughly.

Sources of Content

The actual Content of a Joomla! 5 website is generated from four main sources.

These are: Articles, Modules, Components/Extensions and from Plugin triggers, as illustrated in Figure 5-3.

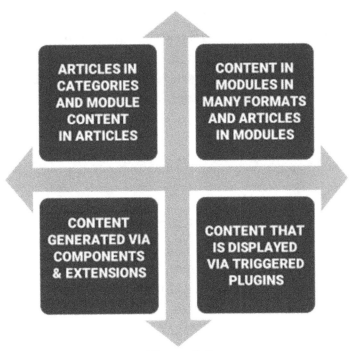

Figure 5-3

Here are descriptions of the four Content sources and how they relate to one another:

Articles from Categories	Articles are the main source of Content on Joomla! 5 websites. Articles are assigned to Categories, or Sub-Categories, and discussed in depth later in this book.
Content in Modules	Much Content on a Joomla! 5 website is generated and displayed by using Modules, which are Content Items that are assigned to a fixed physical location on a webpage. Chapter 12, "CONTENT: Modules," offers complete information on Modules, including what kind of information they can display for routine or creative Content. Modules are the "Sticky Notes" of Joomla! Put something on them and conditionally place them everywhere or anywhere.
Content from Components/Extensions	Components and specific Extensions are the "mini-applications" that generate and display information on a website. There are thousands of Components available, and many of those used on Joomla! 3 and 4 websites could be in the process of modification to work with Joomla! 5.
Content from Triggered Plugins	Plugins generate Content when something happens on the website that "triggers" them into action. As previously noted, Plugins tend to operate all by themselves without Administrator involvement. Plugins act as silent partners to many Components and Modules and reside in the background performing their function with no need for Administrator attention.

Components Control Area

Within the default Joomla! 5 installation, there are five Components, as explained below.

Banners	**Banners** are Content elements you can place at various locations on your website. Banners are simple advertisement panels that can be sold on your website, or used for any purpose you want. Banners can be classified into Banner Categories and Banner Clients. Tracks deals with information about how visitors interact with them, re: clicks, etc. Visit Chapter 26, "COMPONENT: Banners," for detailed instructions on their use.
Contacts	The **Contacts** Component is used to list individuals and can be classified into Categories. Typically, these would be used in business websites where a company has many departments and key personnel

	are to be contact points for that department. More about the Contact Component can be found in Chapter 27, "COMPONENT: Contacts."
Multilingual Associations	If you have the "Language" Filter Plugin enabled, this Component can be used to manage a number of various aspects of making your website multi-language functional. Chapter 28, "Component: Multilingual Associations," should be referenced if multiple Languages are to be used on your website.
New Feeds	**Newsfeeds** can be classified into Newsfeed Categories and are simply a way of displaying information from other websites onto your website. You may recognize a Newsfeed by the term: RSS. Chapter 29, "COMPONENT: News Feeds" covers the use of this Component.
Smart Search	The **Smart Search** Component is a level above the ordinary Search function. The Component requires indexing of the entire Content of the website and is explained in Chapter 30, "COMPONENT: Smart Search." It is an extremely helpful feature on websites that have substantial amounts of Content.
Tags	**Tags** operate in Joomla! much in the same way as hashtags do on social media. One or more Tags ("words or phrases"), can be assigned to Content Items. They are helpful on websites that have a large amount of content and when used in conjunction with, enhance the Search and Smart Search. Chapter 31, "COMPONENT: Tags," contains instructions how to implement and use them.

Users Control Area

If you have a website that operates with one or more Super Users, or with Content that is administrated by Authors, Editors and Publishers, the Joomla!4 User Control ("ACL") has the horsepower to manage and control it.

Content administration access can be controlled and limited to different Users or Users in User Groups, with varying degrees of Access Levels, as described below.

Chapter 23, "USERS: Managing Users," and Chapter 24, "USERS: Access, Actions & Permissions," both address the use of managing Access Control ("ACL"). If you or only a handful of people can access all of the Content, you do not need "ACL" to be invoked. But, if you have a blogging or magazine-style website, then implementing "ACL" is something that you will want to master for your website.

Joomla! "ACL" is a complex subject, and its implementation must follow a certain number of steps to properly implement. You might need several tries to get it right, but in the end, you will learn how it functions, how to implement ACL and put it to use on your website.

System Control Area

When the System button is accessed, it opens another layer of website administration that will be frequently accessed. There are many administrative tasks accessible via this Menu screen, and they are explained below. Throughout the Chapter in this book, you will be referred to these Menu Items to perform certain tasks related to website management.

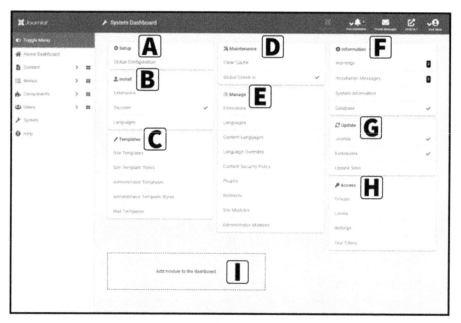

Figure 5-4

Setup	A	This accesses the Global Configuration area of the entire website. Settings that can be changed are: Site, System, Text Filters & Permissions. For the most part, none of these settings need to be changed or modified. However, there may be Exercises included in different Chapters that will instruct you to access this area and make specific changes.
Install	B	This is an important section because it is the gateway for installing Extensions and Templates into the website. It also allows the installation of the various "Language" files for multi-language websites.
Templates	C	This is an important section. It deals with the Templates used on the website for both the Front-End and Back-End. Chapter 17, "VISUAL: Templates," extensively covers Templates and their configuration and uses.
Maintenance	D	Clearing the current website cache, along with any expired cache might be necessary from time-to-time to speed up the website. This is especially needed for websites with massive amounts of Content. Also, the "Global Check-In" function allows the Administrator to

		alter the status of Content Items that have been checked out wherein the User did not log out, thus locking it and restricting others from access.
Manage	E	Essentially, it is the place where Extensions are "Enabled" or "Disabled." "Language" configurations can also be managed here along with Plugins (a form of an Extension), Redirects and both Site and the Administrator Modules.
Information	F	Warnings, Installation Messages, System Information and Database info is accessed in this section. None of these areas will need to be accessed on a regular or frequent basis, unless there are issues directing you to do so.
Update	G	From time to time, Joomla! is updated and this is where you manage that process for your website. Not only does it deal with updates to Joomla!, it also helps with updates for any Extensions that have been added.
Access	H	This area deals with creating website access for both the Front-End and the Back-End. Chapter 24, "USERS: Access, Actions & Permissions," is devoted to this subject. The Users Menu in the Left Admin Menu also gives you access to these same controls.
[Blank]	I	Clicking on this blank module allows the Administrator to add other Joomla! 5 website Module to this screen.

Links to Same Screens

Some of the functions and Administrator locations in the System Menu area are the links to the same controls found in other Menus in the Admin Back-End. They take you to the same screens. This may seem complicated at first, but after a while, you will know where to go directly, or the quickest route, for certain actions you might need to perform.

Help Feature

About all we are going to suggest about the "Help" feature in the Administrator "Home Dashboard" is: *"go look for yourself."* Almost all of the links are the same as those found on the main Joomla! website.

Of greatest interest will likely be the "Joomla! Help" link item. We suggest you visit some of the link items. And, oh yes, make sure you scroll manually to the top of the screen when you open them to see the content.

We might note that the Help Wiki Document is maintained by generous volunteers and sometimes it takes a while for updated help information to be added. As previously stated, don't have high expectations about the help information page content with respect to high levels of details on "how to use Joomla! 5." For example, the help screens do not really go into depth in the same manner as this book does. The Help Screens, for the most part, are simply explanations of the obvious, or explaining what is being viewed vs. "how to" do things, which is why we wrote, not only this book, but the three others we previously authored.

Cautionary Note

When viewing the Joomla.org website Help screens, make sure that the help you are looking at is for Joomla! Version 5, and not Joomla! Version 3 or 4. In many instances, the previous version help screens have been copied over, or the link takes you to the help resources for the older version. Pay close attention to which help document is being displayed and which you are reading.

Also, this book has not taken the easy way out with minimal Content. The instructions and Exercises go into detail, explaining what is being done, how to do it, and then what the end results should look like. To us, this is THE WAY to present Joomla! 5 as a good choice for building both simple and complex websites.

In saying this, it is also strongly suggested that you perform every Exercise in every Chapter, and do so in the order presented. Some Content and Exercises later in the book rely upon, and refer to, actions and Content that has been added in those previous Exercises.

THIS IS IMPORTANT! Complete all the Exercises. Complete them in the order presented.

CHAPTER 6

ADMIN:
Messages, Notices & Warnings

As you perform administrative tasks on the Back-End, it is likely that some sort of message, notice, alert or warning will be displayed after the action is completed. A message could also appear if the action was not completed, or if there was some sort of issue while attempting to do so.

These message displays will appear at the top of the Back-End screen and can be closed by clicking on the **"X"** at the far right side of the message panel.

After Installation

When you completed the installation of Joomla! 5, a *"Congratulations! Your Joomla site is ready,"* should have displayed on the final screen in the installing process. Figure 6-1 is what should be on the screen following a successful Joomla! 5 installation activity.

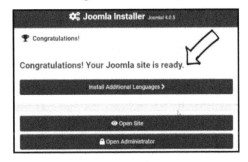

Figure 6-1

After logging into the Back-End, you typically should not receive any configuration warnings. The Message as shown in Figure 6-2 should display. Configuration warnings, if any, could possibly deal with the connections to the server or call attention to outdated, or soon-to-be outdated supporting programs on the server such as versions of "MySQL," or "PHP."

After First Admin's Login

As soon as you logged in as the website's Administrator, the Back-End displayed and a message block appeared asking you to authorize, or not, the collection of information about your Joomla! 5 installation.

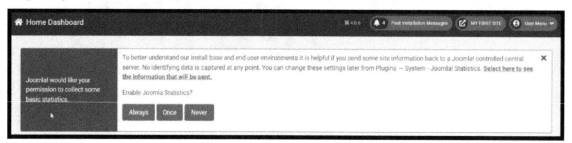

Figure 6-2

The choices of *"Always-Once-Never"* are explained below:

ALWAYS	Will send information to joomla.org whenever a change is made to the configuration of the Joomla! 5 installation.
ONCE	This choice will send the current configuration status, but only one time.
NEVER	Choosing this option will send nothing, ever.
X	By closing the message panel, none of the options are selected. However, this message block will re-appear, so it is suggested that your execute one of the three options. Always close Notifications or Message boxes by clicking on the **"X"** at the far right side of the box.

After these two message panels have been displayed, any further messages, alerts or notifications will be the result of some sort of action taken to execute something that has been created or modified on the Back-End.

Colors Controlled by Bootstrap 5

Because Joomla! 5 used Templates that are built upon Bootstrap 5, the colors for Notifications and Messages are controlled by Bootstrap. This standardizes, for the most part, all Notifications and Message colors across any platform that is using Bootstrap 5. These colors are as follows:

Green	This color is used anytime an initiated action successfully operates to completion, such as: saving, copying, etc.
Blue	Notices are typically blue in color, simply to call your attention to it. Pay attention to these messages and check anything that is indicated.

Yellow	If somethings is amiss, a "Warning Message" may display and it will generally display with a yellow background box. "Warning Messages" do not frequently appear. For example, if a User attempts to Login and does not have an account, a yellow warning will display.
Red	As expected, any "error" or serious "issue" that arises, the Administrator is alerted with a red background box display. When this happens, the Administrator should take action to resolve or cure the issue prompting the display. A "Joomla! Upgrade" notice box is typically red.

It is possible that not every Notification or Message displayed on the Front-End or Back-End of the website will conform exactly to the colors above. Or, as they say, "subject to change without notice." Another factor affecting the colors is the monitor. Not all computer monitors display colors the same or exact colors. Take that that into consideration if you are not seeing "exact shades" of the colors above.

Success Messages

A "Success" Message will always display when the initiated action has completed its processes. When a "Saving" Action has been completed, a "Success Message" will display. *"Success Messages" are always displayed as green.*

If a Content Item of any type is opened and then closed, without making any changes, no message or any type will display. Noting was done, thus this does not merit any sort of message.

Categories, Articles, Modules, Menus, Menu Link Items and all others will display a "Success Message" when the item is "Saved." This is a consistent message scheme.

If a "Saving" action of any type is completed, the green message panel will display, indicating what "successful" action was taken, as shown in the examples in Figure 6-3 for a Category and for an Article:

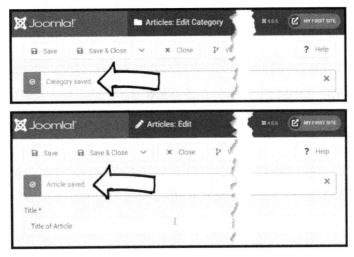

Figure 6-3

Obviously, if a "Save and Close" action is taken, the "success" of the action is the Workspace that was open is closed. Any sort of "Success Message" for this action would be somewhat redundant and a nuisance. The Content Item has "closed," thus the action was an automatic "success."

Alert Messages

If there are any issues whatsoever with a requested action on the part of a Content Item, and something is incorrect, an "Alert" Message will display. Along with the message, the item that is generating the error will be highlighted in "red" to call attention to it.

Here is an example of "Alert" Messages:

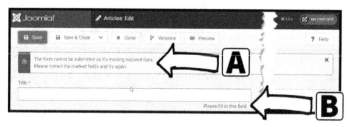

Figure 6-4

A	This is the error message, which also identifies what is wrong or incorrect with regard to content information in the Form Fields, or any other error.
B	This indicates the specific point of the error so it will help in fixing the issue.

"Alert" Messages are always displayed in red, as are the "fault" areas on the workspace that are causing the issue.

Alert Messages for Updates

In the "Notifications" Block on the "Home Dashboard," in the event there are any updates to Joomla!, Extensions, Overrides or Messages, an "alert" will be displayed by a change in color or the affected area.

If all issues are resolved and everything is current, these identification boxes will display a constant "green" color. If there is an "alert" or something that needs attention, the color will change to "red" along with a brief message.

Alerts in the "Notifications" Block are generally very important and should get your attention to resolve and cure any of the noted issues.

Before Updating, Create a Backup

It should be a steadfast Administrator's rule that **IF** an update is required, that a **BACKUP** of the entire website and database is **always performed** before the update is initiated. If not, it is possible that an update could "break" the website to the point where it would not be able to be recovered. There are Extensions that can be added to the website Components that will perform backups with a minimum of effort and allow recovery. If not, the backups should be created within the cPanel or Plesk control panels **BEFORE** the update is initiated. Otherwise, you take your chances of putting your website at risk of being destroyed beyond recovery.

Notification Messages

Notifications generally advise the Administrator about the "System" upon which Joomla! 5 is operating. These can be on-screen notifications, or they can come to the Administrator via email.

For example, if the choice is selected in the "User Options" area, the Administrator can receive an email notification when a new User has registered, providing that feature is enabled on the website.

Notifications can also be "alarms" of sorts, letting the Administrator know that something is wrong, or has gone wrong for some reason or another.

Additionally, Notification Messages can be sent to website Users.

Extensions to Manage Messages

Within the Joomla! Extension's Directory, there are a number of third-party installable Extensions that provides the Administrator with a means to manage and customize any messages or notifications.

At present, most of these are for Version 3 of Joomla!, so *DO NOT USE THEM.*

If you find a Messaging Extension of interest, first make absolutely sure that it is compatible with Joomla! 5 – double check this with the developer to make sure. Using a Joomla! 3 Extension on a Joomla! 5 website could "break" the website to the point where it may not be able to be recovered or restored.

Things Happen, Notifications or Messages Display

It is reasonable to assume that when the Administrator does something, or performs an "action" on the Back-End, there will be a resulting Notification or Message displayed. This is just good management to allow the Administrator to know that everything has worked as expected, or that an "issue" may have arisen that requires attention.

Front-End Users will also see Notifications and Messages displayed under certain occurrences of actions, good or improper. The color scheme for User Notifications and Messages on the Front-End is the same as the Administrator sees on the Back-End.

No Notifications to the Administrator

When a Front-End User does something that will cause a Notification or Message to display, the Administrator *does not* receive a notice about it. This makes sense because the Administrator could be overloaded with minor notifications if the case were the other way around.

The Back-End Message System

Under the Users Menu in the Back-End, there is a link to a "Messaging > Private Messages" feature. This feature allows all Users who have permission to access the Back-End to send a "message" to the website Administrator.

Also, assume that the Administrator has a need to take the website offline for a period of time. One way to let Back-End Users know is to use the "Mass Email to Users" method to send the notification.

Access to both features is found under the "Users" Menu on the "Home Dashboard."

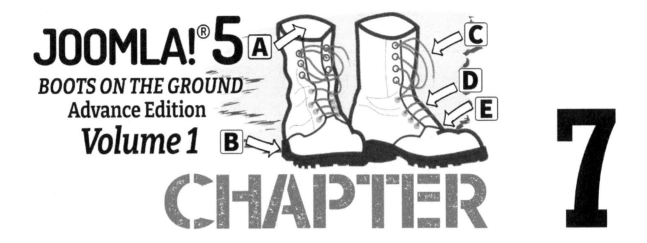

Fast Track Double Time Start

This Chapter has been purposefully included to give you a "Fast Track Start" as a Joomla! 5 website Administrator by accessing and using the Back-End and some of the action steps needed to create Categories, Articles and Menu Link Items. These are the basic actions needed to add Content to a Joomla! 5 website.

The instructions in this Chapter are very fundamental and if you can grasp them early in the learning process, the rest of your Joomla! 5 experience will be easier.

All the details of Categories, Articles, Menus and Menu Link Items can be examined in depth later in the individual Chapters dedicated to them. There isn't any reason for you to wade through the entire book before performing some of the basic tasks of creating Content. Thus, this "Fast Track Start" Chapter is included.

Lace up your Administrator's boots and let's get going.

Accessing the Back-End

For the purposes of this "Fast Track" group of instructions, the assumption is that you are the website's Administrator and the only person permitted to add/edit Content. As the Administrator, you must log into Joomla! 5's Back-End to manage the website and access the various Manager Sections for Content creation and management.

NOTE – THIS IS IMPORTANT!!!

All of the Exercises in this book build upon one another. To get meaningful training benefits, complete all the steps and instructions in the Exercises, _in the exact order presented_. Do not skip around. The

Exercises MUST be performed and completed sequentially as you go through each Exercise in each Chapter progressively.

EXERCISE 7-1: ACCESSING THE BACK-END

Objective: This Exercise will demonstrate how to access the Administrator's area of the website. This is the method the Administrator must use every time to access the Back-End to administer the Content and otherwise manage the website. However, the Administrator may access Content from the Front-End, but that isn't part of the basics involved or discussed at this point. The idea here is to provide the fundamentals as soon as possible while working with Joomla! 5 Back-End.

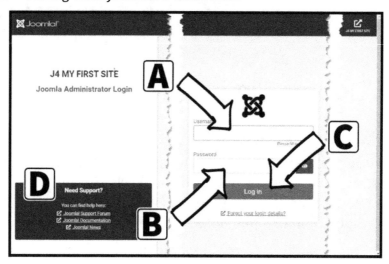

Figure 7-1

Refer to Figure 7-1 for the following:

Step 1		Go to: *http://(domain name)/myfirstsite/administrator* to access the Back-End Login screen. The Back-End is always accessed by adding */administrator* after the domain name in the browser's location bar. The */myfirstsite/* sub-directory is the location into which your Joomla! 5 practice website should have been installed.
Step 2		The Admin Login Page will appear (Figure 7-1). If Joomla! 5 is installed in a sub-directory, the "administrator" path must be in the same sub-directory path as the installation.
Step 3	A B	Log in using the Administrator name and password that you designated when you installed Joomla! 5. Notice that you can view the password that is being entered using the eye icon to the right in the password field. (This feature was not engaged for the screen shot.)
Step 4	C	Execute the "Log In Button." If your User/Password ("U/P"), was correct, the Back-End Control Panel (Figure 7-2) should display. This screen is also called the "Home Dashboard" which, by default, displays the Control

		Panel. Note that the location of the blocks on the control panel may vary, based on the resolution and width of the monitor upon which the webpage is being viewed.
	D	Help is available using these links to the joomla.org website.

Back-End May Change

Because the Joomla! 5 program is always being improved, changes may be made to the Administrator Back-End and Front-End Screens. If changes are made, they will likely be included in future upgrades or updates to the Joomla! 5 version in use. Be aware that this might happen in the future. Should that be the case, the screenshots in this book may be slightly different than those in any future release of Joomla! 5 sub-versions.

After successfully logging into the Back-End, the Administrator's "Home Dashboard" will display, as shown in Figure 7-2. Each of the sections and functions of the "Home Dashboard" will be explained, not only in this Chapter, but within all the Chapters that follow.

Figure 7-2

The "Home Dashboard" Control Panel – Don't Panic!

Every time you log in, the screen shown in Figure 7-2 will open as the starting point to perform Back-End tasks. Various features of the Back-End will be discussed in different Chapters of this book, as their use is required.

Before you experience an *"OMG!!!"* moment when seeing the Back-End for the first time, here's is what you need to know when you log in as the Administrator. The "Home Dashboard" Control Panel is simply the starting point for all Joomla! 5 Back-End tasks. This administrative area is the "gateway" to access any of the functions needed to manage the entire website and its functions/features.

Reviewing the accompanying descriptions of the various areas will be helpful in understanding their purpose and function.

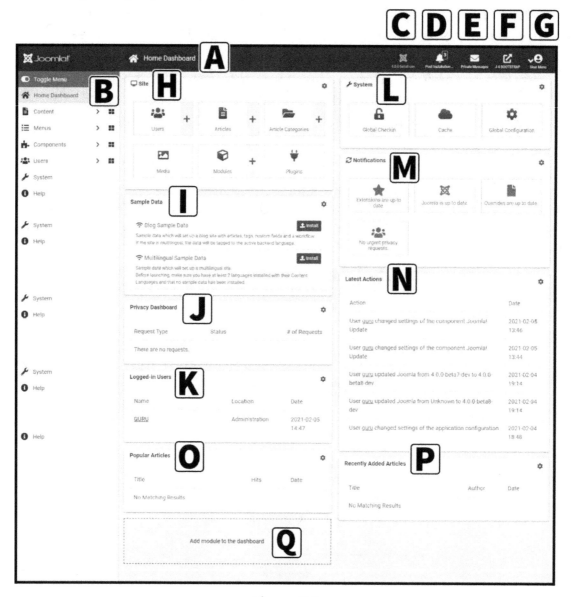

Figure 7-3

Refer to Figure 7-3 for the following:

A	The Control Panel heading will change depending upon what screen you are viewing in the Control Panel, identifying which Manager or Administration Area is being displayed. Clicking the Joomla! logo at the top left of the screen will take you

	back to the Main Screen of the Administrator Control Panel [this screen] from any other screen.
B	The links in this Menu access other important administrative areas. Each of these areas is covered in depth in other Chapters of the book. There are administrative areas in the left Menu that can only be accessed there, while some also have duplicate access links on the main "Home Dashboard" screen.
C	Here you will find which version of Joomla! 5 is installed.
D	The "Bell icon" indicates that Post Installation Messages have been posted for your attention.
E	Private Messages indicate that other Registered Users have communicated with you.
F	The Box/Arrow icon, when clicked, opens a new browser window and displays the website Front-End in a new browser window. This icon typically appears on all Back-End windows.
G	The User Menu opens a workspace where your User information and other settings can be configured, including a change of passwords.
H	The buttons in the Site Panel provide fast access to some of the most frequently used administrative functions that deal with Content, Layout and Website functionalities.
I	The Sample Data Panel offers the option to install Content into the website. It also allows for the installation of some Multilingual Sample Data, if you will be creating a website that uses more than one language.
!!!	Each of the Panels in the Back-End can be Edited or "Unpublished" to suit your preference for the display of this screen.
J	The Privacy Dashboard Panel serves to notify the Administrator of User requests for Privacy Information, which might relate to the website's Privacy Policy.
K	Current Logged-in Users are shown in this Panel.
L	The System Panel provides access to various local platform configuration settings.
M	If there are any updates to Joomla, or to Extensions that use the updating system, it can be managed in the Notifications Panel. If there are updates, the box colors will change to call it to your attention.
N	The Latest Actions Panel indicates actions that have been taken on the website's access or Content.
O	This shows Popular Articles that have been most viewed, which can be configured in the Panel's Edit area.
P	Lists the most Recently Added Articles, the number of which, can be set in the Panel's Edit area.

Q	This Panel allows the Administrator to add more Panels to the Back-End.

Installing the Blog Sample Data

To ensure that the Exercises in this book have functional meaning and give you the proper learning experience, it is necessary to install the Blog Sample Data and discuss what is happening. This is also necessary for the purposes of demonstrations and Exercise in the following Chapters of the book.

EXERCISE 7-2: INSTALLING THE BLOG SAMPLE DATA

Objective: This action will install some basic blog-style Content and Menus onto the website. You do not need to do this for your final working site, but it is suggested you do this here so the following Exercises will make sense and illustrate the different Back-End functions with working examples. Many of the Exercises in this book are predicated upon the installation of the "Sample Data." The "Multilingual Sample Data" is not being installed, and cannot be installed after the "Sample Data" has been added.

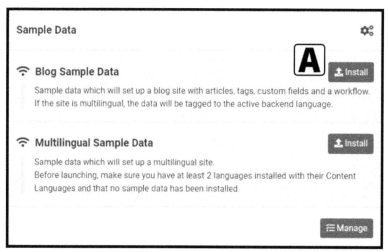

Figure 7-4

Refer to Figure 7-4 for the following:

Step 1	In the Sample Data Panel, execute the "Install" action for "Blog Sample Data" to begin the process of including the "Sample Data" onto the website.

Figure 7-5

Refer to Figure 7-5 for the following:

Step 2	After initiating the action, you will be asked to confirm it (Figure 7-5). Do so by initiating the "OK" action.

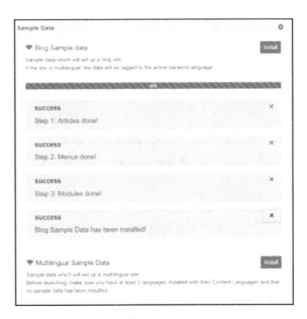

Figure 7-6

Refer to Figure 7-6 for the following:

Step 3	During the installing process, you may see some information display progressively on the screen. During this time, do not leave the browser window, or attempt to initiate any other actions. If you are seeing the screen (Figure 7-6), with the information display, this means that the Sample Data has been successfully added to the website. If the screen is not being displayed, it is possible that the latest Joomla! 5 version's installing message sequences will/have been replaced with the Joomla! logo spinner or another screen. Just be patient during this sequence! The display may change to Joomla! spinning logo in future release candidates. However, these are the four steps involved the addition of the Blog Sample Content processes to become part of the website. This is being included here for informational purposes.

During installation, there may be messages on the screen with a Joomla! logo spinner, indicating the status of the Sample Data installation. Be patient and let the process complete. There will be a green panel display at the top of the screen indicated that the task has been completed. The message will say: "Sample data installed!" Click on the **"X"** in the message panel to close it.

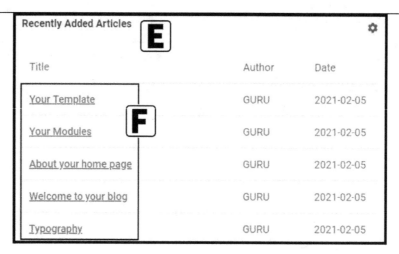

Figure 7-7

Refer to Figure 7-7 for the following:

Step 4	Verification that the Sample Data has been added can be confirmed in the "Recently Added Articles" block on the "Home Dashboard" Control Panel screen (Figure 7-7). These are the "Sample Data" Articles that have been added. A screen refresh may be required to view the populated list – do so to ensure the display is correct.

Refer to Figure 7-8 for the following:

Step 5	Next, view the website Front-End, by clicking the "Front-End" icon as shown in Figure 7-8, at the top right of the screen, and view the new Content in the Main Content Area and Menu Modules that have been added on the right side of the screen.

This button opens the website Front-End

Figure 7-8

Figure 7-9

New Modules & Content Added

After installing the Sample Data, the new Front-End, as shown in Figure 7-9, displays the new Menu Modules and Information Modules and Content that have been added to the Front-End as a result of the above Exercise.

A	A new Menu Module, in a horizontal format, has been added to the top of the screen. This Menu is dedicated to the "Blog Content" that was added as "Sample Data."
B	This is the website "Search" Module which allows searching all of the Content on the website.
C	This Template has a Module, containing an image and text, located at "Module

	Position" = "banner" on the "Home page" of the website. It will only display when the website is opened to the "Home page." It can be "Unpublished." This image, because it takes up so much space, will be "Unpublished" in a latter Exercise.
D	The Template also has a Module that displays the "Latest Posts" at the "Module Position" = "top-a." This Module is displaying the last three Articles that were "Published." They will only display when the website is opened to the Home Page. It can be Unpublished.
E	This displays the website "Breadcrumb" pathway. This Module can be "Unpublished" if the "Breadcrumbs" are not desired.
F	This is a Module with an image and set up similar to "C" in Figure 7-9, but located in a different Module Position.
G	This is the Main Menu Module and contains the "Home" Menu Link Item, which is the default opening page of the website.
H	The User Login Module is located here.
I	The Content displayed in the Main Content area of the Home Page, in this case, are the "Featured Articles," and is controlled by the Home Menu Link Item. Every Article that appears on this "Home" screen are designated as "Featured," in addition to their regular Category assignments. Articles from multiple Categories can be designated as "Featured" and will display here on the front page.
J	The "Popular Tags" Module is displayed in this "Module Position" on the Home page of the website. It can be "Unpublished."
K	The "Older Posts" Module is displayed in this respective "Module Position" on the Home page of the website. It can be "Unpublished."

After Installing the Blog Sample Data

To make things easier when performing Exercises in this and later Chapters, the "Image Modules" located at the "banner" and "top-a" Module Positions should be removed, or "Unpublished." This will make it easier to view the Home screen without the need to constantly scroll down the screen.

Sharing Data with Joomla! Option

During the first login, a request will be made on the screen to share information about your Joomla! 5 instance with joomla.org. Make the choice and execute the appropriate button to clear the message display. It will not appear again after this action.

EXERCISE 7-3: UNPUBLISHING SELECTED MODULES

Objective: This Exercise will guide the Administrator through the process of "Unpublishing" two Modules that appear on the "Home" screen. These are being "Unpublished" for convenience for scrolling the "Home" screen. By doing this, the main screen will be easier to view, with less scrolling, in the Exercises that follow in other Chapters.

Please perform these steps exactly as described. These and similar Administrator actions will be further explained later and in greater detail in other Chapters and Exercises.

Step 1	If not already there, go to the Back-End and log in as the Administrator. The "Home Dashboard" will be the predominate display.
Step 2	In the "Site" Block, click on the "Modules" panel – but not on the **"+"** part, which creates a new Module. Clicking on the main block icon opens the List of Modules on the website.
Step 3	On the list, under the "Position" column, find the Module in the "banner" "Module Position" The name of the Module is: "Image." This might be the first Module listed. If not, search for it on the list.
Step 4	Place the cursor over the green check mark icon. Click on it to put the Module into the "Unpublished" state. The icon will change, indicating the item is no longer "Published."
Step 5	Scroll down the List of Modules and find the Module located in the "top-a" "Module Position" This is the "Latest Posts" Module.
Step 6	Place the cursor over the green check mark icon. Click on it to put the Module into the "Unpublished" state. The icon will change, indicating the item is no longer "Published."
Step 7	Go to the website Front-End and refresh the screen. Notice now that the large banner image is no longer displayed. The image being displayed at the top is associated with the "Your Template" Article.
Step 8	Also note the Modules on the right side are now more conveniently displayed, as is the other Article Content displayed in the Main Content Area.

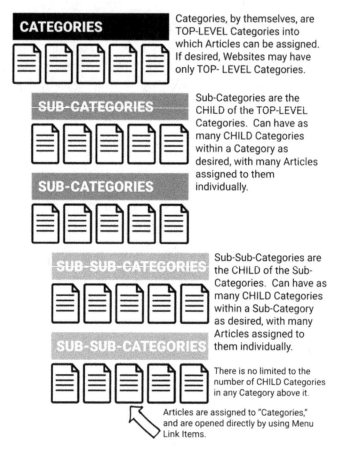

Categories, by themselves, are TOP-LEVEL Categories into which Articles can be assigned. If desired, Websites may have only TOP- LEVEL Categories.

Sub-Categories are the CHILD of the TOP-LEVEL Categories. Can have as many CHILD Categories within a Category as desired, with many Articles assigned to them individually.

Sub-Sub-Categories are the CHILD of the Sub-Categories. Can have as many CHILD Categories within a Sub-Category as desired, with many Articles assigned to them individually.

There is no limited to the number of CHILD Categories in any Category above it.

Articles are assigned to "Categories," and are opened directly by using Menu Link Items.

Figure 7-10

Understanding the Joomla! 5 Content Structure

Most of the Content on a Joomla! 5 website consists of Articles. Articles must be assigned to Categories (Figure 7-10). In fact, in case you forget to make a specific Category assignment, all Articles created are automatically assigned to a default Category called: "Uncategorized."

As part of the "Fast Track Chapter," Categories, Articles and Menu Link items will be created to help you understand the method of doing so, and the relationships between them. When you complete the Exercises below, you will probably be surprised at how easy it was to do something that initially sounds complicated. The actions are really not complicated if you follow the action steps needed to create each element. After that, the same actions are simply repeated steps.

Joomla! 5 has many configuration rules that govern the creation and management of Content. Listed below are some of the general rules pertaining to Categories, Articles and Menu Link Items. Once you have this basic understanding of how Content is created and displayed, you won't have any trouble doing so after this Chapter's Exercises are completed.

Rules Relating to Categories, Articles & Menu Link Items.

Rule 1	Categories are the top level of Content Management for Articles.
Rule 2	Categories can have Articles assigned to them, but only Articles.
Rule 3	Articles must be assigned to a Category, regardless of its level in the hierarchy of Categories.
Rule 4	Articles that are not specially assigned, automatically are designated into a default Category called: "Uncategorized."
Rule 5	Sub-Categories (a child of a Category), can be created and assigned within any Category above it.
Rule 6	Sub-Sub-Categories (a child of a Sub-Category), can be created and assigned within any Sub-Category.
Rule 7	Categories cannot be assigned to multiple parent Categories.
Rule 8	There is no fixed limit to the number of parent or child Categories that can be created.
Rule 9	There is no fixed limit to the number of child Categories that can be created in any Category above it in the hierarchy.
Rule 10	Articles can only be assigned to a single Category, although there may be Extensions that modify this rule which allows an Article to be assigned to multiple Categories.
Rule 11	There is no fixed limit to the number of Articles that can be created.
Rule 12	There is no fixed limit to the number of Articles that can be assigned to a Category.
Rule 13	There is no such element as an Article "child."
Rule 14	Articles can be associated with each other through creation of automatic within-Articles links, or via the use of "Tags" to create a subject or topic commonality among them. "Tags" are not a substitute for Category classification assignments.
Rule 15	A Menu Link Item, within a Menu, is required to directly open an Article for viewing. However, there are a multitude of other types of Menu Link Items can be created to access other type of Content by selecting other types of Content layouts and configurations.
Rule 16	There is no fixed limit to the number of Menu Link Items, nor any limit to a multiple link hierarchy that can be created, so long as each item links to an Article [or some other type of Content]. Mega Menu Extensions greatly enhance this capability.

Rule 17	There is no practical limit to the number of Menus that can be created and made accessible, either directly, or some other interaction among elements to make them visible.
Rule 18	Menu Link Items can be connected to Content other than Articles, and this is covered in Chapter 21, "NAVIGATION: Menu Systems."
Rule 19	A Category must be created, into which an Article is assigned when it is created. Then, to access the Article, a Menu Link Item must be created within a Menu, which connects to an Article to make it visible.

In short, a Category must be created, into which an Article is assigned when it is created. Then, to access the Article, a Menu Link Item must be created within a Menu, which connects to an Article to make it visible.

There is extensive information in the respective individual Chapters in this book that deal with Categories, Articles, Menus, Menu Link Items and Modules.

Links to Components

As previously mentioned, Content also is generated from Components, for example, a Shopping Cart Extension. When Component Extensions are added or that can be linked, that option choice is automatically added to the list of Menu Link Item Types that can be selected when creating the Menu Link Item. So, rather than selecting an Articles link, you select the Component's designated as a link choice, then one of the targets available within it.

The choices of Menu Link Items within the Menus selections will indicate all of the links that can be created for any type of Extension that has been installed. In some cases, the number of Extension-specific links can be extensive.

For a Shopping Cart, a possible Menu Link Item choice could be "New Products." In that case, if that choice is selected, and it is designated as the Home link, it would display "New Products" automatically when the site opens. This is one of hundreds of possibilities for linking Components to Menu Link Items to generate Content display.

Looking at the Hierarchy

As discussed above, Figure 7-10 provides a visual representation of what a typical Content hierarchy looks like in Joomla! 5. Of course, there are any given number of combinations of Categories designated as parents and child. This all depend on your website and the depth and complexity of Content.

The Content organization shown in Figure 7-10 can be compared to a typical file cabinet. Within the drawers are hanging folders that contain file folders, that contain documents, as follows:

The Cabinet	The file cabinet itself can be considered as the Content Component.
File Drawers	The individual file drawers can be thought of as the "Parent Categories."
Hanging Folders	The hanging folders would be "Sub-Categories" of the "Parent-Category."
Individual Folders	Then, the individual file folders within the hanging folders are the "Sub-Sub-Categories" of the "Sub-Categories," and so on. Consider them as "grandchildren" Categories.
Documents	Finally, within these folders, at any Category level, are Documents which consist of Articles within the Joomla! 5 Content hierarchy. Documents ("Articles"), can be placed into any folder at any location in the file cabinet.

Minimize Hierarchy Complexity

Don't make Content hierarchies too complicated. With too many Menus with Menu Link Items that go to too many different Categories ("parent or child"), website visitors can get easily confused and chase their tails trying to find and access Content. Keep the hierarchy as simple and condensed as possible, steering the User to the most important Content. Use of the Category Blog or Category List type of Menu Link Items can an effective way to display a collection of within individual Categories or groups of Categories Articles.

Not all Links Must Go Directly to Articles

As discussed above, not all Menu Link Items must go to Articles. In fact, Menu Link Items can connect to different targets on the Website, which will be explained fully in Chapter 21, "NAVIGATION: Menu Systems."

Another example of this is a situation where a Menu Link Item's target is a Category, at any level in the Content hierarchy. When the link action is executed, it displays a "list view" of all the Articles that have been assigned to that Category. The List of Articles are links that connect to the individual Articles, opening them for viewing. In this case, it was not necessary to create a Menu Link Item to each Article, but rather, only to the Category that contains them, and subsequently the ability to "drill down" into the Articles themselves.

Also, a Menu Link Item can be created that points to a Category List that shows the Sub-Categories within the top Category, which is the Menu Link Item target.

How the Content Structure is Created

Content is generally created for access by executing one of three actions:

Action 1	Create a Category using the Category Manager. Or create a Category at any location within the Category hierarchy you have determined meets the needs of the website.
Action 2	Create an Article via the Article Manager and assign it to any Category.
Action 3	Create a Menu Link Item in a Menu that connects to an Article, assuming the Menu itself already exists.

In the following Exercises, while performing the Actions above, you will only find instructions that cover what is needed to complete the task. On the various Admin Screens, you will see many other controls, options, Buttons, fill-in boxes, and other parameter settings. For the "Fast Track" Exercises, you can ignore most of them. However, later in the book, or our companion books, you will learn more about these items. Right now, the focus will be only on the basics so you will understand the fundamentals of creating Content on a Joomla! 5 website.

While completing the Exercises, go through the steps exactly as outlined and perform only those tasks, nothing else. Later Chapters will provide more detailed action steps to accomplish Content creation of all different types. These future Exercises will build upon previous Content creation.

Additionally, for the most part, Articles are the mainstay of Content. How the Article Content is, or can be, displayed is a different story. Chapter, 8, "CONTENT: Understanding the Front Page & Layouts," will explain the many different combinations of Content visual presentation. Be patient and go through the Exercises step-by-step so you will quickly understand and master the required techniques.

Category and Article Manager Options

Within the administrative management area of a Joomla! 5 website, there are various Managers. Two of the most prominent are those that pertain to Categories and Articles.

The Category Manager controls the creation, arrangement, and management of all the Categories in use on the website. When opened, this Manager opens a screen that lists the entirety of the Categories that have been created, along with "Options" to create New or additional Categories, or Sub-Categories.

The Articles Manger controls the creation, arrangement, and management of all the Articles in use on the website. When opened, this Manager opens a screen, or multiple screens, that lists the entirely of the Articles that have been created, along with "Options" to create New or additional Articles.

In both Managers, there is a link that accesses the "Options" that may be set for all types of Content. These are discussed in detail in Chapter 11, "CONTENT: Category & Article

Options." Note here that the Category "Options" are in the same location in which Article "Options" are set. They are within different tabbed areas in which the "Options" may be set or selected which apply globally.

ABOUT THOSE QUOTE MARKS

Within Exercises, quote marks are used to highlight or place emphasis. When you are instructed to enter Content in any field or area, do so WITHOUT QUOTES, even though the example text in the Exercises includes them for emphasis within the text.

EXERCISE 7-4: CREATING A CATEGORY

Objective: This Exercise creates a single "Parent Category" into which Articles will be assigned. Sub-Categories are created the same way, except they are assigned to a previously created "Parent Category" within the Category hierarchy.

Note: *Arrangement of the blocks on the "Home Dashboard" may appear differently based on the screen width and resolution of the monitor screen being used.*

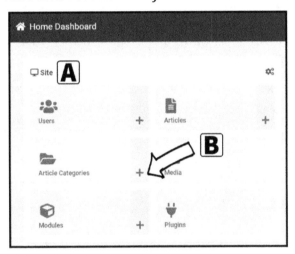

Figure 7-11

Refer to Figure 7-11 for the following:

Step 1		In the "Home Dashboard" Control Panel, locate the Site Panel, which will likely be the topmost block.
Step 2	A	Within the Site Panel, in the Article Categories block, click on the **"+"**
	B	which will open the Category Manager Workspace.

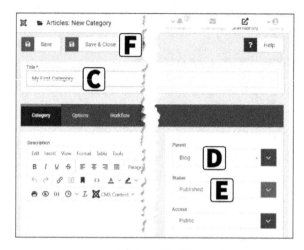

Figure 7-12

Refer to Figure 7-12 for the following:

Step 3	**C**	In the text field, enter: "My First Category" (without the quotes).
Step 4	**D**	In the Parent selection area, located to the right, select the "Blog" option. This assigns "My First Category" as a "child" into a "Parent Category" named "Blog."
		It is not necessary to enter any Description for a Category. Text may be added if desired, but it is not necessary to do so.
Step 5	**E**	Execute the Save & Close action.

Figure 7-13

Refer to Figure 7-13 for the following:

Step 6	**G**	If the action was successful, the on-screen "Success" message will display, indicating the Category has been saved (Figure 7-13). The "Success Message" appears whenever any Content Item has been successfully saved into the system. The message panel does not close automatically, so you much close it with the next Step's action.
Step 7	**H**	Execute the **"X"** action to close the success notification message.
Step 8	**I**	Return to the "Home Dashboard" and click on the Article Categories link

		icon in the Site Panel to open the Administrator's Category List view.

Refer to Figure 7-14 for the following:

Step 9	**J**	Upon returning to the Category List, the new "My First Category" should be visible as shown in Figure 7-14 as a "child" of the "parent" Category named "Blog."

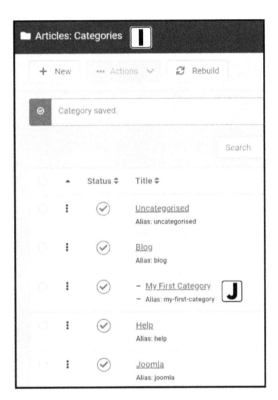

Figure 7-14

About the Save Buttons

Throughout the Administrator Screens, whenever you make entries on an element, you will be required to execute a "Saving" action, as shown in Figure 7-15. But, there are other types of "Saving" actions, that can come in handy on occasion when creating Content.

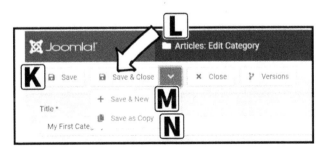

Figure 7-15

Save	K	This action saves your screen and keeps the same screen in view. This is a convenient feature in the event the item contains a lot of information, and it is necessary to pause occasionally. The "Save" action keeps the item open for further and continued editing.
Save & Close	L	When executed, this action saves your data, then it closes the screen and opens a new screen This shows a list of items in the current section that is being edited. This applies to all Content Managers.
Save & New	M	When executed, this action saves your screen, also duplicating it, removing all the data entered. This gives you're a blank screen to create another incidence of the same type (Category, Article, etc.).
Save as Copy	N	When executed, this action saves your screen, and duplicates the screen but, unlike "Save & New," it does not remove the data. When executed, it changes the "Title" and "alias" by adding a numerical suffix. You can change the title, alias and anything else on this copied version and it will not affect the original source element or document.

Save it or Lose it!

If changes have been made to the Content, but one of the four save "Options" have not been executed, and the item is "Closed," the input or changes will be lost. This applies in all instances of Content, be it default or added Components, Articles, Categories, Modules, or settings made within the Content Managers. *To keep the Content, some sort of "saving action" must be executed.*

EXERCISE 7-5: CREATING AN ARTICLE IN A CATEGORY

Objective: This Exercise creates an Article that will be assigned to the "My First Category" created in a previous Exercise. This function is what will likely be used the most frequently on a Joomla! 5 website. Articles are the main type of Content on a website and thus likely the type of Content that will be created more frequently. Articles are assigned to Categories during their creation process.

Here is the process to follow to create an Article and assign it to a previously created Category:

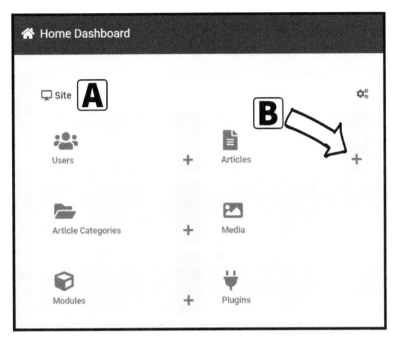

Figure 7-16

Refer to Figure 7-16 for the following:

A	Again, on the "Home Dashboard," within the Site Panel, as part of the Articles access
B	point, click on the **"+"** which will open the Article Manager Workspace.

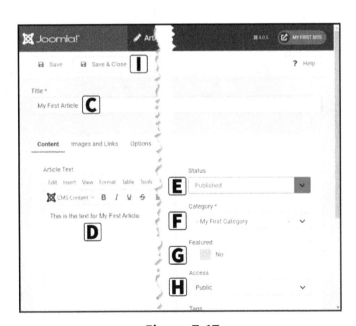

Figure 7-17

Refer to Figure 7-17 for the following:

C	Enter "My First Article" into the Title box. (without quotes). When instructed to add text to a Form Field, which are generally enclosed in quotes in this book for emphasis, do not enter the quotes when you add the text.
D	Enter "This is the text for My First Article" in the Article Text Area (without quotes).
E	In the Status selector, select "Published."
F	In the Category drop down, select "My First Category." Every Article must be assigned to a Category, even if it is the unassigned Category designation.

Something new in Joomla! 5 is the automatic "saving action" that takes place when a Content Item's "Category" is selected. When, for example, a Category is selected for an Article, an automatic "saving action" is triggered and the screen is refreshed – as would occur if the Administrator triggered a simple "Save" action.

G	*Do not* select "Yes" for the Featured selector, it should remain set to "No." This option will be covered in Chapter 10, "CONTENT: Articles."
H	Allow Access to remain selected as: "Public." Additional information on Access Control ("ACL") will be presented in Chapter 23, "USERS: Managing Users."
I	Select the Save & Close option and execute the action.

Immediately after the Save and Close action is initiated, the screen will change to the Article List view, and display the "Success Message." Remember to close the message panel using the **"X"** at the right side.

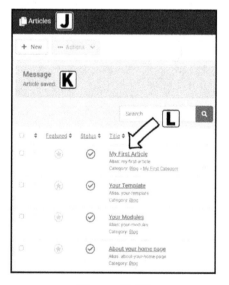

Figure 7-18

Refer to Figure 7-18 for the following:

J	The Articles screen, which lists all Articles that have been created, appears after any saving action has been executed within the Article Manager screens.
K	The "Success" message displays whenever any Content has been saved. Close the message display in the usual manner.
L	The newly created Article will appear on the list, most likely at the top of the list of Articles – if the default setting is based on "ID descending," (This is a "Global Options" setting that can be changed if desired), which refers to the number in the right column. Every item has an "ID" number and is sequentially added when created.

Figure 7-19

Refer to Figure 7-19 for the following:

M	On the Article list, note the information regarding the Category assignment, indicating the top Category is "Blog," with a child or Sub-Category of "My First Category." This is where the Article is assigned within the Content structure. Clicking on any of the links in the Category breadcrumb will take you to that location.

The Article has now been created and assigned to a Category. However, there is yet no way to access the Article, which requires creation and configuration of an action item to display it on screen.

To display an Article, it is necessary to create a Menu Link Item that connects to the Article, to display it when the link is clicked.

ALERT!

THIS NEXT STEPS ARE IMPORTANT!
PLEASE COMPLETE THEM BEFORE PROCEEDING.

Following the Action Steps in the Exercise above, repeat the processes to create two new additional Articles assigned to "My First Category," naming them as follows (do not include the quotes):

"My Second Article" (without quotes), add text similar to the first Article, assigning it to "My First Category" in the section area to the right.

"My Third Article" (without quotes), add text similar to the first Article, assigning it to "My First Category" in the section area to the right.

The resulting Article List should now display, as shown in Figure 7-20, which indicates there are three Articles in the "Blog > My First Category" location. Verify this visually and if not correct, repeat the steps above. Again, note the "order" in which they appear – "ID descending" – which means the "last Content Item created, is the first one displayed."

Figure 7-20

EXERCISE 7-6: CREATING A MENU LINK ITEM TO AN ARTICLE

Objective: The objective of this Exercise is to guide you through the Action Steps needed to create a Menu Link Item, connect it to an Article and assign it to a Menu that has already been created. In this Exercise, the Main Menu will be used. At this point, the Main Menu only contains a "HOME" link, which is required to open the main screen of the website.

Figure 7-21

When the "Sample Data" was installed, there other Menus were created, as you can see when the Menus feature was opened. For the time being, this Exercise will work only with the Main Menu.

Refer to Figure 7-21, make note of the following:

A	If not already there, access the "Home Dashboard," which will open the Control Panel.
B	The "Home Dashboard" is the location within the Control Panel.
C	Click on the "Menus" link, which will open a list showing all of the Menus that have been created on the website.
D	Click on "Main Menu" to open it. For future reference, note the "Home" icon next to the "Main Menu" name, in the "Home Column," indicating that the websites "Home" Menu Link Item is within this Menu. It could be in any existing Menu, but in this case, it is the Main Menu.

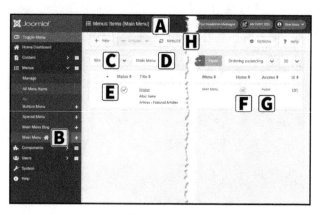

Figure 7-22

Refer to Figure 7-22, make note of the following:

A	Indicates you are viewing a Menu and the name. In this case, the Main Menu is opened.
B	The Main Menu is highlighted, indicated this is where, or which Menu is open. Also, note the "Home" icon. This indicates this link is the visitor-facing Content to be opened with the website is accessed.
C	The Administrator can view either the Site or Administrator Menu using this selector.
D	This selector will allow the Administrator to quickly change which Menu is being accessed, without going back to the "Home Dashboard."
E	The check mark here indicates the Home Menu Link Item, which is set to display "Articles > Featured Articles" is in the "Active" Status. More on this in Chapter 21, "NAVIGATION: Menu Systems."
F	The icon here indicates the Home Menu Link Item, which is set to display Articles > Featured Articles as the screen display when the website is accessed. More on "Featured Articles" in Chapter 10, "CONTENT: Articles."
G	This information column indicates which user group has access to the Menu Link Item, in this case it is: "Public." This means that everyone accessing the website can view the Home Menu Link Item. If set to other access, a User Login might be required to view the Menu Link Item.
H	Rebuild is a utility that will refresh the list of Menu Link Items within the Menu that is being accessed.

At this time, click on the **"+ New"** button at the top left of the Main Menu screen, which will open the "Menus: New Item" Manager.

REMINDER!

Because this Chapter is a "Fast Track" to learning how to perform essential tasks using Joomla! 5, many of the minute details about the tasks involved are not being discussed. These discussions are being deferred to other, subject-specific Chapters later on.

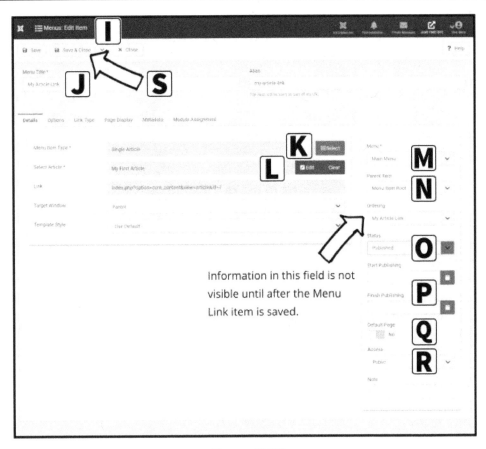

Figure 7-23

Refer to Figure 7-23 for the following:

I	On each screen there is an identifier confirming which Manager is being accessed.
J	Enter "My First Article Link" in this field to name the Menu Link Item, which is how it will be displayed in the Main Menu, that is, in which "order" it will appear within the Menu Module.
	The choice for what type of Menu Link Item, there are many and will be covered in Chapter 21, "NAVIGATION: Menu Systems. For now, complete the following Action Steps, as a continuation of the above:
K	Click on the blue "Select" Button under the "Details" tab in the Workspace.
	On the next window, select "Articles" from among choices or Menu Item Types.

		A list of choices will display, then scroll down and select "Single Article."
	L	In the "Select Article" field, click on blue "Select" button. Ignore "Create" for the time being.
		From the "List of Articles," select "My First Article," which was created previously.
	S	Execute the Save & Close Action.
		The "Success Message" will display on the screen. Close the message.
		Go to the website Front-End and refresh the screen.
		In the Main Menu at the right, note that the Menu Link Item to "My First Article" now appears. Note that it is a "top level" Menu Link Item, that is: It is not a "child" of any other Menu Link Item.
		Click on the link to verify that the correct Article Opens.
K		This field allows the Administrator to make the choice as to what type of Link will be created. There are many "Options" and will be covered in Chapter 15, wherein the Navigation Configurations will be discussed in detail.
M		Indicates which Menu is being altered, or to which a new Menu Link Item is being created. If there are several Menus, it is important to select the proper one. If the wrong Menu is chosen, the error can be easily corrected by opening the Menu Link Item Manager again, and selecting the desired Menu assignment.
N		Because a Menu Link Item can be a "child" of another, it is necessary to designate in field [L], whether the item will be a "parent," a "child" or a "child of a child," etc. This is how multi-level Menus are created by nesting Menu Link Items with each other. In other words, a Menu Link Item that is a sub-item of another Menu Link Item.
O		As is the case with all Content, there is always a choice of making the item immediately visible on the website, or not making it visible for the time being. This is done via the "Published" and "Unpublished" selectors. The setting should be set to "Published."
P		Articles, Modules and Menu Link Items can be assigned a Start ("Publish") and Stop ("Unpublish") Date for viewing. Content can be created for automatic display in the future. The Content can also be set to stop displaying at some point following Publishing. This is an automatic action and can be helpful for displaying or shutting off time-sensitive Content.
Q		If selected, the Menu Link Item and its related Link will be the "Default Home Page" that is displayed when the website it opened. Only one Menu Link Item can be designated as the Default Page. This sets the website's "Home" Page.

R	Whether this link will be available to be viewed by any website visitor, or only to Registered Users is designated in this selection area.
S	Also, as with all Content being created, one of the several Saving actions must be executed to enter the Content into the website database records.
	Go to the website Front-End, using the Button (explained previously), at the top right of the screen.

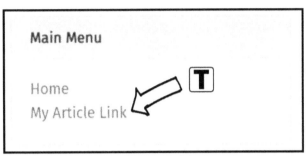

Figure 7-24

Refer to Figure 7-24 for the following:

	A new browser window will open to the website Front-End.
T	The Menu Link Item entitled: "My Article Link" should appear in the Main Menu Module. Click on the Menu Link Item.

Was the Menu Link Item to the Article Created?

At this point, it is necessary to confirm that the Menu Link Item: "My Article Link" has been created, and that it opens the "My First Article," which will display in the Main Content Area.

Figure 7-25

Refer to Figure 7-25 for the following:

Figure 7-25 shows only a portion of the Front-End from the Main Content Area, or Article Display Area of the website.

U	The "Breadcrumb" line repeats the name of the Link, verifying the location on the website being viewed.
V	The "Title" of the Article, which was entered when created, is displayed.
W	All the other items displayed with the Article will be explained in Chapter 10, Content: Articles. Make a mental note here that these items can set to appear, or not, in the "Options" for Articles. This will be explained how to do it globally for Articles or selective on an Article-by-Article basis in Chapter 10.
X	The Content of the Article is displayed here.

Other Viewing "Options" for Menu Link Items

The fundamentals of creating a Chapter and Articles with a Menu Link Item to access it on the Front-End has been briefly covered in this Chapter. However, the Single Article isn't the only option that is available. Two additional Articles were created, which will be included in future Exercises.

This Chapter was intended to get you going on a "Fast Track" to creating a Category, an Article and then a Menu Link Item to view it. That goal has been accomplished.

After progressing through the Exercises in those Chapters, the Content: Category and Article "Options" will be thoroughly covered.

But, before getting into more complicated Exercises, you should understand the Joomla! 5 Front Page and the layout of Content elements. This topic is covered in Chapter 8, "CONTENT: Understanding the Front Page & Layouts."

By the time you reach the Modules, Menus and Templates Chapters, you will have acquired a thorough understanding of Content. From that point on, this book will keep building upon what you have learned previously with more discussions, explanations, and valuable Exercises to provide practical demonstrations of how everything is managed on a Joomla! 5 website.

EXERCISE 7-7: CREATING A MENU LINK ITEM TO A CATEGORY

Objective: In this Exercise, a Menu Link Item will be created that opens a Category, not an Article. The Category screen will display a List of all of the Articles that have been assigned to it. This Exercise covers only a Menu Link Item to a single Category, not a List of Categories, etc., which are different types of links.

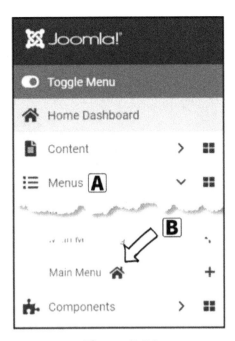

Figure 7-26

Refer to Figure 7-26 for the following:

	Access the Back-End "Home Dashboard."
A	In the left Menu Area, click on "Menus."
B	Select "Main Menu" from among the selections.

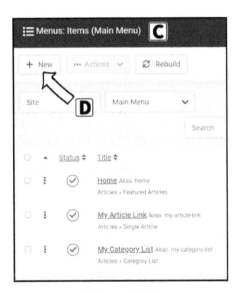

Figure 7-27

Refer to Figure 7-27 for the following:

C	Open the "Main Menu," which will open the List of Menu Link Items that have been

	created within the "Main Menu."
D	Click on the **"+ New"** Button at the top of the screen to create a new Menu Link item within the "Main Menu."

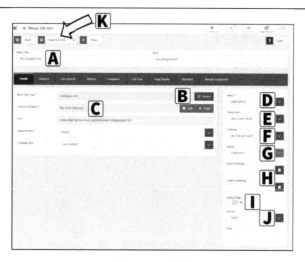

Figure 7-28

Refer to Figure 7-28 for the following:

When the "Menus: New Item" screen opens, there are a number of items that need input, or need to be configured, as explained below:

A	Enter "My Category List" (without quotes), in this field to name the Menu Link Item, which is how it will be displayed in the Main Menu.

The choice for what type of Menu Link Item, there are many and will be covered in Chapter 21, "NAVIGATION: Menu Systems" as referred to previously. For now, complete the following Action Steps, as a continuation of the above:

Step 1	**B**	Click on the "Select" Button.
Step 2		On the next window, select "Articles" from among the choices.
Step 3		Scroll down and select "Category List." This selection will display a list of Articles within a selected Category.
Step 4		In the "Choose a Category" field, click on "Select."
Step 5	**C**	From the List of Categories, select "My First Category."
Step 6		Execute the Save & Close Action.
Step 7		The "Success" panel will appear. Close it.
Step 8		Go to the website "Front-End" and refresh the screen.
Step 9		In the "Main Menu" at the right, note that the Menu Link Item to "My Category List" now appears. Again, this Menu Link Item is a

		"top level," not a "child" of any other.
Step 10		Click on the link. A "listing" of the Articles (by name in reverse order of creation), as created in an earlier Exercise should be displayed from within "My First Category," as previously assigned when created.
C		This field allows the Administrator to make the choice as to what "type" of Link will be created. There are many "Options" and will be covered in Chapter 21 and Chapter 22, wherein the "Navigation" configurations will be discussed in detail.
D		Indicates which Menu is being altered, or to which a new Menu Link Item is being created. If there are several Menus, it is important to select the proper one. If the wrong Menu is chosen, the error can be corrected by opening the Menu Link Item Manager again and selecting the desired Menu assignment.
E		Because a Menu Link Item can be a "child" of another, it is necessary to designate in field [L], whether the item will be a "parent," a "child" or a "child of a child," etc. This is how multi-level Menus are created by "nesting" Menu Link Items with each other. In other words, a Menu Link Item that is a sub-item of another Menu Link Item.
F		The "Ordering" selector allows the "Super User" to have the Menu Link Item display at its inserted location, which is always at the end. Or, the Menu Link Item can be moved to the "First" or "Last" Positions. This will be covered again in Chapters 21 and 22.
G		As is the case with all Content, there is always a choice of making the item immediately visible on the website, or not making it visible for the time being. This is done via the "Published" and "Unpublished" selector. The setting should be set to "Published."
H		Articles, Modules and Menu Link Items can be assigned a "Start" and "Stop" Date for Publishing. Content can be created for automatic display in the future. The Content can also be set to stop displaying at some point following Publishing. This is an automatic action and can be helpful for displaying or shutting off time-sensitive Content.
I		If selected, the Menu Link Item and its related Link will be the "Default Home Page" that is displayed when the website it opened. Only one Menu Link Item can be designated as the "Default Page."
J		Whether this link will be available to be viewed by any website visitor, or only to "Registered Users" is designated in this selection area.
K		Also, as with all Content being created, one of the several "Save" actions must be executed to enter the Content into the website database records.

Go to the website Front-End, using the Button (explained previously), at the top right of the screen. A new browser window will open to the website Front-End.

| L | The Menu Link Item entitled: "My Category List" [L] should appear in the Main Menu Module. Click on the Menu Link Item as shown in Figure 7-29.. |

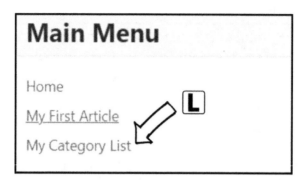

Figure 7-29

Refer to Figure 7-30 for the following:

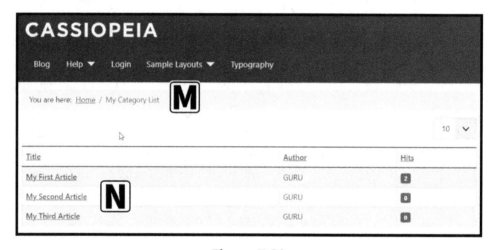

Figure 7-30

| M | The "Breadcrumb" line repeats the name of the Link, verifying the location on the website being viewed. |
| N | The List of all of the Articles in "My First Category" will display, subject to the settings of the Filters, which will be explained in another Chapter. |

Note there are three columns: *Title, Author, Hits.* This display can be reduced to one column by using "Options" settings, which will be covered in later topics.

Was the Menu Link Item to the Category List?

At this point, it is necessary to confirm that the Menu Link Item: "My Category List." Was created, and that it opens the "My First Category," which will display in the Main Content Area, as shown in Figure 7-30.

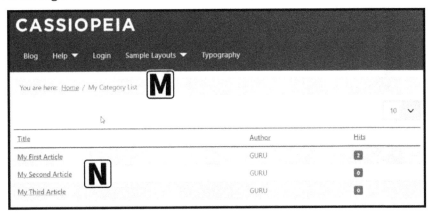

Figure 7-30

Fixing the Logged-In "Session Lifetime"

During the previous Exercises, you may have noticed that when you bounced back and forth between the Admin Back-End Screen and the book, that you may have been required to login several times.

This caused by a "Session Setting" that involves the database session handler. The details of this are not important. What is important is how to stop this from happening because it will likely be a nuisance while performing Administrator actions in the Back-End. The defaults setting is "15 minutes," which may be too short for tutorial experiences.

EXERCISE 7-8: SETTING THE LOGGED-IN SESSION "LIFETIME."

Objective: The objective of this Exercise is to set the "Session lifetime" to a value other than the default, thus providing more time for the Administrator to stay logged-in before the database session automatically executes a "log out" action. By default, the "session time limit" is 15-minutes. While reading this book and working with the Back-End, this time limit may be exceeded, resulting in the Administrator being logged out of the Back-End.

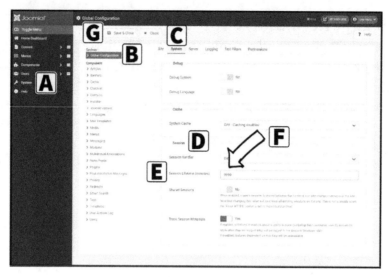

Figure 7-31

Refer to Figure 7-31 for the following:

Step 1		If not already there, go to the Back-End and log into the "Home Dashboard" as the Administrator.
Step 2	A	In the left menu, click on the "System" link.
Step 3	B	On the "System Dashboard," in the "Setup" Block, open the "Global Configuration."
Step 4	C	Click on the "System" tab in the main window area.
Step 5	D E	Scroll down to the "Session" area and locate the "Session Lifetime (minutes)" field.
Step 6	F	In the field, enter "99" (without the quotes). In system-time, this is equivalent to 39 hours. The maximum time limit that may be entered is "9999."
Step 7	G	Execute a Save & Close action.

The session timeout is now set to an extended period of time. If desired, the time (in minutes), may be decreased to meet your own requirements, perhaps only an hour or so.

Adjusting Column List Displays

If you open the List of Articles, there are columns of information about every Article, as well as on the Categories List. This makes viewing some of the information with broken or truncated lines.

To fix this, there is a controlling feature at the top right of the table display, indicating: "9/9 Columns." Clicking on this button will show a dropdown by which some of the columns can be "unselected."

From those available, uncheck the following:

- Access
- Author
- Hits

These columns are not needed at this point, so removing them will not affect any of the Content displays. Also, each "List Display" has its own set of controls.

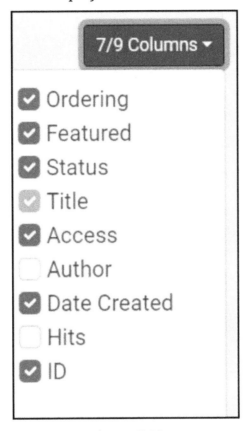

Figure 7-32

Summarizing the "Fast Track"

This "Fast Track" Chapter has been included at the start of the book to provide exposure as to how Content is created via the Back-End and made to display on the website Front-End.

During the above Exercises, an Article Category was created, along with three Articles, all assigned to the same Category. A Menu Link Item was created to access a single Article. Then, another Menu Link Item of the Category List type was created to open a Category showing a "list" of all of the Articles with it. Both of the Menu Link Items were inserted into the Main Menu.

These Menu Link Items demonstrated two ways of accessing Articles on the Front-End by: 1) directly from a Menu Link Item, and 2) via the Category of Articles, the list of which displays links to all of the Articles within the Category.

More detailed information about Categories, Articles and the Menu System will be explained following Chapters. There are individual Chapters dedicated to each of these topics in great detail, along with Exercises that build upon one another to create a complete program of learning the methods of administering a Joomla! 5 website.

Make sure that you have performed the Exercise's in this Chapter before moving forward.

JOOMLA!® 5 A
BOOTS ON THE GROUND
Advance Edition
Volume 1 B
CHAPTER 8

Understanding the
Front Page & Layouts

To help you master Joomla! 5, it is necessary to understand how Joomla! 5 Pages ("screens," "pages" or "webpages"), are terms to be used interchangeably), are constructed and organized, what Modules or Content goes where and how it is accomplished. Finally, how all of those things tie together to comprise a sensible and visually cohesive website.

Unlike most other website programs, Joomla! 5 does not rely on the "one long page" that contains all of the Content. Those websites are designed for mobile viewing but are a real pain on desktop screens. Bootstrap 5, which is used by Joomla! 5 for layouts, resolves the issues and allows desktop sites to display one way and on mobile devices another way, more friendly for the screen size.

If you have seen many of these sites, you will note that their page has the same visual construction and accessing Content in detail is often a "scroll and hunt" trip. This forces you to view a lot of Content before finding the information you are looking for. Actually, these type of pages appear to be more like "scrolling brochures," vs website pages that can contain an abundance of Content that is easy to navigate. Joomla! 5 takes a different approach.

Also, when you painfully scroll up and down the desktop screen on those long Pages, all the animation that is part of the Content pieces, comes back into play. So basically, you must scroll up and down to find what you want and then endure more of the aggravating animation that has been added for "coolness" vs. "functional operation" of the screen's display. In most instances, there are no navigation links to access the individual topic areas of the webpage. You generally will still need to manually scroll back up to the top of the screen, you know, the proverbial "back to top" button. The page designs and layouts are nuisances – except on mobile devices, where they do have some benefit if accompanied by a "hamburger" Menu of links to the Content areas. That's a pretty obvious feature given the pages are designed primarily for viewing on mobile devices.

By comparison, Joomla! 5 displays highly selective Front-Page Content, then provides a multitude of navigation "Options" to drill down into the information you are seeking. For websites with minimal Content, the long "scroll and hunt" "Home" screen might be OK. But for Joomla! 5, this won't do at all. Therefore, an array of different screen layouts, navigation Modules and Menu Link Items take you to detailed Content. This allows complex and Content-rich websites to be created.

You may have noticed on the long scrolling screen layouts that it is very difficult to find detailed information about the company or business. The main part of the website is just a crawling group of content blocks that have the same layouts, etc. Then, when you finally get to the bottom of the screen, you just might find a Menu with Menu Link Items to details Content. This is "after" you have wasted all that time scrolling through the blocks of Content in which you really didn't have much interest.

Here is one point: If you want your website to be a "one-pager," then you can use a Joomla! 5 one-page Template for the page. You can also build the page yourself using a Page Building Extension that allows you to create pages in any style of format. But remember, those "look alike, function alike" pages can get very bothersome both on desktop displays and on mobile devices. Too much motion, left, right, up, down, fade in, fade out, spin, flip, rotate, etc. can make site/page visitors seasick!

The Website Front Page

For demonstration purposes, the Front Page of the default website installation will be used and explained. Once you understand the general scheme of the structure, and how the layout is set up along with the way it can be easily modified, you will be able to manage your website effectively.

Chapter 7 Exercises – Go Back and Do Them!

At this point, as explained in Chapter 7, "Fast Track Double Time Start," Exercises 7-1 through 7-8, should have been completed. If you have not performed those Exercises, please go back to Chapter 7 and do so. Exercises in this Chapter are dependent upon Content that was added in Chapter 7. All subsequent Chapters also rely on Exercises being completed in previous, sequential, Chapters.

This is part of the "Fast Track, Boots on the Ground" method employed in this book's Chapters. Definitive Exercises guide you through successive Content building experiences. Each builds upon the previous Chapters and Exercises in a progressive manner.

Please use this book to your advantage to hone your skills as a website Administrator. Perform the Exercises and gain the skills and techniques needed to master Joomla! 5.

Front Page Geography

First, Content on a Joomla! 5 website is created or generated primarily from the sources as shown in Figure 8-1.

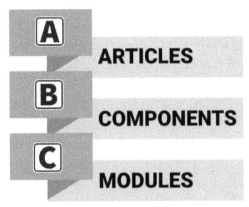

Figure 8-1

Any combination of the Content sources in Figure 8-1 can appear on any website page, in any layout format, using any Template to control the design, look and feel of the page. In addition, there are Extensions available that allow for creation of Site Templates and individual Page Layouts, which allow for some creative ways to display Joomla! 5 pages, or screens. Chapter 19, "VISUAL: Using Template/Page Builders," covers the subject thoroughly. Knowing that, let's examine each part of a Joomla! 5 webpage in detail:

A	On Joomla! 5 websites, Articles are the primary Content elements. They are created using an Article Manager and when displayed, appear in the Main Content Area of the webpage. At this point, the "HOME" Screen is controlled by the "Home" Menu Link Item in the Main Menu, in the right column. The "Home" Menu Link Item is currently set to display the "Featured Articles" when the website is opened. No Articles, in the Sample Content that was added have yet been designated as Featured Articles. Many other website platforms pass themselves off with the term "blog posts," which are essentially, in the overall scheme of things, Articles by any other name. A "blog" piece on other platforms is simple an "Article" in Joomla! 5 parlance, and a group of Articles comprise a collection of "blog posts" and so on.
B	Components are "mini-applications" that operate inside the Joomla! 5 Framework, (or in the Framework layer added by Developers to support their Third-Party Extensions). There are thousands of Components, many of them have been, or are being, modified to work on the Joomla! 5 Bootstrap 5 "Framework." Typical examples of Components are shopping carts, photo galleries, real estate websites, specialized templates with Content, and other similar functional elements. The way a Joomla! 5 website is elevated from plain vanilla to a highly functional one, is by adding

	Components that generate specialized Content. Components can be opened with a Menu Link Item, such as: Gallery displays, Shopping Carts, and more.
C	Modules are remarkably interesting. They are Extensions that can be associated with a Component, or singularly provide Content displays. A Login area is a Module that is not associated with a Component. A Search Module, on the other hand, is associated with a Component ["Smart Search"]. In many instances, when a Component is installed on a website, its Content is usually made functional via a companion Module, along with Content that displays in the Main Content Area of the webpage.
	What makes Modules so effective and powerful is their ability to be located anywhere on a page where the Template has Module Positions. If you recall, Articles can only be displayed in the Main Content Area. Modules have greater flexibility. In fact, Modules can even be placed within an Article, which opens a wide range of unique ways to present Content. Also, a Module can be assigned to a Menu Link Item exclusively. The Module is not visible except when a specific Menu Link Item (can be more than one), is clicked to display an Article or Component. At that time the Module will appear in its assigned "Module Position" Click another Menu Link Item, the Content changes and the Module does not display. See Chapter 12, "CONTENT: Modules" for complete information about their use.

Examining the Front-Page Layout

When a Joomla! 5 website first opens, it is considered the "Front Page." The Front-Page layout and Content are generally associated with one Menu Link Item, typically "Home." However, any Menu Link Item can be designated as the "Home" Page. It does not even need to have the name "Home." It can be named anything you want. It does not need to display only in the Main Content Area.

"Home" is actually used as a straightforward way of telling website visitors that the "start page" of the website is located here ("Home"), and simply serves as a convenient way for them to return to the starting point so-to-speak.

If your website is a Shopping Cart operation, the Menu Link Item designated as "Home" can be the opening page/screen of the Shopping Cart and contain no Articles whatsoever. The "Home" target page can open any "target" Content, as long as there is a Menu Link Item in a visible Menu to open the webpage.

Before discussing the Front-Page Layout, let's perform an Exercise where the "Home" Menu Link Item in the Main Menu is no longer the link that controls the type of Front-Page Layout.

EXERCISE 8-1: CHANGING THE "HOME" MENU LINK ITEM TARGET

Objective: The goal of this Exercise is to demonstrate how to change the Menu Link Item which controls the display of the "Home" opening page of the website.

In this case, it is going to be changed from the "Home" Menu Link Item in the Main Menu to the "Blog" Menu Link Item in the untitled Menu located at the top of the screen.

Then, the "Home" Menu Link Item in the Main Menu will be removed, re-created and then assigned to the "Featured Articles" link. Remember, "Featured Articles" are those that share a dual Category assignment, and display ONLY in the Front-Page Main Content Area.

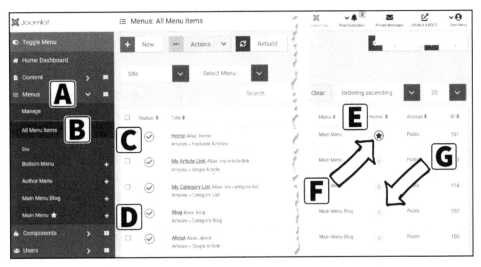

Figure 8-2

Refer to Figure 8-2 for the following:

Step 1		Log into the Back-End as the Administrator and access the "Home Dashboard."
Step 2	A	In the left Menu of the "Home Dashboard," open the "Menus" area.
Step 3	B	Select the "All Menu Items" choice on the list. When you perform this action, you should see a list of all the Menu Link Items for all Menus on the website, regardless of their location or Menu Module screen assignment. Sub-Menu Link Items are also shown.
Step 4	C	Locate the "Home" Menu Link Item, which is identified in the "Home" column on the list. There is only one Menu Link Item that is graphically indicated as the "Home" item by its color.
Step 5	D	Locate the "Blog" Menu Link Item, which is likely directly below the "Home" Menu Link Item on the list.
Step 6	E	Look in the "Home" column in the table and locate the Menu Link Item

	F	with the gold "Home" icon displayed. This indicates which Menu Link Item's target Content will be opened when the website initially loads in the Browser Window.
Step 7	G	For the "Blog" Menu Link Item, place the Cursor over the grey dot icon and click it. The "Set as Home" message box should appear to alert you to the action that will take place when clicking on the icon.
Step 8		When the green Message Box appears, it indicates the action Menu Item set to "Home" was completed. In this case, no Save action is required. Close the Message Box. The gold "Home" icon should now be assigned to the "Blog" Menu Link Item.
Step 9		Go to the website Front-End and close the browser tab display. Then go to the Back-End and click the icon to the top right to re-open the website. Optionally, "refresh" the browser window.
Step 10		The result of the action in Step 9 above should display the new "Home" Front Page and show four Articles within the Article Blog Category format (Figure 8-3). The "Home" button is no longer the default which opens the website. This happened because the Blog Menu Link Item is set as a Category Blog to display all Articles in a singled Blog Category. This is the Default "Home" Page per the Cassiopeia Template and the Blog Sample Data which was installed earlier.

Here are descriptions and information about each element identified in Figure 8-3. Note that these descriptions apply, in part, only to this Template's Page/Screen. Other Templates may have different layouts and physical structures. However, the same general principles apply to most all Templates and Page layouts.

First, the overall structure of this Page is a two-column layout, with the Main Content Area being Column 1; the stacked Module on the right side is Column 2. The location assignments are explained below.

Refer to Figure 8-3 for the following:

A	This is the website name, or Title, inserted as a graphic into the website Template. It can be changed or replaced in the Templates: Edit Style Area of the Template by placing a new graphic, or image, in its place. More about this in Chapter 17, "VISUAL: Templates."
B	The top Menu now controls what is displayed on the website because the "Blog" Menu Link Item has been designated at the "Home" link. It is also configured to display the Category: "Blog Article Content," which it does.
C	The middle area of the page is known as the Main Content Area (within the dashed border box in Figure 8-3), and is generally where Articles are displayed. Also,

Components can/will be displayed in this same area and when that happens, no Articles are likely to display. However, Component Content and Articles could be configured to appear at the same time. This is not an assignable position for Modules to display, however, Module Positions can be added above and below the Main Content Area, which is frequently the case with most Templates. *See:* Chapter 12, "CONTENT: Modules."

D	The Main Menu is a Menu Module, located at the sidebar-right "Module Position" This is typically the Menu that will contain the majority of Menu Link Items to website Content, as you will see when other Templates are installed. It can be named anything, other than Main Menu as the standing naming convention. Before installing the Sample Data, this Menu was in control and "Home" meant the starting page. Adding the "Sample Data" added the top horizontal Menu to access the Content that was added. Now, the "Home" target was changed to the "Blog" Menu Link Item … this makes the "Main Menu" and "Home" contradictory, at least temporarily, which suggests the Menu should have a different name.
E	Located in "Module Position" "bottom-b," the "Popular Tags" Module is displayed with "Older Posts." As a point of information, Modules can be stacked above and below each other in any designated "Module Position" and in any Order. If in the horizontal format, the Modules can be located to the left or right of each other.
F	This Module is obvious. It is a "Login Module" for Users to access any Content that is protected from general access, and the Access Control is set to Registered, meaning a User's Account must be created before access is allowed. After logging into the website, Users are allowed to view the restricted Content.
G	Another Module in the "sidebar-right" location is a link area and contains a Menu Link Item to an "RSS Feed." The Module is named "Syndication," but there is no name on the Module. This is because the "Title" is set to "Hide" in the Module's Control Area.
H	Located at the top, just above the Main Content Area, is a Breadcrumb Module, which indicates exactly where you are located on the website. This Template has a "Module Position" called breadcrumbs and is set to display at the bottom of the screen by default. Breadcrumbs are typically located near the top of a Page, but can be located anywhere there is a "Module Position" Breadcrumbs, being a Module, can be "Unpublished" to not display.

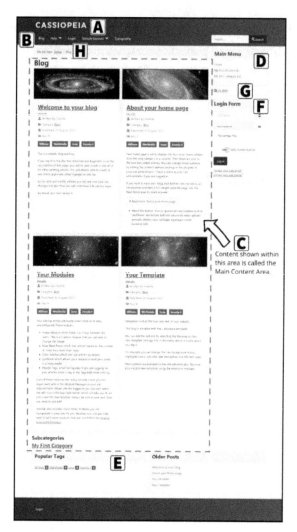

Figure 8-3

What Else Do You Need to Know?

The expression: "A rose is a rose is a rose," does not apply to Joomla! 5 Layouts because layouts are controlled by Templates and there are thousands upon thousands of available and they all have differences.

So, keep in mind during these book Chapters and Exercises, that the techniques will be the same pretty much across the board, while the look and feel of the end product may not be. This is because the Templates can be highly customized to suit a website's purpose, and is based on the skill of the Administrator in creating them.

More on Templates in Chapter 17, "VISUAL: Templates" where additional Templates will be installed on your practice website. Those will also have settings that can be changed and altered for different visual appeal.

Additionally, Chapter 19, "VISUAL: Using Template/Page Builders," will open new horizons for the Administrator to create specialized individual Pages for the website, or create complete Templates to be used for the entire website structure.

Featured Articles

"Featured Articles" are easy to understand. They are Articles that have been designated ("forced" if you will), to automatically appear in the Main Content Area of the website when it is opened – provided that the "Home" page Menu Link Item is set to include "Featured Articles." This is typical for Article Blog styles where the most recent Article is to appear at the top of the display. In fact, in the Administrator "Home" Dashboard, under Content, there is a separate selection named Featured Articles to help manage this Content display.

Here is what happens when an Article gets the "Featured Article" designation. Articles can be created and given the designation of being a "Featured Article," even though it might simultaneously be assigned to another defined Category. This is the only instance where Articles can be assigned to two Categories; its own designated Category assignment and another one named "Featured Articles."

Then the Menu Link Item, the one designated as "Home" or "Default," can be set to also connect to a Category called "Featured Articles." This function gathers up all of the unexpired Articles designated as "Featured," and displays them in a pre-determined order.

The "Featured Articles" can be collected from any number of "named Categories" and displayed using the Menu Link Item that targets the "Featured Articles."

That's how it works. It isn't complicated, but does require attention to what settings are invoked at the time of Article creation. Note that previously "Published" Articles can be set to "Featured" at any time, and be joined with the rest in the designation.

Also, many Articles can be designated "Featured" even though they are scattered among any number of assigned Categories, thus allowing for the Front Page to be a collection of the Articles gathered together from many assigned Categories.

EXERCISE 8-2: RE-DESIGNATING THE "HOME" MENU LINK ITEM

Objective: The goal of this Exercise will guide you through the process of re-designating the "Home" Menu Link Item to control how the website appears when it opens on the screen.

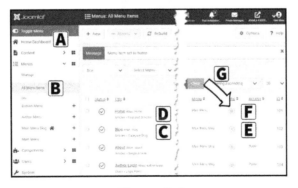

Figure 8-4

Refer to Figure 8-4 for the following:

Step 1		Log into the Back-End Home "Dashboard" as the Administrator.
Step 2	A	In the Left Menu of the "Home Dashboard," open the "Menus."
Step 3	B	Select "All Menu Items" on the list. When you perform this action, you should see a list of all the Menu Link Items for all Menus on the website, regardless of their location or Menu Module screen assignment.
Step 4	C	Locate the "Blog" Menu Link Item, which is now the website's "Home" page designation from earlier.
Step 5	D	Locate the "Home" Menu Link Item.
Step 6	E F	Look in the "Blog" Menu Link Item row in the table and locate the gold "Home" icon displayed. This indicates which Menu Link Item's target will be opened when the website initially loads in the Browser Window.
Step 7	G	On the "Home" Menu Link Item, directly above, place the Cursor over the grey dot icon and click it. The Set Default box should appear. Click on the icon. The "Home" Menu Link Item was set as the "Articles-Featured Articles" type by default during installation.
Step 8		When the green Message Box appears, it indicates the action Menu Item set to "Home" was completed. In this case, no Save action is required. Close the Message Box.
Step 9		Go to the website Front-End and close the browser tab display. Then go to the Back-End and click the icon to the top right to re-open the website. Optionally, "refresh" the browser window.
Step 10		The result of the action in Step 9 above should display the new "Home" Front Page with Article Content in the Main Content Area. This happened because the "Home" Menu Link Item is set as a "Featured Articles" link. When Sample Data was installed, there were four Articles co-designated as "Featured" along with their own respective Category of "Blog," which you can visually verify by looking at each Article's "Details" information.

EXERCISE 8-3: CREATING "FEATURED" ARTICLES

Objective: The goal of this Exercise is to demonstrate how to designate Articles, which are assigned to other Categories, to also be assigned as a" Featured" Article. This Exercise will also demonstrate how Articles from different Categories ["Blog" and "My First Category"], can also be designated as "Featured" to appear together on the same page/screen.

Step 1	In the "Home Dashboard > Control Panel > Site Panel," open Articles.
Step 2	In the "Featured" column on the List of Articles, select the icon to change the Status of the following four Articles to _not-Featured,_ by clicking on the gold "Featured" icon (changing them to grey): • Your Template • Your Modules • About your homepage • Welcome to your blog This can also be performed by selecting all the Content Items by checking their respective boxes in the left column, then going to the "Actions" drop down at the top and selecting "Unfeatured." When clicked, the action completes itself automatically.
Step 3	Because your Articles were the last created, the "Date Created" column heading can be used to sort the list to display them at the top of the list. This is helpful if you have many Articles on a website and need to sort them by their origination date. Click on the Column Heading: "Date Created." The result should be a display that sorted the List of Articles from the "Oldest" to the "Newest." Click the heading again. The List now is in reverse; "Newest to Oldest," which is what you want to display.
Step 4	Open "My First Article."

Figure 8-5

Refer to Figure 8-5 for the following:

Step 5	A B	To the right, toggle the "Featured" setting from "No" to "Yes."

Step 6	Execute a Save & Close action. The Article Saved Message should display. Also, in the Featured Article Column, the icon will change to an orange color.
Step 7	Repeat this process for My Second Article, and My Third Article, also designating those two as "Featured." However, rather than opening the individual Articles to change the setting, click on the grey icon in the "Featured" column. The icons will change color to gold. The two other Articles are now also designated as "Featured" Articles, along with the one changed previously.
	This can also be performed by selecting all the desired Content Items by checking their respective boxes in the left column, then going to the "Actions" drop down at the top and selecting "Featured." When clicked, the action completes itself and saves the new settings automatically.
Step 8	Open the "All Menu Items" under the "Menus" section in the left Admin Menu.
Step 9	On the list of Menu Link Items, under the "Home" column, check to ensure the designation from the Blog Menu Link Item to the "Home" Menu Link Item re-designation was previously accomplished. If not, do this using the circle icon. The icon should change from a grey circle to a gold "Home" image, indicating that this Menu Link Item now controls the Content on the website's opening screen.
Step 10	Go to the website Front-End, perform a screen refresh. The result should be similar to Figure 8-6. Note the order of the Articles. The most recent one you created ("Third") is at the top; the earliest you created ("First") is at the bottom.

Home

My Third Article

Details
Written by Super User
Category: My First Category
Published: 18 February 2019
Hits: 0

This is the text for My Third Article.

My Second Article

Details
Written by Super User
Category: My First Category
Published: 18 February 2019
Hits: 0

This is the text for My Second Article.

My First Article

Details
Written by Super User
Category: My First Category
Published: 16 February 2019
Hits: 6

This is the text for My First Article.

Figure 8-6

Alternate Method of "Featured Article" Assignment

There is an easier alternative method of assigning Articles to the "Featured Category" via the Article List layout. With the full list of Articles displayed within the Article Manager, refer to Figure 8-6-A.

[B] indicates the currently assigned Category for the three Articles that will be also assigned to the "Featured Category." This is their normal Category designation.

[A] is the "Featured" Column and Articles may be assigned to the Category by clicking on the grey icon in the column, which will turn orange when the action is completed.

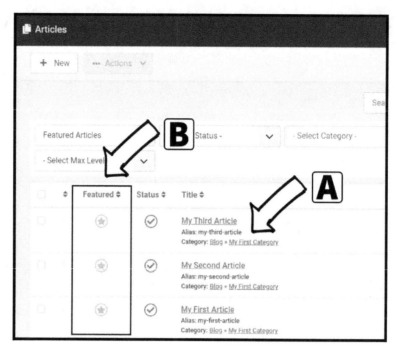

Figure 8-6-A

EXERCISE 8-4: CHANGING THE ORDER OF THE ARTICLES

Objective: In this Exercise, the Order of the Articles will be changed. This is done so the ordering of the Articles, when displayed in any Category List View, will conform to the revised or configured order.

Step 1	If you have configured all three of your Articles as "Featured Articles," their Order can be changed. All Article ordering can be changed in the same manner, regardless of their Category assignments.

Figure 8-7

Refer to Figure 8-7 for the following:

Step 2	Go to the left Admin Menu, select "Content > Featured Articles," that will display them as shown.

Step 3	A	The small blue arrows at the top of the second column allow the changing of the ordering of any Content Item on the list. When you click on the small arrow, the dot icons in front of each Content Item changes from grey to black. The order of Content Items cannot be changed unless this action step is performed.
Step 4	B	Using the icon, drag "Second Article" to the top of the list. Do this slowly and note how other Articles drop down out of the way as you move it. Once you drop an item into place on the list, there is no need to execute any Save action. The reposition is locked in place when the mouse button is released.
Step 5		Go to the website Front-End and refresh the screen. The result should be as shown in Figure 8-8, with the new Article Order of: *Second-Third-First*.

Featured Ordering is Separate

When changing the "ordering" of the "Featured Articles," it does not change the "ordering" of the same Articles within their respective assigned Category. The two "ordering" configurations are completely separated.

If you view the "Home Dashboard" > Content> Categories and filter the list via "My First Category" in the Category List Filter, the "ordering" of the Articles remains in the "order" in which they were created, not in the "re-ordered" configuration of the "Featured Articles order."

Figure 8-8

Many Layout Options

As mentioned previously, every website has a "Home" page, or screen, that is displayed when the website is accessed. The "Home" setting, which dictates the Layout format, has a number of variables available based on the type of Content the Menu Link Item targets.

Here are some rules that apply:

Rule 1	At least one Menu Link Item, in any Menu, must be designated as the "Home" Page, although it does not need to be named "Home."
Rule 2	The Menu Module must be "Published" and visible on the Front-End in any "Module Position" on the Template.
Rule 3	The "target" Content Item must also be in a "Published" status. If not "Published," the "Home" screen will be blank.
Rule 4	The "Home" Menu Link Item can be one of any different Menu Link Item Types that can be created.
Rule 5	The "Home" Menu Item Type is the designator that targets the Content that will initially appear on the Front-End display when the website is accessed,
Rule 6	The layout is not required to be an Article, or multiple Articles (a Category List layout, Category Blog etc., is possible).
Rule 7	The "Home" Menu Link Item can be derived from any Component. Components are alternate types of Content that display in the Main Content Area of the website.

Modules on the website can be directly associated with the "Home" Menu Link Item, which will limit the display of the Module to only that page. They can also be connected to other Menu Link Items in any combination. In fact, Modules can individually be associated with any single or multiple Menu Link Items. This allows the discretionary display of Modules on different website screens. More about this technique in Chapter 12, "CONTENT: Modules."

Sorting and Re-Ordering Article Lists

Sometimes it is necessary to filter, sort, re-order and/or display the List of Articles in several ways. A feature has been included in the Back-End for that purpose and will be discussed in depth in Chapter 10, "CONTENT: Articles."

CONTENT:
Categories

Categories are used as a method of keeping Content organized on a Joomla! website. The idea of Categories is to provide some sort of logical order for managing Content. On websites where there is limited amount of Content, the default "Uncategorized" Category is fine to use. However, on websites that contain a large amount of Content, a Category hierarchy is pretty much mandatory.

Content in both the default in the form of Articles, and those you might add as Extensions, rely on "categorization" as a method of organizing and managing Content. Here are some of the default Components that use Categories:

- Banners
- Contacts
- Newsfeeds
- Users (the Categories are called "User Groups")
- Media (the Categories are called "Folders")
- Extensions (many add-ins also use Categories to organize Content)

However, the most frequent use of Categories is to manage and organize Articles. Articles are the most frequently used to present Content, so it stands to reason that a method of organizing them is needed. In addition to the Components noted above, Categories are almost extensively used to manage Articles.

Rules that Apply to Categories

Categories comply with rules that govern and manage how Content is created and displayed. Here are some general rules pertaining to Categories across the board:

Rule 1	Categories are the top level of Content management.
Rule 2	The very top level Category in any Category Group is specifically referred to as the Parent Category.
Rule 3	Sub-Categories ("Child Categories") can be created or associated within any Category above it (it's "Parent Category").
Rule 4	Content Items may be assigned to either Categories or Sub-Categories.
Rule 5	Content Items *cannot* be assigned to more than one Category or Sub-Category at a time. This is a steadfast rule.
Rule 6	Extensions may exist that will allow multiple Category assignments, but this feature is not part of a default installation. This is a feature that might be added by a third-party Developer. An Extension that may allow Article designations into multiple Categories may be developed at some point, so check the Joomla! Extensions Directory ("JED") to see if such an Extension is available.
Rule 7	There is no fixed limit to the number of Categories that can be created.
Rule 8	There is no fixed limit to the number of Sub-Categories that can be created within a Parent Category.
Rule 9	Sub-Sub-Categories can be created within Sub-Categories, without limit.
Rule 10	Categories and any level of Sub-Categories can include descriptive text that can be displayed when using Category-based page displays.
Rule 11	There is no specific limit to the number of actual Content Items that are allowed to be assigned within a Category at any hierarchal level.
Rule 12	Common sense should prevail when establishing a Category hierarchy, so the organization of Content isn't confusing or difficult to navigate by website Users or Administrators. Extensive "drill downs" through Categories is not a good categorization practice.

Figure 9-1 shows a typical hierarchy of Categories and Sub-Categories. The layers of Sub-Categories can extend to many levels, but should only be created if there is a compelling need for extended Category depth.

Figure 9-1

Keep in mind that a Sub-Category is simply the "Child" of another Category with it's "Parent" above it. A Sub-Category can be a "Parent" of a Sub-Sub-Category.

Content in Categories

Once a Category structure has been created, you can assign Content Items to it. This process of structuring Content is similar to a file cabinet that has drawers. Within those drawers are hanging folders and with those are file folders. As far as a hierarchy goes, this is a four-level deep arrangement:

File Cabinet: = Parent Category

File Drawers: = Child Sub-Category

Hanging Folders: = Child Sub-Sub-Category

File Folders: = Child Sub-Sub-Sub-Category

Content Items: = Any Content at any Category level

Content Items, without limit, may be added to any Category at any level, as shown in Figure 9-2. Keep in mind, a Content Item may only be assigned to one Category, regardless of its level in the Category hierarchy.

Figure 9-2

Content that is created, or generated, through the use of specialized Extensions may have a slightly different method of Category/Content Item arrangement, but all are typically along the same generalized structure as shown above.

Creating Categories

In Chapter 7, "Fast Track Double Time Start," you created a Category ("My First Category"). In this section, you will create another Category, as a "Sub-Category," then assign a Content Item to it.

IMPORTANT NOTE!

If you have not created the "My First Category" at this point, go back to Chapter 7 and complete Exercises 7-3 through 7-6. Also, in Chapter 8, complete Exercises 8-1 through 8-4. Subsequent Exercises in this book are built upon actions taken in previous Exercises. To get maximum benefit, perform them in sequence.

There are eight steps involved in creating a Category in the Content Manager area of the Control Panel, and are demonstrated in detail in Exercise 9-1:

Step 1	Accessing the Content Manager in the Control Panel or, Access the following in the Site Panel on the "Home Dashboard."
Step 2	Opening the Article Categories Manager.
Step 3	Clicking the **"+New"** Button at the top of the screen.
Step 4	Entering a Name for the Category.
Step 5	Entering Description Information for the Category if desired (optional, but not required).
Step 6	Designating the Category as a Parent or as a Child of an existing Category.
Step 7	Enabling the Category by Publishing it.
Step 8	Executing a Saving Action.

About this "Published" Thing

If a Category is set to "Unpublished," any Content assigned within it will not be accessible on the website. A Category should be designated as "Published" before executing a Save Action to make it so, and the Content within the Category visible to website visitors.

However, individual items within a Category can be set to be "Published" or "Unpublished," regardless of the status of the Category itself. However, if set to "Published," and the Category is "Unpublished," the obvious result is the item will not display.

About Access Permissions

Generally, most Content is accessible by all website visitors ("Public"), which is the default setting. However, if there are viewing restrictions to be applied, then one of the optional access permission settings must be selected before executing a Save Action. This is accomplished via "User Access Control" ("ACL"), and is covered in Chapter 24, "USERS: Access, Actions & Permissions."

EXERCISE 9-1: CREATING A SUB-CATEGORY.

Objective: The objective of this Exercise is to create a Sub-Category ("Child Category") and assign it to the "Parent Category" called: "My First Category," that was previously created in another Exercise. This will create a simple Category hierarchy that will demonstrate the methods and the use of the type of categorization.

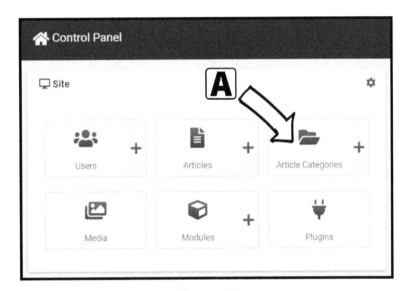

Figure 9-3

Refer to Figure 9-3 for the following:

Step 1		Access the "Home Dashboard."
Step 2	A	In the Site block, click on the Article Categories icon (not the **"+"** symbol). There is no particular reason for doing it this way, other than to demonstrate a different way of opening a Manager on the "Home Dashboard." Obviously the **"+"** icon will create a new Category, but it is best to learn the "long way" of creating one to fully understand the process.
Step 3		Note that the previously created "Parent Category" named: "My First Category" is visible on the list of Categories. This is a Category that was previous created in Chapter 7, "Fast Track Double Time Start."

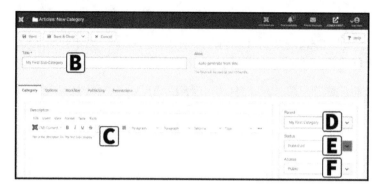

Figure 9-4

Refer to Figure 9-4 for the following:

Step 4		At the top left of the screen, click on **"+New"** to create a new Category.
Step 5	B	When the New Category window opens, enter "My First Sub-Category" (without quotes) into the "Title Field."
Step 6	C	In the "Description" text area, enter: "This is the description for My First Sub-Category" (without quotes).
Step 7	D	Under the "Parent" selector to the right, select "My First Category" to be the Parent Category.
Step 8	E	Make sure the "Status" is set to "Published."
Step 9		This Sub-Category should be viewable by all website visitors, so make sure that "Public" was selected in the "Access" selector. If a Category is not set to "Public," none of the Articles within it will be visible, unless the User has Login Access. The Access Level of the Parent controls the Access of the Child, whether it is a Category or Article. This is another steadfast rule.
Step 10	F	Execute a Save & Close Action.

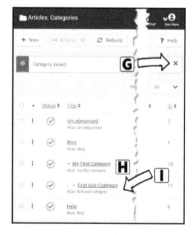

Figure 9-5

Refer to Figure 9-5 for the following:

Step 11	G	After the Save & Close Action is initiated, the screen will return to the "List of Categories," and the green Message "Category saved." Box will display. Close it by clicking the **"X"** to the right.
Step 12		The hierarchy of Parent Categories are automatically listed.
Step 13	H	The Child Category just created should appear under its assigned "Parent Category" of "My First Category," which is, in fact, a Child of the "Parent Category" "Blog."
Step 14	I	Note that the "Child Category" is visually indented under its "Parent Category," indicating it is "sub-" to the Category above. If used, a Sub-Sub-Category, would appear indented below its respective Sub-Category Parent. This method is standardized throughout Joomla! 5 "list views."

The Category building process can be repeated as often, and any time, as necessary to create a Content classification system. Each site has its own requirements, so map out how the Content is to be organized and build the Category structure as needed, at least a preliminary structure.

It is wise to design the Category structure before creating Content in the form of Articles so they can be properly assigned when created. However, you can simply create Articles and save them into the default "Uncategorized" classification and move them into any of the named Categories later.

Adding Content Items

Content Items, in the form of Articles, can be added to Categories that have been created, regardless of their level within the hierarchy. In other Components, different types of Content are added to the Categories created within those Components, such as: Contacts, Banners, etc., or those Categories that are part of Component Extensions that may be installed.

It is important to note here that an Article may only be assigned to one Category, unless an Extension (if available), which allows multiple-Category Article assignments has been developed.

In this Chapter, we are dealing only with Categories and Articles. Categories within Components will be addressed within their respective Chapters. The following Exercise will add Articles into the Sub-Category created in Exercise 9-1.

EXERCISE 9-2: ADD AN ARTICLE TO A SUB-CATEGORY

Objective: The objective of this Exercise is to add an Article into "My First Sub-Category" that was created in Exercise 9-1. Rather than create new Articles, the Articles that were created during installation of the "Sample Blog Content," and located in the default Category "Help," will be *moved* to the "My First Sub-Category." It is also the goal of this

Exercise, to illustrate how to move multiple Articles from one Category to another using the "Batch" method.

Figure 9-6

Refer to Figure 9-6 for the following:

Step 1		In the "Home Dashboard" Area, open Content and select Articles, or access Articles in the Site Panel. Either method will take you to the screen as shown in Figure 9-6.
Step 2	**A**	The result of this action is the displaying of a List of Articles, with their assigned Categories identified. In this case, three Articles are in the "Help" Category. If the list is not showing all Articles, a "Filter" may be controlling the display. Use the "Clear" button at the "Filter Options" selector at the top of the list display area.

Figure 9-7

Refer to Figure 9-7 for the following:

Step 3	**B**	Use the "Filter Options" to narrow the list display by choosing the "Select Category" Filter to the "Help" Category. Then, select all three Articles in the "Help" Category using the check boxes as shown.

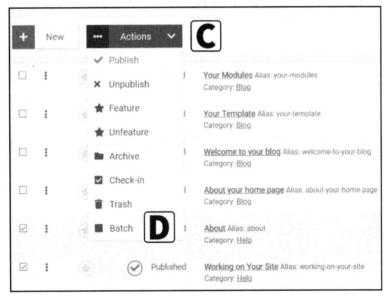

Figure 9-8

Refer to Figure 9-8 for the following:

Step 4	**C**	At the top of the screen, with the boxes checked, under the Actions Menu, click the "Batch" button, which will open a popup window.

Within the popup window (Figure 9-9), take the following actions:

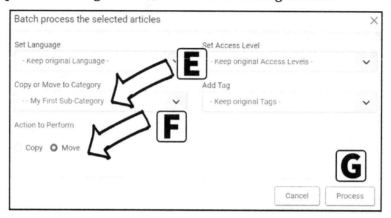

Figure 9-9

Refer to Figure 9-9 for the following:

Step 5		In the section: To "Copy or Move to Category." The selection referred to are the Articles selected previously.
Step 6	**E**	In the dropdown, select "My First Sub-Category."
Step 7	**F**	Select the "Move" radio button as the "Action to Perform"
Step 8	**G**	At the bottom right of the popup window, click the "Process" button to initiate the action. This might take a few seconds or longer to complete, depending upon the number of Articles being moved to the new Category.
Step 9		After the Process Action, the green "Success Message" will appear. Close the message panel in the usual manner.
Step 10		Observe that the "Help" Category is now showing as being empty of any Articles, which is what should be after moving the three to another Category.
Step 11		Execute a "Clear" action for the "Filter Options."

Figure 9-10

Refer to Figure 9-10 for the following:

Step 12	**H**	To verify the "Move" results, use the "Filter Options" and the "Select Category" filter, set to "My First Sub-Category," to set the list display. The result should be three Articles as shown in Figure 9-10.

To verify the consolidation of the Articles under the Category, go to the website "Front-End > Main Menu > My Category List Link" [Figure 9-11 **[I]** and click on it.

This will display the List of Articles previously created and assigned to the Category. The "My Category List" Link is set up as a Category Blog Layout targeting the Articles in "My First Category" previously created. It was also set up to show sub-categories, meaning that any child Categories, if they exist, will be displayed below the list of Articles in the parent Category.

The List of Articles within that "Parent" Category are displayed in Figure 9-11 **[J]**. Note that the "My First Sub-Category" is displayed as a link – which opens that Category's List view automatically.

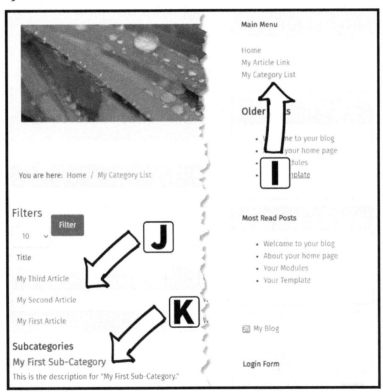

Figure 9-11

Click on the Category Name Heading "My First Sub-Category" **[K]** to open it, showing the Article List in Figure 9-12.

Figure 9-12

The Missing Article?

If you refer back, there were three Articles assigned to the Sub-Category that was selected. However, only two Articles are being shown. Why is this? The answer deals with permissions assigned to the missing Article.

Normally, Content is automatically set to "Public," which means every website visitor can view it. Exercise 9-3 will demonstrate how to change the Permissions that are assigned to a Content Item.

Changing Content Access

If you look at the List of Articles in the Administrator Back-End, you will see that one of the two Articles that were moved to "My First Sub-Category" does not have "Public" access. The "Working on Your Site" Article has it's Access set to "Special," which is a type of User Access Control, as show in Figure 9-13 **[L]**.

If you do not see this column, go to the "column viewing" button at the right of the list and check the "Access" button to force that column to display.

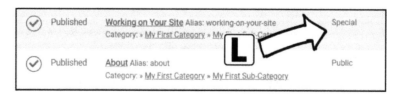

Figure 9-13

EXERCISE 9-3: CHANGE THE ACCESS PERMISSIONS

Objective: The objective of this Exercise is to demonstrate how the "Access" permission for a Content Item is set or designated. "Access" for the demonstration Article is currently set for "Special," which is controlled via User Access Control ("ACL"), and it will be changed to "Public" so that anyone can view the item. To change the Access for this Article, perform the following steps:

Step 1	Access the Article Manager via the "Home Dashboard."
Step 2	Open the "Working on Your Site" Article.
Step 4	When the Article opens, view the controls on the right side of the screen.

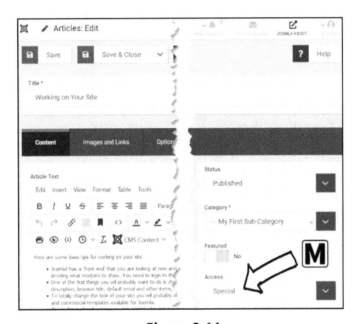

Figure 9-14

Refer to Figure 9-14 for the following:

Step 5		Execute the actions as outlined below.
Step 6	M	In the Access dropdown, change the setting from "Special" to "Public." The "Special" User Group use will be discussed in detail in Chapter 24, "USERS: Access, Actions & Permissions."
Step 7		At the top of the screen, execute a Save and Close Action. The green "Saved Message" will appear, and the List of Articles will be displayed again. Close the Message panel.
Step 8		Go back to the Front-End, refresh the browser window.

Step 9		The three Articles in "My First Sub-Category" should be displayed. Also note that they have arranged themselves in their order of creation, which is the default "Options" setting for Articles.

The "Special" Access Permission

The "Special" Access configuration deals with the permission for Users assigned to certain User Groups the ability log into the Administrator Back-End. The "Special Access Level," by default, includes the Manager, Author, and Administrators Groups. It also includes Child Groups of those Parent Groups.

Comprehensive information about "User Access Control ("ACL")" will be discussed in Chapters 23 through 25.

Rearranging the Order of Article Categories for Back-End Viewing

By default, any List View of Content Items in Joomla! 5 are ordered by the date of entry, or the actual order in which they were entered. In many cases, when viewing a List of Categories, the default display order isn't desired. For example, if you wish the Categories (or other Content Items), to be displayed alphabetically, a change from the default method is required.

The manner or ordering in which Lists of Content are displayed can be set in the "Global Options" for Articles & Categories, with the ability to over-ride the setting within the Content Item itself, or the Menu Link Item that controls it.

Reviewing Filter Options

Before progressing to the re-ordering Exercise, a review of the "Filter Options" is necessary.

All "List Views" have the ability to filter the "List Display" by different means, as explained in Figure 9-15, which is the popup that is visible after clicking the Filter "Options" Action Button.

On websites with a limited amount of "Content Items," List Filtering isn't of any significant importance. However, on more complex websites will a great deal of "Content Items" and a complex array of Categories and hierarchy, the ability to trim down the "List of Content Items" will make administration of them much easier. The "Options" for a Category List View are explained below:

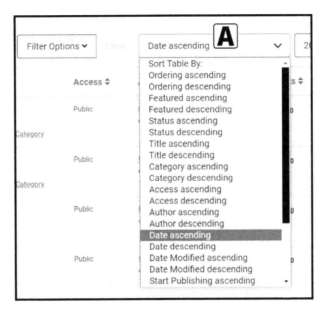

Figure 9-15

Open the Filter "Options" popup window:

Refer to Figure 9-15 for the following:

A	**Ordering ascending**	This is the default setting, generating the "Content Item ID" number from the lowest to the highest ID number value. However, the numbers do not list in pure numerical order, but by value order.
	Ordering descending	This choice reverses the "Content Item ID" list to the largest ID number first.
	Featured ascending	Lists "Featured Articles" by ID number in ascending order from low to high
	Featured descending	Reverses by ID Number the "Featured Articles," from highest to lowest number
	Status ascending	Selecting the Status choice, allows the filtering of the list based on the Publishing status of the Content Item. In this way, for example, only the "Published" Content Items can be displayed, without cluttering the list with all status selections. This option displays the list by A-Z based on the Status Name.
	Status descending	This reverses the above to a Z-A display.
	Title ascending	This choice will display a Content Item List alphabetically by the first characters in the Content Item Name, A-Z. This setting only applies to the Parent Level Content Item.

Title descending	This reverses the above to a Z-A display.
Access ascending	If Access Levels are assigned to the individual Content Item, this setting allows the Content Item List to be ordered by the alphabetical name of the User Access Level, A-Z.
Access descending	This reverses the above to a Z-A display.
Author ascending	Lists by "Author Name" in A-Z order.
Author descending	Reverses the above "Author Name" list in Z-A order.
Date ascending	Sorts the list by the "Created Date" of the item.
Date descending	Sorts the list in reverse order of the "Created Date" from most future to current date.
Date modified ascending	Sorts the list in order of "Modified" from the most recent to the oldest date.
Date modified descending	Reverses the list of "Modified" from the oldest to the most recent shown last ordering.
Start Publishing ascending	Based on the "Start Publishing" date, lists the items in order from current to future date.

IMPORTANT NOTE!

These ordering features only apply to how the "Content Item List" is viewed on the Back-End. It does not affect how they are viewed on the Front-End. Remember, this is a "viewing option" and not a physical positioning or reordering option, which will be covered next.

Rearranging the Order of Content Items Within Categories

Using the Table "Options" above does not change the actual physical order of the "Content Items" as viewed on the website Front-End. It simply changes how they are displayed in the Administrator's Back-End View. The same applies to a "List of Articles" in any given Category. In fact, this same applies to filtering any "Content List" in the Back-End. The Back-End view changes but the Front-End does not.

Content Items (such as Articles), within Categories can be sorted for visibility purposes on the Back-End. However, the Articles can be moved around if a different presentation of their order on the Front-End is desired. This same method applies throughout most of the Joomla! 5 Components that have a Category/Content Item hierarchy configuration.

Using the "Table Options" in a List View can be considered a "soft view" change in the Content order. However, forcing Content Items to assume another location, is actually making a change to the "hard view" of the Content Items in a List. This process explained in Exercise 9-4 below.

EXERCISE 9-4: CHANGE THE ORDER OF A CATEGORY CONTENT ITEM

Objective: The objective of this Exercise is to force a Category Content Item, in this case, an Article, to be relocated to a different viewing location on the website Front-End. If Content Items are displayed as: 1-2-3, this method can be used to force the Front-End order to be 1-3-2, 2-1-3 or whichever order is desired.

At this point, there are insufficient numbers of Categories to be re-ordered. Therefore, the List of Articles will be used to demonstrate the method to be used. Re-ordering functions the same way whether it is a Category or Article. In fact, almost any Content can be re-ordered in the same manner.

Step 1	Go to the website Front-End, in the top Menu, click on the "Blog" Menu Link Item.
Step 2	Note the order of the three Articles that are displayed in "block" format.

1	**"Welcome to your blog: Column 1, Position 1.**
2	**"About your home page" Column 2, Position 1.**
3	**"Your Modules" Column 1, Position 2.**
4	**"Your Template" Column 2, Position 2.**

Note that the "Sub-Categories" link to "My First Sub-Category" is also displayed, but it will not be affected by any re-ordering of the Articles. It is simply a link to the Sub-Category within the "Parent Category > Blog," a modification that was performed in a previous Exercise.

Also, it is possible that the arrangement of these "Blog Articles" within the "Sample Date" may be different in future releases of Joomla! 5. Regardless of their actual "order" or "arrangement," the manner of moving them remains the same. Make naming adjustments to the above as needed if the Article Titles do not match.

Step 3	In the Back-End "Home Dashboard," access the Articles List. Execute a "Clear" action on the Filter Options to remove any sorting of the display from previous Exercises.
Step 4	Use the Filter Options, Select Category and select: "Blog." This will display only the four Articles that are within the "Blog" Category. Any others are located within Sub-Categories as a Child of "Blog." This can easily be remedied by using the "Select Max Levels" selector by setting the option choice to "1." This pares down the list to only those Articles that are directly within the "Blog" Category.
Step 5	Select "Unfeatured Articles" in the "Select Featured" dropdown.

Changing the Order of the Article display on the Front-End is a two-step process:

Step A	Set the conditions of the display sort in the Menu Link Item that opens the view.
Step B	Arrange the actual Order of the Articles in the Article Manager.

The following actions will configure the Menu Link Item to designate the manner in which the Articles in the Category will be Ordered, or arranged.

Step 6		In the "Home Dashboard," open the Menus selector, and then open the "Main Menu Blog" Menu Link Item. This Menu Link Item was created during the installation Sample Data, and opens the Articles and Sub-Categories within the "Blog Category."
Step 7		In the Menu, open the "Blog" Menu Link Item. Then open the "Blog Layout" tab.

Refer to Figure 9-16 for the following:

Step 8	A	Under the "Blog Layout" Tab, in the "Article Order" selector, (found near the bottom of the screen), choose "Article Order" from among the choices in the drop down list, implying that the desired display should be in the "Article Oder," which is the "Order" in which they are physically arranged in their assigned Category.
Step 9	B	At the top of the screen, execute a Save and Close Action. The green Saved Message will appear. Remember to Close it.

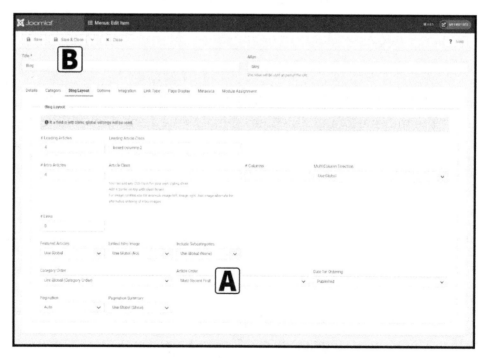

Figure 9-16
Other actions as shown on this screen will be discussed in another Chapter.

The actions below are the next steps needed to move the "About your home page" Article to the top position on the display. Also, these Action Steps will be used to let you navigate through the instructions without use of a figure or illustration to act as a visual guide.

Step 10	In the "Home Dashboard," go back to the Content > Articles selector, either in the left Menu, or in the Site Panel. Notice that the dot icons (column 2) for each item is grey, indicating they cannot be moved and the default settings are in control.
Step 11	In the column heading area, between the check box and the Featured column, click on the "up/down" blue arrows. This activates the "ordering" ability of the Articles, and allows them to be displayed A- or Z-A. The stacked dots in the column for each item are now black, indicating their "order" can be changed.
Step 12	If necessary to do so again, using Filter Options, in the Select Category selector, choose "Blog" as the Category of Articles to display.
Step 13	In the "Select Featured" dropdown, select: "Unfeatured Articles."
Step 14	In the "Select Status" dropdown, select: "Published."
Step 15	At the top of the second column, make sure the blue arrow is pointing "up," and if not, click on it until it displays in that manner.

These steps have now pruned the list down to only those Articles that a "Published" and removed the "Featured Articles," which could possibly result in movement issues if still visible on the list.

Step 17	Click on the dots for "About your home page" Article.
Step 18	With the Article highlighted with a green color, move it slowly to the top and notice that the other Articles slide down below it.
Step 19	When reaching the top, release the mouse and the Article will now be in the top location on the list.
Step 20	The is no Saving Action required. When the item is released, the new Ordering is automatically saved.
Step 21	Go to the Front-End and refresh the screen. The Order of the Articles shown should be the same as those in the manner displayed within the Category itself. The "About your home page" Article should be the very first Article displayed in column 1, Position 1. The other Articles slide right and down > left when an Article is placed above them.

The Order of Articles displayed can be changed at any time, based on the criteria set in the relevant Menu Link Item, and the manner selected within the Category of Articles. There are several ways of pre-selecting the "ordering" and this is first controlled by the applicable Menu Link Item.

Rearranging the Order of Content Items Within Categories

On occasion, it might be necessary to change the order of display for a "List of Categories," such as when a Menu Link Item of the "List all Categories" type is needed to display a list of Sub-Categories within a Parent Category. This can happen frequently on websites that contain extensive Article Content within an array of Categories and Sub-Categories in a complicated hierarchy.

First, it is necessary to create several additional Sub-Categories within the "My First Category" in the List of Categories, as explained in Exercise 9-5.

EXERCISE 9-5: MULTIPLE SUB-CATEGORIES WITHIN A CATEGORY

Objective: In this Exercise, two additional Sub-Categories will be created within an existing Category with an existing "Sub-Category," using the two different methods to accomplish the same results.

Method 1: Save & New

Step 1	On the Back-End, go to: "Home Dashboard > Control Panel > Content > Categories."
Step 2	Open the "My First Sub-Category" item. This is a sub-sub-category of the Parent "Blog Category" located within the "My First Category," which is the first "Child" of the "Blog Category."
Step 3	Under the Save & Close Option at the top, select: Save & New. This Action opens a new, blank, Category Manager screen. Note: this is an alternative method of creating a Content Item, especially when located within an existing Content Item of the same type.

Refer to Figure 9-17 for the following:

Step 4	A	In the Title, enter: "My Second Sub-Category" (without quotes).
Step 5	B	In the Description Area, enter: "This is the description for My Second Sub-Category."
Step 6	C	In the Parent Selector to the right, choose: "My First Category."
Step 7	D	Make sure the Status is set to "Published."
Step 8	E	Make sure the Access is set to "Public."
Step 9		Execute a Save & Close Action. Which will take you back to the List of Categories. The green Category Saved will also display at the top of the screen. Close it.
Step 10		The results should be as shown in Figure 9-18 below.

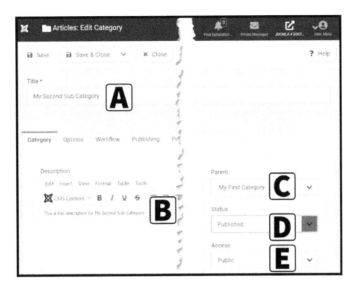

Figure 9-17

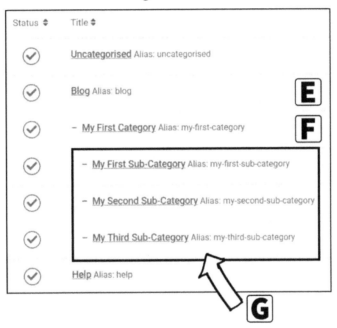

Figure 9-18

Method 2: Save as Copy

Step 1	On the Back-End, go to: "Control Panel > Content > Categories"
Step 2	Open the "My First Sub-Category" Content Category.
Step 3	Under the Save & Close Option at the top, select: Save as Copy. This Action duplicates the current item, adding a suffix number because Content Items cannot have the same Title.
Step 4	Change the Title to: "My Third Sub-Category," (without quotes), and remove the number at the end.

Step 5	Delete any naming text in the "Alias" field. It will regenerate following any saving action execution.
	Alternatively, In the Alias, change it to read: "my-second-sub-category" (without quotes). Normally, you would not concern yourself with the Content Item Alias, but in this case, it is necessary to change it manually. Content Item "aliases" are covered in Chapter 44, "VISUAL: Custom and Alternative Layouts," found in *Volume 2, Boots on the Ground*.
Step 5	In the Description Area, enter: "This is the description for My Second Sub-Category" (without quotes).
Step 6	In the Parent Selector to the right, choose: "My First Category."
Step 7	Make sure the Status is set to "Published." The Status will likely default to "Unpublished" when using this method to duplicate an item.
Step 8	Make sure the Access is set to Public.
Step 9	Execute a Save & Close Action. Which will take you back to the List of Categories. The Category Saved message will also display at the top of the screen. Close it.

Refer to Figure 9-18 for the following:

| Step 10 | On the Back-End, go to: Control Panel > Content > Categories, which will display the List of Categories. |

E	This is the "Parent Category."
F	This is the previously created Sub-Category below the "Parent Category" named: "Blog."
G	These are the three "Sub-Sub-Categories" created above.

Note that all Categories which are indented, indicate they are "Child Categories." Indents are progressive based on their "sub-levels."

Now that there is a "Parent Category" with a hierarchy of a "Child Category" and three Child of Child Categories. Their order can be changed. Make note that by default, the order is "first created, first" with "last created, last" on the Category List Display of "Articles: Categories."

EXERCISE 9-6: CHANGE THE ORDER OF THE SUB-CATEGORIES

Objective: The objective of this Exercise is to rearrange the order of the Sub-Categories within a Category. Currently, the order is first, second, third, by Sub-Category name. The new order will be third-first-second, using the following steps.

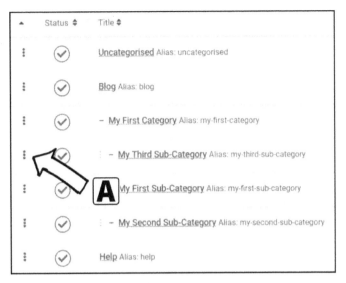

Figure 9-19

Refer to Figure 9-19 for the following:

Step 1	On the Back-End, go to: "Control Panel > Content > Categories," to display the list of Categories.
Step 2	Find "My Third Sub-Category" on the Category List.
Step 3	Place the Mouse Cursor on the dot icon on the left and hold down the button **[A]**. If the icon does not respond, click on the small arrows at the top of the column to make the buttons appear or turn blue in color and is pointing upwards.
Step 4	Slide the Sub-Category slowly up the screen, noting that as an upper item is passed over, it drops down.
Step 5	Release the Mouse Button when the Sub-Category passes over "My First Sub-Category" and it moves below "My Third Sub-Category."
Step 6	The result of the above actions should result in the Category arrangement as shown in Figure 9-19, with their order being: "Third, First, Second."

Figure 9-19

This particular "ordering" method is used throughout Joomla! 5 to permanently move, or arrange the order of any Content Item on a List. It works the same for Categories, Articles and other Content Items that are ordered on a List view.

Remember!
Changing the "List View" ordering via the display options on the Back-End DOES NOT change the order on the Front-End. The Content Items must be arranged in the above manner to create a change is location on the Front-End.

The Front-End View
At this point, while viewing the Front-End, select: "My Category List" in the Main Menu. This will display "My First Category" previously created, at the bottom of the List.

Note there is only one Sub-Category listed, even though there are three Child Categories in existence, as evidenced by the Category List view in the previous Exercise.

This is because the Global Setting for Sub-Categories defaults to one (1) Level only. Additionally, the default setting is to NOT SHOW Categories that are empty, or in this case, meaning they do not contain any assigned Articles. This is a setting that over-rides the display of this Content.

To fix this, the Empty Categories setting needs to be changed, as shown in Figure 9-20.

EXERCISE 9-7: SETTING EMPTY CATEGORIES TO DISPLAY

Objective: This Exercise will demonstrate how to change the default setting that does not allow the display of Categories or Sub-Categories that do not contain Articles, from "Hide" to "Show." Although this Exercise demonstrates how to display a Content Item ("Category") that is empty, that is: no Content Items have been assigned into it. However, as a practical matter, empty Content would normally NOT be displayed.

This reduces screen clutter if the Content Category hierarchy has been created, but many of the Categories have yet to be populated with Articles. These type of Categories," insofar as the configurations go, are considered as "empty," and thus, they are prohibited from displaying by default. This can be changed.

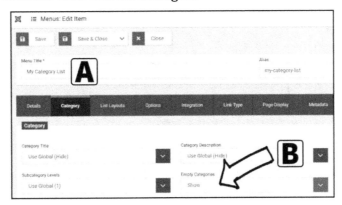

Figure 9-20

Step 1		On the "Home Dashboard," open Menus and select Main Menu.

Refer to Figure 9-20 for the following:

Step 2	A	Open the "My Category List" Menu Link Item. This link is in the Main Menu.
Step 3		Open the "Category" Tab.
Step 4	C	Change the "Empty Categories" setting from "Use Global (Hide)," to "Show." This over-rides the Global Setting.
Step 5	D	Execute a Save & Close Action.
Step 6		Go to the website Front-End, refresh the screen.

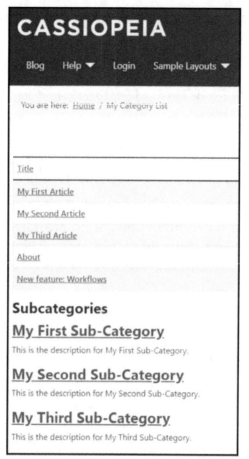

Figure 9-21

Now, when you view the Category Link in the Main Menu, you will see the List of Articles in "My First Category," and at the bottom of the List, all the Sub-Categories will be displayed in the order which was set in Exercise 9-6 above. Make note of the displayed order of the Sub-Categories, which were re-arranged in the earlier Exercise.

This technique can be applied for most all List Items that are displayed on a Joomla! 5 website. However, some third-party Component Extensions may not have this particular feature to change the order of Content items. Their Extension may use another mechanism to achieve the same results.

About Global Settings

Within Joomla! 5, there are Global Settings, which are default settings that will apply to all of the various Content Items. The settings can be changed, and when this is done, the change will apply to all Content Items of the same type, re: Articles, Categories, Menu Link Items, Layouts and so on.

The Global Settings may be over-ridden at either the Content Item Level, individually, or via the Menu Link Item that accesses the Content Item.

See *Joomla! 5: Boots on the Ground, Advance Edition, Volume 2,* Chapter 43, "CONTENT: Global "Options" & Settings," for in-depth information about their use, how they apply and how they can be over-ridden as needed.

Publishing and Unpublishing Content Items

Content Items of all types may be set to "show," or "not show," at any given time. This is controlled by the "Publish" and "Unpublish" function. In other words, a Content Item can be set to display on the Front-end, or not display.

There are two methods to Publish or Unpublish a Content Item, as follows:

EXERCISE 9-8: PUBLISHING & UNPUBLISHING CONTENT ITEMS

Objective: This Exercise will demonstrate two methods of "Publishing" or the "Unpublishing" a single Content Item, as shown below.

Method 1: Using the Status Dropdown Selector in the Content Item

These Actions apply for most all Content Items within the Joomla! 5 Framework, along with most of the Component Extensions.

Step 1	Go to the Front-End, and select "Blog" in the Top Menu.
Step 2	Notice on the layout, the Article: "Your Modules" is displayed. Likely the third Article listed.
Step 3	On the "Home Dashboard," go to: "Control Panel > Content > Articles," to display the List of Articles. Use either the left menu or the Site Panel to do so.
Step 4	Open the Article: "Your Modules," by clicking on the Article Name.
Step 5	On the right side of the screen, change the Status from "Published" to "Unpublished."
Step 6	Execute a Save & Close Action. The "Success Message" should appear. Close it.
Step 7	Go to the Front-End, refresh the screen or select Blog in the Top Menu.
Step 8	Notice that the "Your Modules" Article is no longer visible. And, because the "Leading Articles" number (4) was set in the Category Blog tab, four blocks are available, but only three actual Articles exist for that Category. This is proper in this instance.

Following the steps outline above, almost every Content Item can be set to be viewed on the Front-End, or set to not allow viewing. The Content Item will still be visible on the Back-End so the Administrator can continue to manage the access on the Front-End.

Method 2: Using the Status Icon Selector in the List View

Using this method, the Status of the "My Modules" Article, which was set to "Unpublished" in Method 1 above, will be reversed and set back to Published, but using another method.

Step 1	Go to the Front-End, and select "Blog" in the Top Menu.
Step 2	Notice on the List of Articles, the Article: "Your Modules" is not displayed because it was "Unpublished" previously.
Step 3	On the Back-End, go to: "Control Panel > Content > Articles," to display the List of Articles.
Step 4	On the List of Articles, find "Your Modules." Do not open the Article.
Step 5	Notice in the Status Column that it is set to "Unpublished." This is indicated by an icon that contains an **"X"** indicating "Unpublished."
Step 6	Mouseover the grey **"X"** Mark icon, which will open an information popup. Click on the icon. There may be a slight delay as the item's action is executed, especially if there is a long list of Articles.
Step 7	The Action changes the "Status" of the item.
Step 8	When the selection is made, the screen will automatically refresh itself, and the green "Success Message" will appear at the top of the page. Close that message panel using the **"X"** at the right side.
Step 9	The "Status Column" indicator has also changed to the green icon.
Step 11	Go to the Front-End, refresh the screen, and note the "Your Modules" Article is once again accessible for viewing. Also note that is located in the same "order" location as its assigned location on the Article List.

Status Change is Automatic

Using Method 1, a **Save Action** must be executed because the Content Item is open and must be closed. No **Save Action** is needed when changing settings using Method 2 in any Content Item List View. The selected changes are automatic and instantaneous when the action is performed. There is a difference when making edits within a "workspace" versus edits on the "List" view.

Archiving Categories

"Archiving" is a technique incorporated in the Joomla! 5 that allows outdated Content Items to be saved into a designated location. This is done to: 1) maintain a library of Content Items, and 2) save the Content Item for possible reuse and display again, 3) remove it visually from the List of active Content Items.

Often, Content Items (especially those outdated), are "Archived" to preserve them for potential future re-use or re-Publishing. Exercise 9-9 and 9-10 will guide the Administrator through the process of "Archiving" and "Restoring" Content Items.

EXERCISE 9-9: ARCHIVING CATEGORIES

Objective: This Exercise will guide the Administrator on the method of "Archiving" a Category Item. In this case, it will be a Sub-Category.

Step 1	A	On the "Home Dashboard," go to: "Control Panel > Content > Categories," to display the List of Categories. Use either the left menu or the Site Panel to do so. The result should be a display of the existing Categories, including those created in previous Exercises. Note that on the "Home Dashboard > Site Panel," the term used is "Article Categories," while in the left menu, it is simply: "Categories."

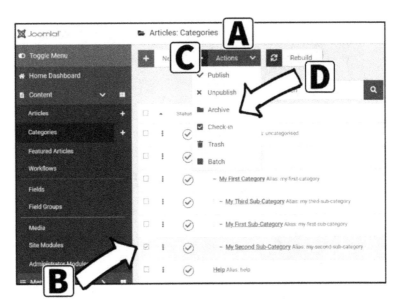

Figure 9-22

Refer to Figure 9-22 for the following:

Step 2	B	Select the checkbox to the left of the "My Second Sub-Category" item.
Step 3	C	Open the "Actions" selector at the top of the screen.
Step 4	D	Select "Archive" on the dropdown list. This action will automatically trigger

		a Saving Action of the list and refresh the screen.
Step 5		The "Category Archived" "Success Message" will display. Close it.
Step 6		Note that the Category "My Second Sub-Category" is no longer displayed on the list.
Step 7		Go to the Front-End, and select "My Category List" in the Main Menu.
Step 8		Notice that the "My Second Sub-Category" is no longer visible below the List of Articles under the "Subcategories" heading.

The Category has now been placed in the website's Archive and can be recovered and restored to its previous location, in the Category hierarchy. The next Exercise will demonstrate how a Category is restored.

EXERCISE 9-10: RESTORING A CATEGORY FROM THE ARCHIVES

Objective: This Exercise will demonstrate the steps involved in restoring an "Archived" Category. The Sub-Category which was "Archived" in the previous exercise will be restored to the "Published" Status.

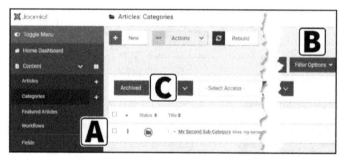

Figure 9-23

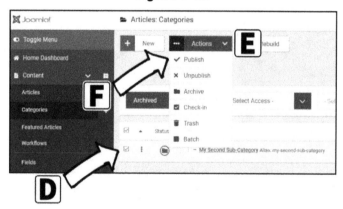

Figure 9-24

Refer to Figures 9-23 and 9-24 for the following:

Step 1	A	On the "Home Dashboard," go to: "Control Panel > Content > Categories," to display the List of Categories. Use either the left menu or the Site Panel to do so. The result should be a display of Categories.
Step 2	B	Click the Filter "Options" which will display a list of available Filters.
Step 3	C	In the "Select Status" dropdown, select "Archived," which will automatically display a list of all of the Categories in the Archive.
Step 4	D	Select the checkbox to the left of the "My Second Sub-Category" item. Alternatively, click on the "folder" icon and execute the action that way.
Step 5	E	After making the selection using the "tick box," open the "Actions" dropdown.
Step 6	F	In the dropdown, select "Publish" as the next action.
Step 7		The Category "Published" "Success Message" will display. Close it.
Step 7		Go to the Front-End, refresh the screen or select Category List in the Main Menu.
Step 8		Notice that the "My Second Sub-Category" is once again visible below the List of Articles. The restoration of an "Archived" Category is complete.

The above processes typically function in the same manner for most all types of Content Items through a Joomla! 5 website. It will likely work the same way for Content Items within Extensions.

Modules are an Exception

Modules **CANNOT** be Archived. They may only be "Unpublished' or "Trashed." There is no function or action that can be taken that will "Archive" a Module.

Deleting Categories ("Trashing")

Categories can be easily deleted, although in Joomla! 5, the term used is "Trash" or "Trashed." This is accomplished by selecting the Category or "Sub-Category," using the checkbox field, and then executing a "Trash" Action via the Actions drop down selector at the top of the screen.

Not Empty, Cannot be "Trashed"

One point to note is that a "Parent Category" cannot be "Trashed" if it has a "Child Category" underneath it. Categories must be completely empty in order to be "Trashed." Another point is that a Category, of any type, cannot be "Trashed" if it has any Content Items, such as Articles, or Images if the Category is in the Media Manager. This applies whether the Content Item within is "Published" or not.

One good point to remember is that a Content Item can be removed from viewing by simply "Unpublishing" the Item vs. "Trashing" it. This way, the Category need not be removed from its List View, but simply set to a different viewing status on the website Front-End.

In the event a Content Item has been "Trashed," it can still be accessed and restored back to its original location. However, if the Content Item is "Trashed" and the "Trash" container is purposefully emptied or deleted, the Content Item(s) are permanently lost and cannot be retrieved. It takes several unique steps, and acknowledgement of warnings, to purposefully empty the "Trash" container so it cannot be accomplished accidentally.

The "Trash" is Protected, in a Way

When a Content Item is deleted, or in Joomla! 5 parlance: "Trashed," it is placed into a holding location, and remain there until one of two additional Action Steps are taken: 1) the "Trash" Container is emptied, which permanently deletes the Content Item from the website, or 2) the Content Item is once again "Published" or" Unpublished," which will restore it back to its original location. Remember, "Trashed" Content Items remain accessible until the "Trash" is purged of any of its Content – which deletes everything within it. **Be aware of that**.

EXERCISE 9-11: "TRASHING" (DELETING) A CATEGORY

Objective: This Exercise will demonstrate the process of deleting a Category by placing it into the "Trash" Container, effectively Unpublishing the Content item.

Refer to Figure 9-25 for the following:

Step 1	A	On the "Home Dashboard," go to: "Home Dashboard > Content > Categories," to display the List of Categories. Use either the left menu or the Site Panel ("Article Categories"), to do so. The result should be a display of Categories. *NOTE:* If no Categories are listed, use a "Clear" action on the Filters, which should result in the Categories being displayed.
Step 2	B	Select the checkbox to the left of the "Help" Category.
Step 3	C	Open the Actions selector at the top of the screen.

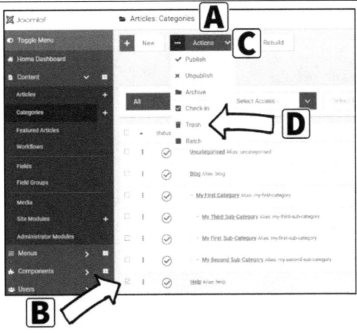

Figure 9-25

Step 4	D	Select "Trash" on the dropdown list. This action will automatically trigger a Saving Action of the list and refresh the screen.
Step 5		The "Category Trashed" "Success Message" will display. Close it.
Step 6		If you change the Filter "Options" in the Status dropdown to "All," the Category "Help" remains on the list, but the circle check icon has been changed to a "Trash Can" icon.
Step 7		In the Filter "Options" in the "Status" dropdown, change the selection back to "Published" and note that the "Help" Category is no longer visible. It has been effectively deleted by being placed in the "Trash" holding location.

EXERCISE 9-12: RECOVERING A "TRASHED" (DELETED) CATEGORY

Objective: The purpose of this exercise is to explain the Recovery Action Steps to restore a "Trashed" Content Item, which recovers a previously "Trashed" or deleted Category.

Refer to Figures 9-26 and 9-27 for the following:

Step 1	A	On the "Home Dashboard," go to: Control Panel > Content > Categories, to display the List of Articles. Use either the left menu or the Site Panel to do so. The result should be a display of Categories.

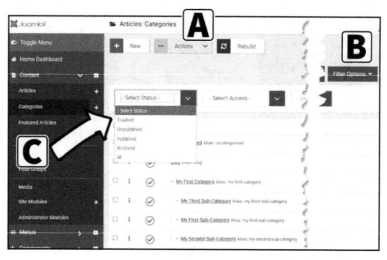

Figure 9-26

Refer to Figure 9-26 for the following:

Step 2	B	Click the Filter "Options" which will display a list of available Filters.
Step 3	C	In the "Select Status" dropdown, select "Trashed," which will display a list of all of the Categories in the "Trash" Container. The result is show in Figure 9-27.

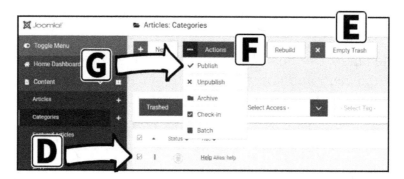

Figure 9-27

Refer to Figure 9-27 for the following:

Step 4	D	Select the checkbox to the left of the "Help" item. Note that the greyed out option to Empty "Trash" **[E]** displays at the top of the screen. Go to the top
	E	Menu and locate the "Empty Trash" button. ***Executing the Empty "Trash" Action will permanently delete the Content Item. DO NOT perform that action.*** However, make a note of how to invoke it. This one action will delete and clear every Category item that is in the "Trash," so always verify your actions.

Step 5	F	After making the selection, open the "Actions" dropdown.
Step 6	G	In the dropdown, select "Publish" as the next action. The Action will take place automatically. Alternatively, clicking on the grey "Trash Can" icon will set the Content Item back to the "Published" Status.
Step 7		The Category "Published Success Message" will display. Close it.
Step 8		Reopen the Category List display by changing the Filter to view only the "Published" Content Items.
Step 9		Notice that the "Help" Category is once again visible on the list. The restoration of a "Trashed" Category is complete.

At this point, Categories have been pretty much explained with regard to what they are, why the exist, how to use them and other related topics.

Also included in this Chapter was the management of Content Items as to their visibility and access.

The next Chapter will deal with the Articles that are assigned to reside within the Category hierarchy.

More in Future Chapters

The manner in which this book is structured is based on progressive learning experiences. As Exercises are completed, with the accompanying explanations, knowledge about the administration of Joomla! 5 is acquired. Each successive Exercise may have repetitive steps but demonstrate different results.

The whole idea of the Exercises is to build, build, and build upon one another to demonstrate the "how" of doing things as the Joomla! 5 website Administrator.

CONTENT:
Articles

Articles are the most common Content Items created on a Joomla! 5 website. There are other sources of Content, usually created from third-party Components, installed as Extensions, but Articles are the most usual form of Content.

Articles are accessed on the website Front-End via a connection from a Menu Link Item. Other Content Items are also opened via a Menu Link Item, but it is a mandatory action to access an Article directly. There is no other direct way to open an individual Article. It must be accomplished by a Menu Link Item, or a direct "hard coded link" embedded in another Article or Module.

The exception to this steadfast rule is the Category List or the Category Blog, which can be opened via a Menu Link Item, wherein there are links to individual Articles are within the Category Article Listing. It is not a direct connection to an Article, but it is another means to access them. There is a significant difference between a Menu Link Item opening an Article and a Menu Link Item opening another type of screen display that may show a List of Articles, which is completely different, yet still access the same Content.

Additionally, within an Article, a link to another Article may be added within the Content area. This is a built-in feature of the new Joomla! 5 platform. However, as noted, it is not a direct way of accessing an Article.

Articles, in "Wordpress" parlance, are "Blog Items." This is simply a rose with another name. The exception being that Articles in Joomla! 5 can be presented in many different ways, other than being a simple "Blog Item."

Articles in the Content Area

When an Article's associated Menu Link Item is clicked, the Article will appear, and it ALWAYS appears in the Main Content Area of the website's Template, as shown in Figure 10-1. Each Template has a Main Content Area, and the Articles displaying in that location will only open at that location when triggered by a Menu Link Item's action. The Main Content Area is where not only Articles appear, but also the Content from Components. This compares to the opposite of Modules, which can be located anywhere on a webpage where a "Module Position" is located, or within Articles or within certain types of Modules.

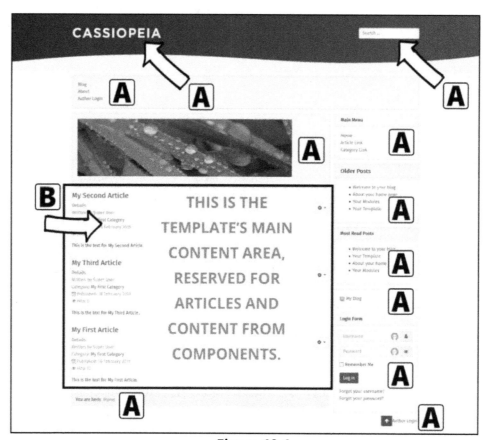

Figure 10-1

Modules in the Content Area

On most Templates, there are "Module Positions" located directly above and below the Main Content Area and they are actually located in fixed physical locations. These are hard-coded locations on a Template into which Modules can be assigned to a physical location on the webpage.

Refer to Figure 10-1 for the following:

A	These are "Module Positions" on the default Joomla! 5 Template. Modules can be placed into any of these locations and can be different on every page. Module visibility is also controlled by Menu Link Items. Modules are discussed in Chapter 12, "CONTENT: Modules." As you may note, "Module Positions" are located pretty much anywhere on any Template screen, but they are/must be hard-coded positions within the respective Template.
B	This is the Content Area located on the default Joomla! 5 Template. Articles appear here by default, as does Content generated via Components, or all other similar sources.

Articles Must be Assigned to Categories

As discussed in previous Chapters, when an Article is created, it must be assigned to an existing "Category" or "Sub-Category." This allows for a classification hierarchy to be created to organize Articles. This isn't a big deal or complicated undertaking for websites with little or limited amounts of Content. However, for websites with large numbers of Articles, a Category Structure should be created. This was discussed previously in Chapter 9, "CONTENT: Categories."

Category Name "Uncategorized"

By default, Joomla! 5 has a fixed, existing Category called "Uncategorized." It is a default Category into which Articles are automatically assigned, unless otherwise designated. Every Article that isn't assigned to a named Category, will automatically be assigned to the "Uncategorized." When that happens, an Article can be easily moved into another Category at any time after that.

In the previous "CONTENT: Categories" Chapter, organization of Content was discussed and how Articles can be assigned. Categories can be created as either "Parent" or "Child Levels" and can be nested within each other to create a hierarchy of organization.

Once Categories have been created, Articles can be assigned into them during creation, or moved into them afterwards. Following the assignment of Articles into a Category, Menu Link Items can be created to allow access to the Articles via any one of these methods.

Method 1	A Menu Link Item directly to an individual Article.
Method 2	A Menu Link Item to the individual Category that displays a List of Articles within the respective Category. This type is called a "Category Blog." There are two types of these: 1) the "Category Blog" itself, and 2) the "Featured Articles" which is a specialized unique "Category Blog" type which has been given another name.
Method 3	A Menu Link Item to a List of Categories, which lists Child Categories that are within a Parent Category. The Menu Link Item connects directly to the Child Category. Otherwise, the link is one as described in Method 2 above. If there are Child Categories that do not contain Articles, there is a control setting to either show "empty Categories" or not, depending upon Article assignments.
Method 4	A Menu Link Item that is connected to a Content Display function of an Extension. These configure webpages for the display of Categories or Articles, or other combinations of Content. There are many such Extensions in the Joomla! Extensions Directory that creates Category/Article displays in different configurations for the Menu Link Item. A shopping cart Extension is a typical example of how Menu Link Items may open such items, such as: product catalogs, products in a category, individual products, and the like.

Using the Article Manager

As part of the Administrator Back-End, there are a number of Managers where Content of certain types are administered. For Articles, this is the Article Manager, as shown in Figure 10-2. This is where everything relating to Articles is controlled. The Content of individual Article's Content is not controlled here. Content is controlled within the respective "Article Workspace."

In a nutshell, there is the Article Manager, that allows access to the individual Articles which opens a specific "Article's Workspace." The Articles are first presented in a list. Usually, the most recent Article is listed at the top unless the default "Options" has been set to display otherwise.

The Article Manager also contains controls that accesses another administration area, called: "Filter Options," whereby settings and configurations can be changed for the display of the Articles listed, as described below:

"Filter Options" and "Options" Explained

Filter "Options" simply control how, and in what manner, Articles are displayed within the Article Manager. Options, on the other hand, contain a wide range of controls for display, configuration and other settings that can be applied globally within Joomla! 5. Filter "Options" deal with how the Content Items within a manager are displayed, while "Options" are hard settings that can be applied to many different types of Content Items. Also, within individual Content Items, or Menu Link Items, there are individual selectors that can override some of the "Options" settings.

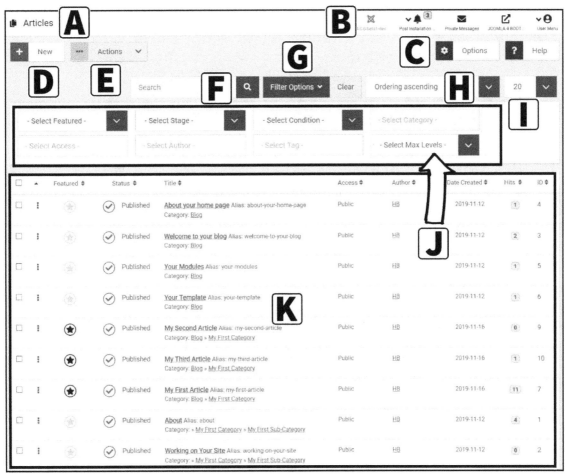

Figure 10-2

Refer to Figure 10-2 for the following:

A	For all Managers on the Back-End, this section identifies the name of the Manager that is being accessed. In this case: "Articles."
B	These items provide information and a quick access to the website Front-End.
C	"Global Options" for Categories and Articles can be set using this access link to the settings. Remember, the Global "Options" for Categories and Articles are exactly the same. *Joomla! 5: Boots on the Ground, Advance Edition, Volume 2,* Chapter 43, "CONTENT: Global Settings & Options," explains these in detail.
D	If a new Article is to be created, this button opens the "Article Workspace."
E	The Actions cannot be invoked until an Article's tick box is selected in the Article List **[K]**.
F	On complex sites with many Articles, it is often convenient to search for Content. This field can be used to do so.

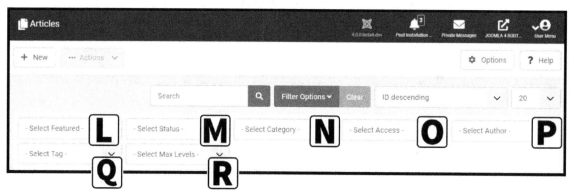

Figure 10-3

G	The Filter "Options" opens an additional layer of Filter(s) as shown in Figure 10-3 above.
H	The order in which the Articles List are displayed can be set here. There are many choices, which are obvious by their named actions. The order deals with how the List of Articles are filtered and displayed for the Administrator. The setting choices do not affect the Front-End display.
I	The number of Articles to be displayed on the List can be set here. There is also a global default setting in another area, that will be discussed in *Joomla! 5: Boots on the Ground, Advance Edition, Volume 2,* Chapter 43, "CONTENT: Global Settings & Options."
J	These are the additional selectors and controls a display when the Filter "Options" is clicked.
K	This is the comprehensive Articles List, with information relative to each Article,

along with some direct action controls for moving, adding to the "Featured" Category List, and to toggle the "Published" state on/off.

Changing Article Access Permissions

Past Joomla! versions allowed the Access to a Content Item, in this case an Article, to be changed in the Article Manager under the "Access" column. This is no longer the case in Joomla! 5. The "Access" setting must be changed within the individual Article Workspace, or Content Workspace itself for other items, re: Categories, etc. It is hopeful this will be changed in the future. This feature might be added back into the layout in the future.

The Filter Options

In addition to the general settings, when the "Filter Options" are selected in the Article Manager, an additional group of settings become visible/available that allows more actions to be implemented and applied to single, multiple or all Articles.

Refer to Figure 10-3 above for the following:

L	The **Select Featured** setting filters the Article List to show either "Featured" or "Unfeatured" Articles, with the default setting being equal to "show all."
M	The **Status** choices deal with Articles that are "Published" and/or "Trashed."
N	The **Category** selector filters the list on the type of Article with regard to any existing Category selected from the list. On large websites, this pares down long lists to the selected Category.
O	**Select Access** filters the Article List based on the "Access" settings for each.
P	**Select Author** organizes the Articles by the writer, or creator of the Article.
Q	If **Tags** are used on the website, the Article List can be filtered based on which "Tag" is being used. When a "Tag" is assigned to a Content Item, it automatically appears as a choice in this selector.
R	If the Category hierarchy has many levels of Sub-Categories this setting allows the Administrator to limit the List display to certain levels. For example, the setting of 1 limits the Article List to those assigned only to top level Categories. If 2, indicated Top Level **+** the next "Sub-Category," etc.

After using Joomla! 5 as an Administrator, in a short time, you will quickly learn how to use the Article Manager and the "Filter Options" to help manage and arrange the Content Items in the various Content Managers found in the Back-End. Don't be afraid to experiment. Using the "Filters Options" will not break anything. You can always reset them back to their default state using "Clear."

The next Administrator level of Content Management is the Article Workspace, which is the screen that opens when an Article is being created, or opened for editing.

Workflow-wise, the Joomla! methodology is:

1	Open the Administration Area "Home Dashboard."
2	A choice of actions is available to access various parts of the Back-End.
2	A "Content Manager Area" Displays based on whichever selection is performed.
3	Next, a "Workspace" is opened where the individual Content Item can be modified.
4	The "Workspace" is closed with a saving action. In fact, it "must" be closed to prevent a "check-out" from preventing others from "checking-in" to the Content Item Workspace. If a saving action is not executed, any changes to the Article will NOT be saved. Also, by not executing a saving action or formally closing the Content Item, it remains "checked-out" to the last user and unavailable to any other Editor.

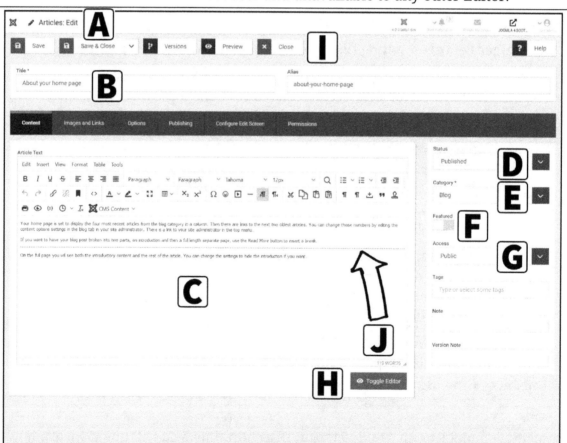

Figure 10-4

Refer to Figure 10-4 for the following:

Figure 10-4 shows the Article Workspace for the "About you home page." You can open it to follow along, or simply refer to the Figure.

A	Indicates the Article Manager's "Edit" feature is being accessed.
B	The "Title" of the Article.
C	The Article Content area, also showing the standard word processing controls. These will change if other Editors are installed and invoked as the active Editor. There are several Editors available that can be easily installed as a website Extension, then designated at the default Editor.
D	The Status setting for "Published" or "Unpublished."
E	Displays, and allows selection of the Articles Category Assignment.
F	Option to select the Article as a "Featured" Article.
G	The choice in this field is to set the viewer Access level of the Article on the website's Front-End.
H	This option switches the Content Editor area from standard word processing style to "html" code configuration. This option is a code-view of actual Content and the associated "html" code being used. It is sometimes needed to switch to this view to make minor corrections to the Content Item's underlying "html" code.
I	This row contains the Saving Action buttons, Versions and Preview, along with the Close action button.
J	The dotted line indicates a "Break" between Intro Text and the Main Body of the Article, which will be discussed later in this Chapter.

"Featured Articles" Category

The steadfast rule is that an Article may only be assigned to one Category at a time. The inclusive use of the "Featured Articles" Category is the only time when an Article can be assigned to two Categories at the same time.

Let's make the distinction here: Articles are always assigned to only one Category. However, the same Article can also be co-designated within the "Featured Articles" Category, which is a special exception for Article display purposes only.

This is the only exception to the one-category rule. It must be qualified that there might be a Joomla! 5 Extension that will allow Articles to be assigned to multiple Categories at the same time. Refer to the Joomla! Extensions Library ("JED"), to double-check on this possibility as one may be available in the future.

Remember, discussions in this book deal with the default Joomla! 5 platform and core file installations with "Sample Blog" Content. Extensions may be added that significantly change some, or part, of the default setup.

Here is the Distinction

While Categories can display using many different Menu Link Item selections, the "Featured Articles" as a Category, can be display using any Menu Link Item set as a "Featured Articles" type. Typically, this is the "HOME" Menu Link Item, but may be named anything else.

This means that when the website opens in the browser window, the "Home" Menu Link Item (which is generally the default), is set to display the "Featured Articles," which is a "Category Blog" Layout, as distinguished from any other type of Content. This displays only those Articles designated as "Featured," regardless of any other Category to which they may be assigned.

This is not done automatically. The "Home" Menu Link Item must be designated to show "Featured Articles" which is the selection that must be made as the "Menu Item Type." This sets the stage for display of the "Featured Articles."

What happens is that "Featured Articles" are displayed on the website opening webpage and the Articles can be part of one, or many other, Categories. The "Featured Articles" is simply a collection of all the co-designated Articles, which could also be scattered among any number of other standard Categories.

In summary, Articles can be assigned to any Category. They can also be individually designated as "Featured" and set to display on the website HOME page in almost any type of layout format. Exercise 10-1 illustrates how this designation is accomplished.

EXERCISE 10-1: DESIGNATING AN ARTICLE AS "FEATURED"

Objective: The objective of this Exercise is to demonstrate how an Article, assigned to any Category, may also be co-designated as a "Featured Article," causing it to appear on the Front-Page of a website. "Featured Articles" can be quickly created via the express route of "Control Panel > Content > Featured Articles," which automatically creates an Articles as such. However, this Exercise will demonstrate how to create a standard Article and then designate it as "Featured," along with its other assigned Category.

Step 1		On the "Home Dashboard," go to: "Control Panel > Content > Articles," to display the List of Articles. Use either the left menu or the Site Panel to do so. The result should be a display of Articles.
		Alternatively, in the Site Panel, simply click on the **"+"** icon next to the Articles link, which will open a New Article Workspace.
Step 2		Using the **"New"** Button at the top, open a "New Article" window. This is commonly referred to as the "Article Workspace." This area functions in a manner similar to any Content editing sections of a website or a word processor, with various "Options" to control Content and appearance.

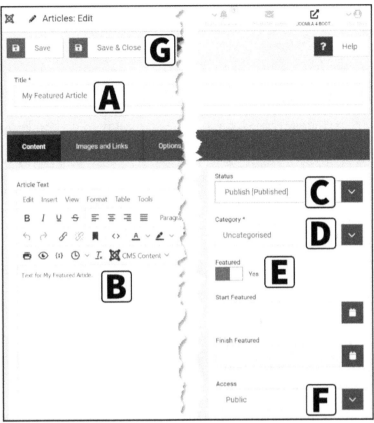

Figure 10-5

Refer to Figure 10-5 for the following:

Step 3	A	Name the Article: "My Featured" Article" (without the quotes).
Step 4	B	In the Content Area, enter: "This is the text for My Featured Article." (without the quotes).
Step 7	C	Make sure the "Status" is set to "Published."
Step 5	D	To the right, in the Category selector, select "Uncategorized."
Step 6	E	Below that, toggle the "Featured" selector from "No" to "Yes." The selector will change color from grey to green and display "Yes."
Step 7	F	Although it should already be set, make sure the "Access" is set to Public.
Step 8	G	Execute a Save and Close Action. The screen will change to the Article List view, and the green "Success Message" will display at the top of the screen. Close the message panel.
Step 9		Go to the website Front-End, refresh the screen, or click on the "Home" Button in the Main Menu so the screen refreshes.
Step 10		Note that the first Article on the list is now "My Featured Article." The other three Articles that are also displayed were each designated as

| | "Featured" in a previous Exercise. Therefore, there are four Articles displayed using a Menu Link Item designated as a "Featured Article" type; in this case "Home." |

Two Categories Displayed

The reason there are Articles from two Categories displayed on the Home page is this:

Reason 1	The Menu Link Item "Home" is set as a Category Blog layout connected to "My First Category," in which there are three Articles.
Reason 2	When an Article is set as "Featured," it automatically displays WITH the Content from the Home Menu Link Item. Thus, there are more Articles displayed as a result of the installation of the Sample Blog Content in an earlier Chapter. Priority-wise, the "Featured Articles" appear before, or above, any other Categorized Articles.

Using "Featured Articles" in combination with regular "Blog" Content, more information can be displayed on the Front-End. Also, "Featured Articles" (as can others), may be set to "Publish" or "Unpublish" on a designated date and time, which is a useful asset for creating future Articles to be "Published" at certain times. This makes the timed-display ("show/not-show"), of Articles a very convenient asset for the management of time-sensitive Content.

Creating Articles

At this point, if you have completed all of the previous Exercises, you should have created four Articles. Creating Articles, as you may have already noticed, isn't a complicated undertaking. It is not necessary at this point, to repeat the process of creating Articles. You can refer to Chapter 7, "ADMIN: Fast Track Double Time Start," and review the basics of Article creation.

With regard to actually "*editing*" Article Content, it is a simple matter of opening the Article Workspace via the "Control Panel > Content > Articles" to display a List of Articles, then opening the specific Article to be edited. Remember to always execute a Saving Action after editing to prevent "locking out" any other editors. The Articles List may also be accessed on the "Home Dashboard" via the "Site Panel > Articles" link.

Rules About Articles

Articles, as do Categories, have a set of rules that apply to them exclusively with which the Administrator should be familiar, such as:

Rule 1	Articles must have a Title. An Article cannot be saved without one.
Rule 2	Articles must be assigned to a Category. The "Uncategorized" Category is the default if no other Category is assigned at the time the Article is created. It is

	still a Category assignment, nonetheless. Articles may be assigned to ONLY one Category. The exception being when Articles are ALSO assigned to the "Featured Article" group. That is the only exception.
Rule 3	Articles must be set to "Published" to be displayed.
Rule 4	Categories within the hierarchy in which the Article is assigned, must also be set to "Published." If an Article is in a Parent Category, the Category must be set to "Published." If an Article is in a Child Category, both the Child and Parent Categories must be set to "Published." These setting requirements apply up and down the Content Hierarchy.
Rule 5	Articles may only be accessed directly by using a Menu Link Item within a "Published" Menu.
Rule 6	Articles may also be accessed via a "Category List" or "Category Blog" Layout, which can be accessed via a Menu Link item within a Menu. These are opened by a different type of Menu Link Item choice than those that might apply in Rule 5.
Rule 7	Articles cannot be nested, that is, they cannot be under another Article, as is possible with the Category Parent/Child configurations. However, Articles may have links within their Content that open other Articles. This is a great topic cross-reference feature, along with "Tags."
Rule 8	Multiple Articles can be assigned to individual Categories or Sub-Categories without any specific limitations.
Rule 9	Article order within a Category can be changed or reordered, which dictates how the Articles display on Front-End under certain parameter settings.
Rule 10	All of the rules pertaining to viewing and ordering Categories also, for the most part, apply to Articles.

Menu Link Items to Articles

As noted above, to open an Article directly, a Menu Link Item must be connected to it, as demonstrated in Exercise 10-2. Article Lists can be accessed by using a different type of Menu Link Item, but to open an Article directly, a single Menu Link Item must be created to do so.

EXERCISE 10-2: CREATING AN ARTICLE'S MENU LINK ITEM

Objective: This Exercise demonstrates how to create a Menu Link Item that opens a single Article as compared to a Category List, or Category Blog List. This is the most ordinary form of Menu Link Item whereby an Article is opened directly via a Menu Link Item in a Menu.

Step 1	On the "Home Dashboard," go to: "Control Panel > Menus" and select

		"Main Menu." This opens the List of Menu Link Items that are assigned to the "Main Menu."
Step 2		At this point, there should be three Menu Link Items on the list: ▪ Home ▪ My First Article Link ▪ My Category List
Step 3		Click the **"+ New"** Button at the top of the screen. This opens a New Menu Link Item screen.

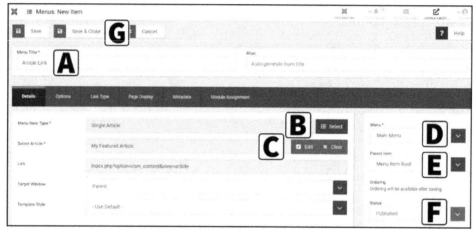

Figure 10-6

Refer to Figure 10-6 for the following:

Step 4	**A**	In the Menu Title field, enter: "Article Link" (without the quotes).
Step 5	**B**	In the Menu Item Type selector, open the selector and go to: "Articles > Single Article." You may need to scroll down to that item.
Step 6	**C**	In the "Select Article" selector, open it and select: "My Featured Article."
Step 7	**D**	To the right, the Menu choice should be "Main Menu."
Step 8	**E**	This should be set to Menu Item Root, and not a sub-Menu Link Item to a "Parent."
Step 8	**F**	The Status should be set to "Published."
Step 9		All other settings, which are the default, should not be changed.
Step 10	**G**	Execute a Save and Close Action.
Step 11		Got to the website Front-End and refresh the screen.
Step 12		In the Main Menu, click the "Article Link" Menu Link Item.

Step 13		The screen should change, showing the "My Featured" Article" only as shown in Figure 10-7.
	H	The Article Link in the Main Menu is confirmed in the location shown in the "Breadcrumb" Module display.
	I	This is the Article with the default "Options" settings shown. These can be changed and is explained later in this Chapter.

Figure 10-7 also shows a default Global Details Setting for all Articles, which displays information about the Article, such as:

Figure 10-7

The **"Author"** of the Article
The **"Category"** into which the Article is assigned.
The **"Date"** the Article was "Published."
The number of **"Hits"** (or views) of the Article.

There are some instances where this information might be helpful. For example, on websites that contain a great number of Articles, written by many Authors, and periodically Published, such as in a "Blog." The number of views may also be important.

However, on smaller websites, with only one or two individuals that post the Content, the Article Details are repetitive and look, shall we say look rather amateurish appearing on every Article.

There are several ways to remove the Details from Article displays:

Method 1 Within the Article	One might assume that these information displays may be controlled on the Article or Category itself. Changing "Options" within a single Article opened directly from a Menu Link Item, has no effect whatsoever upon

Options	the display. The Details data cannot be altered directly in the "Options" setting for either Articles or Categories. However, there are some conditions where these settings, within the Article "Options" might alter the display.
Method 2 Within the Global Options	Another way is to configure the "Global Settings" relative to Articles. These are settings that are invoked for every Article Content Item on a website-wide basis. In this case, every Article. See Exercise 10-3 below for instructions on changing the "Global Settings."
Method 3 Within the Menu Link Item	On an individual Article basis, these settings can be set to not display by using the same Menu Link Item that is used to display it, as demonstrated in Exercise 10-9. This is important, because Method 3 is actually performing the function of Method 1, but not within the Content Item directly, but within its respective Menu Link Item. Why? That's just the way Joomla! works in this regard.

EXERCISE 10-3: SETTING ARTICLE GLOBAL OPTIONS

Objective: The objective of this Exercise will be to change a "Global Settings" for Articles. These are settings that, when invoked, affect *all Articles across the entire website.* In this Exercise the "Articles Details" information when viewed on the Front-End will be set to not show.

As previously explained, it is not possible to modify the "Details" display within the parameter settings of an Article itself. In other words, no over-ride. Joomla! has always functioned where those items are controlled by two other control points in the Back-End: "Global Options" and/or "Menu Link Items." However, there is an exception to this, and is explained in "Article Options" Exceptions below.

Also, in this Exercise, the four items that are under the "Details" heading will be changed. For a complete discussion of the entire "Options" selections, see Chapter 43, "CONTENT: Global Options" & Settings," in *Joomla! 5: Boots on the. Ground, Advance Edition, Volume 2*

Step 1		On the "Home Dashboard," go to: "Control Panel > Content > Articles," to display the List of Articles. Use either the left menu or the Site Panel to do so. The result should be a display of Articles.
Step 2		At the top right of the screen, open "Options" next to the Help Button.
Step 3		On the left Menu Bar, headed as "System," click on "Articles" **[A]**, if it is not already selected. Activating this section is needed to access the proper "Options" that apply to Articles.

Refer to Figure 10-8 below for the following:

Step 4	B	Click on "Articles" in the top tab area.

Step 5	C	Read this information line, which is advising the Article Creator that some of the "Options" for an Article may be controlled by and configured elsewhere: "These settings apply for Article layouts unless they are changed for a specific Menu Link Item or Article." This message was included because of the extensive confusion caused by settings to be at the item level and within Menu Link Items. While it doesn't clear things up, it at least provides a clue as where to go if "Options" do not perform as expected.

It may be necessary to scroll down the screen to perform the following steps:

Step 6	D	Change the "Article Info Title" to "Hide."
Step 7	E	Change the "Category" to "Hide."
Step 8	F	Change the "Author" to "Hide."
Step 9	G	Change the "Create Date" to "Hide."
Step 10	H	Change the "Hits" to "Hide."
Step 11	I	Execute a Save and Close Action.
Step 12		Go to the website Front-End and refresh the screen.
Step 13		Notice all of the "Details" of the Articles have now been removed and the only Content for the Article that is shown are the "Title," the "Published Date" and finally, the Content of the Article.
Step 14		Click on the "Home" Menu Item Link in the Main Menu.
Step 15		Note that the same information has been removed from ALL of the Articles. Why? Because this is a "Global Setting," meaning that it will apply to every Article on the website.
Step 16		IMPORTANT! Repeat Steps 6 through 11, and *reverse the settings* so that each item now indicates "Show" as their "Status." This is important so make sure this step is performed. The following Exercises require the "Options" to be default setting of "Show."

In summary, the "Options" available under the Articles Administration Area are global and they affect every Article on the website. Whenever there is a mention of "global" anything, it means that the setting or action affects everything on the website.

You Can't Do It From Here!

If changing the "Article Details" for one Article is desired, it cannot be accomplished by using the "Global Settings." The setting for the Article is "local," while the other settings are "global." Therefore, an alternative method must be used. It has already been declared that the "Details" cannot be altered within the Article itself, although the settings are accessible. However, if you attempt to change it within the Article Options, ***IT WILL NOT WORK!***

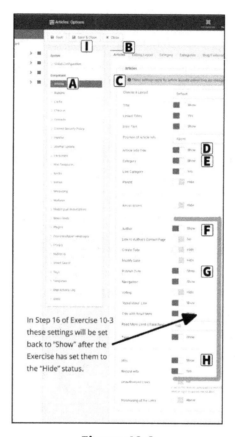

Figure 10-8

At this point, the "Global Options" were used to control the "Details" display within an Article. Those settings were changed, then restored back to the default setting. Make sure these actions, returning them to the "Show" status has been performed.

Using the Menu Link Item to Change Options

Another way is to make the change to an Articles is via the Menu Link Item that opens the individual Article for viewing. This method can be applied to individual Articles vs. the Global application with the previously explained method.

Any Menu Link Item can control the display of the Details of the Article. Therefore, it also controls the Details on a single Article, if the Menu Link Items is of the "Single Article" type.

If the Menu Link Item is for a Category Blog Layout, every Article in the Category is modified. Keep that in mind – the Menu Link Item controls *ALL Details in ALL Articles* to which the Menu Link Item points, either individually or collectively.

The Exercise below will deal with changing the Details of an Article that is opened directly by a Menu Link Item as a Single Article opening action.

EXERCISE 10-4: USING THE MENU LINK ITEM TO CHANGE THE DISPLAY OPTIONS

Objective: The alternate method of changing an Article's Details will be demonstrated in this Exercise by removing all Details. This modification will apply to only the Article to which the Menu Link Item applies. *It will not apply* to the same Articles that are displayed in a Blog format, which are the Category Blog and "Featured Articles" layout choices. This Menu Link Item method must be, and can only be used to change the "Options" for an *individual Article* that is opened directly from a Menu Link Item, which can be in any Menu on the website.

Step 1		On the "Home Dashboard," go to: "Control Panel > Menus > Main Menu."

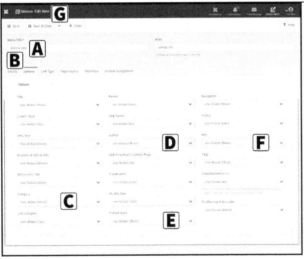

Figure 10-9

Refer to Figure 10-9 for the following:

Step 2	A	Open the "Article Link" that was created in a previous Exercise.
Step 3	B	Open the "Options" Tab in the Menu Bar under the "Title" field in the "Article Workspace." Note that most of the "Options" are set to Use Global ... indicating that the Global Settings are in control. Chapter 43, "Global "Options" & Settings" will discuss all settings in detail.

		In Step 16 of the previous Exercise, these "Options" should have been returned to their default state.
Step 4	**C**	Change the "Category" selector to: Hide.
Step 5	**D**	Change the "Author" selector to: Hide.
Step 6	**E**	Change _all three_ of the "Date" item selectors to: Hide.
Step 7	**F**	Change the "Hits" selector to: Hide.
Step 8	**G**	Execute a Save and Close Action.
Step 9		Go to the Front-End, refresh the screen and click the "Article Link" in the Main Menu.
Step 10		Notice that all of the "Detail" information has now been removed from the "Featured Article."
Step 11		Click the "Home" Menu Link Item in the Main Menu.
Step 12		Notice that the Details for ALL Articles are still showing – this is because their display is still being controlled by the Global "Options" for Articles.
Step 13		Also notice that the Article: "My Featured Article," also is showing the "Details," even though they were disabled, in the previous steps, in the Menu Link Item that opens the Article directly.
		The "Home" Menu Link Item that shows the Category Blog for "Featured Articles" has not been altered, so the Global Settings are still in control.
		Remember, other than using Global, individual Article Details are controlled via the Menu Link Item that displays it, and only it. The Menu Link Item for an individual Article and for Category Blog Articles are different and each has its own set of "Options" controlling how they display using their respective Menu Link Items.
		To change the "Details" in this view of the Article(s), the "Options" must be changed in the Menu Link Item. But ... because this is a "Blog" format, any changes in the Menu Link Item settings (the "tabs" within it), will affect ALL Articles.

While the modification of the Details may seem a bit confusing, it is easier to understand if you keep in mind that the Article itself does not control the display of its own "Details." Those are controlled by: 1) the Global Settings, and 2) the specific Menu Link Item that opens the Article or the Category Blog List, depending upon which performs the function. Also remember that the "Featured Articles" are also in the Category Blog List format, that Menu Link Item will also be in control.

Primary Functions of the Article Options

There are several Option Settings in Joomla! 5 that control different Content Items or the manner in which they are displayed on the website.

When the "Options" are accessed via either the Articles or Categories links in the Control Panel's Content Menu, they are almost the same. All "Options" that are available for one or the other can be accessed in either area.

The "Options" Settings that can affect display of Content via a Menu Link Item is extensively covered in Chapter 22, "NAVIGATION: Menu Option Settings."

Article Option Setting Exceptions

As was mentioned above, the "Options" within a single Article cannot be altered within the Article parameters. They can only be changed via: 1) the Global Settings, or 2) via the Menu Link Item that links to it.

This is a steadfast rule when a single Article is created and accessed directly via a Menu Link Item.

Here's the exception:

When Articles are displayed via a Menu Link Item that is a Category Blog or as "Featured" Articles, the "Options" in the Articles change with an additional parameter added to some of the Option Selections, but not all. There is some selectivity within these options.

In some of the individual Option dropdowns, there is a new choice called: "Use Article Settings." This is a dynamic hand-off of the control of the settings *from* the Menu Link Item *to* the respective Article "Options" within the Article. This new Option is executed by altering the setting of the "Options" within the Menu Link Item that opens the Blog format Category.

For this parameter for the individual Article, the Article "Options" Settings can override both the parameter settings in the Global "Options" and the Menu Link Item, but the "Use Article Settings" handoff must be set to do so.

This is good, because in these two cases ("Category Blog" and "Featured Articles"), the Articles can be customized individually without using the Global "Options" or the "Options" as per the Menu Link Item. When the Menu Link Item hands off this setting responsibility to the Article, this allows greater display customization, as shown in Figure 10-10.

Shown in Figure 10-10 is the default "Home" Menu Link Item, which is a "Featured Articles" Type. This is similar to a Category Blog, but with a different name and the default setting to display them as Featured. There are many "Options" that may be set here to hand off the control of them from the Menu Link Item to the Article itself.

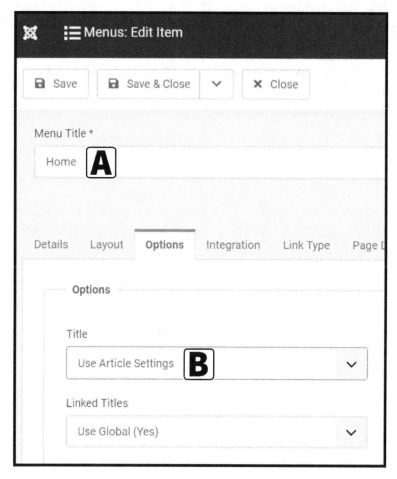

Figure 10-10

Refer to Figure 10-10 for the following:

A	This is the Menu Link Item designated as the Home link, meaning this is the type of webpage that displays when the website is accessed. It is set to be a "Featured Articles" type.
B	These are typical of the settings that can be set to hand-off control *from* the Menu Link Item *to* the Option Parameters within the Article. Not all "Options" can be set to Use Article Settings, but when designated, the "Article Option" overrides both the Global and Menu Link Item Option settings. The configuration settings of: Read More Link, Title with Read More and Tags cannot be handed off to the Use Article Settings option.

Having the ability to change Article "Options" in the Category Blog and Feature Articles is helpful in customizing the visual layout of the Articles as they are displayed on the webpage.

Setting Custom Article Titles

By default, Articles in Joomla! 5, when displayed, show the Article Title, which is the text that was entered into the Title Field in the Article Workspace. For any number of reasons, that Title may not be the one desired to be displayed with the Article. For example, if you give Articles Titles that are control numbers, such as some sort of date coding for internal use, those numbers make no sense as an Article Title, although they may work great for other reasons.

So, to get around this configuration, it is possible to override the actual default Article Title with another, customized Title. To change the Title of an Article, complete Exercise 10-5 below.

Article Title Override

The override of an Article Title can only be accomplished for those Articles that are opened directly via a Menu Link Item. It cannot be used to change the Article Title of those Articles that are opened via any type of Category Link type. For Category type displays, similar title changes may be made, but only for the Category itself, not the individual Articles.

EXERCISE 10-5: CHANGING THE TITLE OF AN ARTICLE

Objective: The objective of this Exercise is to demonstrate how to change the "displayed" Title of an Article without actually changing the formal system Title of the Article. As in setting the Article Display Options, changing the Title of an Article is not accomplished within the Article, but within the Menu Link Item that opens it.

In other Article formats, such as Categories, it is necessary to change the setting for the Menu Link Item that opens it, to allow Article overrides.

In this Exercise, the Article "About" which opens with the "About" Menu Link Item in the "Main Menu Blog," at the top left of the screen, will be modified.

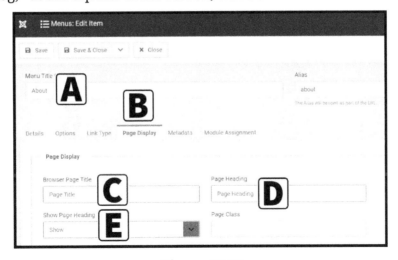

Figure 10-11

Step 1		On the "Home Dashboard," go to: "Control Panel > Menus > All Menu Items."

Refer to Figure 10-11 for the following:

Step 2	A	On the Menu Link Item List, open the "About your home page" Menu Link Item.
Step 3	B	In the tab bar, open the "Page Display" tab.
Step 4	C	In the "Browser Page Title" field enter: "Page Browser" (without quotes).
Step 5	D	In the "Page Heading "field, enter: "Page Heading" (without quotes).
Step 6	E	Set the "Show Page Heading" to "Show."
Step 7		Execute a Save Action. The green "Success Message" will display. Close the message bar.
Step 8		Go to the website Front-End and access the "About your home page," which is a sub-link under "Help" in the top menu. Notice that the browser tab now states "Page Browser" from Step 4 above. Also, that "Page Heading" from 5 above displays in the Article, along with the native Article Title of "About…"

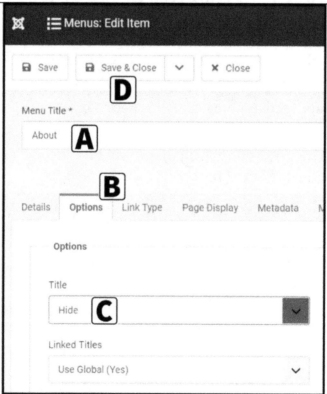

Figure 10-12

Refer to Figure 10-12 for the following:

Step 9	A	On the Menu Link Item List, open the "About your home page" Menu Link Item.
Step 10	B	In the tab bar, open the "Options" tab.
Step 11	C	In the "Title" selector, simply select "Hide" for this field.
Step 12	D	Execute a Save and Close Action. When the screen returns to the List of Menu Link Items, the green "Success Message" will display. Close the panel.
Step 13		Go to the website Front-End and refresh the screen.
Step 14		Open the "About Menu Link Item" in the Top Menu.
Step 15		When the Article is opened, notice that the "About..." Article Title is no longer visible, while "Page Browser" in the browser tab and "Page Heading" for the Article Title now displayed as previously changed.

Changing the actual "Article Title" is a frequent practice on Blogging-type websites where the actual "Article Title" is coded to the Author and other literals. The actual display name of the Article is changed to make it relevant to website visitors. Yet, and internal naming system is used for the "formal" title of the Article. This frequently helps in the cataloging and management of Articles.

Setting Article Display Timing

When Articles are created, by default, they are immediately "Published" unless intentionally set to the "Unpublished" state. If you desire the Article to NOT display immediately, you must manually go to the Article Manager and change the setting to "Publish" on the date desired. This is an absolute nuisance if there are many, many Articles written in advance and to be "Published" and not only different dates, but at separate times on those dates.

To solve this problem, Joomla! 5 Articles have the capability to set both the date/time that an Article will automatically Publish and also to automatically to "Unpublished." Exercise 10-6 demonstrates how this is accomplished.

EXERCISE 10-6: SETTING ARTICLE PUBLISHING PARAMETERS

Objective: The objective of this Exercise is to demonstrate how Articles can be set to automatically Publish and Unpublish on certain dates/times. The "About ..." Article will also be used for demonstration purposes in this Exercise.

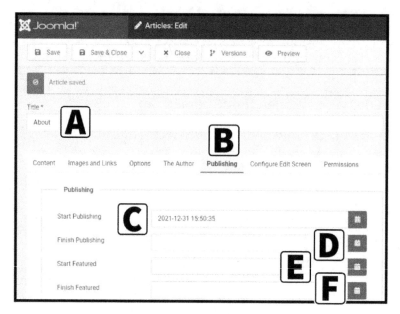

Figure 10-13

Step 1		On the "Home Dashboard," go to: "Control Panel > Content > Articles," to display the List of Articles. Use either the left menu or the Site Panel to do so. The result should be a display of Articles.
Step 2	A	On the Article List, open the "About your home page" Article.

Refer to Figure 10-13 for the following:

Step 3	B	In the tab bar, open the "Publishing" tab and view column choices.
Step 4	C	The "Start Publishing" date/time can be set into this field. If set, the Article will not display until the designated date/time. By default, the "Start Publishing" date is the date the Article was created.
Step 5	D	The "Finish Publishing" date/time is designated in this field. The Article will Unpublish automatically at this time.
Step 6	E	If the Article is to be "Featured," the "Start Featured" date can be set in this field, controlling when the Article starts displaying as a "Featured" Article. The regular and "Featured" Publishing dates "Finish" times may be set separately.
Step 7	F	This can be set as "Finish Featured" the Article as a "Featured Article," thus automatically "Unpublishing" it.
Step 8	G	Execute a Save and Close Action. When the screen returns to the List of Menu Link Items, the green "Success Message" will display.

Time Stamps on Content Items

SET THE SERVER TIME CORRECTLY. During installation, Joomla! 5 uses the local time for the Server Time Zone, depending on where the server is physically located. Heck, the server might be located on the other side of the world, so setting the Website Time Zone is important to display your local time. The Website Time Zone can be set in the Global Configuration > Server setting area as shown in Figure 10-14.

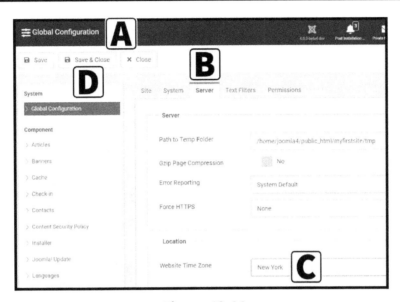

Figure 10-14

Refer to Figure 10-14 for the following:

Step 1	A	On the "Home Dashboard," go to: "Home Dashboard > System" and open the Global Configuration.
Step 2	B	Within the "Global Configuration," open the "Server" tab.
Step 3	C	Set the desired "Website Time Zone." The selection list is rather long, so you may need to hunt a bit to find the proper selection for your location. In our case, being on the U.S. East Coast, New York is the appropriate time zone. Select your time-zone.
Step 4	D	Execute a Save & Close action.

The Article display, whether it is from a Menu Link Item, or a Category List, will now be controlled by the settings in the timer fields, set to your Time Zone. This works very well when one Article should stop Publishing, and another begin, such as Announcements or Notices. It is also a handy feature for pre-writing Articles to be displayed automatically at a later date, especially when the website is used for blog or news Publishing.

If Article Publishing times are unimportant, then nothing needs to be set into the date fields. The default settings will work fine. The Articles will Publish immediately, and remain in the state until changed manually by an "Unpublish" action. However, you should set the Website Time Zone anyway.

Article List Filter Options

While performing Exercises where Category, Article or Menu Link Items are displayed as a list, the list can be awfully long, especially on website with an extensive amount of Content. So, for narrowing down a list, there are Filter "Options" that can be employed, as shown in Figure 10-15.

There is a difference between "Options" and "Filter Options." The "Options" are settings that apply to the Articles and Categories themselves. The "Filter Options" are simply choices that can be applied to how Articles are displayed in the Administrator's Article Manager. The settings employed only affect the screen display, and not the actual Articles, or listed Content Items themselves.

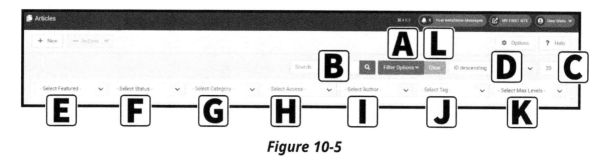

Figure 10-5

Refer to Figure 10-15 for the following:

A	**Filter Options**	When this item is clicked, the filtering choices **[E-L]**, will open. However, based on the resolution or width of your monitor screen, the actual display may vary.
B	**Search**	If the Article List is lengthy, this searching feature can be used.
C	**"20"**	This allows selecting the number of items to display on the List. The default for this number can be set via System > Global Configuration > Site > Default List Limit.
B	**ID descending**	Each item has an "ID" number; this setting allows them to be sorted from low to high or high to low. "ID" Numbers are created by the system and cannot be changed.
E	**Select Featured**	Only "Featured Articles" will be displayed with this filter selected.
F	**Select Status**	This allows the list to be filtered by its Publishing status.

G	Select Category	With items assigned into Categories, the list display can be narrowed to display only those items from the Category selected. Multiple Categories may be selected for filtering.
H	Select Access	Content Items can be set to be accessed only by User or website visitors that are in different Access Groups. This filter can be used to view the items accessible only be certain Groups.
I	Select Author	If there are many Authors, and only their Content Items are to be display, this filter will allow that selection.
J	Select Tag	If "Tags" are used in association with Content Items, this filter will display them based on the "Tag" selected in the filter dropdown.
K	Select Max Levels	Max Levels refer to situations where there are a number of Parent and "Child Category" classifications. Therefore, using a filter can make the task of sorting the Content Items easier.
L	Clear	This button will clear all the choices that are currently set for filtering the list.

The Filter "Options" for Menu List Items are slightly different than those for Categories and Articles but operate in the same manner. The filters are used to narrow the List of Content Items to specific choices. This filtering feature is extremely useful and will likely be used frequently as a website grows with an increasing amount of Content.

Creating Multi-Page Articles

Sometimes Article Content can be quite lengthy. It's often unavoidable. This makes for difficult reading. In fact, most people don't want to read past the bottom of the browser screen. Articles that go on and on and on, likely don't get read beyond the first few paragraphs before the viewer exits the screen. You have likely experienced this when viewing website Articles on mobile devices. It seems like some Article screens will never end. The same with viewing on Desktops and Tablets.

Joomla! 5 has a feature whereby long Content within an Article can be broken down into smaller reading pages thus eliminating the long, scrolling appearance and reduction in the readability. This feature is called "Page Break," giving the Administrator control over the breaks.

Here is how a long Article can be broken down into smaller pages/screens for ease of reading and less screen-scrolling of long Articles.

EXERCISE 10-7: HOW TO CREATE A MULTI-PAGE ARTICLE

Objective: The objective of this Exercise is to break down very long Article Content to a series of smaller reading pages using the "Page Break" Feature. Here are the steps involved in breaking down a lengthy Article into multiple smaller parts using "Page Break" at selected locations in the text:

Action 1	Create an Article.
Action 2	Assign the Article to a Category.
Action 3	Create lengthy Article Content consisting of many paragraphs to text using lorem ipsum dummy text. You can copy/paste some dummy text from here: http://generator.lorem-ipsum.info/
Action 4	Implement the Page Breaks within the Article.
Action 5	Create a Menu Link Item to access the Article.

Obtaining Dummy Text

In the Publishing world, dummy text is frequently used to create mockup layouts. This is called "lorem ipsum" text. There are many sources of this jumbled text. Search Google and you will find many sources. However, we prefer to use: http://generator.lorem-ipsum.info/ to generate the dummy Content needed. The site also gives you the background about the use of dummy text. It's free.

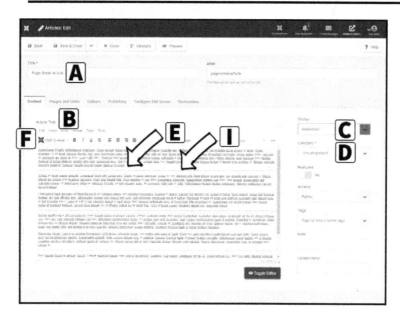
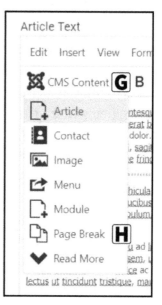

Figure 10-16

Step 1	On the "Home Dashboard," go to: "Control Panel > Content > Articles," to display the List of Articles. Use either the left menu or the Site Panel to do so. The result should be a display of Articles.

Step 2		In the top menu bar, click the **"New"** Button. You may also use the **"+"** in the Site Panel next to "Articles."
Step 3	A	In the Article Title field, enter: "Page Break Article" (without quotes).
Step 4		Go to the http://generator.lorem-ipsum.info/ website and generate six (6) paragraphs of lorem ipsum random text and copy it to your clipboard. The "generate" button is under the text at the left. Select the text and copy it.
Step 5	B	Paste the dummy text into the Article Content area. Ignore the red underline spelling error warnings in the text when they appear. It will have no effect on the test displaying on the Front-End.
Step 6	C	Set the Status to: "Published."
Step 7	D	Assign the Article to the "Uncategorized" Category.
Step 8		Execute a Save Action. The green "Success Message" will display as a result. Close it using the **"X"** to the right.
Step 9	E	Place the editing cursor at the end of the first paragraph.
Step 10	F	Click on "CMS Content" Button in the Editor Menu Bar.
Step 11	G	A dropdown Menu Selection List will display.
Step 12	H	Click on the "Page Break" Action Link. If using the Tiny-MCE default Editor, the link is found under the "CMS Content" section of the Menu. If using the JCE Editor, there is a button at the end of the last line, as shown in Figure 10-16-A.

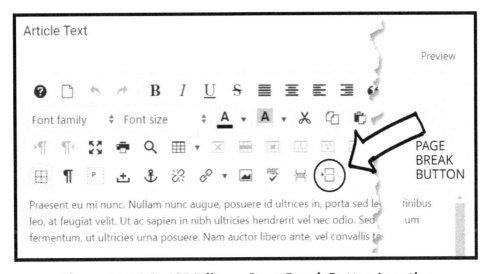

Figure 10-16-A : JCE Editor – Page Break Button Location

Step 13		In the Popup Window, enter "Page Two" in the Page Title field. The first paragraph is automatically designated as Page One, so the first break is

		actually the second page and should be named that way. For the Table of Contents Alias, enter: "Break at Page Two" and execute "Insert Page Break." *See Note 1 below.*
Step 14	I	The result will be an indicator line appearing within the text area at the break location.
Step 15		Place the editing cursor after the second paragraph and repeat steps **H-I**, naming this "Page Three." For the Table of Contents Alias, enter: "Break at Page Three" and Save.
Step 16		Repeat this procedure again, after paragraph three and name it "Page Four." For the Table of Contents Alias, enter: "Break at Page Four" and Save.
Step 17		The Article should now have three dashed lines visible at the locations in which you inserted the page break. The last paragraph, where no Page Break has been entered, is automatically number Page Five internally.
Step 18		Execute a Save & Close Action. The green "Success Message" will display.
Step 19		In the top Menu Bar, click on the blue "Preview" Button, which will open the website in a popup window, displaying this Article.
Step 20		On the right side of the Content Area is an inserted "Article Index" with links to the Pages created above. Also, at the bottom of the Article's text is a "Prev-Next" Navigation. Either one can be used to page through the Content. Navigate through the Content using either, or both, navigation access methods.
Note 1		Notice that the Page Break Article link automatically displays the first paragraph which is actually "Page One." This is why the first Page Break entered was designated as "Page Two." It actually does open the second page of the Article.
Note 2		Selecting "All Pages" will display the entire Article Content on the screen.

At this point in the book, you should be able to create a Menu Link Item to an Article without the Action Steps being illustrated. Try it. If you have trouble, go back and review Exercise 7-5 in Chapter 7 for instructions.

Close the "Preview" screen.

Continue the following steps from the above Exercise:

Step 21		If you have not done so, execute a Save and Close action at this point.
Step 22		Create a Menu Link Item, assigned to the Main Menu, called: "Article Page Break" (without quotes). This should be a "Single Article" that selects the "Page Break Article."

| Step 23 | Execute a Save & Close Action. When the screen returns to the List of Menu Link Items, the green "Success Message" will display. Close it. |
| Step 24 | The Article Page Break link should display in the Main Menu on the Front-End. If it does not refresh the screen to reload the page. |

The Article visibility is now reduced in size by using the "Page Break" feature. Keep this function in mind if you have long Articles on the website, remembering that website visitors do not like to read/scroll the screen to read the Content.

Numbering Page Breaks

In Exercise 10-7, the Page Breaks were Page Two, Page Three, etc. This is not required. The Page Breaks can be named anything and will appear in the order they were created. They do not need to be numbered; regular terms or expressions can be used. In fact, a teaser text can be used. However, also note that the order of the Breaks cannot be changed. The Breaks can be deleted the same way text is deleted by deleting it within the text editing workspace, by removing the "Page Break" marker.

Using the Read More Feature

When displaying Articles in a "Category Blog" type of layout, reducing the amount of visible text may be desired. Articles are typically written with an opening "teaser" paragraph with a link to the remainder of the Article. Remember that the "Featured Articles" Category is actually a Category Blog format.

Creating a Category as a Category Blog Layout

This is important! Make a mental note about it!

The "Read More" feature in an Article can only be used if the Article is assigned to a "Category Blog" Layout. "Read More" cannot be used when a Single Article is selected. Remember this! The link to the Article must display as a "Category Blog" Layout. The "Read More" function will not be active with any other "type" choice.

The Menu Link Item must be set to select a "Category Blog" type of Content, and the Article must be assigned to the "Category Blog" that is selected. In the following Exercise, create a Category of the "Category Blog" type. This is not the "Page Break" function, but setting the environment for the Content that allows the creation of a "Read More" button/link to continue to view/read the remainder of the Article Content.

EXERCISE 10-8: CREATING A BLOG STYLE CATEGORY

Objective: In this Exercise, in order to have an Article display properly with a Read More feature included, it must be assigned to a Category that is a "Category Blog." Follow these steps to create the Category (there is no screenshot insomuch as you have already created Categories in previous Exercises). You should be able to proceed through these steps without visual assistance.

Step 1	On the "Home Dashboard," go to: "Control Panel > Content > Categories," to display the List of Categories. Use either the left menu or the Site Panel to do so. The result should be a display of Categories.
Step 2	Click on the **"+New"** Button in the top Menu Bar.
Step 3	In the Title, enter: "Category Blog Layout" (without quotes).
Step 4	There should be no "Parent" Category, so in the "Parent" Field to the right, make sure it is set to: "No parent," meaning it is itself a Parent.
Step 5	In the Description field, enter: "This is a Category Blog Layout." (without quotes).
Step 6	Execute a Save and Close Action.
Step 7	Confirm the creation of the Category, which should appear at the bottom of the Category List display. Confirm the "Status" as being "Published."

Creating the Article with Introductory Text

Now that a Category Blog Layout environment has been created, into which an Article can be assigned, the Article needs to be created. The "Read More" function may then be included in the Article Content.

Remember: The "Read More" action cannot be used in an Article unless it is within a "Category Blog" designation. **This is an absolute Rule!**

The "Read More" function allows an Author to create "Introductory Text," or what is also known as "Teaser Text" in an Article. This piece of text is typically used to give a brief summary of the Article and to tease readers to continue reading the full Content of the Article.

Demonstrating New Methods

You might notice, as you progress through Exercises, that the same routine steps are not repeated over and over. Some new techniques are introduced here and there to show different actions that are available to the Administration. The "Save as Copy" is one of those examples in the Exercise that follows.

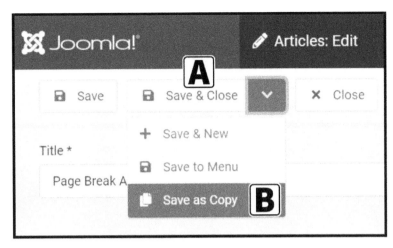

Figure 10-17

EXERCISE 10-9: USING THE "READ MORE" FEATURE

Objective: This Exercise will demonstrate the implementation and use of the "Read More" feature, which places a "continue link" within an Article, that opens the remainder of the text following the opening teaser paragraph.

Refer to Figure 10-17 for the following:

Step 1		Open the previously created Article entitled: "Page Break Article" (without the quotes).
Step 1	**A**	Open the Save & Close Menu.
Step 2	**B**	Execute a "Save as Copy" Action, which will copy the Article and open a new workspace.
Step 3		Change the Title to: "Read More Article" (without the quotes).
Step 4		Clear/delete the text in the "Alias" field.
Step 5		Assign the Article to the existing "Category Blog Layout" Category. Likely located at the bottom of the List of Categories given it was the last Category created. You may need to scroll the Category options in the drop down.
Step 6		When selecting the Category, the screen will automatically process as a "Save" action.
Step 7		Remove all of the "Page Break" markers by placing the editing cursor at the beginning of the paragraph after the marker and execute a Keyboard Backspace. This should delete/remove the marker. Do this for all three break indicators. This cleans the Article of any other "break" features.
Step 8		Execute a Save Action.

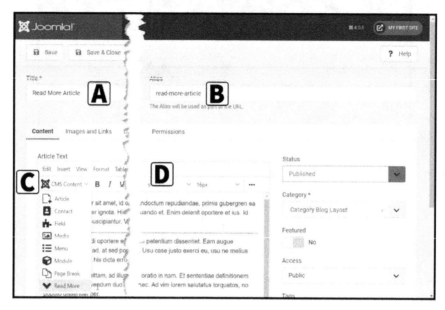

Figure 10-18

Refer to Figure 10-18 for the following:

Step 9		Place the mouse cursor at the end of the first paragraph.
Step 10	C	Open the "CMS Content" Button in the Editor Menu Bar. If using the "JCE" Editor, the button is the second from the right in the bottom button row.
Step 11	D	Click on the "Read More" link item, as in Figure 10-18. A red dashed line will appear between the first and second paragraph.
Step 12		Execute a Save & Close Action.

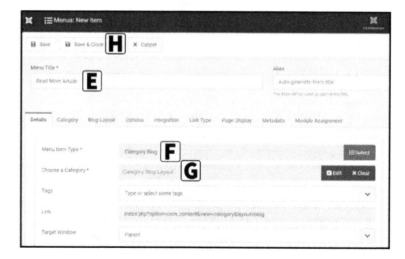

Figure 10-19

Refer to Figure 10-19 for the following:

Step 13	E	Create a new Menu Link Item in the Main Menu named: "Read More Article" (without the quotes). The Main Menu selection is at the right of the screen.
Step 14	F	For the Menu Item Type, within "Articles," select: "Category Blog."
Step 15	G	Select the "Category Blog Layout" Category as the target.
Step 16		Execute a Save & Close Action.
Step 17		Go to the website Front-End, refresh the screen.
Step 18		Click on the "Read More Article" link in the Main Menu.

Refer to Figure 10-20 for the following:

Step 19	H	When the Article opens, you should see the "Read More Link" inserted after the first paragraph of text.
Step 20		Click on the "Read More: Read More Article" Link. The entire Article should display.
Step 21		Return to the "Read More Article" via the Main Menu Link Item.

Notice that the linking text reads: "Read more : Read More Article."

Figure 10-20

Don't Like "Read more ...."

The "Read more: Read More Article" link text can be changed to any custom text desired, although Read more is the term most commonly used on websites. In Exercise 10-10, the text will be changed to "Continue Reading." The name of the Article following can also be changed, but only so that the Article Title will not display after the Read more text. This will also be included in the Exercise. The actions performed to change the name of the Link Item and text will only affect the individual Article. Every Article may have a different custom "Read More" text applied.

EXERCISE 10-10: CHANGING THE READ MORE LINK TEXT

Objective: This Exercise's objective will be to modify the "Read More" Link in an Article to a different term and remove the "Article Title" from the Link. The text for the "Read More" area is changed within the Article's Options. The removal of the Article Title from the "Read More" area is performed within the Menu Link Item that opens the Category Blog layout.

Step 1		On the "Home Dashboard," go to: "Control Panel > Content > Articles," to display the List of Articles. Use either the left menu or the Site Panel to do so. The result should be a display of Articles.

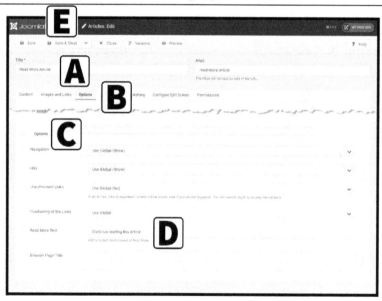

Figure 10-21

Refer to Figure 10-21 for the following:

Step 2	A	Open the Article entitled: "Read More Article."
Step 3	B	Open the "Options" tab in the menu bar.
Step 4	C	Scroll down the "Options" section to the "Read More Text" field which is likely near the bottom of the screen.

Step 3	D	In the field, Read More Text, enter: "Continue reading this Article" (without quotes).
Step 4	E	Execute a Save & Close Action.
Step 5		Go to the website Front-End.
Step 6		If the Article is open, refresh the screen. If not, open it via the Link in the Main Menu.
Step 7		The text should read: "Continue Reading this Read More Article." It still looks wrong with the "Article Title" showing, which is placed into that location automatically by the system.
Step 8		On the Back-End, go back to the "Home Dashboard."
Step 9	F	Access the Menu Link Item "Read More Article" again.

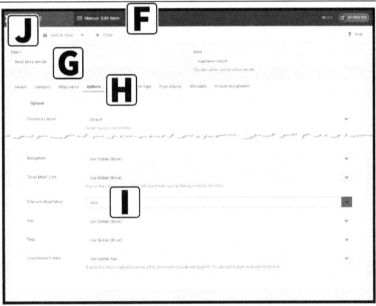

Figure 10-22

Refer to Figure 10-22 for the following:

Step 10	G	Go to the "Main Menu" and open the "Read More Article" Menu Link Item.
Step 11	H	Open the "Options" tab.
Step 12	I	Change the selector for the "Read More with Title" to the "Hide" Option.
Step 13	J	Execute a Save and Close Action.
Step 14		Go to the website Front-End.
Step 15		Refresh the screen.

Step 16	The Article Title should no longer display in the "Read More" field on the screen. Only "Continue Reading this Article" is what should appear in the Link Box.

Note: Actual screen layouts may differ based on monitor screen size and resolution. Keep this in mind when viewing screenshots.

Archiving Articles and Why

Articles, and other Content Items, can easily accumulate and get out of control insofar as managing them on Content List displays. Content Items that have been "Unpublished" or have done so automatically that still display on the list, can create a visual mess. Therefore, a feature is needed that will help tidy up this problem. The Joomla! 5 solution is the "Archive" feature.

Of course, setting Articles to expired or "Unpublished" is one way of having them not display after a date certain, but that might not always be the most convenient method to employ

Archiving allows a website Administrator to remove the "Unpublished" Content Items from the active lists of Content Items. They can also be removed using the "Trashed" feature. However, when "Trash" is emptied, the Content Item is deleted completely and permanently. ***Use the "Trash" and especially the "Empty Trash" features with extreme caution against permanently losing Content.***

An alternative to "Trash" is using the "Archive" feature whereby the Content Items can be removed from the active lists and placed in a storage location, not affected by deletion, unless deletion is performed purposefully.

In the Exercise below, the "Your Modules" Article, which is in the Category named Blog, will be placed into the Archives of the website.

There are two methods that can be used to move a Content Item into an Archive.

Method 1	Within the Content Item, use the "Status" selector, invoking the "Archive" action.
Method 2	On the Content Item List, selecting the item, then using the "Actions" feature to place the item into the Archive.

EXERCISE 10-11: ARCHIVING ARTICLES

Objective: The purpose of this Exercise is to demonstrate how to remove Articles from the "Published" or "Unpublished" Lists into an "Archive" library. This does not delete the Article but simply places it in a storage location where it can be accessed for reference or to be "Published" again.

| Step 1 | A | On the "Home Dashboard," go to: "Control Panel > Content > Articles," to display the List of Articles. Use either the left menu or the Site Panel to do so. The result should be a display of Articles. |

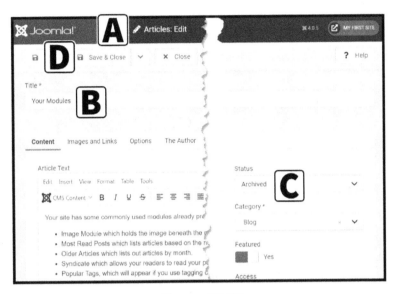

Figure 10-23

Refer to Figure 10-23 for the following:

Step 2	B	Open the Article Content Item: "Your Modules."
Step 3	C	Change the Content Item Status to "Archived."
Step 4	D	Execute a Save and Close Action. When the screen returns to the List of Menu Link Items, the green "Success Message" will display. At the same time, the "Your Modules" will no longer be an Article on the List of Articles.
Step 5	A	To access the "Archived" Content Item, open the Article List again.

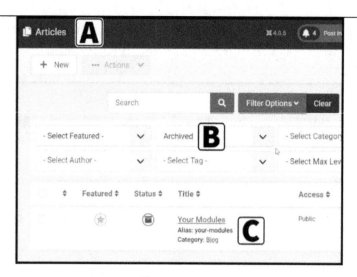

Figure 10-24

Refer to Figure 10-24 for the following:

Step 6	B	Use the Filter "Options" and change the "Select Status" to "Archived."
	C	Your "Modules Article" should display in the List of "Archived Articles."

Refer to Figure 10-25 for the following:

Step 6		The Content Item can be restored automatically with one action.
Step 7	D	On the Archived List View, click on the Archived Folder icon next to the item to be changed, which will display a selector. Choose "Unpublish Item" and the Content Item will return to the "Unpublished" Status. This happens automatically when the option is executed.
Step 8		The Content Item can now be opened, or accessed on the Articles List, and set back to the "Published" Status.

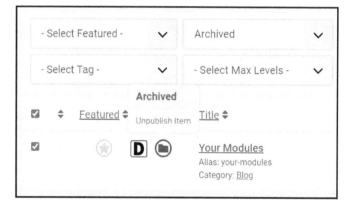

Figure 10-25

"Trashing" Articles

At various times, there is a need to delete an Article, which in Joomla! 5 is defined as "Trash." It involves selecting the Article from the List of Articles in the Article Workspace, then using the Change Status function button at the top of the screen, and when open, clicking on the "Trash" link at the bottom of the dropdown list.

This action is a straightforward function of making the selection, opening the Change Status Menu, and executing the Trash action.

EXERCISE 10-12: "TRASHING" ARTICLES

Objective: The purpose of this Exercise is to demonstrate how to "Trash" an Article and then restore it back to a "Published" condition.

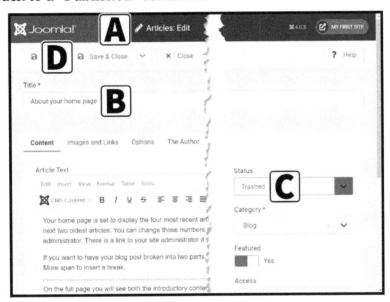

Figure 10-26

Refer to Figure 10-26 for the following:

Step 1	A	Open the "About your home page" Article Workspace.
	B	
Step 2	C	Access the "Status" drop down selector under the "Content" tab.
Step 3	D	Click on the "Trashed" option.
Step 4	E	Execute a Save action. The result of this action places the Article in the "Trash" storage area, thus removing it from being viewed on the Front-End or on any Article lists in the Back-End.
Step 5		Articles may be removed from the "Trash" status by accessing the Article Manager List, selecting the Select Status as Trashed, and clicking on "Trashed" icon next to the Article name, which will sequence to "Published" automatically.

Step 6		Restore the Article back to the active and "Published" status. Simply filter the "Status" list to "Trashed," and click on the "Publish" icon next to the Article name, in an action similar to removing a Content Item from the Archive.

EXERCISE 10-13: ADDING AN ARTICLE LINK INTO AN ARTICLE

Objective: The goal of this Exercise is to demonstration how a Link can be created in an Article to another Article. This can be accomplished to link to many Articles, but only a single Article Link will be shown in the Exercise.

Step 1	A	On the "Home Dashboard," go to: "Control Panel > Content > Articles," to display the List of Articles. Use either the left menu or the Site Panel to do so. The result should be a display of Articles.
Step 2	B	Open the "Your Template" Article.

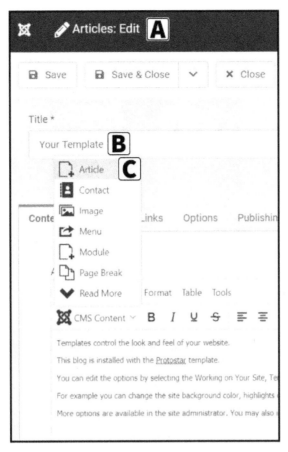

Figure 10-27

Refer to Figure 10-27 for the following:

Step 3		Place the cursor at the end of the Article's text and insert a new paragraph.
Step 4	C	Open the CMS Content dropdown in the Editor Menu Bar and select "Article" if using the default Editor. If using "JCE," click on "chain link" icon and proceed from there.
Step 5		This will open the List of Articles screen.
Step 6		Select the "Welcome to your blog" Article.
Step 7	D	The result should be a link that appears at the bottom of the Article, with the Title of the Article: "Welcome to your blog," as in Figure 10-28.
Step 8	E	Execute a Save & Close action.
Step 9		Go to the website Front-End, in the top Menu and select the "Blog" Menu Link Item and, on the resulting display, open the "Your Template" Article.
Step 10		When the Article opens, click on the "Welcome to your blog" Link below

| | | the Article text. This should open the "Welcome to your blog" Article. |

If the editor's goal is to have several Articles accessible from within an Article, the above action steps may be repeated as many times as needed. This results in a "stack" of "In-Article" Link Items.

Figure 10-28

Adding a Menu Module into an Article

It is possible to add a Menu Module into an Article, by creating the Menu, then inserting its respective Module into the Content by using a "Load Module" feature. See Chapter 11, "CONTENT: Modules," for more information about using this unique technique to embed Modules into an Article.

Please do not attempt to perform this action at this time.

Content Versioning

Something new in Joomla! 5 is "Versioning," whereby previous copies of Content Items are automatically maintained in a library. These versions can be referenced and viewed. They can also be restored, along with other functional settings. The Content Item history copies can be deleted or kept indefinitely along with other choices.

"Content Versioning" is only used for Categories (and Sub-Categories), along with Articles. Modules, for example, do not have this same capability.

This "Versioning" is very helpful if there is heavy editing of Content and the previous version needs to be retained or accessed for reference and/or back-checking purposes. For example, if the site Publishes news-type Content and updates the Articles, the "Version" feature allows editors to access previously "Published" versions of the same Article.

There are two action steps involved in setting up the website for "Versioning."

Action 1	Set a "Global Option" to allow "Versioning" to be implemented.
Action 2	Invoke "Versioning" on the Content Item which must be either a Category or an Article.

EXERCISE 10-14: ENABLING ARTICLE CONTENT VERSIONING

Objective: It is the objective of this Exercise to demonstrate the functional use of the "Content Item Versioning" methods for an Article.

Step 1		On the "Home Dashboard," go to: "Control Panel > Content > Articles," to display the List of Articles. Use either the left menu or the Site Panel to do so. The result should be a display of Articles.

Refer to Figure 10-29 for the following:

Step 2	A	Open the "Options" Manager via the link at the top right of the screen. This opens the Articles: "Options" Manager.
Step 3	B	Open the tab called: "Editing Layout."
Step 4	C	Enable "Enable Versions," if it not already enabled. This button can be found about half-way down the list.
Step 5	D	Set the number of "Versions" to keep. The default setting is "10."
Step 6	E	Execute a Save & Close action.

Figure 10-29

Once "Versioning" has been activated the option to use it with any Category or individual Article is available. Logically, if you are the only Content Editor on the website, "Versioning" isn't a big deal. Nor is it really applicable on a website that has limited Content that is displayed via Categories or by Articles.

When implementing "Versions," think in terms of a larger website with many Articles created by any number of Authors. This is a very helpful tool for Editors that must review and modify Articles written by Authors, who may also make further revisions and so on.

Be Realistic About Versioning

How many times will Articles be edited, and what is the level of necessity to keep older versions? Then, how many previous versions should be maintained. Set the Maximum Versions at a level that is reasonable for the website and the need to maintain older copies of the Content. It is usually not necessary to maintain many back-versions of a Content Item, so use the feature intelligently.

EXERCISE 10-15: USING ARTICLE CONTENT VERSIONING

Objective: This Exercise will demonstrate how "Versioning" is used and applied to a single Article.

Step 1	On the "Home Dashboard," go to: "Control Panel > Content > Articles," to display the List of Articles. Use either the left menu or the Site Panel to do so. The result should be a display of Articles.
Step 2	Open the "Read More Article."

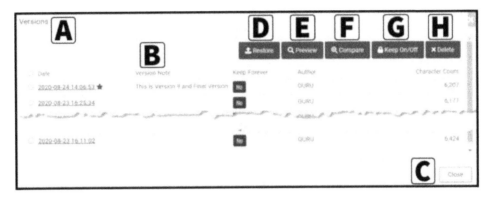

Figure 10-30

Refer to Figure 10-30 for the following:

Step 3	If "Versioning" is used, the "Version Note" field is located at the bottom right of the Article Workspace screen, within the "Content" tab, should be used to enter identification information, re: "This is Version 9 and Final Version." Enter that text, without the quotes, in the "Version Note" field.
Step 4	Execute a Save action.
Step 5	Within the "Read More Article" Workspace, click on the "Versions" button in the very top menu bar. This will open a popup window displaying the "Versions Status" history for the Article.
Step 6	The "Version Note" now displays for the Article currently being edited, as indicated by the "Star" icon next to the Article's editing date.
Step 7	When completed viewing the screen, simply execute "Close" to return to the Article Workspace.

Make Sure you Version!

When using "Versioning" you MUST (or SHOULD), make a Version "Versioning Note" each time before a Save action is executed. Otherwise, only the date will update. The "Version Note" will help you keep track of the most recent version and notate anything special about the changes that have been performed. This can same time when back-checking and helpful to others who may need the info.

Figure 10-30 also shows the tab bar on the "Versions" popup window. There functions are explained below.

The functions described below will only work with a version of the Article selected, or one or more of them selected as the case may apply.

D	With a previous "Version" selected, the "Restore" action moves the older version to the status of the current version being edited.
E	With an Article selected, the "Preview" button displays the Article in a popup window. This is useful for checking earlier Article Content.
F	If two Articles are selected, the Compare action lets you view both on a simulated side-by-side basis to identify the changes between the two.
G	"Keep On/Off" will designate which Article Versions to keep forever."
H	To tidy up the "Version" list, outdated copies of the Article may be deleted by selecting it/them, then executing the "Delete" action.

The Content Editor

The Editor in the Workspace is used for all Content Items and, by default, in Joomla! 5 is called: "Editor-TinyMCE." This Editor contains most of the features typically found in a word processing editor. It is suggested that you spend some time using the Content Editor to familiarize yourself with the different functions.

Throughout some of the Exercises in this book, occasional use of the features of the Content Editor will be used and explained. Many of the presets that are present in the editor relate to the default for website browsers and the Cascading Style Sheets ("CSS") used on the website.

However, at some point, another editor might be needed to complete Exercises.

There are several other Content Editors that can be added to a Joomla! 5 website and can be found on the Joomla! Extensions Directory ("JED"). The "JCE Content Editor" is one of the more popular Editor Extensions used.

Check Out, Check In

When a Content Item is opened by anyone on the Back-End, the system considers the Item as being "checked out." That is: it is flagged as the item's Workspace being opened by someone for editing.

What frequently happens is that a Content Item is "checked out," and editing is performed in the Workspace. The editing is completed, the content has been "saved," then the browser window is just closed, and not "saved and closed." Therein lies the problem.

When the situation exists where there are several editors, and some of the Content Items they accessed were only "saved" and the browser window closed, then a problem arises with anyone else trying to open the Content Item. They will not be able to do so.

The Content Item is then still "checked out" to the last User that edited the Content.

When a Content Item, in this case an Article, is "checked out" and not accessible to the next user, there is a "lock" symbol on the name of the Content item, as show in Figure 10-31.

Figure 10-31

The Solution *to the Issue*

Items that are "checked out" can be "checked in" by the Administrator ("Super User"), other than the person who left it hanging out there. The process is pretty easy, as shown in the Exercise below.

EXERCISE 10-16: CHECKING-IN CONTENT ITEMS

Objective: In the event Content Item is "checked out" and locked and preventing anyone else from opening the workspace, this Exercise will demonstrate how the Content item can be "checked in," making it available for editing.

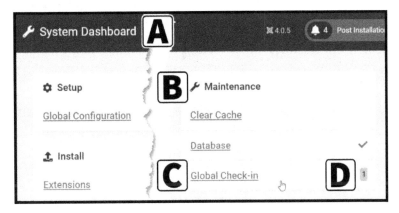

Figure 10-32

Refer to Figure 10-32 for the following:

Step 1	A	On the "Home Dashboard," go to: Control Panel scroll down to System and click on the link, which opens the System Dashboard.
Step 2	B	Locate the "Maintenance" block.
Step 3	C	Locate the "Global Check-in" link.
Step 4	D	To the right, the number indicates how many Content Items are "checked out" and not "checked in." If there is a green checkmark display, that is an "all is OK" message and no items are "Checked-Out" and unavailable to other editors.
Step 5	C	Click on the "Global Check-in" link item. This will open the Maintenance: Global Check-in" Manager.

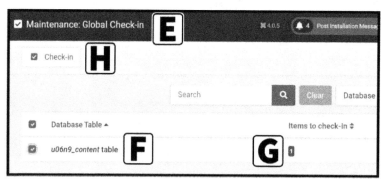

Figure 10-33

Refer to Figure 10-33 for the following:

Step 6	E	With the Manager now open, perform the following steps.
Step 7	F	Select the tick box next to the name of the database table, which may be different for your website than shown in the screenshot.
	G	Indicates the number of "Checked out" items.
Step 8	H	Execute the "Check-in" action.
		The "Success Message" will display. You may close it. Then go back to the Articles list and verify that the item is no longer locked. It should not be.

Many Items Checked Out?

If there are many items checked-out and you only want to check-in the Content Items vs. Modules also as an example. Select only the database table(s) you wish to affect and no others. If there are several and all you want to check-in are Modules that are checked-out, select only that database table.

Where to find More About Articles

There are, of course, many more administrative details that need to be discussed about Categories and Articles. In this book, a purposeful effort has been made to classify actions and Content management into specific Chapters. Here are some examples and where they may be found:

Adding Images to Articles and Modules

Go to Chapter 20, "VISUAL: Images & Media Manager" where these topics are covered.

Layouts for Articles in Category Blogs

Chapter 11, "CONTENT: Category & Article Options" provides detailed information regarding the many ways Articles may be arranged when the Category Blog Layout is chosen via a Menu Link Item.

Using Fonts in Articles and Elsewhere

Joomla! 5: Boots on the Ground, Advance Edition, Volume 2, Chapter 34, "FONTS: Adding & Using Custom Fonts." This Chapter also includes the addition of Google Fonts to the website.

Changing to Different Layouts

Joomla! 5: Boots on the Ground, Advance Edition, Volume 2, Chapter 44, "VISUAL: Custom & Alternative Layouts" are outlined in this Chapter.

Using Multiple or Different Templates

Template use is covered in Chapters 17 through 19, in this book, which includes use of Style Sheets ("CSS"), along with Template and Page Builder Extensions.

For other specific topics, please consult the Chapter Table of Contents or the Index.

CONTENT:
Category & Article Options

If you can imagine a website with many, many Content Items in the form of Categories and Articles, and that each one has a multiple of configuration settings that must be set manually by the Administrator. It is easy to see that it could be a nightmare to manage. The need to set a dozen or more configuration "Options" each time a Category or Article is created would not be any fun at all.

To help with configurations and consistency, along with continuity of layouts and formats, Joomla! 5 has "Options" for many Content Item groups, along with their related alternative layouts. Of course, some of this is like a "Rubics Cube," when "Options," individual Content Item "Options" and Menu Link Item "Options" are all trying to do the same thing.

In this Chapter, the "Options" will be explained in detail to give you an understanding of what they do, how they apply to their respective Content Items, and the variables that might be involved. In situations where "Options" might apply to multiple layouts and design considerations, Exercises will be presented to guide you through the processes of setting and administering the "Global Configurations."

Options Apply to Everything

Every type of Content on a Joomla! 5 website has "Options" that can be configured and applied on a Global Basis to all Content Items. In addition, Content Items have overrides that can be applied at the Content Item Level or modified within the Menu Link Item that opens it, which then functions act as an over-ride to the "Global Option" settings.

Understanding Options

The "Options" are complex and wide-ranging. They control the default conditions upon which almost everything on a Joomla! 5 website is based. It is probably possible to write an entire book on "Options," how they are used, apply to Content, can be over-ridden by the Content Item, or the Menu Link Item which opens them for viewing.

The best way to understand "Options" is to compare them to construction of a large building. The contractor just doesn't scrape the ground and starting laying cinder blocks. Nope. They dig holes, put it footers, drive metal pilings and do all sorts of things so the building has support. That is what "Options" do for Joomla! 5 – they set up the foundation so the Administrator can build upon them, making modification when and if necessary.

In the book, *Joomla! 5: Boots on the Ground, Advance Edition, Volume 2*, Chapter 43, "CONTENT: Global Options & Settings" covers "Options" in great detail. This Chapter will be limited to those "Options" that only affect Categories and/or Articles. The "Options" for those two Content Items are similar and affect each other.

Where are the Global Options

The "Global Options" themselves can be opened from almost any Content Item. When executed, the "Options" which will automatically open to the "Options" for that type of item. From there, the "Options" for everything else can be accessed by just moving from tab to tab at the top, or Content Item to Content Item in the left menu. Figure 11-1 illustrates how to open the "Global Options" feature.

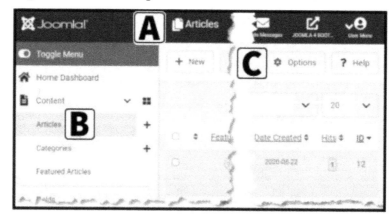

Figure 11-1

A	The Categories or Articles list view should be open, or any Article should be opened to access the "Global Options" via the "Options" button.
B	Select Article Categories or Articles from the left Menu or the Article Categories Articles block on the "Home Dashboard," or have any Category or Article open.
C	Click on the "Options" button at the top right. This button takes the Administrator to the same control area, regardless from where the initial access is initiated. The only notable difference is that the "Options" that are displayed will be those from the source of the action, *re:* "Article Options" will be opened when "Options" is selected from an Article or an "Article List View."

MOST IMPORTANT: Article Categories & Options

The "Options" Settings for Categories and Articles are the most significant that affect Content Items and User Access. The "Options" are also shared by other Content Items. In fact, these "Options" are applied "globally" across the website and more specifically, for Article Categories and Articles collectively.

To find out the "Options" for any feature or element within Joomla! 5, when that feature or element is opened, simply open the "Options" using the button to the top right and proceed from there to configure – keeping in mind that these "Options" will apply globally across the entire website. However, in this instance, the primary application of these Global "Options" is directly with Article Categories and Articles.

Offscreen "Options" Tab

When accessing the "Options," it is suggested that you Toggle Off the left Administrator Menu using the Toggle Menu button. This will allow the screen to display the full "Options" selector tab bar. With Toggle On, the entire bar may not be visible on some smaller monitor widths. There is a slide bar under the tabs to use to access those tabs not displayed. The number of Global "Options" is nine (9).

The Article Category and Article "Options" in Detail

In the Articles "Options" tab bar, there are nine selection areas. Each has a distinct set of "Options" that may be configured, that will then apply across the entire website and control Content, display and visual appearances for Article Categories and Articles.

TAB: Articles

The "Options" under the Article Tab sets the default configuration for individual Article displays, and how some selections function when an Article is created, as shown below. When viewing the Article Options, note that some "Options" are already set, which is the default configuration for the Article settings. There is no need to modify these settings.

Choose a Layout	If "Custom Layouts" have been created (likely not), choosing them can be done here via the drop down. This is the Article's Alternative Layout option under the Article's "Options" tab in the Article Workspace. *Joomla! 5: Boots on the Ground, Advance Edition, Volume 2*, Chapter 44, "VISUAL: Custom & Alternative Layouts," explains how this is accomplished. If no Custom or Alternative Layouts have been created, only the "default" selector will be available.
Title	This Shows/Hides the actual Title of the Article, which can be replaced by an Alternative or Custom Title, or no Title at all.
Linked Titles	If the Article Title shows in any type of Article List on the Front-End, and this is set to "Show," the Article Title will be a direct link to the respective Article by itself.
Intro Text	Intro Text is the short paragraph that appears before the remainder of the Article text. Intro Text is typically above the "Read More" break within an Article which is manually inserted by the Administrator.
Position of Article Info	This defines where the Details of the Article appear, either Above or Below the Content Text. Details show such information as the author, relevant dates and more. However, when "Below" is chosen, the Article Info splits with some above and some below. This cannot be readily changed without performing an over-ride on the Template files.
Article Info Title	Options to "Hide" or "Show" the Articles Info Title, which in the default installation is the Details heading above the Article Info.
Category	Option to display the name of the Category into which the Article is assigned.
Link Category	If the Category is shown, it makes it an Active Link to the respective Category List.
Parent	Allows the display of the "Parent Category" of the Article's Category, should there be a Category Hierarchy being used.
Associations	Hides or Shows the Associated Article's Flags or URL "Language" Code. This is only functional on websites that use more than one language. This also require a "Language Associations" Plug-In activated. See Chapter 28, "COMPONENT: Multilingual Associations."
Author	"Hides" or "Shows" the Author's Name.
Link to Author's	If the Author has a "Contact Page," this will create a Link to that

Contact Page	page. Note that a "Contact Page" for the Author must exist in the "Contacts" Component.
Create Date	"Hides" or "Shows" the Date the Article was originally created.
Modify Date	"Hides" or "Shows" the Date the Article was last modified.
Publish Date	"Hides" or "Shows" the Date the Article was first Published.
Navigation	Navigation in Article are links to additional Articles in the same Category. These are the familiar "Previous" and "Next" links displayed under the Content Text.
Voting	If Article Voting is used, allows is to "Hides" or "Show" it.
"Read More" Link	Provides a choice to "Hides" or "Show" the "Read More Link" in an Article that includes the break between teaser and Content text. This link within the Article can be formatted and enhanced for visual appearance and actual text that displays.
Title with "Read More"	Choice to show the Article Title as part of the "Read More "text.
"Read More" Limit (characters)	The actual "Read More" text, controls the number of characters to display before the actual break in the Article.
"Tags"	If "Tags" are implemented and included within an Article, this is the choice to Hide or Show them.
Record "Hits"	This allows the number of "Hits" to be recorded in the Article List.
"Hits"	"Hides" or "Shows" within the Article Info, the number of times an Article has been accessed.
Unauthorized Links	If this "Options" is set to "Show," the "Intro Text" for restricted articles will display. When the "Read More" link is clicked, it will require users to log in to view the full Article. If set to "Hide," Articles that the User is not permitted to view (based on viewing access levels for the article via "ACL") will not show.
Positioning of the Links	If links are associated with the Article, there is a choice to show them either Above or Below the Content Text. They may also not be displayed by using the "Hide" selection.

TAB: Editing Layout

The Editing Layout tab opens the "Options" that are and can be set on the actual Article Workspace screen. Many "Options" are set as the default, just as in the Article Options, but they are different in nature insomuch as these "Options" toggle the display of the selectors on/off as desired.

Allow Captcha on Submit	The "Captcha" Plugin must be selected and configured in the Plugin Manager to be used when submitting forms, to help eliminate improper Form submissions by intrusive spam bots.
Publishing Options	This setting prevents other Back-End Users from changing certain Fields in the Article Settings, such as: Created By, Created By Alias, Created Date, Start Publishing and Finish Publishing.
Article Options	This setting also prevents other Back-End Users from changing the actual Article Options.
Edit Screen Options	Displays or does not display the Edit Screen tab.
Article Permissions	Displays or does not display Article Permissions tab.
Multilingual Associations	This allows the use of multiple languages on the website and creating associations between Content Item.
Enable Versions	There is the "Options" to track "Versions" of Articles. This setting enables or disables Version Control.
Minimum Versions	This controls the number of "Article Versions" to be maintained, along with other intuitive settings.
Frontend Images and Links	Images and Links can be set to show when the Article is being edited via the Front-End. This will allow Editors to enter Images and Links as described below.
Administrator Images and Links	This will control whether the Images and Links Slider will show in the Article Manager Add/Edit Screen.
URL A Target Window **URL B Target Window** **URL C Target Window**	Three Links can be inserted into Articles. This controls the manner in which the Links, when selected, are displayed on the screen, re: Parent Window, New Window, Popup Window, or Modal Popup. This applies to all three URL Options.
Intro Image Class	If an "Intro Image" is used, this sets the

	alignment or "Float" location.
Full Text Image Class	This sets the "Float" setting for the Intro Image. "Float" is left, right, centered.

TAB: Category

The "Options" that apply only to an individual Category, when they are created, can be preset on a "global basis" using these settings.

Choose a Layout	The setting in this field allows Blog or List Layouts to be applied. This designated the default Layout of either Blog or List. If Alternative Layouts are created, they will also appear here as an Option to set as the Default Layout.
Category Title	Option to show the Category Title.
Category Description	Option to show the Category Description if it was entered wen the Category was created.
Category Image	If a Category Image was inserted, this controls the display.
Subcategory Levels	If an extensive Category Hierarchy is created, the number of Levels to be displayed is designated in this field.
Empty Categories	Sometimes, Categories are created but no Articles are assigned. This setting controls whether an empty Category is displayed on a Category List.
No Articles Message	If there are no Articles in an empty Category, this message can be set to appear – only if Empty Categories is set to "Show."
Subcategories Heading	If the Content Item is located (assigned), within a Sub-Category ("Child"), the name of the Sub-Category's display can be set here.
Subcategories Descriptions	Option to show the Sub-Category Description if it was entered when the Sub-Category was created.
# Articles in Categories	This designates the "Number of Articles" count to be displayed, or not.
Tags	If "Tags" are being used, allows them to be displayed, or not.

TAB: Categories

These "Options" apply for the Articles Categories globally, unless they are set differently in the individual Category or Menu Link items, which can override the settings below. These settings are similar to the Category settings above, but act on multiple Categories vs. just one.

Top Level Category Description	The Description of the Top Level Category, if entered when created, can be set to show, or not.
Subcategory Levels	If an extensive Category Hierarchy is created, the number of Levels to be displayed is designated in this field.
Empty Categories	Sometimes, Categories are created but no Articles are assigned. This setting controls whether an empty Category is displayed. "Hide" is the preferred state for Categories that do not have Content assigned to them.
Subcategories Description	Option to show the Sub-Category Description if it was entered when the Sub-Category was created.
# Articles in Category	This displays the Number of Articles within the Category

TAB: Blog/Featured Layouts

Blog and Featured Layouts consist of Articles within Categories. Blogs and the Front-End Featured Articles usually consist of several Articles and can be arranged in various formats using the "Blog/Featured Layouts" Options.

Remember, these "Options" only apply to the Category Blog and the Featured (Blog) Layouts – they are not Global Settings that apply to everything. Also, although these are Global Options, applying to all Categories and Articles, they may be modified within the Content Item themselves (albeit there are some limitations), or within the Menu Link Item that opens the respective Content.

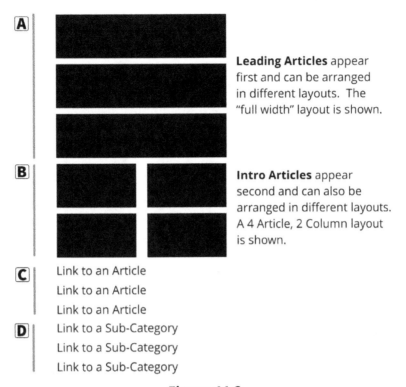

A Leading Articles appear first and can be arranged in different layouts. The "full width" layout is shown.

B Intro Articles appear second and can also be arranged in different layouts. A 4 Article, 2 Column layout is shown.

C Link to an Article
Link to an Article
Link to an Article

D Link to a Sub-Category
Link to a Sub-Category
Link to a Sub-Category

Figure 11-2

It is helpful, before reviewing the "Options" for the Blog/Featured Layouts, to gain some knowledge of the mechanics of the layouts as shown in in Figure 11-2.

Of course, a Blog Layout is something that must be applied to be relevant to the Article Content being displayed. Generally, the Global "Options" that apply first to all Blog Layouts helps to get the Content configured visually. The Menu Link Item that opens a Blog Layout is typically one that designates that Articles from a specific Category is displayed. All Category selections display the same, which is in conformance with the Global "Options" for the Blog/Featured Layouts.

In Joomla! 5, the default Global "Options" can be over-ridden to change the appearance of the Articles by making changes to the Menu Link Item which opens the Category. Therefore, it is actually possible to have separate layouts for each different Category Blog Menu Link Item. This is a powerful feature.

Refer to Figure 11-2 for the following:

# Leading Articles	A	Leading Articles are those that display at the beginning of the Content Area. This sets the number of Leading Articles. Because this is a Blog Layout, the "Read More" Feature can and should be used to only display preliminary text and not the entire Article Content. If the layout is selected to be full width, any number of Articles can be designated. If the layout is a boxed type in multiple columns, the number should be equal to a multiple of the columns.

209

Leading Article Class		This is a "CSS' designation that provides the coding needed for various and different types of layouts for Leading Articles presented in a Blog format. The available "CSS" Classes are listed in Chapter 18, "VISUAL: Style Sheets."
# Intro Articles	B	Intro Articles typically are displayed in Columns below the Leading Articles. This sets the number of Intro Articles to display.
Article Class		This is a "CSS' designation that provides the coding needed for various and different types of layouts for Articles presented in a Blog format (other than that of a Leading Article). The available "CSS" Classes are listed in Chapter 18. "VISUAL: Style Sheets."
# Columns		Sets the number of Columns in which the Leading Articles are presented. Set as "1" will make the Articles display full-width. Any other value will make the layout appear in a multicolumn format.
Multi Column Direction		When multi-columns are used, the "order" of the Articles can be down the first column, then to the top of the next, down to the bottom and back to the top in the next column again. Or, alternatively, the order of Article display can be horizontal, from left to right, dropping to the next row in sequence and so on. These settings are "Down" or "Across."
# Links	C	Designates the number of Links to additional Articles within the Category beyond Leading and Intro Articles. These display below the Intro Articles, if any. If none, display will be below the Leading Articles. It is actually possible to set the Leading and Intro Article values to "0" which will display only links to Articles.
Include Subcategories	D	This displays the Sub-Categories that are the Child of the "Parent Category" being displayed in the Blog or Featured Format.
Linked Intro Image		If an "Intro Image" for an Article is used, this setting can allow or forbid its use as a "Global Option." That does not mean it disallows it completely. Overrides can be applied at the Content and Menu Link Item level.

TAB: List Layouts

List Layouts refer to how the lists of Categories or Articles are displayed in their respective Managers. The settings "Options" are as follows:

Display Select	This Option controls the display of the number of items on the List Layouts. The User has an "Option" of selecting the number of items to show, but this setting can disable that feature.
Filter Field	This presets the Filter for the display of the List Items by Title, Author, Hits, Tags or Month "Published." Setting this sets the default order of the List display.
Table Headings	Give the "Options" of showing, or not showing, the List Table Headers.
Date	Provides the "Options" of displaying the List by Created Date, Modified Date or "Published" Date of the Content item.
Hits	Can be set to show, or not show, the "Hits" or view count of the Articles.
Author	Can be set to show, or not show, the Article Author on the List.

TAB: Shared

These "Options" only apply for the Shared "Options" for List, Blog and Featured Layouts. However, overrides can be set in the respective Menu Link Items.

Category Order	In this Layout, the Order of the Categories can be determined by: No Order, Title Alphabetical, Title Reverse Alphabetical or Category Manager Order, which is according to the Order column configuration in the respective Category Manager.
Article Order	Like the Category Order, the Articles can be designated to appear in a certain order, such as: Most Recent First, Oldest First, Title Alphabetical, Title Reverse Alphabetical, Author Alphabetical, Author Reverse Alphabetical, Most Hits, Least Hits, Ordering (according to the Order column configuration in the respective Article Manager) and Ordering Reverse.
Date for Ordering	Items can be sorted by the following Date choices: Created, Modified or Published.
Pagination	If there are multiple pages in the List Displays, and if the Articles will not display on one screen page, Pagination Links are needed, such as: Auto (links shown if needed), Show (forced) or Hide.

Pagination Summary	This "Hides" or "Shows" the number of total pages involved in the display of the Articles.
Featured Articles	Featured Articles can be excluded from the Article List Display using this Option.

TAB: Integration

The Integration "Options" specify how Articles will integrate with the other Joomla! 5 Extensions. These "Options" generally control the display of "News Feeds" if they are used on the website.

Show Feed Link	This pertains to the "RSS" Newsfeed and whether to show the link or not.
Include in Feed	If the Article has "Intro Text," this is a choice to include it or not.
"Read More" Link	If the Article has a "Read More" button, this is a choice to include it or not.
Remove IDs from URL's	This removes the source IDs from the URL in the browser location bar.
Edit Custom Fields	Allows, or not, the creation of Custom Fields.
Enable Workflow	This allows the Administrator to affect any "Workflows" that may have been created.

TAB: Permissions

This "Options" setting applies to the Permissions regarding Access and Editing of Articles by Authors. This actually applies only when there are a number of Authors involved in creating and editing Content Items. If only the Administrator serves in the Authoring or Editing capacity, these settings do not apply. They primarily apply to Access Groups into which Authors and/or Editors have been assigned.

The Permissions can be set for each Access Group, either for the Default Groups or Groups that might be added to expand the Access Control ("ACL") configurations. The following "Options" apply for every Access Group.

It should also be pointed out that only the Administrator, or website Administrator can change any of the ACL settings that might apply to any User Group.

Each Group's Individual Permissions

To change the Permissions, the User Group must be selected in the left column, then the settings for each Permission Status can be made. The changes to settings do not apply globally to all Groups. Each User Group must be modified separately. Groups may also be set to "inherit" permissions from their Parent Group.

Configure ACL & Options	Users are allowed to change the "Options" and Permissions.
Configure "Options" Only	Users are allowed to change the "Options" but not the Permissions.
Access Administration Interface	Users are allowed to access the Administration Interface.
Create	Users can/cannot Create Content.
Delete	Users can/cannot Delete Content.
Edit	Users can/cannot Edit Content.
Edit State	Users can/cannot change the "Published" State of the Item.
Edit Own	Users may Edit only the Content Items they created.
Edit Custom Field Value	Users can/cannot Edit any Custom Field Value.
Execute Transition	Users can/cannot Edit any of the Transitions that are involved in any Workflow associated with the Content Item.

Component & Other Options

If you have studied the "Options" above, which apply primarily to Categories and Articles, understanding other "Option Settings" should not a problem. Every Component in Joomla! 5 has its own set of "Options." When using Components or installed Extensions, it's a smart move as an Administrator, to make yourself as familiar as possible with the "Options" available for the Component or Extension.

Therefore, when looking at adding other Content to the website, when you access a Component or Menus, take a quick look at the "Options" that are available to the Administrator to manage the Content.

There are not that many "Options" available, and certainly those that are, present themselves intuitively in what they apply to and the possible configurations. Chapter 43,

"CONTENT: Global Options" & Settings," within the *"Joomla! 5: Boots on the Ground, Advance Edition, Volume 2,"* book covers those "Options" in detail, and also, those which were not discussed in this Chapter.

However, during other Chapters and other Exercises, "Options" might be addressed as part of demonstrating how the Component or Menu or added Extension's functions may be managed or enhanced. In such a situation, an attempt will be made to explain the "Options" and how they may apply or affect the Content at issue.

JOOMLA!®5 Ⓐ Ⓒ Ⓓ Ⓔ
BOOTS ON THE GROUND
Advance Edition
Volume 1 Ⓑ
CHAPTER 12

CONTENT:
Modules

Modules are Content Items (of many different types), that can be added to a website into pre-established locations on the webpage. They are the movable parts of a Joomla! 5 webpage. More accurately, they are similar to a "Sticky Note" that can be placed anywhere on a webpage where there is a "Module Position" designated. These locations are hard-coded physical positions that are part of the Template being used for the webpage.

Modules are powerful. They can be used creatively to display many distinct types of Content using the default installation Modules, and those added as Extensions for specialized Content.

Modules Added as Examples

Keep in mind that, at this point, the "Sample Blog" Content was added to the default installation. This added additional Modules to the Content Layout of the "myfirstsite" project. These Modules were in addition to those included in the default installation.

Unlike Articles, which may only appear in the Main Content Area, Modules can be placed in any position on a Template where "Module Position" code has been included. This makes Modules, as Content Items, very flexible. Additionally, Modules may be placed within Articles, making them an even more versatile type of Content Item.

Many Templates have a considerable number of "Module Positions" into which you can assign Modules. Templates typically have "Module Positions" that are next to each other horizontally. One interesting feature of "Module Positions" is that they can be stacked one on top of each other. This adds incredible flexibility for creating page layouts. More about "stacking" later in this Chapter.

Another neat aspect of "Module Positions" is that the assigned Module can be set to spread to fill an entire area. In the case of horizontal "Module Positions," if one Module is assigned, it takes up 100% of the space. If two are assigned, each takes up 50% of the space and so on. This allows for some nice looking and highly functional layouts for displaying generated Content display via Modules. This type of expanding is possible because of the "grid system" of Bootstrap 5, which is integrated into the Joomla! 5 core program.

Template Developers take advantage of Bootstrap 5 and they connect their "Framework," operating above the core Joomla! 5 Framework, and utilize Bootstrap 5 to create very powerful and visually attractive Templates.

Modules in the Default Installation

Modules are Extensions. This means that Modules can be added to Joomla! 5 at any time via the Extension Installer. There are literally thousands of Extensions available, many of them are Modules. Some are Modules that are part of a Component or installed as part of a Package that might consist of a Component, Module and Plugin combination.

Perhaps one of the most powerful type of Modules is the one in which "Custom" Content can be added, and that Modules can be placed anywhere on a Template layout where "Module Positions" are located. The "Custom" Module can also be included within an Article. The actual Content of the "Custom" Module can be virtually anything – it has that much flexibility!

Here are the Module Types that are available through the default configuration when Joomla! 5 in initially installed:

	KEY	**D** = Installed by Default. **SB** = Installed via "Sample Blog" Action. **A** = Available from Default install to Add to website.
Articles-Archived	**SB** **A**	When Articles have been Archived, this Module is used to show a List of Archived Articles by calendar months in which the Archive was initiated.
Articles-Categories	**A**	Displays a List of Categories within a selected Parent Category.
Articles-Category	**A**	Displays a List of Articles from within a single Category.
Articles-	**A**	Shows a List of the most recently "Published" and current

Latest		Articles.
Articles-Most Read	A	Shows list of "Published" Articles with greatest number of page views.
Articles-Newsflash	A	Displays list of Articles from a specific Category.
Articles-Related	A	If Meta Keywords are applied, can display a list of Articles that are related by virtue of the keywords.
Banners	A	Displays list of Banners from the Banners Component.
Breadcrumbs	D	Displays the Content pathway of Content being viewed.
Custom	A	Creates a Module into which custom Content can be added.
Feed Display	A	Can display a syndicated feed from another source.
Footer	A	Places a Footer on the webpage.
Language Switcher	A	If using multiple Languages, allows to switch between them.
Latest Users	A	Displays a list of the latest Registered Users.
Login	A	Adds a Login Form.
Menu	A	Adds a Menu to the Front-End of the website.
Random Image	A	Displays a random image from a Media Folder.
Smart Search	A	Adds a Module to Smart Search the website.
Statistics	A	Displays Users and Articles on the website.
Syndication Feed	SB	Menu added with the Sample Blog.
Tags-Popular	A	Displays tags used on the website.
Tags-Similar	A	Displays links to items with similar Tags.
Who's Online	A	Displays list of Users who are online and accessing Content.
Wrapper	A	Allows the addition of an "iframe" to embed an external website.

Rules that Apply to Modules

Modules have their own set of particulars that govern how they function and display. Here are a few general rules that apply to Modules:

Rule 1	A Modules must exist via the default installation, or be installed as an Extension, or be part of a Component that uses or includes its own Modules.
Rule 2	A fixed "Module Position" must exist on the Template in order to place ["assign"], a Module on a Template's webpage.
Rule 3	A Module must be "Published" or enabled for it to display Content. Modules may also be set to "Publish" or "Unpublish" on specific dates and times.
Rule 4	A Menu Link Item cannot be created specifically to open a Module, but there are Extensions that allow that action to be performed. There are also some rare exceptions to this rule.
Rule 5	Some Components have Menu Link Items that do open a Module directly, but this is part of the feature installed with the Component, not a normal function of the Default Components.
Rule 6	Modules are typically associated with a Menu Link Item. That is, when a Menu Link Item is clicked, to open an Article as an example, the Module will also display in its "Module Position" when that action is executed. This setting is accomplished on a Module-by-Module basis.
Rule 7	Specialized Menu Link Item types can be created that open special Modules directly. This runs contrary to Rule 4 above, but these exceptions are unique and created for specific purposes vs. generalized applications.
Rule 8	A Module may associate with more than one Menu Link item. In fact, a Module could associate with every Menu Link Item on a website, or only on a select number of different Menu Link Items. The association combination options are unlimited.
Rule 9	More than one Module of the same, or different, type can appear in "Module Positions", either in separate locations on the webpage or in the same position location. Each duplicate Module may associate with different Menu Link Items. For example, Custom Module Types may be added/located on any webpage in any, or as many, positions desired.
Rule 10	The exception to Rule 2 is that Modules themselves may also be placed within an Article. This technique is demonstrated in an Exercise later in this Chapter.
Rule 11	It is also possible to place a link to an Article within a Module, thus allow some exception Content flexibility.
Rule 12	Modules CANNOT be placed within other Modules. Period. Full Stop.

Naming Modules

Like all other Content Items, when a Module is created, it must be given a "Title" – which can be anything such as a generic name, a location identifier or a number. Modules can also be named along the lines of what the Module Content displays. For ease of access, it is always advisable to give Modules a "Title" that relates to the Content display it offers. This makes it easier to find the Module on the List of Modules if there are many in use – which is not unusual on larger websites.

Formal Module Titles can be set to hide, which means whatever the name given to it, the name does not need to be displayed when the Module is visible on the website. Only the actual Content of the Module will be displayed, without the Title. This is accomplished on the Module Workspace screen, by changing a simple on/off toggle from "Hide" to "Show," or the other way around. Remember to execute a Saving action is required to have it take effect.

An Alternative Title can be created which may then be displayed rather than the Formal Title. This works the same way for Modules as it does for giving Articles an alternative Title to display. So, Modules may have any name for convenience, but it may have another name, or Title, which displays with it on the screen.

Displaying Modules on a Template

When a Module is created, the default setting is: "Published" and the display is set to show "On all Pages." You already know what "Published" and "Unpublished" does to a Content Item. How it works with the Menu Assignment Manager is explained below and shown in Figure 12-1.

EXERCISE 12-1: ASSIGNING MODULES TO MENU LINK ITEMS

Objective: This Exercise will provide guidance on how to assign the display settings for Modules to Menu Link Items. This action sets "conditional display" criteria for the Module as a "show, no-show" combination across ALL of the Menu Link Items on the website. Modules may have this "conditional display" setting applied to it in many different combinations, as explained below:

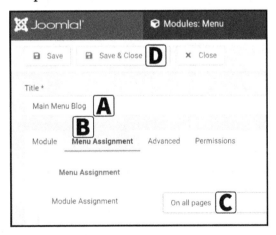

Figure 12-1

Step 1		On the "Home Dashboard" Control Panel open the "Modules Section."

Refer to Figure 12-1 for the following:

Step 2	A	When the List of Modules displays, open the "Main Menu Blog" Module.
Step 3	B	Click on the "Menu Assignment" tab.
Step 4	C	The display choices will appear in a menu with four available options:

	Option 1	**On all pages** The Module will display on every webpage on the website in the "Module Position" in which it is assigned.
	Option 2	**No pages** The Module will not display on any pages. If you choose this option, the Module also will not be able to be displayed within an Article. This is the setting to use for a Menu that will contain Menu Link Items that may be accessed by links within Article or Module Content vs. from a Menu. This Module would typically be assigned to a non-existent "Module Position" such as: "outerspace," which will not display the Module on any website page or screen.
	Option 3	**Only on the pages selected** When this option is selected, a List of all Menu Link Items will be displayed to choose from, with further "Options" at the top of the List. It is a matter of selecting additional options, or making selections from the checkboxes List to display the Module on ALL selected pages.
	Option 4	**On all pages except those selected** The last choice is the opposite of Option 3, in that the Module will display on all webpages EXCEPT for those Menu Link Item webpages that are selected using the checkboxes. Example would be: "All screens except the Home screen."

Step 5	D	When any "Option" is selected, a Saving Action must be executed.

If the Module is to be "Published" within an Article, which is possible, then use the "CMS Content" function. Remember that if the Module is to be exclusive to display "at all times" within an Article, it should be assigned to a non-existent "Module Position" The use of a unique "Module Position" name should be assigned to the Module, re: Outerspace#, etc., as noted above.

Also, if the Module is embedded into other Content, the Module itself must also be set to the "Published" state to be displayed when the Content Item is displayed. It is not necessity for the Module to be assigned to a "Module Position" if it is to be embedded within an Article or another Module.

Finding "Module Positions" on Templates

Previously, it was mentioned that a Module can only be assigned to a "Module Position" which is hard-coded into the particular Template being used to display a webpage via Joomla! 5. The exception to this, of course, is when a Module is being inserted into an Article..

The "Module Position" locations are hard-coded into a Template by their designers. There is nothing the Administrator need do to place a "Module Position" onto a Template. They are already in place.

If necessary, the Administrator may add new "Module Positions" to Templates. It takes some coding skills do accomplish that, so if you don't have those skills, do not attempt to do it. Chapter 47, "ADMIN: Library of Over-Rides" in *Joomla! 5: Boots on the Ground, Advance Edition, Volume 2* covers over-rides exclusively with examples.

The biggest problem is finding out where the positions are located on the Template's layout, and what they are called or named. Every Template has "Module Positions," but they may not be in the same location on each, nor might they have the same name. In short, every Template has its own unique "Module Positions", and the challenge is to find out where they are and what they are named.

For example, one Template may have a "Module Position" named: "right." While another Template might have a similar "Module Position," but it is called: "sidebar-right." It is a reasonable assumption that Templates created by the same developer might use the same naming conventions, or maybe not. Which is exactly the reason the Administrator needs to identify "Module Positions" on every Template being used on the website.

Fortunately, Joomla! 5 has a feature to facilitate finding the "Module Positions" on any Template, as was demonstrated in Exercise 12-1.

EXERCISE 12-2: FINDING "MODULE POSITIONS" ON A TEMPLATE

Objective: This Exercise will provide guidance on how to determine where "Module Positions" are located on any Template that is installed on the website.

Step 1	Open the "Home Dashboard > Control Panel > System," (near bottom of left menu), which opens access to more Administrative areas of the Back-End.

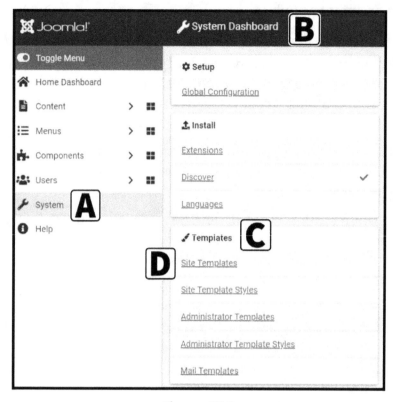

Figure 12-2

Refer to Figure 12-2 for the following:

Step 2	A	In the left menu open the "System" link to open the "System Dashboard."
	B	
Step 3	C	Locate the "Templates" Block.
Step 4	D	Click on the "Site Templates" link.

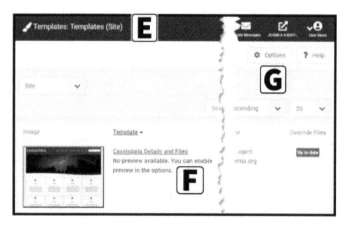

Figure 12-3

Refer to Figure 12-3 for the following:

Step 5	E	The "Site Template" screen will appear showing one Template. If the site has more Templates installed, they will also be displayed on this screen.
Step 6	F	The Template name and a note should display, which is the default Template added during the Joomla! 5 installation: Note that the comment is indicating there is "no preview enabled."
Step 7	G	On this screen, click on the "Options" button at the top right of the screen, which will open to the screen as shown in Figure 12-4.

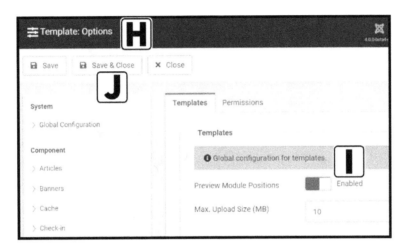

Figure 12-4

Refer to Figure 12-4 for the following:

Step 8	H	Access the Templates "Options" Block.
Step 9	I	Change the "Preview Module Positions" to "Enabled."
Step 11	J	Execute a Save & Close Action.
Step 12		The result of these actions will display the Templates List screen and now the "No preview" icon in the "Preview" Column has changed to the "Preview" icon, and the link is active to view the Template's "Module Positions".
Step 13		Click on "Preview" icon in the "Preview" Column.

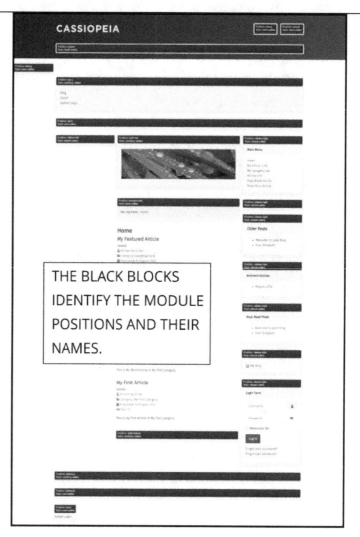

THE BLACK BLOCKS IDENTIFY THE MODULE POSITIONS AND THEIR NAMES.

Figure 12-5

Refer to Figure 12-5 for the following:

Step 14	View the "Module Positions" and familiarize yourself with the name and location on the Template. When you view the individual Modules, these positions will be the ones selected for the "Position" choice in the Module Workplace.
Step 15	When viewing is completed, close this Browser window.

As mentioned, "Modules Positions" and their names may be different for each Template. The ones shown in Figure 12-5 are for the default "Cassiopeia" Template only. If you have/use several Templates, repeat this process for each to determine which template has which "Module Positions" and their names. It is usually not a bad idea to do a "print screen" to get a hard copy of the Template's "Module Positions" and their names.

Multiple "Module Position" Assignment

An individual Module cannot be designated to display in more than one "Module Position" within a Template at a time. They can be assigned to more than one Menu Link Item, causing it to display, or not display, based on the action assigned to the Menu Link Item. However, it will still only display within the designated "Module Position" in every instance.

One more notable feature of Modules is that multiples of the same Module may be created and used on the same website. Not only that, these same-same Modules may be "stacked" within the same "Module Position." This occurs frequently when using the "Custom Module" type.

An Extension may exist that would allow a single Module to be assigned to multiple positions at the same time. Check the Joomla! Extension Directory ("JED") to check if one might be available.

Also, Template and/or Page Builder Extensions may be used which can use the same naming conventions for "Module Positions." Why? Because the created Template and/or Pages built by the Administrator can have the naming convention somewhat standardized between them, thus no issue.

Another thing to keep in mind when using Template or Page Builders, the actual Modules can be placed into those webpages without concern to assigning them individually to "Module Positions." More about this in Chapter 19, "VISUAL: Using Template/Page Builders."

Types of Modules

By default, during installation, a number of default "Module Types" were created. Additionally, during installation of the "Blog Sample Data," additional Modules were added. Listed below are the Modules after "Sample Data" was installed with their function and use explained.

By way of adding Extensions, additional Modules may be added to the List. This can be by individual specialty Modules, or Modules that are part of a Component that is being installed.

Articles-Archived	When Articles have been archived, this Module can be used to show the List of the Archives by calendar months in which the action was taken.
Articles-Categories	This module allows the display of a list of Categories from within a single parent Category. If the parent has five child Categories, it will display those five based on the designation of the parent.
Articles-Category	More selective than Article Categories, this Module allows the display of Articles from within one or more Categories. This is done on a Category-selective basis.

Articles-Latest	This displays a list of the Most Recently "Published" and current Articles within a "Module Position" As new Articles are created, they display on the list within the Module.
Articles-Most Read	As users view Content, this Module displays the Content that has been the most accessed. Of course, it can't really tell if they read the Content. It simply just shows Articles that have the highest number of actual page views ("clicks").
Articles-Newsflash	Allows display of Articles from a specific Category. This is similar to a Category Blog display, but allows the placement of the Module anywhere. The number of Articles to be displayed can be fixed.
Articles-Related	Using meta keywords, Articles can be related to one another. If the current Article has Keywords, the Module will display all other Articles with the same Keyword. Allows for a cross-referencing Articles from within other Articles.
Banners	If Banners are created and categorized in the Banners Component, the individual Banner can be displayed in this Module. More than one Banners Module may be placed on a webpage.
Breadcrumbs	This is also called the *pathway*, which simply shows the current location with the links or Content location used to get there. Helpful on large websites with many areas of Content; not so much on smaller, limited Content websites.
Custom	This is a nifty and frequently used Module whereby "html" coded designs and layouts can be displayed on webpages within a Module or many Modules on the same webpage. Special images can be included, along with text, and it can be visually styled using "CSS" coding.
Feed Display	If you want Syndicated Feeds from another website to appear on yours, then the Feed Display Module can be used to collect and display the feeds in a Module Position.
Footer	By default, the Footer Module shows the Joomla! copyright information at the bottom of the page. It can be set to not display by setting its status to "Unpublished."
Language Switcher	If the website is configured in several languages, this Module offers users the opportunity to change from the current "Language" to any other available language.
Latest Users	If your website has registered Users and a feature to sign up, this Module allows the display of the Latest Users added to the website.
Login	Displays the Login Module on the webpage.

Menu	A website can have many, many Menus. This Module allows the designation of the Menu That will appear in a "Module Position" and associate with which Menu Link Item. A Menu Module can be set to display after a Menu Link Item in another Menu is clicked.
Random Image	The Random Image Module is used to display the images randomly from the selected directory, typically from within the Media Manager. The link to the source of the images may be external to the Media Manager.
Smart Search	Using the Smart Search functions, the Module allows users to execute advanced searching features on the website.
Statistics	This Module shows information about your server: number of Articles, and the number of Users.
Syndication Feeds	If you want to create an outbound Feed for other websites to use to display your Content, this Module, if displayed on a webpage, allows you to do so. The Syndication Module only "feeds" the webpage on which the Module is located/positioned.
Tags-Popular	The most commonly used "Tags," within specific time periods, can be displayed using this Module.
Tags-Similar	If Content Items have similar "Tags," the closeness of which can be specified, the Module will display links to the other Content Items.
Who's Online	Displays the Registered Users (if logged in) and guests who are currently on the website. Can be displayed by number of, by usernames, or both.
Wrapper	Perhaps the most misunderstood and misused Module in Joomla! The Wrapper is an "iFrame" window that displays a website using its URL. It can display an entire website within the Wrapper. However, the link functionalities of the displayed URL can go awry very easily because they are not intended for your Wrapper display, but for that particular website. Before getting too excited about using the Wrapper Module, lower your expectations of what it can do and display.

Common Sense in Module Placement

Given the wide range of Modules available, some thought should be given to where on a website screen it should appear. Some Modules, in the wrong location, look out of place. So, when adding Modules and assigning them to a "Module Position" give some thought to how it looks and how it fits into the visual display of the particular screen.

Moreover, if a Template is responsive for displaying on mobile devices (which it should be), placement of Modules in logical locations on the desktop, might not make sense on the mobile device.

Adding a Module to a Template Position

It is already established that Modules, to appear on any website screen, must be assigned to a pre-determined "Module Position" on the Template in use. Given this fact, the following Exercise will demonstrate how: 1) a Module is created, 2) how it is assigned to a "Module Position," and 3) how it can be relocated within the "Module Position."

EXERCISE 12-3: ADDING A MODULE TO THE WEBSITE

Objective: This Exercise will demonstrate how a Module is created, added to a "Module Position," and associated with a Menu Link Item on the Template. In this case, the new Module will be added to the right column of the default Template. Here are the steps involved:

Step 1		Open the "Home Dashboard > Control Panel > Site > Modules," which will open the Module Manager. The shortcut to creating a Module, or any other Content Item, is to click the **"+"** on the respective block. Or, with the List of Modules screen open, click the **"+ New"** to create a new Module.
Step 2		The next screen displays a List of "Module Types" that are installed and available for inclusion onto the website screens.
Step 3		Select the "Custom" Module type. This type of Module allows the Administrator to create customized Content to be displayed when the Module's display is active with a Menu Link Item.

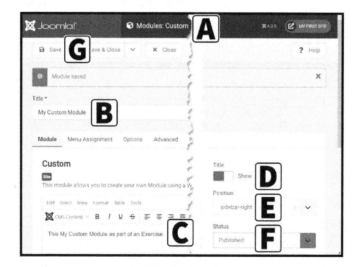

Figure 12-6

Refer to Figure 12-6 for the following:

Step 4	A	The Module Workspace opens as: "Modules: Custom," and has a blank Module displayed.
Step 5	B	For the Title, enter: "My Custom Module" (without quotes).
Step 6	C	Enter "This is the Content of My Custom Module." into the Module Content Area.
Step 7	G	At this point, execute a Save action. It is suggested that when creating Content Items, that frequent "Save Actions" are executed.
Step 8	D	In the right column, make sure the "Title" is set to "Show."
Step 9	E	Open the "Position" drop down, scroll down and select "sidebar-right" as the desired position of the Module on the website screen.
Step 10	F	Set the Status to "Published," if it is not already in that Status.

Do not make any further configuration settings at this point.

Step 11	G	Execute another Save action, if needed.

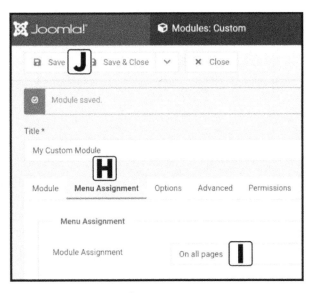

Figure 12-7

Refer to Figure 12-7 for the following:

At this point, it is necessary to decide about the display of the Module in association with the many Menu Link Items that already exist on the website. Here are the choices that may be selected:

On all pages	The Module will display on every website screen.
No pages	The Module will not display at all. Akin to

229

		"Unpublished." However, if the Module is inserted into a Content Item, the "No pages" choice should be made rather than "Unpublish," which would force the Module to not display at all.
Only on the pages selected		Module will appear only on the website screens that are selected among the List of Menu Link Items.
On all pages except those selected		Module will appear on all website screens *EXCEPT* those are selected among the List of Menu Link Items.
Step 12	H	Open the "Menu Assignment" tab.
Step 13	I	"On all pages" is the default. Do not change it at this point.
Step 14	J	Go to the website Front-End and refresh the screen. Note that the "My Custom Module" now displays in the "right-sidebar" and it displays the text that was entered.

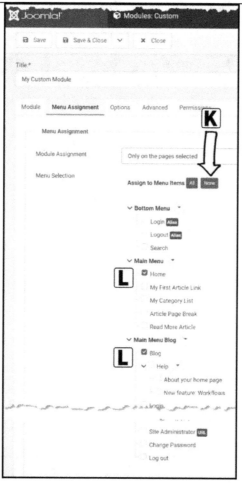

Figure 12-8

Refer to Figure 12-8 for the following:

Step 15		Return to the Module Workspace in the Back-End.
Step 16	K	In the Menu Assignment tab, select Only on the pages selected. This will open a List of all Menu Link Items which exist on the website.
Step 17	L	Click "None" from the choices. This clears the selection from all Menu Link Items, which is easier than removing from them one-by-one manually, especially if there are many Menus and many Menu Link Items.
Step 18	M	On the Menu Item List, select both "Home" and "Blog" as the choices. Note that these are Menu Link Items, each in a different Menu.
Step 19	N	At this point, execute a Save & Close action.
Step 20		Go to the website Front-End and refresh the screen. Note that the My Custom Module now continues to display in the right sidebar. "Home" is the default home page for the website, this the display is correct, because it was selected in the Menu Assignment. It may be necessary to scroll the screen to find the Module.
Step 21		In the top Menu, select "About." When the screen re-displays, note that the Module is no longer visible in the right sidebar.
Step 22		In the same top Menu, select "Blog." When the screen re-displays, note that the Module is now visible in the right sidebar. This is consistent with the choices made in the Menu Assignment.
Step 23		Click on other Menu Link Items in the Main Menu and the Top Menu, which should result in the Module not showing in the right sidebar. It should only appear when the Home and Blog Menu Link Items are selected, because these are the Menu Link Items that were selected to "only show when..." conditions.

The "Popular Tags" and "Older Posts" at the bottom of the screen are not actually Menus. They contain system generated links based on certain parameters on the individual Articles, thus those are not actual Menu Link Items. They also did not display on the Menu Assignment choices.

Inserting a Module into an Article

In a manner that is similar to inserting an Article Link into an Article, a Module can be embedded within an Article. However, a Link is not displayed. The actual Content of the Module is displayed within the Article. For example, if the insert is the Login Module, it will be displayed within the Article exactly the same as it would appear on the screen in its assigned Module Position.

There are three ways of embedding a Module into an Article, as follows:

Method 1 Load Module CMS Content	This method uses a built-in process whereby the action is selected in the "CMS Content" feature, then the Module itself is selected. This automatically uses Method 2 below to insert the Module using the default Editor only. The "JCE" Editor, if used, has buttons to complete this function.
Method 2 Load Module using ID	Method 2 is to enter a code manually with the Module ID Number, such as: {loadmoduleid ##}, where ## is the Joomla! 5 system ID Number of the Module. This ID Number is usually found at the far right of the list screens for Categories, Articles, Modules, etc. When shown the "braces" [the "{" or "}"] must be included in the text that identifies the Module.
Method 3 Load Module using Position Name	Alternatively, you can enter this manually: {loadposition -name-}, where -name- is the Name assigned to the "Module Position" However, this needs care because multiple Modules may be in the same position, thus all of them will display. See note Naming Unique "Module Positions"."

Guide to Cross-Placements

As mentioned Modules, of any type, can be inserted into Articles. Also, that links to other Articles can be inserted into Articles. Modules, in general, cannot have insertions or links added to them. However, the "Custom Module" may take advantage of these cross-placements of Content.

Here is a table of helpful guidelines about cross-placements:

Articles into Articles	Links to other Articles can be added to any Article, but only as links. If the target Article is "Trashed" or "Unpublished," the link remains but will result in a "not found" error.
Modules into Articles	Modules inserted into Articles will display the Content of the Module. This will not be a link, but the actual Module Contents will show.
Articles into Custom Modules	Links to Articles can be added to any Custom Module, but only as links. The actual Content of the Article will not display within the Module.
Modules into Custom Modules	Modules as Content cannot be added into Custom Modules. However, links to existing Modules can be added, but only as links.
Contact Link	A Contact Link can be inserted into both an Article and a Custom Module.

Custom Field	Custom Fields can be added to Articles and Custom Modules, along with various Components.
Media	Media can be added to Articles and Modules and other Content as the source location within the Back-End.

Don't Get Excited

In the "CMS Content" dropdown in any Article, you may have noticed there is an option called Modules. This is a quick method of adding a Module into an Article. When clicked, a List of Modules displays, and this allows the Administrator to click-select a Module for insertion, using Method 1 as noted previously.

There are also three other bits of information that can be obtained when the Modules popup window opens:

Use 1	To find the ID Number of the Module to use the "{loadmodule ##}" method. This is the number to the far right.
Use 2	To find the "Module Position" for the Module to use the "{loadposition -name}" method, where -name- is the exact name of the Module Position.
Use 3	To find the Module Title to use the "{loadmodule mod_name}" method, where name is the Title of the Module to be inserted.

If you have the proper information, a Module can be inserted into an Article by entering the appropriate code, using either the "Module ID Number," the "Module Position" assignment or the Module Title. However, the direct selection method is much faster and easier.

Naming Unique "Module Positions"

There are incidences where a Module is created, that is NOT assigned to any "Module Position" on a Template, yet it will be used in special situations like a Module in an Article, and the Module is not intended to be displayed in a Template's actual named "Module Position"

In this case, a unique Module Name can be easily created. At 200mph Media Group, LLC, we humorously use "outerspace" as a "Module Position" Name, re: outerspaceA, outerspaceB, etc.

The "{loadposition outerspaceA}" (or whatever name), can then be inserted into the Article. No "Module Position" named "outerspace..." needs to exist on a Template to assign a Module to it. Simply designate the "Module Position" to the Module by typing in the bogus

"Module Position" name. The name is a faux name for the sole purpose of using it at a location other than in an actual Template's Module Position.

EXERCISE 12-4: INSERTING A MODULE INTO AN ARTICLE

Objective: The purpose of this Exercise is to demonstrate and define procedures for inserting an existing Module into an Article, using different methods.

Using the "CMS Content" Method, or Module ID Number

Step 1		On the "Home Dashboard," go to: "Control Panel > Content > Articles," to display the List of Articles. Use either the left menu or the Site Panel to do so. The result should be a display of Articles.
Step 2		Open the "My Featured Article" Content Item.
Step 3		Place the Mouse Cursor at the end of the Article Text and insert a hard return.

Refer to Figure 12-9 for the following:

Step 4	A B	Open the "CMS Content" dropdown in the Editor Menu Bar and select Module. Be aware of the differences between the default Editor and the manner in which the "JCE" Editor accomplishes this task.
Step 5		This will open the List of Modules.
Step 6		Scroll down and select the Module entitled: "Login Form." Click on the green button bar with the Module name. This inserts the Module into the Article, indicating the Module ID Number.
Step 7		Execute a Save Action.
Step 8		Go to the website Front-End, and click the "Home" button.
Step 9		View "My Featured Article." Notice that the same Login Module shown on the right side of the screen is now embedded into the Article. This has effectively inserted a working "Login Module" into the Article. Any Module can be inserted with an Article or another Module in the same manner.

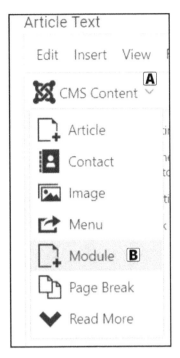

Figure 12-9

Stacking or Ordering Modules

As stated in **Rule 9** previously, as applies to Modules, several Modules may be assigned to the same "Module Position" on a Template. In the case of the Default Template, one "Module Position" is entitled: "sidebar-right." "My First Module" was assigned to that "Module Position" Within the default Template with the "Sample Blog" Content added, there should be six Modules assigned to the "sidebar-right" Module Position.

What if this isn't the exact desired location for the Module? What if the Module should appear at the top of the right column *aka* "sidebar-right?" This can be accomplished through the process of Stacking the Modules in the desired "Order of Display." Exercise 11-5 explains how this is accomplished.

EXERCISE 12-5: STACKING OR ORDERING MODULES

Objective: The objective of this Exercise is to explain and demonstrate how Modules that are assigned to the same "Module Position" on a Template, may be placed in a selected "Order" within the location. The stacking or ordering action that will be taken is to move the "My First Module" from location two, to location one within the sidebar-right Module Position.

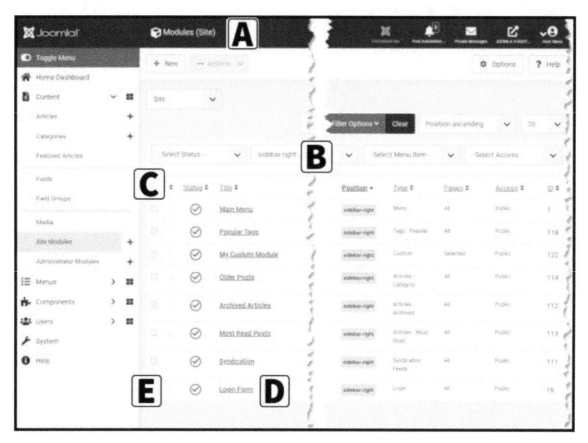

Figure 12-10

Step 1		Open the "Home Dashboard > Control Panel > Site > Modules," which will open the Module Manager.

Refer to Figure 12-10 for the following:

Step 2	A	The next screen displays a List of Modules, and all "Module Positions." If the list is short, use the "Clear" button to remove any selectors that may be affecting the number displayed.
Step 3	B	Next, filter the List by "Select Position" as "sidebar-right." This will display the list of all Modules assigned to that Template Module Position.
Step 5	C	To the left of the "Status" column, click on the blue double arrows at the top of the column. This enables Modules to be relocated in the "Module Position" The black vertical dots in that column will indicate that the Module can be relocated within its current Module Position.
Step 6	D	Locate the Module entitled: "Login Form."
Step 7	E	Click and Hold the Mouse Button on the three vertical dots in the Column.
Step 8		Visually locate and note the topmost Module in the section of "sidebar-right" Location.

Step 9		While still holding the Mouse Button down, slide the selected "Login Form: Module" up until the topmost Module drops down below it.
Step 10		Release the Mouse Button. The Login Module should now be located at the very top of the list of Modules in the "sidebar-right" position. No "saving action" is required. When the mouse button is released, the Content Item drops into the selected position and an automatic "list refresh" occurs.
Step 11		Go to the website Front-End. Refresh the screen. Visually confirm that the relocation was accomplished.

The Login Form Module should now appear at the top. It should remain in that location in the "Module Position" for every Menu Item to which the Login Module is designated to display. Also, the Login Module is designated to show on "all pages," which is an obvious choice for this particular Module.

Using Multiple Instances of the Same Module Type

In theory, as many multiples of the same Module may appear on a website screen. However, as a practical matter, only those Modules that make sense visually should appear. A typical example of this is the Custom Module.

Many instances of the Custom Module may be added to any website screen. Why would you want to do this? The Custom Module is very versatile and may contain any type of Content, such as: text, images, text Content and so on. Thus, many or several Custom Modules can be used.

To do this, simply create the Module desired and assign it to a "Module Position" then assign it to a Menu Link Item.

Remember, you cannot assign a Module to multiple "Module Positions" at the same time. Modules may only be assigned to one "Module Position" at a time. However, they can be assigned to any number of Menu Link Items, which creates various display possibilities.

Possible Extension Available

It is very possible that, at some point, a Plugin Extension may be developed and made available whereby Modules may be assigned to Multiple "Module Positions" using a selector of some sort.

If a Module with the same Content is to be located at a different "Module Position" for a different Menu Link Item, another – or a duplicate – must be created, positioned and then assigned. Why? A single Module cannot be assigned to multiple "Module Positions". They may be associated with multiple Menu Link Items for viewing purposes, but not based on their location on the Template.

Adding Another Menu & Menu Module

Adding a new Module is a straight-forward process. Modules are Extensions and may be added by way of any one of four methods, as described below.

Method 1	Download the Extension file directly from the Joomla! Extension Directory, then install it via the "Upload Package File" method. This is the simplest and easiest method. However, it usually only works if the Extensions is "free" with no costs involved. The Extension installer file is automatically downloaded to the designated location on your computer.
Method 2	Via the website Back-End, under System > Extensions > Install, then use the "Install from Web" feature. Developers may set up their Extensions from within the joomla.org website in the form of a "directory," similar to the "JED." One of the requirements is that the Extensions obtained/installed in this manner, also have automatic "updating" notices and installation features on the Back-End when/if the Developer upgrades or updates the Extension. *One word of caution:* Make sure the Extensions are compatible with Version 5 of Joomla! If they are not, the website may break and NOT BE ABLE TO BE RECOVERED!
Method 3	Using this method, the installation file is installed/uploaded via FTP, or via the website server control panel, to the "tmp" folder. Then the file is called up from that URL location on the website Back-End itself. This is pretty much a "last resort" method of installing an Extension, used if Method 1 or 2 above fail to install the Extension.
Method 4	This seldom used method can be used when the Developer places their Extension on their website location and provides the URL. The installer can be connected to the Extension via a weblink. The link is likely connected to some sort of permissions so that only one user can access the Extension for installation. This method also can pose some security risks, so caution is advised when consider this method for installing any Extension.

Adding Menus & Menu Modules

Menus, when installed, are actually composed of two parts. First is the Menu itself where it is created and when Menu Link Items are added. Second is the Menu Module, which is the object that can be placed within any "Module Position" on the Template, or within an Article or another Module.

Here is a review of the method of Menu and Menu Module creation and facts you should know:

Method 1 Menu-Module	The first method is from within the Menu Manager itself, which is accessed via the "Home Dashboard" Menu by opening the "Menus" and then the "Manage" link. This opens the Menu Manager. From there, a Menu simply need to be named and then saved.
	Following this, another action must take place, from within the Menu Manager. This consists of executing a action button that was automatically created which, when invoked, will create the required Menu Module for the Menu. After that, it will need to be configured. This will all be discussed in the Exercises below.
Method 2 Module-Menu	This method involves creating the Menu Module first. Then performing the actions in Method 1 in reverse. The goal here is to connect the two together because a Menu itself cannot exist without an accompanying Menu Module, nor can a Menu Module be used without a Menu to display the Menu Link Items. This will also be demonstrated in the Exercises below.
Special Note	Menu Modules can be displayed in two configurations: Horizontal or Vertical, the latter being the default. Template "Module Positions" usually have a "Menu" location wherein it is coded to allow for a Horizontal Menu with drop-down Sub-Menu-Items to be used. Otherwise, some "CSS" code "Classes" must be added to the Module to make it display in a certain manner, be it vertical or horizontal, and to configure it's appearance.

EXERCISE 12-6: CREATING A MENU - MENU-FIRST-MODULE-SECOND

Objective: This Exercise will demonstrate the most convenient method to create a Menu and accompanying Menu Module. The Menu is created first, followed by creation of the "Menu Module" and designating its "Module Position" of the Template.

Step 1		Open the "Home Dashboard > Menus > Manage," which will open the Menu Manager.
Step 2		Click on the **"+ New"** button at the top of the screen.
Step 3		Enter the Menu Title as "Menu Method 1" (without quotes).
Step 4		In the other two fields, enter the same name.
Step 5		Execute a Save & Close action.

At this point, the screen returns to the Menu Manager and displays the new "Menu Method 1" Menu, and the option to create the Menu's Module. This button is on the right side.

Figure 12-11

Refer to Figure 12-11 for the following:

Step 6	A	The Menu Manager will display all Menus created.
Step 7	B	Locate the newly created menu: "Menu Method 1."
Step 8	C	To the right, find the action button named; "Add a module for this menu."

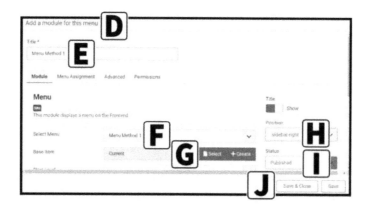

Figure 12-12

Refer to Figure 12-12 for the following:

Step 9		Click on the button to execute the named action. A modal window will open.
Step 10	D	The "Add a module for this menu" creation panel should open.
Step 11	E	Enter: "Menu Method 1" to name the Module.
Step 12	F	Select "Menu Method 1" in the "Select Menu" field.
Step 13	G	The Base Item should indicate "Current."
Step 14	H	Assign the Menu to the "sidebar-right" Module Position.
Step 15	I	Make sure the Module is "Published."
Step 16	J	Execute a Save & Close Action. The buttons are located at the bottom of the Modal Box.

At this point, you may view the website Front-End, but the Menu Module will NOT be displayed. Why? At least one Menu Link Item must be added to the Menu to trigger the actual display of the Module. Menu Link Items will be added after the next Exercise.

EXERCISE 12-7: CREATING A MENU - MODULE-FIRST-MENU-SECOND

Objective: This Exercise will demonstrate the alternative method to create a Menu and accompanying Menu Module. The Menu Module is created first, designating its "Module Position" of the Template. Then the actual Menu is created, followed by addition of the Menu Link Items.

Step 1		Open the "Home Dashboard."
Step 2		Click on the "+" button in the Modules Panel.
Step 3	A	Scroll down and find the "Menu" panel and click on the "+" button. This opens the Menu Module Manager panel.

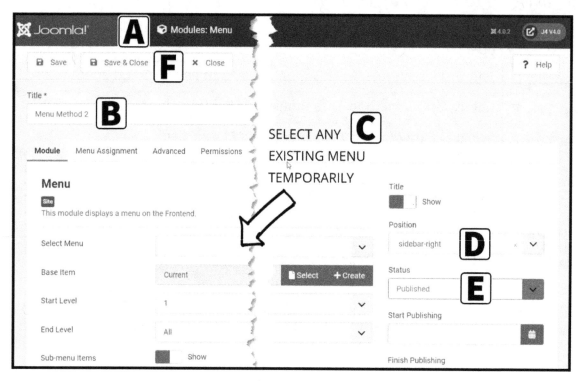

Figure 12-13

Refer to Figure 12-13 for the following:

Step 4	B	Enter the Module Title as "Menu Method 2" (without quotes).
Step 5	C	Because no Menu named "Menu Method 2" yet exists, any choice of Menus can be used temporarily in the Module. The selection will be changed after the Menu is created. In other words, you will need to return to this Module and connect it to the Menu, which will be created next.
Step 6	D	Select the "Sidebar-right" as the Module Position.
Step 7		No other settings need to be changed. Allow them to remain in their default configuration.
Step 8	E	Set the "Status" to: "Published."
		All other settings, which are the default, for the Menu Module can remain the same.
Step 9	F	Execute a Save & Close action.

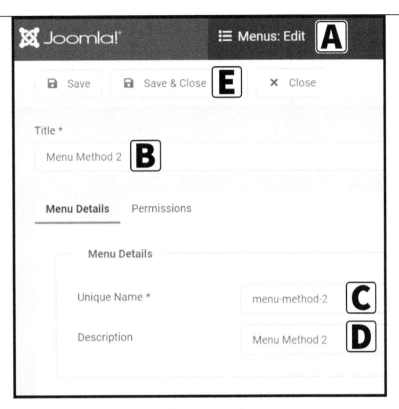

Figure 12-14

Refer to Figure 12-14 for the following:

Step 10		Open the "Home Dashboard" > Menus > Manage, which will open the Menu Manager.
Step 11	A	Click on the **"+ New"** button at the top of the screen which will open the Menus: Editor screen.
Step 12	B	Enter the Menu Title as "Menu Method 2" (without quotes).
Step 13	C	In the other two fields, enter the same name.
Step 14	D	For the "Unique Name," enter: "Menu Method 2" (without quotes), which will change to all lowercase hyphenated upon saving.
Step 15		For the "Description," enter: "Menu Method 2" (without quotes),
Step 16	E	Execute a Save & Close action.
Step 17		Open the "Home Dashboard" and then re-open the Module Manager.
Step 18		Find the "Menu Method 2" Module.
Step 19		In the "Select Menu" field, select the just-created "Menu Method 2" as the Menu to be associated with the Module.
Step 20		Execute a Save & Close action. No other settings need to be changed.

Again, if no Menu Link Item has been created in any Menu, the empty Module will not display on the Front-End. A Menu Link Item must be added to each of the Menus to force them to display in the "Sidebar-right" location on the Front-End.

EXERCISE 12-8: ADDING MENU LINK ITEMS TO MENUS

Objective: This Exercise will demonstrate the two methods that can be used to add a Menu Link Item to any Menu. It is necessary to add Menu Link Items to any created Menu, regardless of the method employed. A Menu or Menu Module will, by default, NOT display if it is empty of any Menu Link Items.

Menu Method 1

Step 1	Open the "Home Dashboard" and access "Menus > Method 1."
Step 2	Click the **"+New"** button at the top.
Step 3	In the "Title" field, enter: "Method 1" (without quotes).
Step 4	Select "Articles > Single Article" as the Menu Type.
Step 5	Select the "Working on Your Site" as the Article choice.
Step 6	The "Status" selection should be: "Published."
Step 7	Execute a Save & Close action.
Step 8	Go to the website Front-End.
Step 9	Click on the "My First Article" link because the "Menu Method 1" Module is set to display only when that Menu Link Item is actioned.
Step 10	Find the "Menu Method 1" Menu and click on the "Method 1" Menu Link Item.
Step 11	This will open the "Working on Your Site" Article.

Menu Method 2

Step 1	Open the "Home Dashboard" and access "Menus > Method 2."
Step 2	Click the **"+New"** button at the top.
Step 3	In the "Title" field, enter: "Method 2" (without quotes).
Step 4	Select "Articles > Single Article" as the Menu Type.
Step 5	Select the "Typography" as the Article choice.
Step 6	The "Status" selection should be: "Published."
Step 7	Execute a Save & Close action.

Step 8		Go to the website Front-End.
Step 9		Click on the "My First Article" link because the "Menu Method 1" Module is set to display only when that Menu Link Item is actioned.
Step 10		Find the "Menu Method 2" Menu and click on the "Method 2" Menu Link Item.
Step 11		This will attempt to open the "Typography" Article. However, because the Article has restricted access to only "Registered Users," the Article will not open.

While the Menu appears with a link to an Article, it cannot be viewed unless the User attempting access has logged in. Be aware of this restriction when creating Menus that contain Menu Link Items to "only" Restricted Content. It might be better to restrict access to the Menu itself, which reduces frustration for site visitors viewing a Menu which contains link to Content Items for which their access is restricted.

Horizontal or Vertical Menus

By default, Menus assigned to locations such as left or right sidebars, or within an Article or another Module are typically displayed in a vertical orientation.

If assigned to the "Module Positions" named "Menu" the default layer is horizontal. This uses "CSS" code that associates with the "Module Position" when a Menu Module is assigned to it. The switch from vertical to horizontal happens automatically because of the style sheet coding for the "Module Position," or for the "Module Class" designation.

The challenge is not relative to setting up a vertically oriented Menu, but to place a horizontal Menu at other "Module Positions" besides "Menu." An example of this would be to place a horizontal Menu at the bottom of the website screen.

At this time, it is not convenient to locate a Menu Module at the bottom of the website page without some extensive manipulation of the Template. This requires an "over-ride" to be created, which is too much of an advanced subject to tackle at this point.

In Chapter 47, "ADMIN: Library of Overrides," the subject of creating a Menu "Module Position" at other locations on the Template will be addressed. Additionally, Chapter 54, "VISUAL: Using Mega Menu Extensions," will deal with this subject, providing that a Third-Party Developer has created one and made it available either as a free or pay-to-download Extension. See *Joomla! 5: Boots on the Ground, Advance Edition, Volume 2*, for the above Chapter references.

The subject of using different Menus in different visual orientations may also be discussed in some of the other more advanced Chapters.

Relocating Menus on the Webpage

Because all Menus are displayed through the use of Menu Modules, and we know that Modules can be located at any point on a Template screen through the use of "Module Positions", it stands to reason that Menu Modules may be relocated to any Module Position.

Along with this relocation is the possibility that the actual "Module Position" has been coded to display a Menu in a certain manner. This is the case with the "Menu Module Position" on the default template, which has attached coding that displays the top "Blog" Menu horizontally. All others simply use the default vertical format.

Of course, when locating Menu Modules on a screen, some common sense must prevail. Menus should be located in convenient positions so that website users can access them easily for navigation. For Example, websites that have Menus that are links to the less important parts of the site, could have some Menus located at the bottom of the screen.

In fact, there are some great "Mega-Menu" Extensions that can be utilized for exactly that purpose either for the Main Menu, or for supplemental Menus located at other "Module Positions." You can be sure that Developers will be making these Mega-Menu Extensions available before long.

Display Conditions for Modules

When a Module is assigned to a "Module Position" it is usually set to "Published" and to be displayed at all times. This means that when any other Menu Link Item is clicked, the Module will continue to display.

What if it is desired to have the Module only display only under certain conditions, such as when a specific Menu Link Item is selected? Modules can be set to show, or not show, based upon which Menu Link Item is selected in any active Menu. There are unlimited combinations of "show-no-shows" that can be created for Menu Link Items between any number of individual Menus.

To acquaint yourself with other "hide/show" possibilities, review the other possible "Module Assignment" options, as follows:

On all pages	This choice is obvious.
No pages	This choice is also obvious.
Only on the pages selected	This shows a Menu/Module, only when certain Menu Link Items are triggered.
On all pages except those selected	This is the reverse of "Only on the pages selected" choice, which excludes rather than includes, Menu Link Items.

The following Exercise will provide guidance on how the above display conditions can be accomplished.

EXERCISE 12-9: CONDITIONAL DISPLAY OF MODULES

Objective: The objective of this Exercise is to present the procedures used to "conditionally" display any Module on the website. "Conditionally" means that when a certain Menu Link Item is clicked, a Module will or will not display at its assigned "Module Position" on the Template. In this Exercise, the two Modules in the "sidebar-right" location [Menu Method 1 and Menu Method 2], will be set to "not show" when "My First Article Link" in the "Main Menu" is clicked. Proceed to accomplish this as follows:

Part A: Only on the pages selected

Step 1		In the "Home Dashboard," within the "Site" panel, click on "Modules." You are not creating a "new" Modules so do not click the **"+"** icon/button. Just click on the main panel for Modules.
Step 2		Filter the display by choosing: "Select Status" and "Published" to ensure the list is easier to view and find Modules. The "Search" may also be used. For this Exercise, search for "Menu Method 1."
Step 3		Open the "Menu Method 1" Module, by either using the "Search" feature or simply opening it by clicking on the Title on the list.
Step 4		When open, select the "Menu Assignment" tab, which will show that the Module is currently set to display "On all pages." This means the Module will always show for every Menu Link Item that is clicked, no exceptions.
Step 5		Click on the dropdown and then select "Only on the pages selected." When that action is executed, it will display every Menu and every Menu Link Item on the website. This means the Module will always show, EXCEPT when the selected Menu Link Items are chosen.
Step 6		At the top of the list are, click on the "None" button. This will automatically de-select every selection on the list. Consider this as "clearing the Menu Link Assignment" for this Module.
Step 7		Scroll down and find "Main Menu" and select "My First Article Link" within that Menu.
Step 8		Execute a Save & Close Action.
		Go to the website Front-End, refresh the screen. The "New Module 1" should NOT display.
Step 9		Click on the "My First Article Link: in the Main Menu. When that action is taken, and because of the conditional setting applied, the "Menu Method 1" will display. Click on ANY OTHER Menu Link Item and the Module will no longer display.

Part B: On all pages except those selected

Step 10		Open the "Menu Method 2" Module.
Step 11		Open the "Menu Assignment" tab.
Step 12		Select the "Open on all pages except those selected" option.
Step 13		At the top of the list are, click on the "None" button. This will automatically de-selected every selection on the list. Consider this as "clearing the Menu Link Assignment" for this Module.
Step 14		Scroll down and find "Main Menu" and select only "Home" within that Menu.
Step 15		Execute a Save & Close Action.
Step 16		Go to the website Front-End and refresh the screen.
Step 17		Click on some of the other Menu Link Items in different Menus. The Method 2 Menu Modules displays when each is clicked.
Step 18		Click on "Home" within "Main Menu." "Menu Method 2" no longer displays, or does a "no-show." This is the "condition," that it will show on "all" Menu Link Items EXCEPT those selected. Selecting any other Menu Link Item in any Menu will allow the "Method 2" Menu Module to display; but when "Home" is selected, it WILL NOT show.

Practical Use of Conditional Module Displays

By example, assume that you had a certain Module to display but you only wanted it to display when the "Home" screen opens. However, when a website visitor clicks on any other Menu Link Item, it would NOT display. Of course, given the variables available with "show-no-show" combinations, they can be configured any way desired.

Assume that a Custom Module has been created with an announcement for an event and the panel is a graphic image. Also, that the Module has been assigned to a "Module Position" directly above or below the Main Content Area of the screen.

Let's assume the condition is that the announcement Module would only display when the "Home" screen is displayed, regardless of what type display is configured. When clicking on any other Menu Link Item, the announcement Custom Module will not display.

Solution:

The steps below are for sequencing information only. It is not an actual exercise to perform, although you may walk through the steps below without actually executing them.

Step 1	Within the "Menu Assignment" tab when the announcement Module Workspace is opened, select the option of "Only on the pages selected."
Step 2	Clear all selections using the "None" button at the top.
Step 3	Select the Menu Link Item which is the designated "Home" selector, regardless of what type of page display it is set to control.
Step 4	If a Save & Close were executed, the Module would then be conditioned to display ONLY on the "Home" screen and hidden when any other page or screen is accessed. Any combination of display settings may be applied, but this specific use is common for the presentation of announcements or date-specific display graphics.

The Conditional Display can be configured for every Module on the website as needed for any desired screen display.

Do Not Hide the Home Menu

It is suggested that the Menu that contains the "Home" Menu Link Item should NEVER be set to hidden. That Menu Module should always be displayed to ensure proper website navigation features are available at all times.

Module Content

Most Modules have predetermined Content, based on its contemplated informational use, or how it was designed to display Content from a Component. Looking at the list of possible Modules that may be added to the website reveals the many different types available with the default installation and those added with the "Sample Blog" install as performed in Chapter 7.

The only Module that allows customized Content to be added into the Module is, obviously, the Custom Module. This Module can contain almost any type of Content.

Also, make a mental note, that some Modules associated with Component Extensions that have been installed may have a wide range of settings and controls which may alter their display.

Module Naming Conventions

Some "Module Position" names follow a standard convention, some do not. Many custom Templates have unique "Module Position" names. By using the method explained in Exercise 12-1, the physical location and name of all "Module Positions" can be determined for any Template installed on the website.

It is always a good idea, after installing a new Template, to first become familiar with its "Module Positions."

If two or more Templates are used on a website, some Modules may need to be duplicated and assigned to the "Module Positions," having different names, on each Template. If a Template has a different name for a "Module Position," a new Module must be created and assigned to that space. Individual Modules cannot be assigned to different named "Module Positions" on different Templates at the same time.

Practical Applications of Modules

In other Chapters in this book, Components and their related Modules will be discussed and demonstrated. Rather than go through a series of Module Exercises in this Chapter, we will include those through the remainder of the book. This way, the demonstration of a more practical use and application of Modules can be demonstrated, as well as their extensive options.

CONTENT:
Field Groups & Content Fields

Within the creation of Content in the form of Categories or Articles, there is a way to expand the information. This is accomplished through the use of "Field Groups" and "Fields." This is a feature whereby additional input fields can be added to Categories and Articles. When included, Authors can enter information into these fields, thus expanding the Content with a systematic approach.

The same Content could be added using the Content Workspace Editor, but the consistency could be haphazard and inconsistent. Having specific information fields, this input becomes more consistent and easier to include when creating Categories and Articles.

This Chapter addresses the "Field Groups" and "Fields" created in such a way that the Administrator can quickly grasp the basics and understand their use.

By definition, "Fields" are simply Content Items that can be added to Articles, Contacts, etc. that should be used having consistent formats. This can be very helpful. For example, if every Article written by Content Editors, have a specific credit or byline located at the end of the Article with contact information. This is but one example of how "Fields" can be used.

Using the Features

First, as in other areas of a Joomla! 5 websites, this feature includes the ability to manage the Field Groups and Fields. Let's first define what they are:

Field Groups	In this case, the "Field Groups" are just another name for "Categories." This is a method of categorizing how the "Fields" are organized. If there are a great number of "Fields," having them organized into logical "Categories ["Field Groups"]," is the way to do it. To be able to add any "Field" to an Article, a "Field Group" must exist into which the "Field" is assigned. This "Field Group" then appears as a "tab" within the Article Workspace.
Fields	These are the individual "Fields" of information that will be added to either Categories or Articles. Their "types" are discussed below.

Fields are Everywhere

As a point of clarification, Field Groups and Fields may be created within the three major Content areas of Joomla! 5. Fields can be used to display additional information within Categories/Articles, Contacts and Users Components.

However, Field Groups and Fields created for Contacts, for example, cannot ALSO be applied/used for Users. Each has their own concentration of Field Groups and Fields. The Fields are dedicated to their own Content type. They are not interchangeable between the different Content types.

Organizing Fields

Before launching into creating Fields, create a plan. Do you need Field Groups ("Categories"), to set up a hierarchy of classifications? Then, what Fields will be assigned to which Field Groups, and so on. Follow these steps when you plan to implement Field Groups and Fields:

Step 1	Determine and create the primary Field Groups. When created, the Groups show up as tabs within the Category or Article creation Workspace. No Field Group, no tab displays. Also, if there is no Field within the Field Group, it will also not appear as a tab. There is no over-ride to "show empty Field Groups."
Step 2	Determine, create and assign Fields to their respective Field Groups. These Fields will appear within the assigned tab in the respective Workspaces. A Field must be assigned to a Field Group [tab display in Workspace], otherwise the field will not be visible.

No Sub-Field Groups

Unlike Categories, which may have "Child" or "Sub-Categories," the same does not apply for Field Groups. No Sub-Field Groups may be created in either the Articles/Categories, Contacts or Users Component areas.

Of course, the actual Field Groups and the Fields are dependent upon what type of information will be displayed on the website and how it will be organized. There isn't any generic approach that can be applied. The Field Groups and Fields will depend strictly upon the customized Content needs of the website.

Planning the Field Groups & Fields

Planning how Field Groups and Fields will be utilized on a website is important. It can also get confusing when dealing with those that apply to Articles or Categories, then for Contacts, then for Users. Each set of Field Groups and Fields is different, yet they are all created in a similar manner. That is the only commonality between them. Each Field Group/Field is used in a different manner in the Contact types.

Creating Field Groups

First, remember that a Field Group is simply a "Category" by any other name. Therefore, a structure can be created which organizes the Fields into "groups," which makes administration easier. It also makes the implementation of including the Content within the Articles easier through separation through the use of the Field Groups.

In the following Exercise, two Field Groups will be created: "AVAILABLE" and "COMING." These fields will be added to Articles to create references to the source of the Article Content and its accuracy.

EXERCISE 13-1: CREATING FIELD GROUPS

Objective: The goal of this Exercise will be to create two Field Groups to be used within Articles. What is going to be created are two field groups and then Fields within the Field Groups. It will be a book catalog, with an image of the book, the author's name and where the book can be purchased. When creating an Article, the information about the book can be included within it by adding Content into the Fields within the Field Groups.

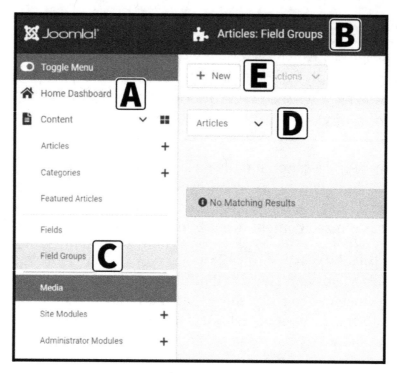

Figure 13-1

Refer to Figure 13-1 for the following:

Step 1	A B	On the "Home Dashboard," go to: "Content > Field Groups," to display the List of Field Groups. The Field Group, "The Author," was included when the "Sample Data" was installed in Exercises in Chapter 7.
Step 2	C	The Workspace screen is identified as: "Articles: Field Groups."
Step 3	D	The Field Group is to be created within the "Articles," not the "Categories," which is the other choice of Field Group type.
Step 4	E	Select the **"New"** button, which will open the "Articles: Edit Field Group" Workspace.
Step 5		In the "Title" field, enter: "AVAILABLE" (without the quotes).
Step 6		Execute a Save & New action.
Step 7		In the "Title" field, enter: "COMING" (without the quotes).
Step 8		Execute a Save & Close action.
Step 9		The results of the above actions should display a list of two Field Groups: "AVAILABLE" and "COMING." "The Author" Field Group was created when the "Sample Data" was installed in Chapter 7.

As you might note, creating Field Groups is near identical to the actions needed to create "Categories" into which Articles are assigned. In fact, "Field Groups" are just another name for "Categories" but are being used in another Content Component for management of Content.

Creating Fields

The next series of actions is to create the Fields that will be assigned into the various Field Groups. There are fifteen different types of Fields that may be created and assigned to a Field Group, as follows:

Calendar	Creates a "calendar selector" for a data field to into which a date is inserted based on User selection.
Checkboxes	Checkboxes create pre-defined values that may be chosen based on the selection criteria.
Color	This options will allow a User to select a color.
Editor	An Editor Box is opened with this option for entering text and or adding images.
Integer	The start and stop value of the list can be created, with increments between, whereby the Author may chose the value.
List	Creates a List of Values which are added to allow the Author to select a value on the List, which may be anything desired.
List of Images	The selection of the folders on the website from which images within it may be displayed.
Media	This is similar to the List of Images, a single image is displayed after it is selected from within the Media location, or uploaded at the time of creation.
Radio	These are buttons, from which only one selector item may be chosen from among those created.
SQL	This field can fetch information from the Joomla! 5 website database and show the output. If you are not familiar with "MySQL" coding, suggest you do not attempt to use this Field.
Text	This is a standard one-line data field for entry of text, similar to a one-line Form Field.
Text Area	This is a multi-line data field for entering paragraphs of text, similar to a multi-line Form Field.
URL	Multiple website URL locations may be entered in this type of field.
User	A single User from among the selection can be chosen for display.

User Groups	Similar to the above, except this will allow the selection of a group of Users vs. simply an individual User.

Also, when creating a Field, it is necessary to 1) assign it to a Field Group, 2) designate the Viewing Access Level for the Field, and 3) assign a Language, if the site has multiple "Language" features activated. See Chapter 28, "COMPONENT: Multilingual Associations," for more information about using Languages.

What should be noted here is that the Field Groups can be added to Articles that are viewable by the "Public" User Group. However, the Field Groups can be designated to be viewed only by "Registered Users," which means they must be logged into the website to view the Content. This is a clever way of adding Content that can only be viewed by Registered Users and not the guest-type website visitor.

It doesn't take much of an imagination to figure out that a different combination of Field Groups, Fields and their viewing permissions assigned to different User Groups, can be used to selectively control the display of information.

So, with that knowledge, the following Exercises will take you through the process of creating the Fields within the Field Groups.

EXERCISE 13-2: CREATING FIELDS

Objective: The objective of this Exercise is to demonstrate the creation of Fields and assign them to the Field Groups as desired. In the first group, there will be four Fields created: BOOK IMAGE, BOOK TITLE, AUTHOR(S) and WHERE TO BUY.

These Fields will be created separately in both the "AVAILABLE" and "COMING" Field Groups.

On the Workspace screens for the Fields, there is an option [right side] to select a "Category." This is not a Category within the Fields Group. It refers to Categories that are associated with Article Content. The default is **"ALL"** which results in the obvious. Otherwise, the Field Groups and Field can be limited to be viewed only within certain Content Categories, if desired, thus increasing the functionality of the Field Groups, Fields and their connection with Content by way of Category association.

Fields Within the "AVAILABLE" Fields Group

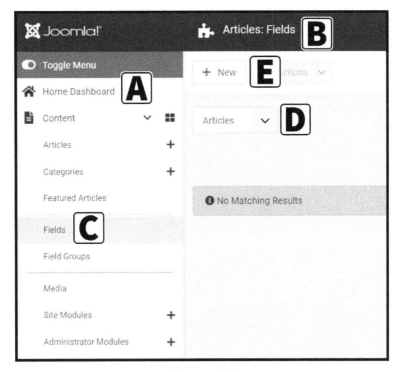

Figure 13-2

Refer to Figure 13-2 for the following:

Step 1	A C	On the "Home Dashboard," go to: "Content > Fields," to display the List of Fields. Initially, there should be only one Field: "About the Author," which was added when "Sample Data" was installed.
Step 2	B	The Workspace screen is identified as: "Articles: Fields."
Step 3	D	The Field is to be created within the "Articles," not the "Categories," which is the other choice of Field Group type. The existing Field was added when "Sample Data" was installed in Chapter 7.
Step 4	E	Select the **"New"** button, which will open the "Articles: Edit Field" Workspace.

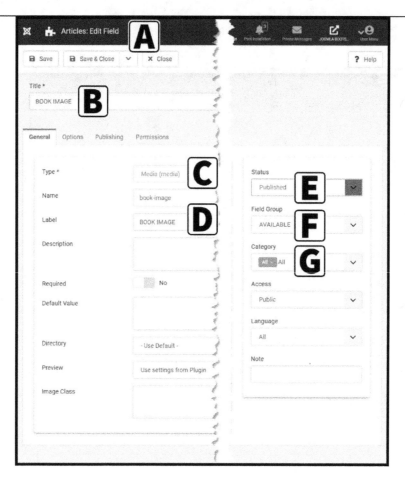

Figure 13-3

Refer to Figure 13-3 for the following:

Step 5	A	The Workspace screen should be the "Articles: Edit Field."
Step 6	B	In the "Title" field, enter: "BOOK IMAGE" (without quotes).
Step 7	C	For "Type," select: "Media."
Step 8	D	For the "Label," enter "BOOK IMAGE" (without quotes). This field will populate itself automatically but the text can be changed manually.
Step 9	E	Make the "Status" to "Published."
Step 10	F	In the "Field Groups" field, to the right, select: "AVAILABLE," a Field Group that was previously created.
Step 11	G	Make sure that **"ALL"** is selected in the "Category" field. This makes the Field inclusive of all Content Categories. If the Field should be limited to only one Category, this is where that designation should be made.
Step 12		Execute a Save & Close action.
		The result should have the "BOOK IMAGE" field display on the List of

		Fields and the "Field Saved" "Success Message" Panel is also displayed. Close it before proceeding.

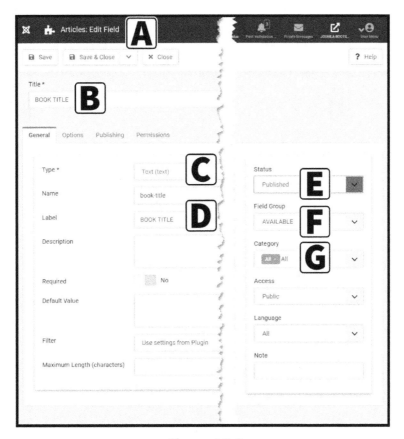

Figure 13-4

Refer to Figure 13-4 for the following:

Step 13	A	Select the **"New"** button, which will open the "Articles: Edit Field" Workspace.
Step 14	B	In the "Title" field, enter: "BOOK TITLE" (without quotes).
Step 15	C	For "Type," select: "Text."
Step 16	D	For the "Label," enter "BOOK TITLE" (without quotes). The text can be changed manually.
Step 17	E	Make the "Status" to "Published."
Step 18	F	In the "Field Groups" field, to the right, select: "AVAILABLE."
Step 19	G	Make sure that **"ALL"** is selected in the "Category" field.
Step 20		Execute a Save & Close action.
Step 21	F	The result should have the "BOOK TITLE" field display on the List of

		Fields and the "Field Saved" "Success Message" Panel is also displayed. Close it before proceeding.

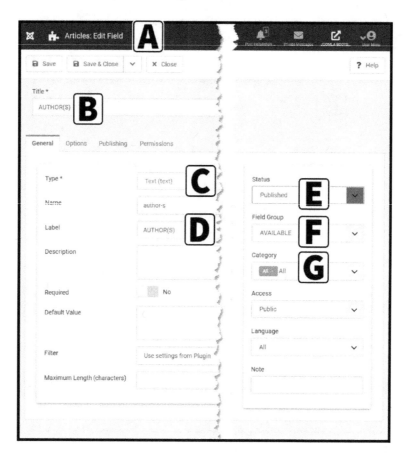

Figure 13-5

Refer to Figure 13-5 for the following:

Step 22	A	Select the **"New"** button, which will open the "Articles: Edit Field" Workspace.
Step 23	B	In the "Title" field, enter: "AUTHOR(S)" (without quotes).
Step 24	C	For "Type," select: "Text."
Step 25	D	For the "Label," enter "AUTHOR(S)" (without quotes). This field will populate itself automatically, but the text can be changed manually.
Step 26	E	Make the "Status" to "Published."
Step 27	F	In the "Field Groups" field, to the right, select: "AVAILABLE."
Step 28	G	Make sure that **"ALL"** is selected in the "Category" field.
Step 29		Execute a Save & Close action.

	The result should have the "AUTHOR(S)" field display on the List of Fields and the "Field Saved" "Success Message" Panel is also displayed. Close it before proceeding.

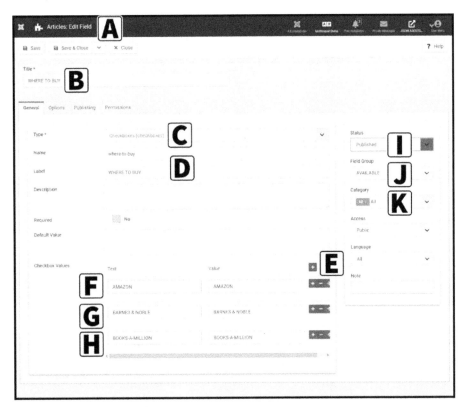

Figure 13-6

Refer to Figure 13-6 for the following:

Step 30	A	Select the **"New"** button, which will open the "Articles: Edit Field" Workspace.
Step 31	B	In the "Title" field, enter: "WHERE TO BUY" (without quotes).
Step 32	C	For "Type," select: "Checkboxes."
Step 33	D	For the "Label," enter "WHERE TO BUY" (without quotes). This field will populate itself automatically, but the text can be changed manually.
Step 34	E	At the bottom of the screen, in the "Checkbox Values" section, click on the green **"+"** button.
Step 35	F	In the "Text" Field, enter "Amazon US" (without quotes).
Step 36	F	In the "Value" Field, enter "Amazon US" (without quotes).
Step 37	E	Click on the green **"+"** button.

Step 38	G	In the "Text" Field, enter "Amazon UK" (without quotes).
Step 35	G	In the "Value" Field, enter "Amazon UK" (without quotes).
Step 36	E	Click on the green "+" button.
Step 37	H	In the "Text" Field, enter "Barnes & Noble" (without quotes).
Step 38	H	In the "Value" Field, enter "Barnes & Noble" (without quotes).
Step 39	I	Make the "Status" to "Published."
Step 40	J	In the "Field Groups" field, to the right, select: "AVAILABLE."
Step 41	K	Make sure that **"ALL"** is selected in the "Category" field.
Step 42		Execute a Save & Close action.
		The result should have the "WHERE TO BUY" field display on the List of Fields and the "Field Saved" "Success Message" Panel is also displayed. Close it before proceeding.

No settings need to be configured under the "Options, Publishing or Permissions" tabs. The default settings are sufficient.

Also, on the List of Fields view, note that there is an informational column that indicates which Field Category the individual Fields are assigned, meaning that the list view may be filtered by Field Groups if desired.

The above Exercise has now created Fields within the "AVAILABLE" Fields Group. The same Fields, for demonstration purposes, should be created in the "COMING" Fields Group, although they could be completely different from the previous Fields in the "AVIALABLE" Field Group.

Fields Within "COMING" Fields Group

Step 1	A C	On the "Home Dashboard," go to: "Content > Fields," to display the List of Fields.
Step 2	B	The Workspace screen is identified as: "Articles: Fields."
Step 3	D	The Field is to be created within the "Articles," not the "Categories," which is the other choice of Field Group type.
Step 4	E	Select the **"New"** button, which will open the "Articles: Edit Field" Workspace.

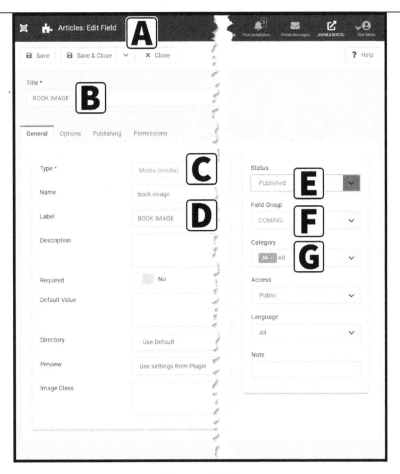

Figure 13-7

Refer to Figure 13-7 for the following:

Step 5	A	The Workspace screen should be the "Articles: Edit Field."
Step 6	B	In the "Title" field, enter: "BOOK IMAGE" (without quotes).
Step 7	C	For "Type," select: "Media."
Step 8	D	This field will populate itself automatically, but the text can be changed manually. If an error is displayed, put a "-1" at the end (without the quotes).
Step 9	E	Make the "Status" to "Published."
Step 10	F	In the "Field Groups" field, to the right, select: "COMING."
Step 11	G	Make sure that **"ALL"** is selected in the "Category" field.
Step 12		Execute a Save & Close action. If an error message displays, in the "Name" Field, enter: "book-image-2" (without the quotes). Execute the Save & Close action again.

		The result should have the "BOOK IMAGE" field display on the List of Fields and the "Field Saved" "Success Message" Panel is also displayed. Close it before proceeding.

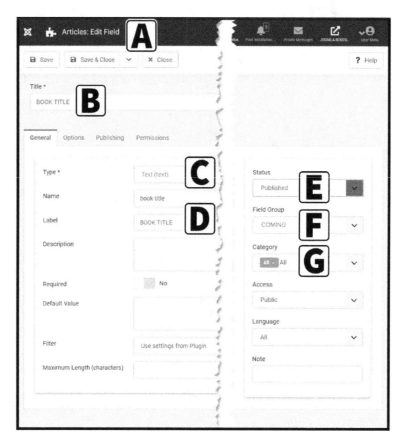

Figure 13-8

Refer to Figure 13-8 for the following:

Step 13	A	Select the **"New"** button, which will open the "Articles: Edit Field" Workspace.
Step 14	B	In the "Title" field, enter: "BOOK TITLE" (without quotes).
Step 15	C	For "Type," select: "Text."
Step 16	D	For the "Label," enter "BOOK TITLE" (without quotes). This field will populate itself automatically, but the text can be changed manually.
Step 17	E	Make the "Status" to "Published."
Step 18	F	In the "Field Groups" field, to the right, select: "COMING."
Step 19	G	Make sure that **"ALL"** is selected in the "Category" field.
Step 20		Execute a Save & Close action. If an error message displays, in the

		"Name" Field, enter: "book-title-2" (without the quotes). Execute the Save & Close action again.
Step 21	**F**	The result should have the "BOOK TITLE" field display on the List of Fields and the "Field Saved" "Success Message" Panel is also displayed. Close it before proceeding.

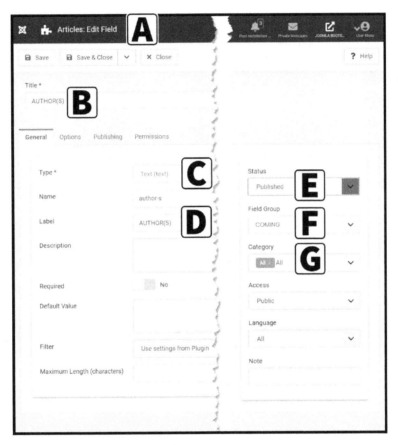

Figure 13-9

Refer to Figure 13-9 for the following:

Step 22	**A**	Select the **"New"** button, which will open the "Articles: Edit Field" Workspace.
Step 23	**B**	In the "Title" field, enter: "AUTHOR(S)" (without quotes).
Step 24	**C**	For "Type," select: "Text."
Step 25	**D**	For the "Label," enter "AUTHOR(S)" (without quotes).
Step 26	**E**	Make the "Status" to "Published."
Step 27	**F**	In the "Field Groups" field, to the right, select: "COMING."
Step 28	**G**	Make sure that **"ALL"** is selected in the "Category" field.

Step 29	Execute a Save & Close action. If an error message displays, in the "Name" Field, enter: "authors-2" (without the quotes). Execute the Save & Close action again.
	The result should have the "AUTHOR(S)" field display on the List of Fields and the "Field Saved" "Success Message" Panel is also displayed. Close it before proceeding.

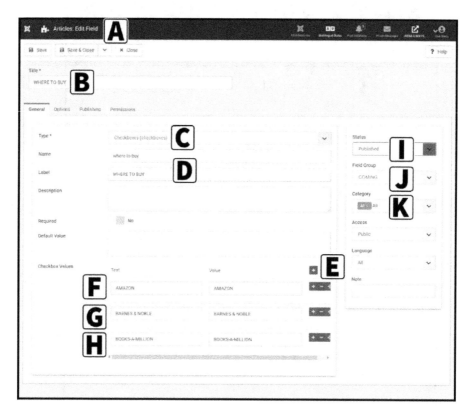

Figure 13-10

Refer to Figure 13-10 for the following:

Step 30	A	Select the **"New"** button, which will open the "Articles: Edit Field" Workspace.
Step 31	B	In the "Title" field, enter: "WHERE TO BUY" (without quotes).
Step 32	C	For "Type," select: "Checkboxes."
Step 33	D	For the "Label," enter "WHERE TO BUY" (without quotes).
Step 34	E	Click on the green "+" button.
Step 35	F	In the "Text" Field, enter "Amazon" (without quotes).
Step 36	F	In the "Value" Field, enter "Amazon" (without quotes).

Step 37	E	Click on the green "+" button.
Step 38	G	In the "Text" Field, enter "Barnes & Noble" (without quotes).
Step 35	G	In the "Value" Field, enter "Barnes & Noble" (without quotes).
Step 36	E	Click on the green "+" button.
Step 37	H	In the "Text" Field, enter "Books-a-Million" (without quotes).
Step 38	H	In the "Value" Field, enter "Books-a-Million" (without quotes).
Step 39	I	Make the "Status" to "Published."
Step 40	J	In the "Field Groups" field, to the right, select: "COMING."
Step 41	K	Make sure that **"ALL"** is selected in the "Category" field.
Step 42		Execute a Save & Close action. If an error message displays, in the "Name" Field, enter: "where-to-buy-2" (without the quotes). Execute the Save & Close action again.
		The result should have the "WHERE TO BUY" field display on the List of Fields and the "Field Saved" "Success Message" Panel is also displayed. Close it before proceeding.

No settings need to be configured under the "Options, Publishing or Permissions" tabs. The default settings are sufficient.

The above Exercises have created four Fields within the "AVAILABLE" and the "COMING" Field Groups. The "WHERE TO BUY" field selections are different in each Field Group.

The Results

At this point, there have been Fields created within the two Field Groups. These data fields may now be used in Articles and each Field Group will appear as a tab within the Article Workspace as shown in Figure 13-11. They cannot be used in "Categories" because they were not created within the "Category" group.

You will note the tabs above the Article Content section. By clicking on the tab, it opens the Field within the Field Group as identified by the tab. In this case, they both appear identical because the same Fields have been created within each Field Group being used. Also, note that ALL of the Fields created display when the respective Tab is opened. These Fields then simply act like a "form" to be filled out by the Author.

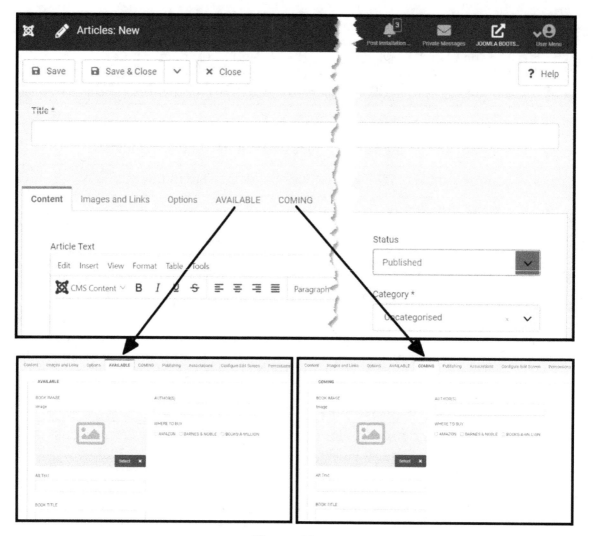

Figure 13-11

Here's the most important point about Field and Field Groups. They are "available" for use, but their use is not required. In other words, Articles can be written without the inclusion of the Fields.

If the Field information is not populated or content added to the Fields, it will not appear in the Article. If any bit of information is added, the Fields will automatically appear within the Article, either above or below the text Content.

The location of the Field data display can be designated to appear before or after the Content within the Article. This allows various configurations to be created and they will be demonstrated below. This option can be invoked on an Article by Article basis to be "Above, Below or Split."

One Field Group Only

A single Field Group may be used only one time within an Article. However, if several Field Groups have been created and are available, each individual Field may be used, but only once each per Article. In this case, "AVAILABLE" fields can be used only once; "COMING" fields can only be used once.

Articles with Fields

In the following examples and Exercises, two Articles will be created with their Fields populated. Several options will be included in the layout creations and how the Fields are used.

EXERCISE 13-3: CREATING ARTICLES WITH FIELD CONTENT

Objective: The objective of this exercise will be to create two Articles, one using the "AVAILABLE" Field Groups, another using the "COMING" Field Groups.

Before proceeding:
Before creating Articles below, please create the following Article Categories:

1. **BOOKS** – as a "Parent" Category.

2. **BOOKS AVAILABLE** – as a "Child" Category to "BOOKS."

3. **BOOKS COMING** – as a "Child" Category to "BOOKS."

The steps needed to create Categories is not being repeated here. At this point in the book, as a Joomla! 5 website Administrator, the process of creating Categories should be "second nature" and a task that is easily performed.

When completed, check the List of Categories for the following:

- BOOKS
- BOOKS AVAILABLE
- BOOKS COMING

The Articles created below will be assigned to one of these two categories, and there will be Menu Link Items created that will open the Categories to display the List of Articles assigned to them.

Refer to Chapter 9, "CONTENT: Categories" if you need to review the steps and actions needed to create Categories, or Chapter 10, "CONTENT: Articles."

Article with "AVAIALBLE" Fields

Step 1	A	On the "Home Dashboard," go to: "Control Panel > Content > Articles," in the left menu, or click the **"+"** symbol in the "Articles" button area of the Site Panel of the "Home Dashboard."

Step 2	B	In the Title field, enter: "ARTICLE – BOOKS AVAILABLE" (without quotes).
Step 3	C	In the Article Content area, enter a paragraph of two of text. Can be "lorem ipsum" text if desired, which is what is used in the Article example.
Step 4	D	Execute a Save action after adding the paragraphs to lock in the content of the Article.
Step 5	E	Open the "AVAILABLE" tab, which is the Field Group that was created in an earlier Exercise. This opens the Fields Workspace for the "AVAILABLE" Field Group.

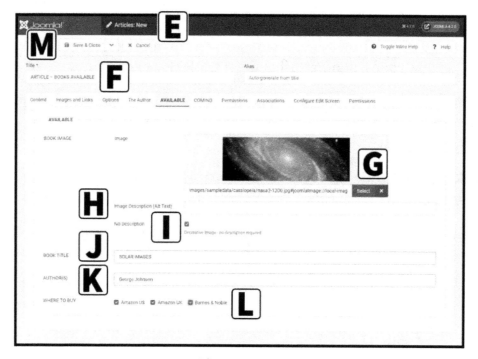

Figure 13-12

Refer to Figure 13-12 for the following:

Step 6	F	In the "BOOK TITLE" field, enter: "SPACE IMAGES" (without quotes).
Step 7	G	In the "BOOK IMAGE" Field, click on the "Select" button. This will open the Joomla! 5 Media Manager, wherein there are folders with images, or you can upload your own image.
Step 8		Open the "sampledata > cassiopeia" folder and any "640 x" image by clicking on it. When the check mark appears on the image, click on the "Insert" button at the lower right. When that action is completed, the "AVAILABLE" Fields will appear and the image is shown in place.

Step 9		Execute a Save action. It is wise to do this after adding an image into a Field.
Step 10	H	In the "Image Description" Field, enter: "Description of the Image." (without quotes). This is the "ALT" description for an image, if used.

Note that there is an over-ride for the required description by ticking the "No Description" box, indicating that this is a "Decorative Image – no description desired."

Step 10	I	Do not check the "No Description" choice.
Step 11	J	For the "Book Title," enter: "SPACE IMAGES" (without quotes).
Step 12	K	In the "Authors" field, enter: "George Johnson" (without quotes).
Step 13	L	Select all tick boxes in the "Where to Buy" Field.
Step 14	M	Execute a Save & Close action.

At this point, the Article has been created and the Fields within the "AVAILABLE" Field Group have been created. It is now necessary to create a Menu Link Item so Users may access the Article on the Front-End.

Step 15		On the "Home Dashboard," go to: "Control Panel > Menus" and open the "Main Menu."
Step 16		Click on the **"+New"** button at the top left of the Workspace.
Step 17		For the Menu Title, enter: "FIELD GROUP DEMO" (without quotes).
Step 18		For Menu Item Type, select: "Single Article."
Step 19		Select the "ARTICLE-BOOKS AVAILABLE" in the next field.
Step 20		At the right, make sure "Main Menu" is selected.
Step 21		Set the "Status" to "Published."
Step 22		Execute a Save & Close action.
Step 23		Go to the Front-end and refresh the screen.
Step 24		In the "Main Menu," select: "FIELD GROUP DEMO."
Step 25		The "Field Group Article" should display in the Main Content Area showing the Fields from the Field Group above the main Content of the Article and should include the image and the information inserted/selected in the other fields.

Observations – Field Group Article:

Here are several observations to be made on the resulting "Field Group Article," that includes the "AVAILABLE" Fields Group and the "Fields" as selected in the Exercise.

First	Notice that the Fields are displayed above the Content text. Each Field may be located above or below the Content Text, which allows for some creative use of the Fields. An Exercise below will demonstrate how to change this location.
Second	This is an obvious glitch or serious error in the Template CSS coding because there is a round bullet in front of each Field Name. This is an obvious error. Please refer to Chapter 47, "ADMIN: Library of Overrides" in *Boots on the Ground, Advance Edition, Volume 2* for instructions on how to change and/or correct this issue.
Third	Field Labels are displaying. Field Labels can be set to "NOT SHOW," and this will be covered in an Exercise below
Fourth	The image was added in its uploaded size. The size of the image may be changed in the Media Manager and instructions on how to do this can be found in Chapter 20, "VISUAL: Images & Media Manager."
Fifth	Within the Article, the "AVAILABLE" Field Group may only be used one time, conforming to the Rule that only a single Field Group may display within an Article. However, more than one, if different, Field Group may be displayed.

Customizing the Display of Fields

As noted above, the display of the Fields within the Field Groups can be customized. The Field Labels can be set to "Hide," or not display. Each individual field may also be configured to display either above or below the Content Text within the Article. The location is absolute to above or below. It cannot be set to display between, for example, separate paragraphs of text.

The below Exercises will demonstrate how to customize the Fields.

Each Field Configuration is Separate

The customization of Fields is performed on an individual basis. This means that the settings or configuration for each must be individually set based on the desired results. There are no global settings within the Field Groups that can be set. However, the default settings are: A) Field Labels are set to "Show," and B) the location of all Fields is set to be "Above" the Content Text by default.

EXERCISE 13-4: REMOVE LABELS FROM FIELDS

Objective: The objective of this Exercise is to demonstrate how to remove, or set to "hide" or "not display" the Field Label of a Field, in this case, the "Image" Field.

Step 1	On the "Home Dashboard," go to: "Control Panel > Content > Fields," and select "BOOK IMAGE" in the "AVAILABLE" Field Group.
Step 2	In the "BOOK IMAGE" Workspace, open the "Options" tab.
Step 3	Scroll down to the "Display Options" section.
Step 4	Set the "Label" button to "Hide" from the default "Show" option. The configuration setting will change.
Step 5	Execute a Save & Close action.
Step 6	Go to the website Front-End and refresh the screen.
Step 7	Access the "FIELD GROUP DEMO" in the "Main Menu."
Step 8	Notice now that the "IMAGE" Field Label no longer displays, but the bullet still appears – this will be fixed in an Exercise in Chapter 47, "ADMIN: Library of Overrides" *Boots on the Ground, Advance Edition, Volume 2.*

Each individual Field, regardless of "Type," may have the option to "Show" or "Hide" the Field Label set using the above steps or sequence of steps.

EXERCISE 13-5: POSITION OF THE FIELDS

Objective: The goal of this Exercise is to demonstrate the methods or action steps needed to relocate Field positions from the default "Above" the Content Text, to a location designated as "Below," or after the Content Text. The "WHERE TO BUY" Field will be relocated from "Above" to "Below."

Step 1	On the "Home Dashboard," go to: "Control Panel > Content > Fields," and select "BOOK IMAGE" in the "AVAILABLE" Field Group.
Step 2	In the "WHERE TO BUY" Workspace, open the "Options" tab.
Step 3	Scroll down to the "Display Options" section.
Step 4	Set the "Automatic Display" selector from "Before Display" to "After Display Content." The default setting may be "Before Display Content."
Step 5	Execute a Save & Close action.
Step 6	Go to the website Front-End and refresh the screen.
Step 7	Access the "FIELD GROUP DEMO" in the "Main Menu."
Step 8	Notice now that the "WHERE TO BUY" Field has now been relocated after the

| | Article Text from its previous location of "Before." |

Each individual Field, regardless of "Type," may have the option to relocate the display from "Before" to "After" if desired.

Article with "COMING" Fields

In the exact same manner as in the Exercises above, the "COMING" fields may be added to Articles, either as a single Field Group, or in association with the "AVAILABLE" Field Group.

When a second, or subsequent Field Group's Fields are used in an Article, they will, by default, display: A) "Before" the Content Text, and B) immediately below the Fields from the previous Field Group.

The order of display is in the same order as the Field Group order in the tab row. The "order" may be changed within the Field Groups List by changing their order on that list.

This is done in the same manner as relocating the Categories or Articles on a list, or rearranging the "order" of Modules. Perform this re-ordering in the column to the left of "Status."

When used in combination, several Field Groups and their respective Fields may be used to insert information "Before" or "After" the Content Text. This can be done selectively so there is some wide latitude on how the information is displayed.

JOOMLA!® 5
BOOTS ON THE GROUND
Advance Edition
Volume 1

CHAPTER 14

CONTENT:
Weblinks

In previous versions of Joomla!, there was a Component entitled: "Weblinks." Back in the early days of the internet, website Administrators did a lot of "chest-thumping" about the number of "links" on their website that connected to other websites. This was almost at a pandemic level of use. As a result of the popularity of "weblinks," a Joomla! Component was created and included in the default installation. That is no longer the case. "Weblinks" have been relegated to the level of being an optional add-in Extension level and are no longer part of the Components that are added during installation of Joomla! 5.

The "Weblinks" Extension is also one of the very, very few Extensions that have been created by the Joomla! Developer Team. Most all Extensions are typically created by Third-Party Developers.

ABOUT THE "Weblinks" COMPONENT

The use of the "Weblinks" Component is self-explained. It is a Component that must be installed after the Joomla! 5 website is established. It is installed in the same manner as all other Extensions. The file is sourced, downloaded and the Extension install procedure is implemented. When completed, the "Weblinks" appears within the Components Menu. It does not show or display on the "Home Dashboard" area. The "Weblinks" Component is accessed in the same manner as all others via the left Menu, under "Components."

Weblinks Parts

The "Weblinks" Component consists of four major parts, as explained below. Note the similarity of organization that is established for "Weblinks," which is very similar to that of the "Contacts" Component, as follows:

Links	These are the actual "URL" links that will connect to other websites. They can be categorized, have "ACL" features along with "Publish/Unpublish" settings. The browser target window can be designated. Images may also be added. Because they are near-like Contacts and Articles, "MetaData" can also be added.
Categories	Categories are used to establish a hierarchy of "Weblinks" which may also contain "Child" Categories, similar to the same method as explained for Categories that apply to Articles. These Categories have no relationship or integration with any other Category as they relate to their respective Content Items.
Fields	Similar to "Content Fields," these can be added selectively to each "Weblink" that is created. As in "Content Fields," there are the same "types" of Fields available to be included with any "Weblink" that is created. They can be very helpful in narrowing the definition of, or information about, the "Weblink" that is being created.
Field Groups	The "Field Groups" are just another term for "Categories," but named differently to distinguish them as applying to only "Fields." These are sometimes necessary to create a logical order among large numbers of "Weblinks."

Obtaining the "Weblinks" Extension

As previously mentioned, the "Weblinks" Component is one of the very few Extensions that are sourced directly from the Joomla! Developers, or the Development Team. It is their work product and does not derive itself from any third-party. Which is great. This reduces the complications that might be associated with it.

Use the "JED" to Obtain the Component

Obtaining the "Weblinks" Component installation files is very easy, and the steps involved are outlined below:

Step 1	Access the joomla.org website location.
Step 2	Under the "Download & Extend" Menu Link Item at the top, select "Extensions" among the drop-down selections.
Step 3	In the Search field, enter: "Weblinks" (without the quotes), then execute the search action. A number of "Weblink" type Extensions will appear for

	download.
Step 4	Scroll down and find the "Weblinks" Extension with the Joomla! logo. It also indicates that it is an "OFFICIAL EXTENSION." The box will also indicate it is compatible with J!3, J!4. If not noted, it will also work with J!5.
Step 5	Click on the Extension's box to access the Extension download screen.
Step 6	At this point, you can view the Extension Demo and view the Documentation associated with the "Weblinks" Extension.

Note: Because this is a Package ("Pkg") file, take note that it includes a Component, Module and Plugin. It may be necessary to take further action with each of those items after installation to utilize the "Weblinks" on a website.

Step 7	Click on the "Install" button at the top to initiate the install process.
Step 8	The action will initiate a screen scroll, and when at the bottom of the screen, execute the "Install" action again.
Step 9	Monitor the download. The Joomla! logo will display during this time.
Step 8	When the download is completed, the Extension should be installed via the normal procedure, as discussed in previous Chapters, which will add "Weblinks" to the Component list, and also add a "Weblinks" Module and an associated Plugin. If there is a Plugin that needs to be activated, the system will alert you to that required action when attempting to use "Weblinks."

At this point, the assumption is being made that the installation of "Weblinks" on your Joomla! 5 instance has been successfully completed.

Spelling/Terms for Weblinks

You might see "Weblinks" or "Web Links" as the descriptive term on the Joomla! website. For standardization, "Weblinks," as one word, is the term that will be used in this book. However, the "Web Links" term will be used when the Back-End screen displays it exactly that way.

How to Display Weblinks

The individual "Weblinks" can be displayed in several different ways, which is why the Component can be useful. It can be displayed as a regular Component in the Main Content Area. It may also be selectively displayed within a Module assigned to any logical Module Position. Each will be demonstrated in the Exercises below.

However, it is necessary to be informed on the different methods, through Menu Link Items, by which the "Weblinks" can be displayed. While using the different methods, compare them to how Articles are handled and managed. "Weblinks" are keenly similar to Articles except their display simply contains links and descriptions, and possibly images, versus textual content. These will be demonstrated below. Here are the display choices for "Weblinks:"

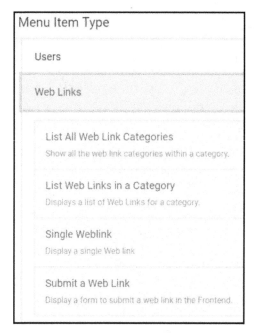

Figure 14-1

List All Web Link Categories	This option will display all of the "Parent" Categories within the "Weblinks" Component, including any "child" or "Sub-Categories" that may have been created. Empty "Weblink" Categories can be set to "not display."
List "Weblinks" in a Category	All of the "Weblinks" within a selected individual "Weblink" Category are displayed using this choice.
Single Weblink	This displays a single "Weblink" that may be enhanced with extended text and images within the description. Images such as those for logos and/or products can be included. The display can be very creative, such as something that might be used for advertising a product or a service on another website. It may also be used as a link-back to some type of Content on your own website.
Submit a Web Link	If a Menu Link Item is created of the type to "Submit Weblink," executing this link will open a form into which the "Weblink" information can be entered, including into specific "Weblink Categories." The creator must log into the Front-End

	to access the submission form. This obviously requires the User to have "Registered" User permissions, along with "allowed" permissions for various actions. These permissions can be "fine-tuned" to other User Groups and configuring their permissions to submit "Weblinks" after log in.

Creating Weblinks

In the Exercises below, "Weblinks" will be created, but not in the order as displayed above, or how they appear in the Menu to access them. The Exercises will be performed in this logical use-sequence order:

1. Create a "Weblink" Category – if more than "uncategorized" is required.

2. Create a "Weblink" Field Group – if groups are desired.

3. Create a "Weblink" Field – if fields are desired.

4. Create a Weblink.

The logical process is to create "Weblink" Categories, Field Groups and Fields before creating an actual "Weblink" itself.

General "Weblink" Plan

In the following Exercises, the creation of the "Weblink" elements described above will be included, along with the creation of a new "Registered" User Group that will have permissions to log into the Front-End of the website and create "Weblinks." This means that the "Public" or "Guest" Users will not be able to submit "Weblinks;" only those that have "Registered" and are in the designated User Group will be able to do so. The default for use of the "Submit Weblink" is reserved for the Administrator. However, privileges can be extended to any "Registered User" through the use of the "ACL" configurations.

In addition, the "Submit a Weblink" Menu Link Item, that will be located in the "Main Menu," will not be visible to any Users, other than one that is "Registered."

EXERCISE 14-1: CREATE A "WEBLINK" CATEGORY

Objective: This Exercise will demonstrate the method used to create a "Weblink" Category. A default "Weblink" Category of "Uncategorized" exists, but it is not the same as the "Uncategorized" that is used with Articles; same concept but not the same element. While sharing the same name, they do not share the same hosting space for their designated Categories. The Category creation in this Exercise applies only to those for Weblinks.

Step 1		On the "Home Dashboard," go to: "Components > Web Links," to open the choices within that Components Sub-Menu.

Step 2		Open the "Weblinks > Categories" link to open the "Weblinks Category" workspace. A list of the existing "Weblinks Categories" will display, showing the default of "Uncategorized."
Step 3	A	Select the **"New"** button, which will open the "Web Links: New Category" Workspace.

Refer to Figure 14-2 for the following:

Step 4	B	In the "Title" field, enter: "Weblink Category One," (without the quotes).
Step 5	C	Select the "Category" Tab. Enter a description of this "Weblinks Category" as follows: "This is the first Category created within the "Weblinks" Component." (without the quotes).
Step 6		Do not, at this time, enter any information under the "Options," "Publishing" or "Permissions" tabs.
Step 7		Do not make any changes in any selection options on the choices of configuration at the right side.
Step 8	D	Execute a Save & Close action.
Step 9		As a result of Step 7, only the "Uncategorized" and "Weblink Category One" should appear on the list that is displayed.

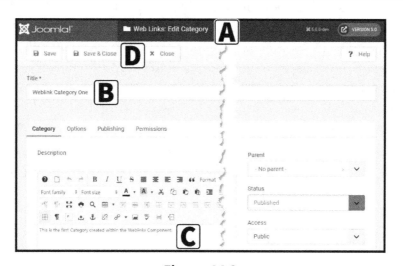

Figure 14-2

EXERCISE 14-2: CREATE A WEBSITE FIELD GROUP

Objective: This Exercise will demonstrate the method used to create a "Weblink Field Group." No default Field Group exists. Each Field Group must be created and assigned to a "Field Group Category." The Field Group creation in this Exercise applies only to those for "Weblinks." The "Field Groups" that are used with Articles are not the same and cannot be interchangeably used.

Step 1		On the "Home Dashboard," go to: "Components > Web Links," to open the choices within that Components Sub-Menu.
Step 2		Open the "Weblinks > Field Groups" link to open the "Weblinks Field Groups" workspace. The message: "No Matching Results" should display, given that none have yet been created, or installed by any Extension or addition actions of the "Sample Data."
Step 3	A	Select the **"New"** button, which will open the "Web Links: New Field Group" Workspace.

Refer to Figure 14-3 for the following:

Step 4	B	In the "Title" field, enter: "Field Group A," (without the quotes).
Step 5	C	Select the "General" Tab. Enter a description of this "Weblinks Field Group" as follows: "This is Group A for "Weblinks" Category One." (without the quotes).
Step 6		Do not, at this time, enter any information under the "Options," "Publishing" or "Permissions" tabs.
Step 7	D	The "Status" setting should be: "Published."
Step 8	E	The "Access" should be set to: "Public."
Step 9	F	Execute a Save & New action.
Step 10		As a result of Step 7, only the "Field Group A" should appear on the resulting list that is displayed.

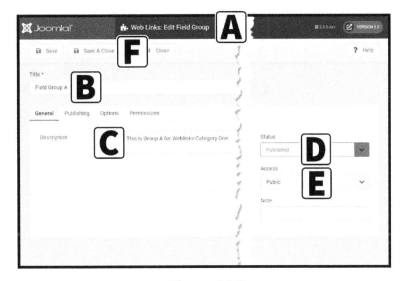

Figure 14-3

EXERCISE 14-3: CREATE A "WEBLINK" FIELD

Objective: This Exercise will demonstrate the method used to create a "Weblink Field." One default "Field Group" exists entitled: "Link Name." Each new Field must be created and assigned to a "Field Group Category." The Field creation in this Exercise applies only to those for "Weblinks." The "Fields" that are used with Articles are not the same and cannot be interchangeably used.

Step 1		On the "Home Dashboard," go to: "Components > Web Links," to open the choices within that Components Sub-Menu.
Step 2		Open the "Components >Weblinks > Fields" link to open the Fields workspace. One Field, "Link Name" might already be on the list displayed. Disregard this Field.

Refer to Figure 14-4 for the following:

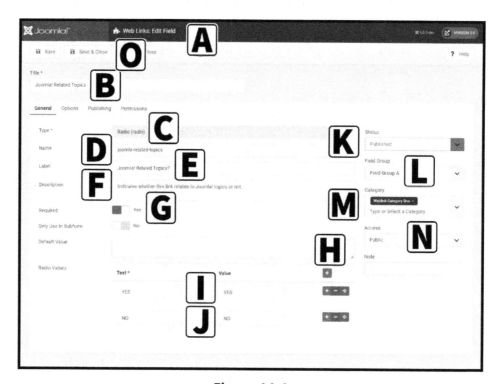

Figure 14-4

Step 3	A	Select the **"New"** button, which will open the "Web Links: New Field" Workspace.
Step 4	B D	In the "Title" field, enter: "Joomla! Related Topics" (without the quotes).
Step 5	C	In the "Type" field, select: "RADIO (radio)."
Step 6		Execute a Save action.

Step 7	E	For the "Label," enter: "Joomla! Related Topics?" (without the quotes). This are the words that will appear to the left of the link's input field. By default, this is usually the same as the Link's "Title," but can be changed to anything, as was done in this example.
Step 8	F	In the "Description" field, enter: "Indicates whether this link relates to Joomla! topics or not." (without quotes).
Step 9	G	Toggle the "Required" field to: "Yes" (without quotes).
Step 10	H	Scroll down to "Radio Values" and click on the green [+] to the far right. This will open new input areas below.
Step 11	I	In each field block, enter "YES" (without quotes).
Step 12	H	Click again on the green [+] to the right of the last input area. This will open new input areas.
Step 13	J	In each field block, enter "NO" (without quotes).
Step 14		Execute a Save action.
Step 15		The results, at this point should be two choices for the Radio Button type. Radio Buttons allow only one of the items to be chosen, regardless of the number of choices available.
Step 16	K	In the choices in the right column, select the following, in addition to making sure the Field is "Published."
Step 17	L	For the "Field Group," select: "Field Group A."
Step 18	M	For the "Category," select: "Weblink Category One." This permits limiting certain Fields to specified "Weblink" Categories, or multiple Categories.
Step 19	N	Access should remain set as "Public."
Step 20		Do not, at this time, enter any information under the "Options," "Publishing" or "Permissions" tabs.
Step 21		Do not make any changes in any other selection options in the right.
Step 22	O	Execute a Save & Close action.
Step 23		As a result of Step 14, the link should display and "Field Group A" should appear with "Link Name" under the "Field Group" on the list that is displayed.

EXERCISE 14-4: CREATING WEBLINKS, TWO METHODS

Objective: This Exercise will demonstrate the creation of a "Weblink" by two distinctly different methods:

Method 1 will be a "Weblink" created by the Administrator ["Super User"] in the Back-end. This method would typically be used when the Administrator is the only creator of Content on the website.

Method 2 by a designated Registered User via the website Front-End. This activity may also be performed by other Users that have appropriate permissions with respect to the "Weblinks" Component, re: create, edit, etc. This method can be used when additional Content Editors have permissions to add "Weblinks" to the website.

Method 1: "Weblink" by Administrator via Back-End

Step 1		Log into the website Back-End "Home Dashboard" as the Administrator [Super User].
Step 2		On the "Home Dashboard," go to: "Components> Web Links," to open the choices within that Component's Sub-Menu.
Step 3		Open the "Components > "Weblinks" > Links" to open the "Links Workspace." There should be no "Weblinks" listed and the screen will display a message indicating as such, with a link button to "Add your first Web Link."
Step 4	A	Click on **"Add your first Web Link"** or select the **"New"** button at the top of the screen, which will open the "Web Links: New Field" Workspace.

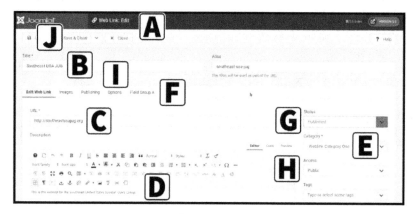

Figure 14-5

Refer to Figure 14-5 for the following:

Step 5	B	In the "Title" field, enter: "Southeast USA JUG" (without quotes).
Step 6	C	In the "URL" field, enter: "southeastusajug.org" (without quotes).

Step 7	D	Enter this into the "Description" field: "This is the website for the Southeast United States Joomla! Users Group." (without quotes).

Notice that, above the Description field, there is no "Field Group" displayed, even though one has already been created. The next step will resolve that issue.

Step 8	E	In the "Category" field, select: "Weblink Category One." This will automatically trigger a screen refresh, after which, the "Field Group A" Tab will display. Because "Field Groups" are associated with "Field Group Categories," they do no display until formally assigned, and then added automatically.
Step 9	F	Click on the "Field Group A" Tab. Each "Field" in the Group will be listed. In this case, it should only be one.
Step 10		Toggle the selection to "YES," because the links is related in some way to a Joomla! topic.
Step 11	G	In the right column, the "Status" should be "Published."
Step 12	E	In the "Category" field, double check to confirm that is displays: "Weblink Category One."
Step 13	H	Set the "Access" to "Public."
Step 14	I	Access the "Options" tab in the "Web Link: Edit Workspace."
Step 15		In the "Target" field, select: "Open in new window."
Step 16	J	Execute a Save & Close action.

The "Weblinks" Module that displays the "Weblinks" created in this, and the next, Exercise will be created below in Exercise 14-4. It is a specialized form of a "Menu" but created specifically to display "Weblinks" on the website.

Creating the "Weblinks" Menu Link Items

As with any Content Item, any "Weblink" that is created must have an associated Menu Link Item to open it directly, or open the individual "Weblink Category" in which it is assigned, or open the "List of "Weblink" Categories." The Exercise below will create a "Weblinks" Menu within the previously created "Main Menu".

EXERCISE 14-5: CREATING A "WEBLINKS" MENU LINK ITEM

Objective: This Exercise will demonstrate how to create a single Menu Link Item to a single "Weblink." First, a new User will be created. Then, the Menu Link Item to a "Single Weblink" will be created in the "Main Menu." This new User is needed because, at this point, only the Administrator is the only User that can successfully log into the website Front-End.

Creating the New User

Step 1		If not already there, Login and open the "Home Dashboard" on the website Back-End.
Step 2		In the left Menu, open: "Users > Manage" to open the "List of Users." The User that will be added will also be used as part of Chapter 32: "ADMIN: Workflows," in *Joomla!4: Boots on the Ground, Advance Edition, Volume 2.*
Step 3	A	At the top of the screen, click on the **"+New"** button that will open the "New User" creation Workspace.

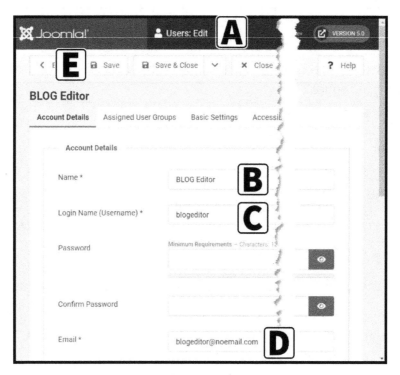

Figure 14-6

Refer to Figure 14-6 for the following:

Step 4	B	For the "User Name," enter: "Blog Editor" (without quotes).
Step 5	C	For the "Login Name (Username) *" enter: "blogeditor" (without quotes).
Step 6	D	For the "Email," enter: "blogeditor@noemail.com" (without quotes) which is a non-existent email address. Because the new User will not need to verify their email address, any email can be inserted here for demonstration purposes ("@noemail.com").
Step 7		Scroll down and set the "User Status" to "Enabled."
Step 8	E	Execute a Save action. The "Success Message" should display.

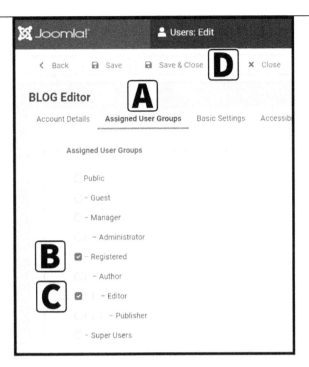

Figure 14-7

Refer to Figure 14-7 for the following:

Step 9	A	Open the "Assigned User Group" Tab.
Step 10	B C	Assign this new User to: 1) the "Registered" Group, and 2) the "Editor" Group.
Step 11	D	Execute a Save & Close action. The "Success Message" should display.
Step 12		In the "Home Dashboard" click on "Global Configuration" to the right, which will open the "Site" configurations area.
Step 13		Scroll down the "System" list and click on "Web Links," which opens the "Web Links Manager Options" screen.

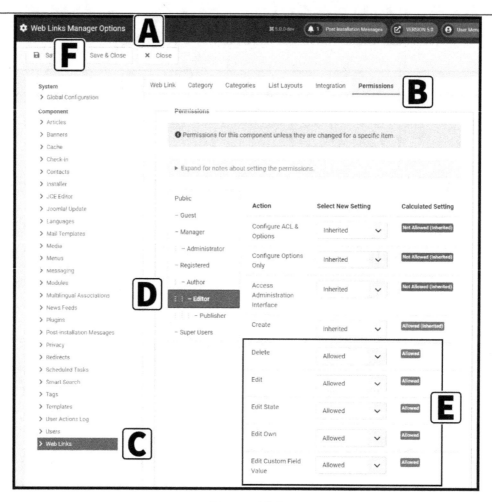

Figure 14-8

Refer to Figure 14-8 for the following:

Step 14	B	Open the "Permissions" Tab.
Step 15	D	Click on the "Editor" Group.
Step 16	E	Make these modifications to the "Permissions" by setting the to "Allowed" (green indicator), for the following "Actions:" • Create • Delete • Edit • Edit State • Edit Own • Edit Custom Field Value
Step 17		Execute a Save & Close action.

The "blogeditor" User now has Front-End access as "Registered" along with the allowed permissions for modification of their own "Weblinks." This User will be utilized in

Exercise 14-6.

Creating the Menu Link Item

Step 1		If not already there, Login and open the "Home Dashboard" on the website Back-End.
Step 2		In the left Menu, open: "Menus > Main Menu" to open the "List of Menu Link Items" in the "Main Menu."
Step 3	A	At the top of the screen, click on the **"+New"** button that will open the "Menus:" creation Workspace.

Refer to Figure 14-9 for the Following:

Step 4	B	In the "Title" field, enter: "Single Weblink" (without quotes).
Step 5	C	In the "Menu Item Type" selector field, when the window opens, select: "Web Links > Single Weblink."
Step 6	D	In the "Select Weblink" field, open the drop down and select: "Southeast USA JUG," which should be the only item displayed.
Step 7	E	In the right side choice, set the "Menu" to "Main Menu."
Step 8	F	In the right side choice, set the "Status" to "Published."
	G	In the right side choice, set the "Status" to "Public."
Step 9		Execute a Save & Close Action.
Step 10		Go to the website Front-End and refresh the browser window.
Step 11		In the "Main Menu," the "Single Weblink" item should display.
Step 12		Click on the "Single Weblink."
Step 13		The resulting display should be the "Southeast USA JUG" page with the "Joomla Related Topics" element displayed, along with the live link to the target website and the description that was entered when the "Weblink" was created.
Step 14		Clicking on the website link will open a new browser window and display the URL's target website.

The above creates a link to only a "Single Weblink," which can be cumbersome if there are many links to create. There are two other types of links that can be created, which are: 1) a single "Weblink Category" and 2) a "List of "Weblink" Categories," both of which can be used for multiple "Weblink" displays if they have been assigned within "Weblink Categories" during creation.

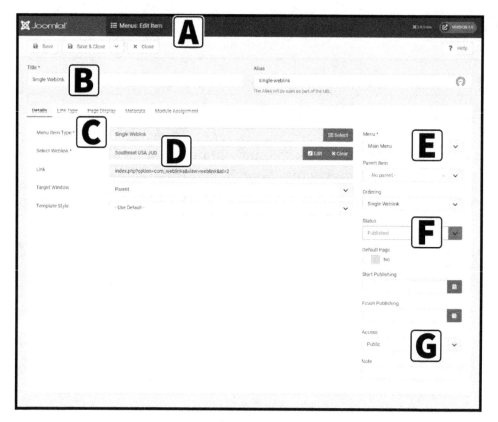

Figure 14-9

The above has demonstrated how the Administrator can create a "Weblink" via the website Back-End, then create a Menu Link Item to affect the ability to display it within a designated Menu.

The alternative method of "Weblink" creation is for a "Registered User" to be allowed to create them via the Front-End, and this is explained below. However, a Menu Link Item must be created in the "Main Menu" that will trigger the Workspace for creating a new "Weblink."

EXERCISE 14-6: CREATE A "SUBMIT WEBLINK" ITEM

Objective: This Exercise will demonstrate the creation of a Menu Link Item in the "Main Menu" that functions to open the "New "Weblink" Workspace." This Menu Link Item must be created by the Administrator on the website Back-End.

Step 1		If not already there, Login and open the "Home Dashboard" on the website Back-End.
Step 2		In the left Menu, open: "Menus > Main Menu" to open the "List of Menu Link Items" in the "Main Menu."
Step 3	A	At the top of the screen, click on the **"+New"** button that will open the "Menus:" creation Workspace.

Refer to Figure 14-10 for the Following:

Step 4	**B**	In the "Title" field, enter: "Submit a Weblink" (without quotes).
Step 5	**C**	In the "Menu Item Type" selector field, when the window opens, select: "Web Links > Submit a Weblink."
Step 6	**D**	In the right side choice, set the "Menu" to "Main Menu."
Step 7	**E**	In the right side Menu, set the "Status" to "Published."
Step 8	**F**	The "Access" selector should be set to: "Registered," which will limit the "Status" of the User who has permissions to create a "Weblink" on the Front-End.
Step 9		Execute a Save & Close action.

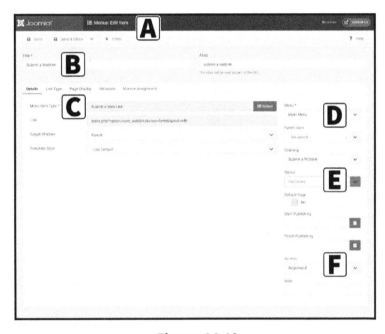

Figure 14-10

Method 2: "Weblink" by Registered User via Front-End

This is the alternative method of creating a "Weblink" entry by a "Registered User" logging into the Front-End and submitting the form.

Step 10	Go to the website Front-End and refresh the browser window.
Step 11	Login as: "blogeditor" using the password entered when the User account was created.
Step 11	After login, within the "Main Menu," the "Submit a Weblink" item should display.

| Step 12 | Click on the "Submit a Weblink." This opens the Workspace, which is displayed in a vertical format without the "Tabs" for the different configuration options as seen on the Back-End. |

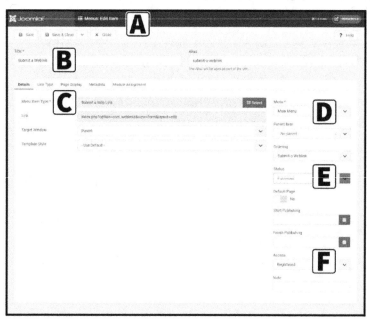

Figure 14-11

Refer to Figure 14-11 for the Following:

Step 13	In the "Title" field, enter: "My First Weblink" (without quotes).
Step 14	In the "Category" field, select: "Weblink Category One."
Step 15	In the "URL" field, enter: "southeastusajug.org" (without quotes).
Step 16	In the "Description" field, enter: "This is My First Weblink." (without quotes).
Step 17	No additional information is needed. Scroll own to the bottom of the screen and execute a Save action.
Step 18	The "Success Message" should display.
Step 19	Go to the website Back-End and, in the left Menu, access: "Components > Web Links > Links," which will display a list of the existing "Weblinks."
Step 20	Confirm that "My First Weblink" is on the list.

Note also that both of the "Weblinks" on the list have been assigned to the same "Weblink Category" entitled: "Category One," which will be used in the next Exercise. Also, this method only allows the "Registered User" to create a "Weblink" within an existing "Weblink Category."

Displaying "Weblinks" in a Module

Another way of displaying "Weblinks," other than via a Menu Link Item, is to display a pre-configured "Weblinks Module" in a standard "Module Position" on the webpage layout.

By default, a "Web Links Module" was created when the Extension was initially installed. This Module now needs to be configured to: 1) locate it into a "Module Position" and 2) select the "Weblinks Category" the Module should display. In this case, it will be in "Category One" which already exists.

EXERCISE 14-7: CONFIGURING A "WEBLINKS" MODULE DISPLAY

Objective: This Exercise will demonstrate the configuration of the "Weblinks Module" to display immediately below the "Main Content Area" of the webpage, and display the "Weblinks" from "Weblink Category One," which was created previously. The target "Module Position" will be "sidebar-right."

Step 1		Log into the website Back-End as the Administrator [Super User].
Step 2		On the "Home Dashboard," go to the "Site" Panel and open the "Modules" block. This will display a list of all website Modules.
Step 3		Use the "Filter Options" and select "Web Links" in the "Select Type" drop down.
Step 4		The "Web Links" Module will display.
Step 5		Click on the "Title" of the Module to open it's Workspace.
Step 6		In the "Category" field, select: "Weblink Category One."
Step 7		In the right column, set the "Position" as: "bottom-a" which is the "Module Position" below the Main Content Area.
Step 8		The "Status" should be set to: "Published."
Step 9		The "Description" selector should be set to "Show."
Step 10		All other configuration choices should remain as the default.
Step 11		Open the "Menu Assignment" tab.

For the purposes of visual simplicity, the "Web Links Module" will only display under the condition that the "Blog" page is displayed, which is selected within the "Main Menu Blog" Menu Link Item, in the top banner area of the webpage.

Step 12		At the top of the Menu Items section, select: "None," to clear the selections that may already have been selected.
Step 13		Scroll down to the "Main Menu Blog" list of Menu Link Items.
Step 14		Tick the box next to the "Blog" Menu Link identifier.

293

Step 15		Execute a Save & Close Action.
Step 16		Go to the website Front-End. It should automatically be open to the "Home" screen. If not, click "Home" in the Main Menu Module.
Step 17		Click on the "Blog" Menu Link Item in the top Menu.
Step 18		Scroll down to below the Main Content Area.
Step 19		The "Web Links" Module should now display, showing two "Weblinks" along with their "Descriptions" to the right.

Additional Use for Weblinks

There are many obvious uses for "Weblinks" on a website. One that is often overlooked is using this Extension to create a library of links to various pages on the website itself. Nothing prohibits the use of links to locations of Content Items within the website itself.

This is actually a method of creating a Menu, but doing so using a different Component. Of course, the different type of Menu Link Items can be created that does the same thing, but creating internal links this way, reduces those that appear in the conventional Menu display.

In this way, keeping the visible Menu Link Items and Menu Modules to a small number, with one or two connected to a "Weblink" Module with a listing of links to website internal pages is accomplished. While not the optimum way to do this, it can be used in this manner if absolutely necessary.

CONTENT:
Adding Extensions

One of the most outstanding features of Joomla! 5, and previous versions, is that they are "extendable." It all starts with the basic or "default" installation which has enough to create an operational website with essential functions. Articles, Menus and more can be created to display Content. But for most websites, this just isn't enough. To meet that challenge, Joomla! was designed so that Extensions can be added, resulting in thousands being created by individual Developers.

What started out to be a six-cylinder engine to run Joomla!, can be "extended" to sixteen-cylinders to crank up the ability to create virtually any type of website. Extensions can change the entire makeup of a website by presenting more Content and allowing it to be displayed in many different ways, all on top of the basic features provided.

Previous Chapters have outlined the "core" Joomla! 5 installation, which is more than sufficient to create and deploy different types of general-content websites. But there is a point where the default installation runs out of options and more features are needed.

This is where Extensions come into play. Using Extensions, Administrators can add features, functions and unique Content displays along with a whole range of related parts that enhance the overall website.

In this Chapter, Extensions will be discussed, and Exercises will guide you through the relatively simple process of adding them to the website. Demonstrations will also be addressing how the Administrator may configure the Extensions via the "Home Dashboard."

Where Extensions Come From

The Developers that work on the Joomla! 5 website coding, DO NOT develop Extensions as part of their Joomla! 5 volunteer role. They may do so independently, but their involvement with the Joomla! project does not involve creating Extensions. The Joomla! 5 team does not generally develop Extensions, beyond those included in the default installation. Yes, they do add Extensions on occasion, but they do so to improve the basic configuration, not to add "extended features."

Extensions are created by independent, third-party Developers, which is where they come from. Mostly independent Developers create Extensions, then share them with the Joomla! community via the Joomla! Extensions Director ("JED"). The "JED" lists thousands of Extensions that can be added to the website. These Extensions are used on hundreds of thousands of website across the world.

Shortage of Extensions

Because Joomla! 5 is still a relatively new version, the number of Extensions available at this time might be limited. However, you can be assured the Extensions that are highly popular and used by many Joomla! 3 & 4 websites in the past will be reworked and reprogrammed to be compatible with Joomla! 5.

One thing that is important to the Administrator is that the Extension MUST be compatible for use with the Joomla! 5 platform. Extensions created for previous version will not likely install properly. It is also possible that attempting to do so might "break" the website, requiring a complete re-installation.

Many Developers create Extensions and then contribute them to the Joomla! community. They do this because developing Extensions to perform certain functions, or to display certain Content formats, is good practice in programming.

Other Developers have created successful businesses out of Extensions they have created that work alone or in unison with others. It is safe to assume that if you want an Extension to do something specific, it is likely available somewhere in the "JED." The "JED" classifies Extensions by Category, and some searching will narrow them down so you can select the most appropriate one for your website's needs.

Also, if you are coding savvy, you may be able to further modify these Extensions by creating "overrides," which is another name for "customizations." Chapter 44, "Custom & Alternative Layouts, and Chapter 47, "Library of Overrides" both address the topics of changing the default configurations of Extensions. They can be found in *Boots on the Ground, Advance Edition, Volume 2.*

The Joomla! Extensions Directory ("JED")

Extensions are primarily obtained via the "JED," wherein Developers list their Extensions and links are provided to their website for download. Of course, many of these Extensions are "for sale," so anticipate the need to make payments for some of them.

To access the "JED," go to: joomla.org then, open the "Download & Extend" Menu Link Item in the Main Menu, followed by accessing "Extensions" in the drop-down sub-menu. After that, search & seek the type of Extension desired. There is even a Menu Link Item in the sub-menu called "Compatible with Joomla! 5," which is the location where Extensions within that group are now listed within the "JED" classification of Extensions.

Always look for Joomla! 5 Compatibility

When searching Extensions, always, always, always make sure you confirm that the Extension is configured to work with Joomla! 5. Extensions are "version specific," which means exactly what it implied. If it is not apparent, **DO NOT** attempt to install the Extension. The "JED" may show compatible Extensions with a "J!5" icon.

Commercial vs. Non-Commercial Extensions

"To pay or not to pay," that is the question. There are many, many Extensions that are absolutely free to download and use. They are donated to the Joomla! community by Developers. Other Extensions require a fee, a subscription or a membership to the Developer's website. The "JED" delineates the difference as "free download" or "paid download." But here is where things get fuzzy.

You might come upon an Extension that fits the function just the way you want, and it is listed as "free download." You follow the "JED" page links to the location to download the Extension, where you might immediately run into one of these four situations:

Situation 1	All is well. The Extensions is, in fact, completely "free" and can be immediately downloaded via the "JED" link or the Developer's website. The Extensions is the "full version" with all features, without any restrictions on use whatsoever.
Situation 2	The Extension is "free," but you must register as a User on the website, which will require an email confirmation. When you click on the link in the email received, you gain access to the site and may log in and download the Extension. The conditional requirement is that you become a "registered user" on the website.
Situation 3	The Extension, which was listed as "free download" is, in fact free, but you must pay for a membership to access the download area on the

	Developer's website. Technically, the Extension is "free," but the rub is that you must pay for a subscription to the website to download any Extensions. This "membership" combination comes in many forms, so be aware that payment may be required, but not for the Extension itself, but to access the download area, or to pay for support, or to obtain the Extension with a term period for delivery of upgrades. There are many variations to this method of providing "free" Extensions, which themselves are available at no direct cost, but the cost to access the download area is another thing altogether.
Situation 4	The Extension is "free," but it is a stripped down version with missing features to make it fully functional. There are many Extensions that fit into this scenario. The Extension, with basic functions, is available "free," but the meat and potatoes versions require some sort of payment, or membership or subscription. There are many, which claim the ability to extensively customize, but only provide the basic features. To get all of the bells and whistles that you wanted, there will likely be some sort of pricing scheme involved.

More Information About Extensions

There are some other scenarios for downloading and using Extensions, whether they are "free" or "paid" versions – regardless of what form the payment takes. These situations deal with the use of the Extension on the website(s) themselves. Here are those possible wrinkles that may be included with Extension use:

Situation 1	The Extension can be used on an unlimited number of websites.
Situation 2	The Extension may only be used on a specified website. The website must be identified with the Developer at the time it is acquired. It is to be used strictly on the declared website. After download and installation, there may be some sort of license key entered, or a registration required where in the domain is identified and a license code issued, which is entered into the Extension via the Administrator's Back-End. In this case, should the Extension be used on another domain name website, a new payment and license must be obtained.
Situation 3	The Extensions is limited to use to a certain number of websites, and you must list and/or get a license key for each installation. This is easy enough to do in most cases. You log onto the Developer's website, enter the domains for the use of the Extension and get a license key. The key is entered in the Extension's Manager after installing it on the website. This situation isn't widely used, but there are some instances where the number of website uses is limited.

Situation 4	There are other limitation, such as the number of times the Extension can be downloaded; the subscriptions are in tiers whereby the updates are allowed for different time periods based on the level of subscription purchased; no updates or upgrades are offered after the initial download; or downloading of upgrades or updates are limited to specific lengths of time, again base on the payment level of the subscription.

Is the Extension Supported?

Another point to consider about Extensions is the level of "support" from the Developers. Usually, "free" Extensions have little or no support from the Developers. Or if you want support, it is fee-based. However, with more complex Extensions, support is essential, and without it, if you are not a code savvy Administrator, you may have difficulty in getting the Extension to function properly.

When purchasing an Extension with a subscription required, you should expect a certain level of support include with the subscription. In most cases, the support is excellent with proper responses within a reasonable time. In other cases, requests for support are never answered. There are also instances where the responses are curt and do not answer the question, such as: "Read the instructions," etc. Also, some support is simply posting requests on a "forum" location and hoping someone will respond with an answer, which might be someone from the Developer's staff, or just another user.

Monetary Units When Purchasing

If you are in the United States, be aware of the value difference in the British Pound (GBP) or the EuroDollar (EUD) as it compares with the value of the U.S. dollar

Exactly what is the Purpose of Extensions?

Extensions enlarge the capabilities of the website. They are "added on," and thus "extending" the functions and features of the website. They work on the building-block principle where the Joomla! core sets the foundation, then Extensions are added to expand capabilities.

There are six types of Extensions in Joomla! 5. Each Extensions installs the same way via the Administrator Back-End by the Administrator designated as the "Super User." Based on the type of Extension, they may need to be configured by the Administrator, or simply enabled for use – such as Plugins.

Some Extensions actually install with multiple parts. For example, a Component may also install a Template, Modules and Plugins. The Administrator should always check to make sure the proper parts are "enabled" to "Published" or otherwise configured to perform the desired functions.

File Types for Extensions

Extensions that can be installed into Joomla! 5 fall into five types, as follows:

"pkg"	A "Package" file is one that contains all the necessary parts to install a complete Extension. The Extension could contain a Component, Modules, Plugins and even Templates. They are typically bundled into one file that incorporates all parts during the installation process.
"com"	This prefix indicates that the Extension is a Component – a "mini-application" that runs inside of the Joomla! 5 Framework. Any new Components will appear on the dropdown list in the Left Menu on the "Home Dashboard," and are accessed by clicking on the Component name. This method is the only way to access a Component, regardless of type.
"mod"	Modules are added using files with this prefix and generally only consist of a single Module that is used for specific types of Content display. The Module is then listed and named in the "Modules – Select a Module Type" Manager.
"plg"	An Extension that is a Plugin is generally a companion to something. Plugins perform actions when "triggered" by something else. Usually, there is no configuration needed after a Plugin in installed other than to "enable" it.
"tpl"	While typically not frequently referred to as an "Extension," Templates, in fact, are. They are installed the same way but have a specific location on the website Administrator area. Make no mistake, a Template "IS" an Extension, so be aware of that when dealing with installing, using and uninstalling them. Templates have a special requirement when uninstalling and is covered in Chapter 17, "Visual: Templates."
Language	Extensions that install an additional "Language" into the website are typically prefixed by an indicator of their language. They are likely "pkg" file types, but are not so named. A typical name for a French "Language" Extensions could be: fr-FR_joomla_lang_full_3.7.0v1.zip. See Chapter 28, "Component: "Language" Associations" for information about the use of this Extension.

Different Functional Types of Extensions

Extensions used on Joomla! 5 website fall into six types, as shown in Figure 15-1. Each Extension has unique functions and characteristics regarding how the Content is displayed or accessed by website visitors.

Each of these is explained in detail in other Chapters in this book, and discussed and used in Exercises that teach practical skills on their implementation and use. At this point, all that is needed is the understanding of "what" these Extensions are and what they do.

All Extensions install the same way, albeit they may be sourced from different Developers under different acquisition methods, *re:* "free" or "paid" downloads as discussed previously. The mechanics for every type of Extension's installation are identical, regardless of their type and use.

COMPONENTS

Components are mini-applications that run inside Joomla! 4. There are hundreds of Components available. A Form Building Feature is a Component.

MODULES

Modules are physical elements that can be assigned different locations on the page that display content or functions, or executable actions.

PLUGINS

A Plugin executes "actions" that take place when something, such as a Menu Link Item "triggers" the Plugins predetermined "actions."

TEMPLATES

Templates are Extensions with the page/screen designs with layouts and Module Postions. More than one Template may be used on a website if desired.

LIBRARIES

Libraries are packages of code that do not typically require any interaction by the website's Administrator.

LANGUAGES

These are Extensions that allow the use of multiple languages on a website that viewers may select, provided that feature has been enabled.

Figure 15-1

Sources of Extensions

There are several methods of installing Extensions onto a Joomla! 5 website. But it should be repeated: Each Extensions installs the same way and there are four processes of doing so, as explained in detail below.

Install from Web	This options connects the Extension Installer directly to the "JED," where all Extensions are accessible. Once you find one there, it can be selected and installed via the standard method. One note here is that only the Extensions that use Joomla!'s automatic update notification method can be installed using this method. Extension Developers that do not use that feature are not listed in the "JED." There is some sort of requirement for Extensions to qualify to be downloaded via this method.
Upload Package File	This is where the Administrator has sourced and downloaded the Extension file(s) to the local computer. The next step is to then to click on the Extension Installed, which automatically executes the installing the action. This is likely the most popular method of adding new Extensions to a Joomla! 5 website.
Install from Folder	This is a more complicated method than any others. It requires the Extension Installation Files to be uploaded to a folder on the website server, typically after the Administrator has downloaded it and used a File Transfer Program ("FTP") to move the file to a designated folder on the server. The default is the "tmp" folder at the installed location, which is the same folder used when installing Extensions by any method. It indicates the content is typically in the folder "temporarily" for installation purposes.
Install from URL	This method is rarely used and involves installing an Extension from a "URL" file link to the installer file. The link is located on the Developer's website, or some other location accessible via the internet. At this time, there are no known instances for this method available to install any Extension on a Joomla! 5 website.

Steps Involved to Install Extensions

For every Extension, there are several action steps involved in adding it to a Joomla! 5 website. While some methods have a different route to obtain an Extension for installation, the fundamental methods and processes are the same, regardless of how the Extension is obtained.

The process below makes the assumption that the Extension will be installed using the "Upload Package File" method.

Action 1	Locate the Extensions via the "JED" or on the Developers website.
Action 2	Download the Extension installer file, usually a "zip" file, to the Administrator's computer. If the files says "UNZIP FIRST" as part of the name, perform that action step before the next action. Unless the file contains the "UNZIP FIRST" message, it is not necessary to "unzip" the file.
Action 3	Use the Back-End Extension Installer feature to add the Extension to the website. For a normal "zip" file, selecting the file is all that is required. For "UNZIP FIRST" files, you must open the folder and install all of the parts individually. There may be several, so the Administrator must make sure to install each.
Action 4	When initiating the installing action, the Joomla! logo will appear on screen as a spinner, especially while the file uploads from the computer to the server. The Extension continues to install, and a "success message" is displayed when the action is completed.
Action 5	The Extension, or it's parts, must be configured and/or enabled to use it on the website.

Degree of Difficulty

If this were an Olympic Event, the degree of difficulty for installing an Extension would be a 2, because it is really easy to accomplish.

Other than the additional steps to configure the Extension, the installation is straightforward and not particularly difficult. Most Extensions just cruise right along and install in a jiffy, without undue drama or difficulty.

However, there are times when, for complex technical reasons, an Extension cannot or does not install using the preferred conventional method. Joomla! 5 recognized this and has provided other methods for installing Extensions.

Status Indicator Images

Extensions that are installed, along with Categories, Articles, Modules and more have their "Status" indicated using three images, as follows:

GREEN CHECKMARK: The item is active, Published or enabled for use.
RED "X" CIRCLE: The item is inactive or disabled.
LOCK SYMBOL: The item is critical to the website operation and cannot be removed or uninstalled. The item is in a "protected" state. It is also used to indicate an item is "checked out" to the last user.

Adding a New Content Editor

The Exercise below will add a different Content Editor that can be used on the website in all of the Content Workspaces. The "JCE Editor" is a very popular and full-featured add-on that extends the editing capabilities. This installation was previously included in Chapter 7, but it is being repeated here with detailed information about the installation process.

EXERCISE 15-1: INSTALLING "JCE EDITOR" FREE EXTENSION

Objectives: The goal of this Exercise is to provide information on how to install the JCE Editor, Free Version. This Editor has been previously mentioned as a possible alternative to the default Editor. JCE also has a "Pro" version, and it is suggested that if you are comfortable with the "Free" version, upgrading should be considered.

Part A – Obtaining the Extension

Step A-1	Access the Extension Directory ("JED") on the joomla.org website.
Step A-2	In the "Search" field, enter "JCE" (without quotes).
Step A-3	Click on the "JCE" panel when it appears. Notice the notification message that it is compatible with Joomla! 5. Also note that it is a "free download" Extension. The product screen will then appear.
Step A-4	On the right, click on the "Download" button. The screen transfers to the "JCE" website, promoting the "Pro" version of JCE.
Step A-5	Scroll down and download the "latest" version, the one that has the highest version number. This will download the "pkg_jce_####.zip" file to the Administrator's computer folder designated to receive downloaded files.
Step A-6	Go to the download location on the computer and verify the file is present and proceed to Part B – Installing the Extension.

Extension Compatibility Version

When selecting and downloading Extension, always check to make sure that it is compatible with the Joomla! 5 version. Do not attempt to install any Extension that does not identify itself as compatible with Joomla! 5. Do not do it if not so noted. The website might "break" and not be able to be restored, so use extreme caution and make sure the Extension is Joomla! 5 compatible.

Part B – Installing the Extension

Now that the "JCE" free version has been downloaded, the next step is to install it into the Joomla! 5 website using the action steps below.

Step B-1	If not already there, go to the Back-End and login as the Administrator to access the "Home Dashboard."
Step B-2	In the left Menu, open the "System" location.
Step B-3	In the "Install" block, click on "Extensions." **Reminder:** Make sure the Extension is compatible with Joomla! 5.
Step B-4	In the tab area, click on "Upload Package File" tab.
Step B-5	Click "Or browse for file" to access the computer's directories.
Step B-6	Go to the folder in which files are downloaded and fine the "pkg_jce_####.zip" file and click or double click on it.
Step B-7	This starts the installation process, indicated by the logo spinner. Sometimes Extension installs happen quickly.
Step B-8	When completed, the "Installation of package was successful" message panel will display. Close it.
Step B-9	Review the information on the page, which encourages you to obtain the "Pro" version of "JCE." That can be done later. For now the "Free" version will be used.

Part C – Activating the "JCE Editor" for Use

The Extension has now been obtained, downloaded and properly installed for use on the website. However, the current Editor is the "default" Editor that is being used in all Workspaces. The JCE needs to be designated at the "default" Editor. Follow these action steps to accomplish this action.

Step C-1	If not already there, go to the Back-End and login as the Administrator to access the "Home Dashboard."

Step C-2	Access the "System" area of the Back-End.
Step C-3	In the "Setup" Panel, select "Global Configuration."
Step C-4	Open the "Site" tab. It will probably be open by default.
Step C-5	Find the "Default Editor" selector and open the drop down.
Step C-6	Select "Editor – JCE" from among the choices available.
Step C-7	Perform a Save & Close action.
Step C-8	The "Configuration Saved" "Success Message" will appear.
Step C-9	Without going through each Step, go to Content > Articles and execute a **"+New"** Article action step.
Step C-10	The new "JCE" Editor should appear in the Workspace. Spend some time looking at the icons and determining what they do, or what function they perform. Some are obvious, others may need further inspection to understand their function.
Step C-11	Investigate the tabs along the top of the "JCE" Editor. Familiarize yourself with the content of the tabs.
Step C-12	Scroll down to the bottom of the "JCE" Editor.
Step C-13	Note that these button are the same as what appeared under the "CMS Content" tab in the default "TinyMCE" Editor. They perform the same functions. With this Editor, there is no "CMS Content" drop down.
Step C-14	Also note at the top of the Editor, at the right, there are three tabs, one of which allows a "Preview" function to look at the Content Item before actually Publishing it.
Step C-15	Open any existing Article. When the Workspace opens, refresh the browser window. There might be a slight delay before the "JCE" opens as it maps its way into the Article Workspace.

This concludes the action steps involved to install and activate the "JCE" Editor, Free Version. If the "Pro" version is purchased, simply go through the same Action Steps as outlined above. The "Free" version does not need to be removed or uninstalled to install the "Pro" version.

"JCE" is a fun Editor to use. It has many features that allow Editors to create visually appealing Articles, along with images and photos. However, the "CMS Content" feature as found in the default Editor, is not the same in "JCE." When needed, the difference between the two has been identified and explained.

New "Home Dashboard" Panel

In addition to the newly installed Extension appearing in the left Menu under the Components link, they can also be found elsewhere. This is typical in Joomla! 5 where there are two ways, methods or location in which to be able to access Components, Modules, Categories or Articles, etc.

In the case of Components, a new Panel is added to the "Home Dashboard." It is called "3rd Party" and lists the Extensions that have been added which are not part of the Joomla! 5 "default" installation. However, not all Extensions will be listed here. Only those that conform to certain Joomla! 5 configurations regarding updating will be included.

Pay attention to this happening after installing Extensions, especially for those that will be accessed frequently. The "3rd Party" Panel will give you access that is one click faster than the left Menu. However, there is a difference in that within the "3rd Party" Panel, the Extension's Manager is opened. In the left Menu, the Component's "sub-parts" are accessible via a sub-menu link item. Deciding which to use will be something the Administration will decide upon after repeated use.

Where is JCE Administration?

The "JCE" Editor is a Component. It has parts, but the main Manager is within the website Components area. They may be accessed in that Menu directly verses opening the Component Manager before accessing the part. Either way, the end result is the same. Administrator's, after a time using the Back-End access points, will develop their own style and method of administration.

Uninstalling Extensions

It is a reasonable assumption that if an Extension can be installed on a Joomla! 5 website, it should also be able to be removed, or uninstalled. The answer to this is affirmative – any Extension can be uninstalled. The exception are those that are essential to the installation, in which case, they are locked and cannot be removed or uninstalled.

It is always a good administrative policy to remove, or uninstall, any Extensions that are not being functionally used on a website. As the Administrator, you may occasionally install and Extension for operational and functional testing. Then, you find it does not perform as expected, etc. It is a smart move to uninstall the Extension. Don't let unused Extensions remain on the website.

Two Ways to Do This

There are two ways to render an Extension inoperative. This includes Components, Modules, Plugins, Templates, Languages and Libraries.

Danger! Danger! Danger!

Make sure when rendering Extensions inoperative or performing an uninstall, that the *Extension is not part of the website's "core" files.* This could render the website inoperative and possibly, with no way to recover. Use some caution when uninstalling. Be careful as to which Extension that you remove by the "uninstall" method.

Two Methods to Disable/Uninstall and Extension

Disable the Extension Does not remove it.	With this method, the Extension is simply disabled, or "Unpublished," as the case may be. This way, the Extension can be re-activated at any time because it remains part of the website. It is not actually removed.
Uninstall the Extension Physically removes it.	This action completely removes the Extension from the website. It cannot be re-activated without re-installing it. Everything pertinent to the Extension is physically removed, thus the need to re-install.

Disabling/Unpublishing Actions

EXERCISE 15-2: DISABLING AN EXTENSION

Objectives: The goal of this Exercise is to demonstrate how to disable an Extension buy "Unpublishing" or "disabling" it.

Step 1		If not already there, go to the Back-End and login as the Administrator to access the "Home Dashboard."
Step 2	A	In the "Site" Panel, open the "Modules" Manager.

Refer to Figure 15-2 for the following:

Step 3	B	Search for the "Older Posts" Module, which currently appears on the right side of the screen, in the "sidebar-right" Module Position.
Step 4	C	The "Older Posts" Module should be the only one displayed.
Step 5	D	The "Position" of the Module on the Template is indicated.
Step 6	E	The pages the Module is configured for display. This action will affect the Module display on every page to which it is assigned.
Step 7	F	In the "Status" column, note the icon indicating that the Module is, in fact, "Published" thus making it viewable based on the "Menu Assignments" for the module.

Refer to Figure 15-3 for the following:

Step 8	G	Hover the mouse over the "Checkmark" icon. A notice will popup indicating that if clicked, the item will be "Unpublished."
Step 9	G	Click on the "Checkmark" icon to "Unpublish" the Module. When this action is executed, the process of changing the "Status" of the Module automatically takes place. The "Module Unpublished" Message will display when complete. Close the message.
Step 10	G	The "Checkmark" icon will have changed to a grey "X" indicating that the item is "Unpublished."
Step 11		Go to the website Front-End and refresh the browser window.
Step 12		Note that the "Older Posts" Module no longer appears in the "bottom-a" Module Position, under the Main Content Area.

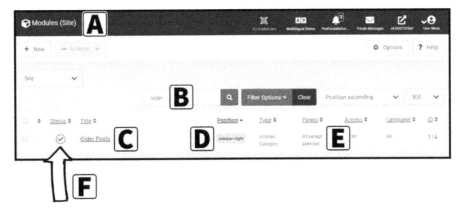

Figure 15-2

Figure 15-3

To "Republish" the Module, simply perform the same action steps. Because the Module is in the "Unpublished" Status, the only option is to "Publish" it, and the same process accomplishes this.

Make note also that this all took place in the "Module Manger" and not within the Module itself. If the "Module Workspace" is accessed, the "Status" setting may be selected there, with the additional step of performing a "saving" action to invoke the change in "Status." It is easier to do this in the "List" view of Content Items.

Installing an Extension

To demonstrate the processing removing/uninstalling an Extension, it is necessary to first actually install one, obtained from the "JED." Once this action is completed, an Administrator can proceed to reverse that action.

EXERCISE 15-3: OBTAINING & INSTALLING AN EXTENSION

Objectives: This Exercise will demonstrate how to install an Extension onto the website. There is an Extension called: "FlexiContact," that will be used, which is one of the types that has both a "free" and a "paid" or "pro" version. The "free" version will be used in this Exercise.

Obtaining the Extension, "FlexiContact"

Step 1	Go to the Joomla.org website.
Step 2	Open the "Download & Extend" directory on the top Menu, then the "Extensions" location.
Step 3	Open the "Browse Extensions" area.
Step 4	Open the "Compatible with J!5."
Step 5	With the "J!5" compatible Extensions displayed, enter "FlexiContact" in the search box at the top.
Step 6	At the top of the display, two images should appear for the "FlexiContact" Extension. A "free" version and a "paid" version.
Step 7	Click on the image for the "free" version. The "Plus" version is the pay-for version. **NOTE:** The "J!4" version of this Extensions will install without issues in Joomla! 5.
Step 8	On the next screen, scroll down to access the "Download" button and execute the action.
Step 9	Scroll down the next screen, at the bottom, and execute the "Free Download" for the "FlexiContact" Component. You may also download the User Guide if desired.
Step 10	The Component Extension should download to the file location on

		your computer that has been designated to accept downloaded files.
Step 11		Go to the download folder and verify that the "com-flexicontact_###.zip" file is located there.
Step 12		Now that the Extension has been obtained, no further action is needed at this point.

Installing the Extension "FlexiContact"

Step 1		If not already there, go to the Back-End and login as the Administrator to access the "Home Dashboard."
Step 2		Access the "System" area of the Back-End.
Step 3		Open the "Extensions" link in the "Install" Panel. This will open the "Installer."
Step 4		Open the "Upload Package File" tab.
Step 5		Click on the "Or browse for file" button.
Step 6		Go to the "Downloads" folder and click on the "com_ ..." file for the Extension. Then click on "Open" to begin the installing action.
Step 7		The Joomla logo may appear during the download and installing process.
Step 8		When completed, a "Success Message" will appear at the top of the screen. Close it.
Step 9		Return to the "Home Dashboard."
Step 10		Open the "Components" list on the left Menu.
Step 11		"FlexiContact" should be on the list of Components.
Step 12		Open the "Configuration" location within the "FlexiContact" Component, where you will find an array of features that can be set or configured.

Removing/Uninstalling an Extension

After performing the Steps in the previous Exercise, the installation of the "FlexiContact" Component is now complete.

Next, assume that this Extension is no longer needed and should be removed from the website, thus from the list of Components. The following Exercise will accomplish the complete removal, or "Uninstallation" of the Component from the website.

To completely remove an Extension, different action steps must be taken beyond simply "Unpublishing" or altering the visibility of the Extension. The Exercise below will explain this process.

EXERCISE 15-4: REMOVING AN EXTENSION

Objectives: The goal of this Exercise is to demonstrate how to perform the actions necessary to completely remove, or "Uninstall" an Extension from the website. Because it is not advisable to remove "default" Extension, an Extension Component will be "Uninstalled" that was added previous: "FlexiContact."

Step 1	If not already there, go to the Back-End and login as the Administrator to access the "Home Dashboard."
Step 2	Access the "System" area of the Back-End.
Step 3	In the "Manage" block, click on "Extensions."
Step 4	In the "Search" field, enter "flexi" (without quotes). The result will be that the "FlexiContact" will be displayed. Also, notice at the top of the screen that none of the buttons are active.
Step 5	Click on the "check box" to the left of the Extension's name. When that action is performed, the buttons at the top of the screen now become active.
Step 6	Click on the **"X Uninstall"** button.
Step 7	Click "OK" in the panel asking for confirmation of the "Uninstall" action request. This is a double-check to ensure that the action is what the Administrator intends.
Step 8	Several "success messages" will display. Read them, then close the message panels.
Step 9	To confirm the removal, go to the "Components" link in the left Menu. The "FlexiContact" Component should not be listed.

The above Exercises have guided you through the process of acquiring, installing and uninstalling an Extension. This is the same process that is applied for every Extension to be added to a website. The only variable is the method of acquisition of the Extension.

Special Actions after Uninstalling

In some cases, "Uninstalling" removes the Extension from the access points in the "Home Dashboard," but does not physically remove the files from the website folders. This is particularly true in the case of "Uninstalling" Templates. This issue will be covered in Chapter 17, "VISUAL: Templates." It isn't a big deal but may present issues when re-installing the same Extension and could "throw errors" when attempting to do so.

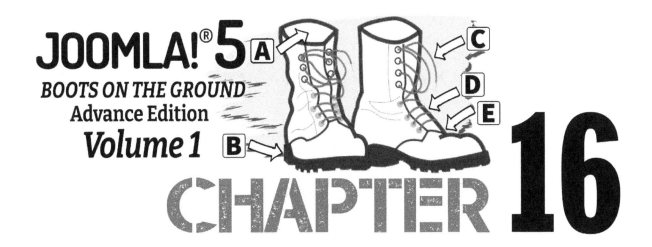

CONTENT:
Specialized Extensions

When building and configuring a Joomla! 5 website, the probability of including Extensions of one type or another is very high. Extensions expand the use and functionality of the website. They add features. They add functions. They help in managing Content. They are a key for the development of websites that have both expanded form and function. They also allow the control of the visual aspects.

What makes Extensions so vitally important is their ability to take a "plain vanilla" website and make it something very specialized and functional. For example, adding a "shopping cart" Extension to the website. For your information, there are a number of excellent "cart" Extensions that can be purchased and added to a Joomla! 5 website. These shopping cart features have been specifically created to work perfectly on the Joomla! platform.

There are hundreds of other types of Extensions that are available which can be easily added to a Joomla! 5 website that will greatly enhance its function.

How and Where to Obtain Extensions

As explained in previous Chapters, Joomla! 5 Extensions are secured through the joomla.org "JED" or directly from Extension Developers, although the "JED" is actually the "path" by which Administrators are led to the Developers. The "JED" is a "directory" and the "download" links contained in the "JED" are actually links to the Developer's websites.

So, the "how and where" of obtaining Joomla! 5 Extensions is that you start with the "JED" and proceed from there.

The "JED" isn't the only way to find or locate Joomla! 5 Extensions. Of course, internet search engines can provide links to the same or similar Extensions, so don't be afraid to look there.

Types of Extensions

Just a cursory tour of the "JED" will be enough to grasp the sheer depth and number of Extensions available to be added into a Joomla! 5 website. At the time of this book's writing, the number was somewhat limited, but as time goes by, more Developers will upgrade their products to work with this new version.

Figure 16-1 is a screen shot of the "JED," indicating there are over 6,000 Extensions available in a large variety of "use" Categories, as shown. Not all, of course, are compatible with Joomla! 5, but that list continues to grow.

Again, ALWAYS make sure that the Extension you are considering for the website is compatible with Joomla! 5. Joomla! 3 Extensions WILL NOT WORK. Do not attempt to use them. Use Joomla! 5 specific Extensions only. This cannot be over-emphasized. Using an Extension that is not compatible and can break your Joomla! 5 instance to the point where it cannot be recovered.

Figure 16-1

Using a Specialized Extension

Specialized Extensions are simply those that are designed to do something very specific and very complex. Examples of these are: shopping carts, real estate, auto sales and the list goes on.

One thing all Specialized Extensions have in common is that they all install into a Joomla! 5 website the same exact way. There are some things to be aware of, as explained below:

Trial Versions/Free Versions	These are generally "stripped down" versions of the Extension. They are comprised of the minimum capabilities of the Extensions, missing some of the more desirable or advanced features. There are, however, Developers that do give their products away at no charge, or simply ask for a donation. We appreciate and recognize their generosity.
Pro or Full Versions	The "upgrade" version of Extensions are the "pro" or "full" versions. This is likely the version that must be purchased as an upgrade from the "trial" or "free" versions. They usually are one-time payment, with annual renewal for support and upgrades. Many are limited to one or a few website use only. The "Developer" or "Agency" versions have more generous restrictions on use.
Quickstart Packages	This Specialized Extension include everything within the *.pkg* file. They include the Joomla! 5 program and the Specialized Extension itself, along with the Content and Images included with the demo Template. You must install the package into a "clean" location on the website, with no Joomla! 5 version installed. After extracting the "zipped" file on the server, the Joomla! 5 program is installed WITH the Extension, and all its parts.

Formats for Extensions

Depending upon what the Developers have created with regard to an Extension, They [the Extensions], are provided in different file formats that are understandable by Joomla! 5.

For more information about Extension file formats, please review Chapter 15, "Content: Adding Extensions."

Interesting Sidebar

We were looking at a Template that works with one of the Page Builder Extensions. It had a neat background image group running as a parallax video. It did not come with the Extension files. When asked about the rotating image background, the Developer told us where to download it. It worked for us perfectly. This is a prime example of making sure the images come along with any Specialized Template that you add to the website. We initially assumed the images came with the Template, but were wrong. Be prepared to go a bit beyond the ordinary to make your Extension installation appear the same way as the demo version you may have viewed.

What You See Isn't What You Get

If you shop around for a Specialized Extension and you see one that you like, then purchase and install, you might be disappointed with the result. Why? Most of the Specialized Extensions do not come with the Content, the Images or the same Layouts as you saw on the Developer's website. What you saw there is a prime, number one, demonstration of the product and it's capabilities.

When the Specialized Extension is downloaded and installed, there is usually an incredible amount of work needed to get your version to begin to even look anything close to the sample you saw.

The solution to this problem is to use the Developer's "Quickstart" Package. Many developers offer these type of packages. It is often a wise choice to make when the Administrator wants the Specialized Extension to function and appear the same way on their website as the Developer's demo website.

QuickStart Over Standard Installation

If a "quickstart' version of a Specialized Extension is going to be used, it CANNOT be installed over, or into, an existing website. The "quickstart" includes the Joomla! 5 operating platform, so it must be a fresh or clean installation. This will install Joomla! 5, the Extension, the Template, etc. After installation, should the Joomla! 5 version needed to be updated, a message to that effect will be displayed. However, the Joomla! 5 version within the package may not be the latest, so be prepared to run a quick Joomla! 5 upgrade after install.

Investigate, Investigate, Investigate

Do not make immediate assumptions that a certain Specialized Extension is "exactly what you want," when doing your research. A fatal flaw in a feature might be as simple as the inability to collect State Sales Tax in a shopping cart, when it is required in your State for online orders. Or the ability to calculate shipping costs to international destinations.

It is suggested that all of the desired features needed for your Extension first be reduced to a written list. Then, when reviewing Extensions, go through the list and check off those that apply.

Also, be aware that some Developers provide, for their Specialized Extensions, certain Plugins and Modules that are either free or require purchase. These are usually unique items that fit into a niche within their Extension. We have seen great Extensions which require the purchase of additional Modules or Plug-ins to maximize the functionality of the Extension.

Another factor to consider is that third-parties might have created additional Extensions that be added to a Specialized Extension to enhance and/or improve it. The "JomSocial" Extension falls into that category. There are an abundance of third-party Extensions that can be added to a website that integrate into the "JomSocial" platform. Just be aware of the availability of third-party features that may be added to existing Extensions.

The "Social Web" Extensions is another category that third-party have piled on with well-over four-hundred eighty (480+) Extensions just for displaying Content pulled from various social media platforms. Some interact directly with the Social Media accounts.

In other words, the third-party Extensions give almost every other Extension a greater footprint and functionality on any website choosing to use them. Always make through assessments of need and functionality prior to installing an Extension add-on.

With a new version of Joomla!, we cannot repeat this often enough: "Make sure the Extension is Joomla! 5 compatible. If not, the Extension may break the website upon attempts to install it."

Visitor-Facing vs. Administrator-Facing

Extensions can be classified into two broad categories: those which will be used to display content to website visitors on the Front-End, or those which only the Administrator "will see" or actually uses to administer the website.

Usually, Extensions that are "Templates" are the visitor-facing that provide visual or content that is designed to be viewed on the Front-End, which comprises the large majority of Extension uses.

On the other side of the website, the Administrator Back-End, there are many Extensions which facilitate the administration of the website. These generally apply to how "Content" is created or managed via the Back-End.

A new group of Extensions called: "Page Builders," have now appeared which operate on an operating layer designed by the Developers. The actions of these Extensions serve a couple of purposes.

First, the Administrator uses the Extension to either build/create/format or otherwise design individual website pages, thus the "Page Builder" label.

Second, the actual results of the same Extension creates a "view" for visitors on the Front-End. Different Templates and different Page Layouts can be created based on website Content display requirements.

Developers are now taking Extensions further by providing "themed templates" that integrate with their Page Builder Extensions, thus giving them a greater ability to create Specialized Templates for Administrators to use on websites.

For more information about Templates, see Chapters 17 through 19, which addresses Templates, Style Sheets and the Template/Page Builders. These are "Specialized" Extensions for the experienced Administrator.

Know what you want, then find it

The first series of steps to take in finding in Extension is deciding what you want it to do. Exactly, what does the website need and how does it make the website better? Once that determination has been made, finding out the particulars is the next step.

Search the "JED" for the "type" of Extension desired, then start doing research. Visit all of the Developer websites and review their Extensions and look at the "demos" if they have any available.

Remember, however, that the "demos" of Extensions are perfect, set up to show off the features of it in the best way possible. The Developers are "selling" the Extension to you, so make sure you understand what it does and how it can be applied to the Content of your website.

An Extension should not be added to your website just because you think it is "neat." That is the last reason. The top level reason should be about how it will make accessing website Content better or easier for visitors.

It's all in the details

Making sure the Extension will do the job on your website is your responsibility. Once you have acquired it, especially if it cost money, you can't ask for a refund because you make the wrong choice. Research the Extension and its features before making any purchase. Make sure it will do what you want it to do for your implementation plans. Pay attention to the details!

Here's an actual case study:

We had to add a UK based shopping cart operation into a Joomla! 3 website. After getting it all running, the client all of a sudden wants to have "worldwide international shipping" fees added to the cart checkout. Great! The cart default installation did not have such a feature. It was set up for UK shipping rates only.

Fortunately, there was an Extension available for that particular shopping cart that did provide that feature. Of course, it cost money, and then it had to be configured.

This is a good example that: 1) if we knew that the client wanted international shipping rates involved, and 2) if we knew we might have picked another shopping cart, and 3) we found (luckily!), an Extension that works with the cart.

So, when you have a complex or unusual configuration requirement of feature need, make sure that every detail and element is checked before making the commitment to the Extension. Investigate and try to anticipate some of the "hidden needs" that an Extension might require for any functional application.

Support is Important

Another key element of Extension acquisition is what kind of support is available should it be needed. Of course, you have no way of knowing if the support service is any good, but you can make some assumptions.

If the Developer is a large operation, chances are their support is good. If the support is "only" a forum onto which you post issues and other users "might respond," then you might want to shy away unless the Extension is absolutely critical.

If your Extension is purchased, or if you buy a support term such as 3- or 6-months, chance are the Developers will have decent support. After all, they did take your money and if you need them they should be there.

The Extension Developers that offer a number of Extensions and an array of Extensions that a functionally inter-related, chances are, support will be available.

Country of Origin

Another consideration is the "country of origin" for the Extension. Experience has shown us that most of the Extension Developers are in Eastern Europe or Middle Asia locations. That is not saying it's a bad thing. There are great Developers located in those locations.

What can be problematic is response times for support tickets. For Middle Asia locations, it is a 12-hour time difference between the U.S. and perhaps more for Europe. Keep this in mind when requesting support. Allow for the time differences. Urgent support requests might be handled that way by the staff, but only on the time zone of the support center. It is not reasonable to expect them to be on a 24-hour operation.

Many of the bigger and better Extension Developers also have operating locations in Western Europe, England or in the U.S. The location of their support is very helpful when requesting support and expecting a timely response.

VISUAL:
Templates

When a website visitor accesses a Joomla! 5 website, their device screen is generated by Content created/entered by the Administrator or other Editors via the Back-End. How the display is accomplished is by "Templates," which control the physical and visual aspects of the website. In other words, the "Front-End" of the website. How the Content is laid out on the screen and the "Navigation Controls" are all part of the Template, including the locations wherein Modules are positioned on each screen.

By way of a review, a "CMS" website is one that separates Content from design and layout. This way, the Content Administrators can enter Content, and not be concerned about the details of color, page arrangement, appearance, and other visual aspects of the screen. Content Administrators are generally not very good at website design, so a "CMS" is perfect for their use. These Editors enter the Content and then save it. When that action is performed, the Content appears on the website, controlled by the Template's layout and visual parameters, which is the result of the work product of the website designer.

What "IS" a Template?
A "Template" is an Extension that has been designed as the key element to display webpages or screens on a Joomla! 5 website. Almost every website, particularly those based on the Joomla! platform, use Templates to display Content.

Not all templates are the same. For example, a "Wordpress" Template [called "theme"], will not work on a Joomla! 5 website. Templates are dedicated for use on their respective "CMS" platforms. Also, don't assume that any Joomla!-based Template can be used on Joomla! 5. They cannot. Templates are dedicated to specific versions of the platform because of the unique manner in which the system operates. The Template receives coded instructions from the base program and each version of Joomla! is different.

How Templates Function

A Joomla! 5 website cannot function without at least one Front-End Template designated as the "default." This is what website visitors see when accessing the Front-End for the first time. From that point onward, it's open game insofar as adding and using other Templates on the website, and the purpose of this Chapter is to, to demonstrate how that can be accomplished.

A Template consists of many files to define its structure and help it operate upon the Joomla! 5 Framework. The "Default Template" does that. Chances are when you add a third-party Template, it will have its own "Framework" upon which it operates, and that "Framework" functions on top of the one for Joomla! default. More about that subject in Chapter 19, "Using Template/Page Builders."

How Templates Work

Templates consist of files containing code that manage various aspects of its operation and appearance, and quite often, specialized function and/or Content. The "visual" part of the Template is controlled by the all-important Cascading Style Sheets ("CSS"), or Syntax Cascading Style Sheets ("SCSS"). More about these in Chapter 18, "Visual: Style Sheets."

When a User visits a website, the default Template fires up, the "CSS" kicks into action, and the webpage or screen displays. Then, based on the visual architecture of the template and the "CSS/SCSS" associated with it, the Content appears.

Here are some points of knowledge you should know about Templates:

- Templates are Extensions.
- Templates are not available in the Joomla! Extensions Directory ("JED").
- Template Enhancements are sometimes available in the "JED."
- Components may also contain their own Templates.
- Templates are typically obtained from private Developers.
- Templates install exactly the same way as other Extensions.
- One Template on a website must be designated as the "default."
- Templates can be assigned to different webpages via the Menu Link Item Assignment method.
- Most third-party Joomla! 5 Templates are built upon a "Framework" other than the default that was originally installed.

- If a Template uses a special "Framework," it is typically installed along with the installation of the Template Extensions. If not, it must be installed before the Template is added to the website.

- There are Joomla! 5 Extensions available that will allow the Administrator to create Templates or individual Pages/Screens that can be globally or selectively used on the website.

- There are Extensions available that allow changes in Templates without actually changing Template Files, that is: manually creating 'overrides."

- Templates have built-in "overrides" that can change the Template configuration and display, re: colors, column layouts and the like.

Where to Get Templates

As previously stated, Templates are generally not available via the "JED," so they must be obtained from third-party developers, or from website shops that sell or distribute them. If you search the internet for "Joomla! 5 templates," you will get many results, where you will find both free and pay-for Templates.

The best way to approach the Template shopping experience is to have in mind the kind of Template and the "look and feel" that you want from it. Then, visit the website offering Templates, look for their Joomla! 5 versions, view the demos (most all Template websites have demos available), and if you like one, make an acquisition decision.

Content has First Priority

When choosing a Template, don't pick a Template and then fill it with Content. Know your Content, then choose a Template that will work the best. However, there are business-specific Templates that are specialized and only require the Administrator to put Content into it. There are thousands of these types available under many hosting plans by many hosting providers. Be aware that it is possible that several hundred or more other websites might be using the same Template and the same images. These business-theme Templates can be modified to suit the needs of almost every website layout and Content requirement.

Templates, Free or Otherwise

Templates are available from providers under these typical scenarios:

Free to Download and Use

This is the most generous source of Templates. Some Developers have created a free Joomla! 5 Template(s) and distribute it/them free of charge without limitations. While these might be hard to find, there are some available. In Exercise 13-1 below, a source of two of these Templates is identified and will be used for instructional purposes.

Free to Download Limited Version, Pay for Full Version

This class of Templates allows a "free" download of a limited version, or it is sold at a reduced price. The full version, or what is commonly called a "Pro" Version, can be obtained at an increased cost, or a higher fee on a per-Template basis, or if you upgrade your membership level on the website.

Pay per Template

This is where Templates are acquired through direct purchase of the Template on a one-at-a--time basis. Administrators simply buy one Template from a source. If only one or two Templates are needed, this type is fine.

Restricted/Limited Use

This is where a Template is acquired and the domain on which it will be used must be designated. Sometimes the number of domains may be several, but they must be identified for specific use. Other paid Templates allow unlimited use, but some are restricted to single and/or only a few domains. Be aware of this when purchasing Templates.

Template Membership Clubs

Rather than buying Templates *ala carte*, a "Club Membership" is required and based on which level, it determines how many Templates may be downloaded. If many Templates are required, this is often an advantageous way of obtaining them. These websites usually have many different membership levels, so determine which best fits your needs and/or possible future needs of Templates from this source.

Version Compatibility Check

When seeking and selecting a Template, ***make absolutely sure*** that it is built to operate on the Joomla! 5 platform. Templates for any other platform will NOT work properly. Double check compatibility before purchasing. Attempting to use incompatible Extensions/Templates has the possibility of permanently "breaking" the website. It is wise not to be reckless when installing Extensions – check them closely.

Template(s) Come with Components

For most modern Templates for Joomla! 5 take advantage of the excellent features built into the platform, along the Developer's platform layered on top of the core. Components, Modules and Plugins often come with the Template. This is frequently the case of the "Themed Template," where they are designed for a specific type of business or industry, a "beauty shop" for example.

Generally, the download file is designated as a "*.pkg*" which means that more than just the Template is "packaged" into the downloaded installer file.

Desktop and Mobile Templates

If you have a mobile device and have accessed website with it, you already know that some websites do not display well, or properly, on the device. In many cases, the website, and it's Template's width, is hard-coded and the mobile device simply shrinks the big desktop site down to miniature size. That problem was solved a long time ago, especially with the introduction of "Bootstrap." Joomla! 5 uses the latest version of "Bootstrap 5," upon which to build the website structure.

This technique makes the websites "responsive." That is, the site adjusts itself based on the width of the browser being used. On a desktop, the wide version displays. On mobile devices, the Template adjusts, according to built-in width-adjustment rules, and the Content displays nicely, shifting to a vertical display of the Content. On mobile devices, much of the Content will "stack" itself vertically and not horizontally. Thus, the devices display react to the screen's width and the Content is accessible by scrolling the device screen vertically.

Template Frameworks

Joomla! 5 has a Template "Framework" that is installed by default. The default Template is coded for the "Framework" for the Front-End. A separate, uniquely distinct, Template is likewise coded for the Administrator's Back-End.

Some independent Template developers build theirs on the default "Framework," but most have their own more advanced version of a "Framework," upon which their Templates are built and coded. This allows them to include features that make them work better, display better and can be administered in many ways such as: changing colors, changing global layouts, changing individual page/screen layout, restructuring the layout and adding Module Positions as needed for unique – and often fun! – features for the Administrator to use.

For a quick understanding, refer to Figure 17-1 for a quick visual understanding of the default Joomla! 5 "Framework," and how third-party "Frameworks" are used in companionship and harmony with it.

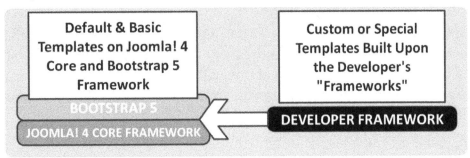

Figure 17-1

The Developer's "Frameworks" take advantage of the Bootstrap 5 integration with the Joomla! 5 core "Framework." This technique allows Joomla! 5 to be used as the base or trampoline from which the Developer's "Framework" and bounce off and create some fantastic Templates.

Aside from Templates themselves, there are also Page/Template Builders that work of the same principals. Chapter 19, "Visual: Using Page/Template Builders," covers their use.

There is nothing the Administrator needs to do or worry about to integrate all this together. It does so by itself when installed. When you add a Template Extension that is built on a third-party Framework, both are installed at the same time. Also, the Developers have already made sure their "Framework" works with Joomla! 5 perfectly.

Updates Not Affected

One great advantage of using third-party Frameworks upon which a Template is built, is they are not affected by Joomla! 5 updates. Sure, the default Template can be modified with "over-rides," but still, having a Template with more features and controls that functions "on top" of the default Framework has many advantages. One of those is that Joomla! 5 core updates do not affect the Third-Party Template.

Installing Templates

Let's apply this integration and install a couple of "freebie" Templates into the "myfirstsite" location. The first course of action is to locate and download a "free" and unrestricted use Template.

Obtaining and Downloading Templates

As with all other Extensions, Templates, being Extensions themselves, must be obtained, downloaded, and then installed into a Joomla! 5 website via the Extensions Installer Manager. Templates are rarely referred to as being "Extensions," but they actually are, so keep that in mind. It's just a matter of semantics.

Front-End and Back-End Templates

Joomla! 5, just as its predecessor versions, uses two templates. One Template applies to the visual display on the visitor-facing Front-End of the website. The second is used on the Back-End to display the Administrators "Home Dashboard" workspaces where the entire website is managed and administered.

At present, there are a number of Front-End Templates available for use on the Front-End. A new, or alternative, Back-End Template has not been released by any of the Developer websites. It is highly likely that one will be available for consideration in the future. There has been for previous Joomla! versions so it is a reasonable assumption another will surface for Joomla! 5 use.

There are no combo-Templates that modify both the Front-End and the Back-End at the same time. Templates that apply to each are individually installed.

Based on the above, the following topics and discussions will deal only with the Templates that are, or would be, used on the Front-End. This is the most important Template(s) anyway, so the information presented will help with the administration and use of more than one Template on the website.

Installing Templates

Templates ARE Extensions. They are installed exactly as other Extensions, although they are treated and administered separately from Modules, Components, Menus, etc. Templates are in a class all by themselves and have a number of unique considerations that the Joomla! 5 website Administrator should be aware of and have working knowledge.

Template or Quickstart Template

When sourcing and downloading Templates, its important that you be aware of the two types that are typically being offered by Template Developers. These are the: 1) Template as a free-standing Extension and 2) Quickstart Template Package. What is the difference?

The Template Extension, by Itself

The "Template," when sourced for downloading, implies that it is an Extension of the "Template" type, that can he installed via the standard processes, into an existing website, and then assigned to various Menu Link Items for display. In other words, this is a free-standing Template that is intended to be installed into an existing Joomla! 5 website.

The Quickstart Template Package

The "Quickstart Template," is actually both a Template and the Joomla! 5 platform. This type of Template ["Quickstart"], is intended to be the installation files for BOTH Joomla! 5 and the Template simultaneously.

Basically, the "Quickstart Template" IS NOT intended to be installed onto an existing Joomla! 5 website. It is intended to be used as the file that will be used to initially install Joomla! 5 on a website server. It contains both the Joomla! 5 core files and the named Template. The latter is installed at the same time as the core Joomla! 5 platform.

In summary, a "Template" is intended to be installed on an existing Joomla! 5 website. A "Quickstart Template" is intended to be used as the initial installer to add a Joomla! 5 website to a server location. It cannot, and should not, be installed on an existing website.

Update Likely Needed

It is possible, after a "Quickstart Template" has been installed, that the Joomla! 5 version may be recently outdated and require an "update" action. No big deal! Just click on the highlighted notification block on the "Home Dashboard" and execute the steps required.

Obtaining a Free Joomla! 5 Template

As with all other Extensions, Templates, being Extensions themselves, must be obtained, downloaded, and then installed into a Joomla! 5 website via the Extensions Installer Manager. This is accessed via the Administrator "Home Dashboard."

At this time, there have been a limited number of Joomla! 5 compatible Templates made available by Template Development Companies. Remember – the Joomla! organization ("Open Source Matters, LLC"), does not build or provide Templates, other than the two included within the program's default installation.

There are several "free" Joomla! 5 compatible Templates being offered for use. We have researched and tested most of them and have selected two templates offered by "Joomlart.com" called: "JA Purity III" and "JA Stark" which will be used to demonstrate the installation and use-configuration of multiple Templates.

No Affiliation

The 200mph Media Group, LLC, does not have any working relationship with "Joomlart" and is not compensated for mention or use of their Templates as featured in this book. We have paid subscriptions to some of their Extension/Template products.

A Usable Joomla! 5 Template

The main Templates that will be used for demonstration in this Chapter is "JA Stark" and "JA Purity III" which are available "free" from the Developers at "joomlart.com." However, a User account is required, and the following are instructions for creating an account, which will allow the downloading of their "free" Extensions. These Templates, because they are "free," do not have any limits to their use and may be used on working websites without any fee.

EXERCISE 17-1: CREATING AN ACCOUNT AT JOOMLART.COM

Objective: The goal of this Exercise is to create a user account at "***joomlart.com***" for the purposes of downloading "free" Templates for use in demonstration Exercises. See the disclaimer above.

Step 1	Open a browser window and go to "joomlart.com"
Step 2	Click on the "Login" button at the top right of the screen.
Step 3	On the next screen, at the bottom, click in the "Signup here" link.
Step 3	Enter your "email address," a "username" and a "password."
Step 5	Agree to the "Terms and conditions."
Step 6	Execute the "FREE SIGNUP' action.

Step 7	An account has now been created and the next screen will allow you to navigate the website as a "logged in user."
Step 8	In the top Menu, which shows the affiliated companies that will allow the use of the same login, click on the "Joomlart" link button, which will take you to their website.

Before proceeding to download any products it is suggested that a familiarization tour of their website, their Templates and Extensions is in order.

Recall the mention that Template Developers often use their own "Framework" upon which to build their Templates and Extensions. The use of the Templates from "Joomlart," includes the automatic installation and implementation of their "T3 & T4 Frameworks" upon which their Template is built.

Additionally, "joomlart" has a "Page Builder," which is a Component Extension that allows the construction of individual website screens. These can be considered as "mini Templates" for use on a single website page vs. a Template, which manages the layout and appearance of the entire website. A limited version of the "Page Builder" can be downloaded "free."

Download Selected Templates & Extension

On the "Joomlart.com" website, perform the following actions to download two "free" Joomla! 5 compatible Templates, along with the "T4 Page Builder" Extension. It is possible the screen layout at "joomlart.com" may have changed and the instructions below might not apply. However, make every attempt to follow similar action steps to download the two Templates and the Extension.

Here is what's going to be accomplished:

Two of "joomlart.com" Templates will be downloaded and installed. Each Template uses a different "Framework" upon which it operates. This will be discussed as the Exercises progress. Also, their Page Builder Component for Joomla! 5 will also be installed.

EXERCISE 17-2: DOWNLOADING TEMPLATES & EXTENSION FILES

Objective: The goal of this Exercise is to obtain two "free" Templates and one "free" Component and install them into the website. The JA_Stark Template and the T3 Framework, the JA_Purity-III Template and the T4 Framework, and the T4 Page Builder Component will be downloaded from the "joomlart.com" website.

Step 1	If not already logged in, log into your user account at "joomlart.com"
Step 2	Open the "Products > Joomla Templates" section in the top Menu, and to the left of the green "All Tags" button in the product selection Menu, select the **"Free(6)"** button and click on it.

Step 3	This displays a list of choices. Click on the graphic panel for the "JA Stark" Template.
Step 4	Click on the "Get it now!" button in the "Quick Info" panel.
Step 5	Among the choices, select "JA Stark Template," making sure that the selection *IS NOT the "quickstart" type.* The "Type" should be identified as a "Template" and NOT a "Quickstart."
Step 6	Go back to the "Free Joomla Templates" using the link in the "Breadcrumbs" Menu to do so.
Step 7	On the resulting screen, open the "Purity III" Template screen. Make sure you have not selected "JA Purity II."
Step 8	Download the "Purity III" Template Type using the download button to the right – making sure that you have *NOT selected the "Quickstart" type.*
Step 9	On the same screen, download the "T3 System Plugin."
Step 10	Click on the "Joomlart" Menu Link item in the Breadcrumbs Menu to return to a previous screen.
Step 11	Scroll down to the" T4 Page Builder & T4 Framework" section and click on the "View All" name.
Step 12	Use "Download" to obtain the "T4 Framework for Joomla 4" file.
Step 13	Use "Download" to obtain the "T4 System Plugin" file.
Step 14	Use the Breadcrumb pathway go back one screen.
Step 13	Click on the "T4 Framework" button. A list of "T4" download items will display.
Step 15	Click on the "T4 Page Builder" button.
Step 16	At the bottom of the list, download the "T4 Page Builder Package," which will include the Extension, the Plugin and the Article Integration feature.

At this point, two Templates and one Extension should have been downloaded to the default location on your computer.

The actual layouts and location on the source website may not be exactly as noted above. If there is a difference, simple search for the specific file name.

EXERCISE 17-3: INSTALLING TEMPLATES & EXTENSIONS

Joomla! 5 has an automatic built-in method that is used to install Extensions of any type. By following the action steps below, the two Templates and the Page Builder Package Extensions can be easily installed.

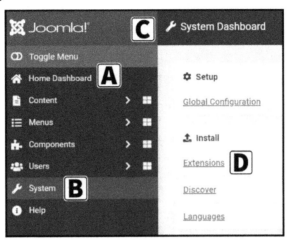

Figure 17-2

Refer to Figure 17-2 for the following:

Step 1	A	Access the "Home Dashboard."
Step 2	B	Access the "System" Administration Area.
Step 3	C	The "System Dashboard" should display.
Step 4	D	Execute the "Extensions" action within the "Install" Block.

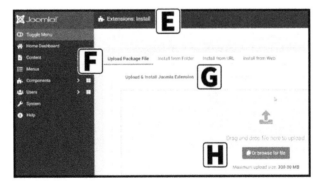

Figure 17-3

Refer to Figure 17-3 for the following:

Step 5	E	The "Extensions: Install" screen should open.
Step 6	F	Select the "Upload Package File" tab option.

Step 7	G	The "Upload and Install Joomla Extension" area should display.
Step 8	H	Click on the "Or Browse for file" if you do not have the ability to drag 'n drop images into the designated area.
Step 9		Browse your computer to access the location of the two Templates and the Extension downloaded previously.

NOTE: *The "J!4" version of these files will install properly into Joomla! 5. Make sure the "T3" and "T4" plugins have been installed as noted below.*

Step 10	Select the "JA Stark" Template, which will automatically start the installation process.
Step 11	When completed, a "Success" message will display, along with information about the Extension.
Step 12	Click on the "Or Browse for file" again.
Step 13	Install the "JA Purity III" Template.
Step 14	After the "Success" message displays, open the "Or Browse for file" link again.
Step 15	Install the "T4 Framework" previously downloaded.
Step 16	Repeat the installation actions to also install the "T4 Pagebuilder Package" file previously downloaded.

At this point, both the "T4 Framework" and "T4 System Plugins" should have been installed, along with the JA_Stark and the JA_Purity-III Templates. Also, the "T4 Page Builder" Component should also be accessible under the "Home Dashboard," Components Menu.

Step 17	Go to the "Home Dashboard > System > Site Template Styles," then click on the "Purity III – Default" Template.
Step 18	An error message will display, noting that "Purity III requires T# Plugin to be installed and enabled."
Step 19	Go back to "joomlart.com" and access the "T3 Framework" download area and click on "T3 Framework," NOT the old version which is identified.
Step 20	Download the "T3 System Plugin."
Step 21	Install the "T3 System Plugin" via the Extension Installer.
Step 22	Go back and attempt to open the "Purity III Template," which should now open properly because the "T3 System Plugin," which it requires, been installed.

This "error resolution" activity has been included to demonstrate how easy it is to resolve these sort of issues when installing Extensions.

Unique Website Pages/Screens

Ignoring page Content for the moment, what makes pages/screens on a website different from each other is the construction of the Module Positions and the Cascading Style Sheet that is applied. Additionally, Joomla! 5, Bootstrap 5 also controls some of the visual aspects and layout configurations.

It is very possible that [aside from Content], every page on a website can have a completely different layout and color scheme based on the combination of Templates and Style Sheets. This is what gives Joomla! 5 websites their functionality and character. It also allows the pages/screens to be designed to be appropriate to the Content, such as business-themed Templates.

An example of this would be a corporate website where there are separate pages/screens for the various departments. Each department has its own page, in its own unique layout and colorization. Thus, each has their own Template variation which makes this possible. This type of website configuration happens more frequently than imagined. Bigger, more complex and Content-filled websites usually are set up and designed in this manner. The authors of Content simply create the Articles and the Template, and/or Page Builders, and their configuration settings takes care of the visual display.

Page/Screen Construction

There are two parts of a Joomla! 5 website page/screen that determine how Content is to appear and how it looks. These two parts are: fixed Content Containers and Modules in fixed Module Positions.

The main fixed Content Container is the Main Content Area, which is where Articles are generally displayed. It is also the area in which the Components, or at least most of them, are generally displayed. This isn't a steadfast situation, but more likely than not, the main Content area will be primarily utilized by Components.

Surrounding the Content Container area, based on hard-coded fixed Module Positions, are the Modules which can be assigned. These Module Positions can be above, below, left, or right of the Content Container. Just knowing this, it is very reasonable to assume that almost any variation of layout is possible for any website page/screen. Add to this the color variations, along with the style of the actual Content within the Content Container and within the Modules displayed, gives rise to the possibility of unlimited appearances.

Templates Control Display

What ties all the above together are the Joomla! 5 Templates. Each Template contains the actual physical construction of the page/screen, along with the fixed "Module Position" designations and the Cascading Style Sheets ("CSS") to control colors and appearance.

Bootstrap 5 controls most of the functionality of the layouts and the default display configurations, which are generally not of a big concern to the website Administrator.

Most quality, modern templates, which are built upon Bootstrap 5 and their respective Frameworks, have Administrator controls which over-ride the default settings that allows changing of almost all of the Template's parameters.

On desktop displays, the general layout of Templates is based on a "horizontal" visual format, which can include "columns" of layouts, along with "stacked" Content. However, on mobile devices, the display configuration is "vertical" whereby most all of the Content is "stacked," which includes Articles and Modules. The reason for this is obvious: to optimize the display of Content for any screen size width. Chapter 32 in the *"Boots on the Ground, Advance Edition, Volume 2"* book covers this topic under: "Joomla! 5 on Mobile Devices."

Multiple Page Layouts Using Templates

Knowing that Templates can be modified and configured, it gives rise to the concept that every webpage can be different. Through the use of one Template, the layouts can be modified by the use of different types of Modules. The page construction stays generally the same, but the Modules can vary on each.

This is how appearance is modified when using only one Template. However, there is another, more creative way, in which the appearance of pages on a Joomla! 5 website can be different – and these differences are notable.

Switching Templates

It is possible to use more than one Template on a Joomla! 5 website. This is accomplished by installing additional Templates [compatible with Joomla! 5], and assigning the Templates to different Menu Link Items in the various Menus being used on the site.

Basically, Template 1 [the designated default Template in use], is assigned to the Menu Link Item that is designated as the "Home" item. This, of course, can be set for any kind to available Content layout, but it is the "default" Template for the "Home" Menu Link Item assignment.

Then, for every other Menu Link Item for which the Template and its layout are to be different, the Template is "assigned" to the Menu Link Item. If three Templates are used, each Template has its own respective Menu Link Item assignment. This is how Templates can be switched between Content on the website pages/screens.

Each "page" can also be modified outside of the Template structure. This will be discussed and explained later.

EXERCISE 17-4: ASSIGNING TEMPLATES TO MENU LINK ITEMS

Objective: The goal of this Exercise is to demonstrate how a Template is assigned to a Menu Link Item, causing it to be displayed when the link is initiated.

Step 1	If not already there, go to the Back-End and log in as the Administrator. The "Home Dashboard" will display.
Step 2	Open the "System" link in the left Menu.
Step 3	In the "Template" block, open the "Site Template Styles" which will display the screen: "Template: Styles (Site)." All of the Templates that have been installed previously will display on the list.
Step 4	Look at the "Pages" column. This will indicate the Menu Link Item assignments for each Template. None of the newly installed Templates should have any assignments noted in this column, as confirmed by the "Not assigned" notation.

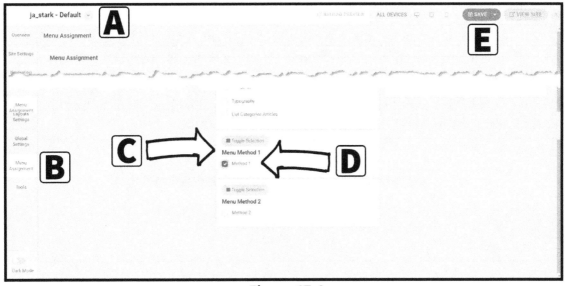

Figure 17-4

Refer to Figure 17-4 for the following:

Step 5	A	Open the "JA Stark" Template by clicking on its name.
Step 6	B	Look to the left and find the "Menu Assignment" tab in the vertical menu and click it. The screen that opens should list all available Menus and all of the Menu Link Items in each.
Step 7	C	Find the "Menu Method 1" and "Menus Method 2" Menus. Each Menu has one Menu Link Item in each.
Step 8	D	In the "Menu Method 1" Menu, select "Method 1." Do not make any

		assignment to the "Menus Method 2" Menu.
Step 9	**E**	Execute a Save & Close action [pull down the Save button], at the top right of the screen. The Template now is assigned to display ONLY when that Menu Link Item's action is executed.
		If necessary, exit this Template screen after a "Save" action by using the browser's "Back" button to return to the "Home Dashboard."
Step 10		Go to the website "Front-End" and refresh the screen.
Step 11		In the "Main Menu," click on the "My First Article Link." This is necessary because the "Menu Method 1" Menu is assigned as a Module to only display when the "My First Article Link" is clicked. This is an example of interactions that may be configured between Menu Link Items and Modules, and now a Template.
Step 12		When the "Menu Method 1" Menu Module displays, click on the "Method 1" Menu Link Item in the Menu.
Step 13		Observe the resulting page. It has changed completely because a new and different Template is displaying the page. And, because of the differences between the default and this Template, the display is completely changed, including Content, Menus and "Module Position" Displays. This will be addressed below.

In the next part of this Exercise, a different Template will be assigned to the "Method 2" Menu Link Item within the "Menu Method 2" Menu Module.

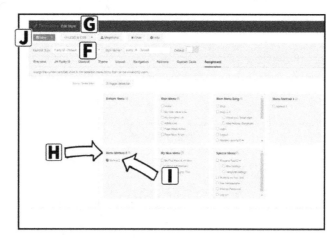

Figure 17-5

Refer to Figure 17-5 for the following:

Step 14	Open the "Purity III" Template by clicking on it's name.
Step 15	Look to the tab bank and find "Assignment" tab along the top and click it.

Step 16		In the "Menu Method 2" Menu, select "Method 2."
Step 17		Execute a Save & Close action [pull down the Save button], at the top left of the screen. The Template now is assigned to display ONLY when that Menu Link Item's action is executed.
Step 18		Go to the website "Front-End" and refresh the screen.
Step 19		Click on the "Home" Menu Link Item in the top Menu displayed on the "JA Stark" Template. This takes the website back to the default main Template.
Step 20		Click on the "My First Article Link" in the Main Menu.
Step 21		Find the "Menu Method 2" Menu in the right column and click on the "Method 2" Menu Link Item.
Step 22		Observe the resulting page. It has changed completely again because now a new and different Template is displaying the page. And, because of the differences between the default and this Template, the display is completely changed, including Content, Menus and "Module Position" Displays. This will be addressed below.
Step 23		Click on the "Home" Menu Link Item in the top Menu, which will return the Front-End to the default "Home" Template.

The above discussions and Exercises address only the ability to add Templates and to selectively use them. Other aspects of multiple Template use are very extensive with regard to Module Positions, Modules, configuration, and the like. It is not possible to fully address these subjects within the limitations of this book.

Just be aware that when switching Templates on a website, not all of the information, Menus and/or Modules will transfer laterally to the newly selected Template and may require additional configuration efforts, as briefly discussed below.

Another observation is the difference in the "admin screens" within the Template Workspace. Neither of these two Templates used the standard Joomla! 5 "saving" buttons. If you install future Templates the action buttons are different.

Different Template, Different Modules

One of the main problems between Templates is the configuration of the Module Positions in the webpage construction and the naming conventions used. For example, the default Joomla! 5 Template has a "Module Position" named: "Sidebar-right." The "JA Stark" Template, for the same "Module Position" calls it: "Sidebar-R." The "JA Purity III" Template designates this same location as: "Sidebar-2."

Now then, knowing that Modules CANNOT be assigned to more than one "Module Position" at a time, this automatically flags this as a major issue with page layouts when switching Templates between pages/screens.

Of course, one could "hack" every Template being used on the website to change all of "Module Position" names to the same name in each Template. That creates a lot of work, and a lot of complications should Templates be updated, and the "Module Position" names become over-written. Then there is the issue of changing all of the "CSS" that might apply. This is simply asking for trouble.

In some cases, the Template "hacking" might work fine, but one can easily see how it could create a real nightmare scenario of many different Templates are being used and issues arise. It will take a lot of work of configure them all.

The other way is to make duplicates of each Module to be used on the different Templates and reassign them to new Module Positions as needed. This might be fine for Module Content that is automatically generated by a Component or Plugin, but doesn't work too well for Custom Content in the Module, where the Module-duplication is the only way.

Of course, using the latter means that every time a change is made to the Custom Module Content, it must be made in EACH of the other Modules that display the same Module Content on different Templates.

No Standard Naming Convention

There is no standard method of naming Module Positions the same on various Templates. Yes, by coincidence, some Module Positions are consistently named, re: Main Menu, Search, Login, etc., but these are limited. Also, some Templates have many more Module Positions than the default or those created by other developers, consistency in naming is almost an impossible task.

There is one possible method of making sure that Custom Module Content can be displayed on various Templates in their respectively named Module Positions, as explained below.

Front-End and Back-End Templates

Joomla! Version 4 operates on two Templates. One is for the management and administration of the website and is referred to as the Back-End. This is where the Administrator manages everything. The other Templates is for the display of Content on the Front-End.

There may be multiple Back-End and Front-End Templates assigned to the website structure. However, at this point in time, there is only one Template available for the Back-End. There are increasing numbers of Templates that can be acquired [free or purchased], for the Front-End.

Additionally, there are several Template creating software products that are available to create your own Custom Templates for the Front End. There are also "Page Builders" which can create individual website pages/screens that can be highly customized with respect to layout and Content. Page Builders cannot easily be converted or applied to operate like Templates because their focus is on the individual page/screen construction. This is a "build one page at a time" process.

Template & Page Builders

Previously, it was noted that there are many Templates available from Developers via several methods, most of them the pay-to-use type. This involves purchasing a Template, or subscription for access, which is a complete and ready-to-use Template. These are installed exactly the same way as any other Extension. Most of the Templates also have an administration area where the Template's parameters can be configured. This allows for some customization within the parameters allowed to be modified. Some of these Templates have limitations on these modifications, and some have administration features that allow the Template to be extensively modified. This is possible through the use of Bootstrap 5 and the Developer's Frameworks, which works above and in conjunction with the Joomla! 5 Framework.

The alternative to purchasing third-party Templates, many of which are now available based on a business-type theme, is to build your own. If starting from nothing, this can be a big undertaking and requires an elevated level of knowledge about Joomla's Templates and the coding involved, along with a high degree of skill in writing "CSS" that accompanies the Template files. It takes a lot of work to create a complex and highly responsive Template.

There is now available, as both free-standing software products and as internally installed Extensions, "Template Builders" and "Page Builders" that can create self-made Templates. Also, the Page Builders allow the creation of individual pages to be created and used that do not affect other Template pages. The investment in these products is minimal and provides the opportunity to create an unlimited number of website pages for self-use or for clients.

Obsolete Products

The Themler and Artiseer Template Builders you may run across are successors of each other and do not work particularly well with Joomla! 5. These two have been replaced by a product called *Nicepage*.

Another product, *TemplateToaster,* was previously a Joomla! Version 3 compatible program and has now been upgraded to function with Version 4, but is not yet indicating it is compatible with Joomla! 5.

At present, *TemplateToaster* and *Nicepage* are two very versatile Template Builders that operate as stand-alone software products that are installed on desktop systems. All others install as Extensions within the Joomla! 5 installation. Instruction on the use of these two products is too extensive to be included within this book. Likewise with the Extensions that install as Template Builders or Page Builders. Each has many configuration possibilities along with customization settings that are very technical and require complex instructions.

Once you have acquired some skill and knowledge about Joomla! Templates and their construction, parts and components, you might want to explore each of the Template Builder and Page Builder products.

VISUAL:

Style Sheets

In the Joomla! 5 scheme of things, the control of website appearance and display is accomplished by Templates and their associated Style Sheets. They work together to cause display of the visual layout and the colors and a number of other parts of the webpage. Every Element on the screen is controlled by a Style Sheet and the related code, referred to as "CSS."

Because Joomla! 5 also works with Bootstrap 5, another type of Style Sheet is also being used with the code being referred to as "SCSS." For the most part, the "SCSS" is not something with which the Administrator need be involved. It is a default set of style coding the is particular to Bootstrap 5. The standard "CSS" is the type which can be changed and/or modified to produce different results in the Templates display.

Within this configuration, multiple Templates (and their "CSS"), can be used to change page layouts and displays individually. This means that multiple Templates can be used on a single website. Templates are assigned to Menu Link Items on a selective basis and can be best understood as displayed in the graphic below:

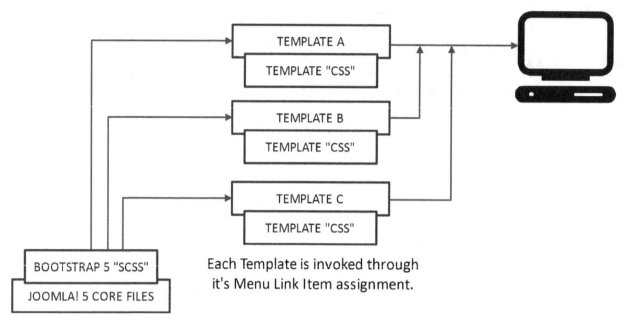

Figure 18-1

This shows that the Joomla! 5 Core Files and Bootstrap 5 feed into each Template, which also has its own "CSS" that applies to them individually. Multiple Templates, when used, are assigned to separate Menu Link Items. When a Menu link is selected, the website screen display changes based on the Template's layout and how the "CSS" is coded to display the visual aspects of the Content Elements.

Among website Templates, one must be designated as the "default." It doesn't make any difference which one, but one must be designated. The "default" also means that ALL Menu Link Items will display the Template. If other Templates are used, and assigned to other Menu Link Items, those control themselves and display Content based on that respective Template's configuration.

The "default" Template display is connected automatically to every Menu Link Item in every Menu. When a second Templates is used, it is connected to at least one Menu Link Item. When associated with the second Template, the Menu Link Item it is also disassociated with the "default" Template.

What Bootstrap 5 Controls

For simplicity sake, without delving too deep into Bootstrap 5, this is the code that controls how a website is displayed on different size screens. Based on 12-column fluid layout configuration, the displays adjusts Content in the columns on the right and place them "below" as the screen size gets smaller.

Conceptually, if there were 12 Modules, for example, all next to each other on one row (on a large monitor), when the same display is viewed on a mobile device with the smaller screen, the Modules would automatically align with 12 stacked one on top of the other.

Incrementally, as the screen width decreases, Bootstrap 5 keeps moving the right side Modules down below others until only the first Module is on top of the eleven others in order. This is pre-determined by the "SCSS" in Bootstrap 5.

Mobile First

If there is a full screen of content on the desktop, Bootstrap 5 takes control of all Elements and moves them down and/or makes them wider to accommodate the size of the smaller screen. In fact, Bootstrap 5 operates on the principle of "Mobile First" when it comes to page layout and design. We all know what a non-mobile website looks like on a phone device. It's terrible. However, the same website layout can be made to display properly on small devices with Bootstrap 5.

Most all Joomla! 5 Template Developers design on the "Mobile First" principles which adapts the display based on the width of the viewing screen.

Should the Joomla! 5 Administrator be concerned with making these configurations? No. The Template deals with this all on its own with an integration of Bootstrap 5 AND the Template Framework and the "CSS."

Default "CSS" Elements on all Templates

Within the "standard" of "CSS" coding rules established by an international organization, and integrated into all viewing browser, there are a given set of "values." These Elements can be viewed here, at the W3C Schools website:
https://www.w3schools.com/cssref/css_default_values.asp

This is a table that shows the "CSS" Element, the default values that should be set, and has a "Try it" link that demonstrates how the "CSS" performs. Play with some of the "Try it" buttons and look at the code and the results. It helps to understand the relationships.

This default settings are built into every popular web Browser. Based on what the "value" settings might be for any given "CSS" Element, the display of the webpage responds accordingly.

On the left side are the "CSS Reference" links. Look at some of them, especially the color Elements to get an idea of the default color settings. Entire books have been written on "CSS" and there is an abundance of information available online. No attempt will be made to duplicate that information in this Chapter.

Typography in Webpages

The actual display of heading, text and Content on a Joomla! 5 webpage comes under the heading of "typography," which are established standards. Every browser is coded to "parse" certain "CSS" Elements. The "W3C Schools" example explains the Elements and their supporting coding.

The "Sample Blog Data" that was previous installed has a sample of the "typography" that is applied to the "Casseopeia" Template. This can be viewed under the "Typography"

Menu Link Item in the top, horizontal Menu. What is shown are but a few samples of the "CSS" Elements and resulting display.

The "h" Elements, of which there are six in each Template, can be individually coded as to size, font, color, weight and other "CSS" values. So can the other Elements as shown.

Here is a listing of the "CSS" that is being applied to the Heading 1 ("h1") Element:

---

h1

box-sizing : border-box;

font-weight : 700;

line-height : 48px;

margin-bottom : 8px;

margin-top : 0px;

font-size : 40px;

font-family : -apple-system, "Segoe UI", Roboto, "Helvetica Neue", Arial, "Noto Sans", sans-serif, "Apple Color Emoji", "Segoe UI Emoji", "Segoe UI Symbol", "Noto Color Emoji";

Figure 18-2

The other "h" Elements have similar coding but with different values as to the "font-size" and so on. You can refer to the "W3C Schools" description of the Element's values for information about what they actually control.

Every single line of Content on a Joomla! 5 website is controlled by some sort of "CSS" coding. These are fixed values that were installed as part of the Template. Every Template has its own "CSS" file that controls the display of "CSS" Elements. As an example, the "h" headings on different Templates, even though installed on the same website, can be completely different as to size, font, color and so on. This is what "CSS" allows Template developers to do, but on a scale that goes far beyond simple "h" Elements.

Standard "CSS" Elements

In the above discussion, the "h1" Element was briefly discussed.

"CSS" codes like "h1, h2, p, ol" and others, are called "selectors." When creating Articles or other Content in which "CSS" can be assigned, there are other "selectors" in the default files, such as:

h1	Top level heading Element.
h2	Secondary level heading Element.
h3 h4 h5 h6	These are all additional secondary heading Elements that can be used, based on the content structure of heading and text. Each can be configured differently to enhance the display of Content.
p	This is the "CSS" Element that defines a "paragraph" of text, which applies to all default text.
ol li	An "ordered list" is on that has the items displayed as: 1. List Item 2. List Item 3. List item The "ordered list" can be any type of number or an alpha character, but not a "bullet" image.
ul li	An "unordered list" is on that has the items displayed as: • List Item • List Item • List item The "unordered list" can be any type of "bullet" image, but not a number or an alpha character.

A more comprehensive list of "CSS" Elements can be found at the link below. Spend some time viewing this list to get a familiarization with the names of the Elements. For any given "CSS" Element, there can be assignment of values that affect how Content Items that are so designated will display on the Front-End.

https://www.w3schools.com/cssref/css_default_values.asp

The above website is an excellent place to spend time to get familiar with "CSS" and the Elements and values that can be assigned to them, and what the expected results should be.

Fixed or Variable Size References

Without going into great "CSS" detail, within the webpage there are Elements which rely on size settings. This can be the size of the font, the width of the page or an Element on the page, or other related content. The control of the size is in the "CSS" coding assigned to the Element.

Basically, sizing on webpages is set in "pixels," the value used for measurement of monitor screens. This is a fixed, hard-coded value. Which means, the Element, a font-size as an example, will remain at 18px regardless of the size of the screen. A nice large heading (72px), on a large screen will look just fine. But the same view on a lower resolution device screen would be massive. It would look awful.

Therefore, two other value settings have been included, which are the "em" and the "rem."

px	This is a *fixed-value size* that displays in the same size regardless of the size of the screen and is relative to the pixel resolution of the screen. It is "16px" of screen space on any size screen.
em	This is a *variable size* based on a percentage-size of the *"parent"* Element.
rem	This is also a *variable size* but it is based on the percentage-size of the *"root"* Element.

Let's apply these to a "font-size" value of 16px, which is the default size of the "root" Element provided by the browser. Don't worry about that setting, you can't change it. Here is how "em" and "rem" work using the 16px value as an example.

What is a parent value? If a font is within a "table layout," and the "CSS" for the "table" has a font-size setting, then the value being applied is "relative" to the font-size setting as establish in the "table" settings. Assume the font-size for the "table" is 18px, and an "em" setting is .777, the resulting size is equal to 14px. If set at 1.333, the resulting size is 24px.

If there is no "font-size" setting specified in the "CSS" for the "table," the "root" value now controls and the "rem" setting is the new variable factor. In this way, font-sizes can be controlled in several ways, relative to their location within the page's "CSS" structure. This can all get very complicated, which is why it is suggested that you study the "W3C Schools" resources to learn more about "CSS" and "Bootstrap" Element coding.

px	16px is the default font-size value for the text display.
em (parent)	The relative values are dependent upon whether the Elements "parent" has a font-size setting. Setting "em" at 100% results in the obvious; setting it at 150% results in a font-size display of 24px. 150% is the same as 1.5000em. Either setting can be used. In fact, if the desired font-size is the same as the "parent" value, no identical value need be assigned.
rem (root)	Absent a "parent" font-size setting, the relative values are established from the "root" font-size setting, re:

> 16px in this example. Setting "rem" at 100% also results in the obvious; setting it at 150% results in a font-size display of 24px. 150% is the same as 1.5000rem. Either setting can be used. In fact, if the desired font-size is the same as the "root" value, no identical value need be assigned.

Examining the "CSS" for a Template

First, there is no particular reason that the "Bootstrap 5 SCSS" files need to be modified unless you are building or creating an entirely new Template. In fact, there are Extensions that allows this activity to be performed by the Administrator, as outlined in Chapter 19, "VISUAL: Using Template/Page Builders."

The "SCSS" of Bootstrap 5 is utilized by the Template/Page Builders, but it is typically not modified or "recompiled" by the Extension. However, the "CSS" within the Template/Pagebuilder "Framework" is/can be modified to change the appearance and layout of the screen Content.

On the other hand, it is possible to change the "CSS" applied to an existing Template not created using a Template/Page Builder. The obvious question now is: "Where is this done?"

Access via the Back-End

The most convenient way to access and examine the "CSS" files that control the display of the Front-End is via the Template's area of the Back-End, as follows:

Step 1		If not already there, access the "Home Dashboard."
Step 2		In the left Menu, access: "System > Site Templates," which will display the three Front-End Templates.
Step 3		In the default Cassiopeia Template, click on: "Cassiopeia Details and Files." This opens a list of the folders and files that are within it's installed directory/folder.
Step 4		Click on the "css" folder name. This will display the folders and files that control the visual aspects of the Front-End when this Template is being viewed.
Step 5		Click on the "template.css" file name, near the bottom of the list.
Step 6		What is being shown is the actual code for every "CSS" style that is applied to every Element.
Step 7		Scroll down the page and look at some of the Elements and their code. If you don't understand "CSS," this stuff can be very complicated.

Step 8	PLEASE DO NOT MAKE ANY CHANGES TO THE "CSS" CODE.
Step 9	Notice that there are many references to "rem" font-sizes which scales the Content associated with that Element either up or down as a "relative" size.

How "CSS" Works with Templates

Within the Joomla! 5 scheme of things, Templates and "CSS" files are always associated. The coding of the layout in a Template makes reference to "CSS" files and the Elements therein. Then, the "CSS" file contains the Element settings that cause the Template to display the Content in a certain way.

When a Template starts to display, in addition to calling upon all the other resources, it reaches out to the various "CSS" files that are "linked" to it, and parses the instructions for the "CSS" Elements into a visual display. Every piece of Content on a Template screen has some controlling "CSS" that makes it display. This can be the "default" that is controlled by the "root" settings. Or the display can be controlled by the "CSS" setting that is caused by the "parent" of the item being displayed.

Even better, the "inline styles" can also control the display. An "inline style" is something as simple as a bold word or italicized text within a paragraph. Only that text is affected, but it is within an assigned "CSS" Element's tag, a paragraph <p> as an example. Thus, the "inline" designation, which is an over-ride of its "parent CSS" for specific words.

More than one "CSS" Style Sheet

There are typically more than one Style Sheet linked to a Template. Bootstrap 5 has several Sheets that are applied in the background. There are other "CSS" Style Sheets that are applied to on-screen Content. Many of these Style Sheets are lengthy and have some very complex coding of the "CSS" Elements.

When Third-Party Components are added, they too will have Template layouts that apply to only the Content generated by them. As a result, there are also more "CSS" Style Sheets that are called upon for the page display.

This generally works whereby the default Template is used, with its respective "CSS" Style Sheet. Then the Component, which displays within the Main Content Area of the screen also has its own "CSS" Style Sheets that come into play. This is a typical example of how many "CSS" Style Sheets can be applied to the same screen display at the same time.

Other Types of "CSS"

There are three ways in which to apply "CSS" to a content Element, as follows:

Via an External Style Sheet	This is a separate file that is specified and calls the "CSS" code into play when a page is displayed. The Style Sheets are linked by a lines of code in the "head" section of the website's

	main webpage.
Via Internal or Embedded "CSS"	This is where the "CSS" is part of the file that displays the Content. It can be injected at any point in the file, but is usually in the <head> section. This "embedded" Style coding can supplement any other "CSS" that might be applied to the specific webpage.
Via Inline "CSS"	If something is selected on the page, usually via a Content editing workspace, and its "CSS" assignment is different, it is considered to be an "inline" application of the "CSS." A bold word in the middle of a sentence is an example. So would a line of type that has been selected and set to display in italics. These are both "inline CSS" uses.

Without delving into the code of the "CSS," here are some examples:

Internal/Embedded	This code example changes the color for the <p> (paragraph) tag, and this code can be inserted into the <head> section of the webpage.
	
	`<style type="text/css">`
	`p {color: #F00000;}`
	`</style>`
	
	More "CSS" Elements can be added to the code and it will only apply on the screen into which it is embedded. This is a "block" of "CSS" code that is inserted into the page, thus it is considered "internal" to that page/screen only.

Inline	This is a **bold** word. Another example is applied in this way: <p style="color: #F00000;">This is a paragraph of text.</p> and applies until the "closing" tag </p> is listed.

More about application of "CSS" is found at the "W3c Schools" website, including the use of Styles, Closing Tags and how other Elements are properly coded. As previously stated, the entire "CSS" knowledge base and application is very extensive.

Books with more pages than this one have been written on the subject of "CSS," along with hundreds of thousands of web references. In fact, a search for "css selectors" can return over 2,800,000 pages – which is a lot of reading, and is why the reference above to "W3c Schools," the official world-wide "bible" for "CSS" coding. It is an Administrator's valuable resource if modification of "CSS" might be required to change a Template's display appearance.

Because this book is not written as a "CSS" primer, and the many online references to it, no attempt is made to replicate that information. However, in other Chapters and Exercises, some individual "CSS" modifications may be used and demonstrated.

Two Types of Style Sheets

For a Joomla! 5 website, there are typically two types of style sheets that are in control. The first is the Style Sheet(s) that apply to the Bootstrap functions that manage the page and display mechanics. The section is the Style Sheet that is associated with a Template. This Style Sheet controls the page layout and visual aspects of the page and its Content elements.

Bootstrap Style Sheets

There are dozens of Bootstrap connected Style Sheets, far too many to describe and illustrate here. It is worth noting that the Joomla! 5 Administrator likely has no need to access or modify any of the "CSS" or "SCSS" files within the Bootstrap file sections. These files control how the webpage reacts to different screen sizes, and this is done on a fixed-rule method for different sizes. It all happens in the background, so Users are not aware of what is going on.

The Bootstrap Style Sheets contain and conform to certain rules which makes the webpage react based on screen width. This is the application of the "Mobile First" concept of webpage design. This is also one of the reasons that "multi-column" page layouts have been phased out. The "sidebar-left" and "sidebar-right" layouts fell out of favor quickly after Bootstrap started being used.

Sidebars are still being used, but not for things like Menus, because they would move out of location too much. Menus are now typically displayed horizontal across the top, and Bootstrap converts them to a "Hamburger" looking button when the screen width reaches a certain value. The Menu is then accessible in a "fly-out" when the "Hamburger" is swiped, tapped or clicked.

Figure 18-2 below shows the same webpage with a name heading and horizontal Menu and how the display changes when the screen width is reduced from a very large desktop to a mobile phone device:

Figure 18-2

Figure 18-3 displays the Menu on a Mobile Phone Device when the "Hamburger Menu" icon at the top right is tapped, displaying the Menu, in this case, it is being displayed on the left side:

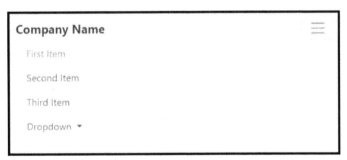

Figure 18-3

As shown above, the Menu display changed from horizontal on the Large Screen to a "Hamburger" icon in Figure 18-2, then when tapped, the Menu displays vertically on the smaller screen as in Figure 18-3. All of these changes were accomplished by Bootstrap

351

and was also accomplished automatically, with no change in any code in any Style Sheet, be it Bootstrap or that of the Template.

Template Style Sheets

Template Style Sheets, as previously stated, control the layout and appearance of the webpage. They do not control the mechanics and manipulation of the Content that happens when the webpages are viewed on different screen sizes (widths). The Template Style Sheets control the Content Elements and how they appear visually, not how they react to changes in screen width display.

Bootstrap controls how a webpages are displayed on different screen widths, the function of the Template Style Sheet can be considered.

The Template Style Sheet controls the layout and visual aspects of ALL of the elements on the page. This includes images, text, Module layouts, and every other piece of Content. The "CSS" settings are the fixed-codes that apply to each element based on their "ID" or their "class." Again, refer to the "W3C" website for specific information about each of the possible elements and the codes which can be applied.

Third Party Templates

The default Joomla! 5 Template is very limited as to which color can be changed by the Administrator. Third-Party Templates, however, typically do not have such a limitation. In fact, they have gone one step further and integrate Bootstrap with their own Framework, and then add control which will actually change the "CSS" that is applied on-screen via the Template. Some of these actually allow the Administrator to make extensive and a wide range of changes to the visual appearance of the website page.

Because this is a Template, and the settings apply to every page that is displayed, there are limits to webpage displays. For example, if the "paragraph text" is set to display in blue, it will display in blue on every webpage that is created and assigned to the Template via the associated Menu Link Item.

Also, the website banner and other images, color blocks, heading sizes and colors, along with many more page elements can be changed – but only on a global basis within the Template. All the settings apply to every page.

Problem Solved

The ability to make more than global changes via a Template has been solved. The introduction of Template & Page Builders introduced a whole new world of both physical layout and visual controls for webpages.

Using actual Template and Page Building Extensions and Tutorials on their use, can be found in these *Boots on the Ground* future volumes, to be Published in 2023:

VISUAL:
Using Template/Page Builders

In previous Chapters, numerous references have been made to Extensions called: "Template Builders" and "Page Builders." This Chapter devotes itself to topics about these Extensions consisting of useful information about each.

It has already been established that Joomla! websites consist of a "Site Template" and a "Style Sheet" that operate with the "core" files, along with those of Bootstrap 5, to generate website pages/screens. The look and appearance of the webpages is dependent solely upon the "Site Template" being applied. "Site Templates" are associated with Menu Link Items, which permits several different "Site Templates" to be used on a highly selective basis.

The problem with this approach, is the Administrator is virtually "stuck" with what the "Site Template's" coding provides. The only way to make changes is to create "overrides," but this isn't an undertaking for those not experienced with website coding.

The "Site Templates" can be dramatically modified to create a desired final layout, but often this effort requires an advanced knowledge of "CSS" and even "SCSS" and Bootstrap. Modifying "Site Templates" is usually a difficult undertaking.

Commercially Available Templates

There are an incredible number of Joomla! 5 Templates available from third-party Developers. These include both "Site Templates" and those that are theme-based. These are either free, or available via some sort of method of payment be it per-Template, per-Subscription or per-Membership as discussed in Chapter 17.

Some Templates' styles are generic in that they may be used for any type of website. The current, and increasingly more popular approach, is to create Templates that are specific for a certain theme or industry, re: *education, beauty shop, restaurant, political, etc.* These come with theme-specific images where an Administrator need only to insert the appropriate text and replace some photos for their business.

Content from Articles

Some "themed" Templates are really "Site Templates" or "Page Builders" in disguise. Joomla! operates on a Category plus Article plus Menu Link Item arrangement to display Content. The "themed" Templates are webpages with blocks of text inserted that are not generated via the standard Joomla! 5 "Articles" structure. Therein lies the difference. Templates typically display Articles as the Content, while the Page Builders display "blocks" of Content (text and images), which may only be edited within the "blocks," which are not Articles.

Not to be misleading, it is necessary to point out that a standard Joomla! 5 Article can be inserted into any part of most "Page Builder" layouts. Not all "Page Builders" have that feature wherein an Article can be placed into any part of the webpage. If that feature is important to the website's Content objective, make sure the "Page Builder" that is selected allows Articles to be embedded. When that action is permitted, the Article can be edited at the source, which is via the Joomla! 5 Article Workspace. Joomla! 5 Modules may also be inserted in the same manner and edited in the Modules respective Workspace.

Anyway, there is an affirmative tradeoff in using one or the other. For example, if the website is primarily a "blogging" type of site with input from many authors, then the "Template" method of display management is probably the route to take.

Creating a website using "Page Builders" where the Content is going to be created by multiple Authors and displayed on different pages in different type of Blog Layouts, the Administrator will have a lot of work to do to create the webpages. The upside is that some very graphically enhanced and visually interesting pages can be created.

Brochure Style Websites

If the website is a "brochure" style, promotional, or self-serving, then the "Page Builder" use is very appropriate. Using a "Page Builder," allows the Administrator to create some very nice looking "Blocks" of Content, and most Extensions provide these in pre-configured layouts. The "Block" is dragged into position, the image and/or text changed, rinse and repeat, and the "page" has been "built." Some of the "Page Builder" self-promotions actually lay claim to "hundreds" of these Content "Blocks." Most of these claims are true.

Developer Template Framework

Another factor that plays into the realm of Templates is the Developer's "Framework" which operates with/above the core Joomla! "Framework." This allows customized Template development that is independent of the limits of Joomla! 5.

For "themed" Templates, how this is implemented is simple. The Developer "Framework" is integrated into the Content Editor Workspaces. When an Article is open for editing, there is an option to switch from the "default editor" to the "Framework" Editor, thereby changing control of the editing process. The "builders" are integrated into the Article Workspace. The modifications work only for the individual Article being modified.

This is great, because the Administrator gets the best of both features. First, the core Joomla! 5 Content hierarchy management system. Second, the expanded features that are available using the Developer's "Framework" to create and modify not only the Content, but the look, feel and style of the Article's layout.

When a Developer's Template is installed, their "Framework" is also installed, or should be installed prior to the Templates. This was the case with the "T3-" and "T4-Frameworks" in an earlier Chapter. Without naming them all, there must be close to a dozen different Developer "Frameworks" that can be installed that "operate" above the Joomla! 5 core "Framework."

The Joomla! 5 website Administrator requires no knowledge whatsoever about "Frameworks" and how they function. "Frameworks" typically operate as "Plugins" and require no Administrator intervention to function properly. Plugins simply run in the Background automatically when Joomla! 5 starts, which "triggers" the Plugin into action.

Website Layouts Past and Present

Before the invent of mobile devices, webpages generally had "Site Templates" that typically configured the screens with left- and right-sidebars and a Main Content Area, along with above and below "Module Positions."

Developers started building websites with the Main Menu in a horizontal view along the top of the screen. Then, it moved to the left-sidebar location. Then, it got "trendy" to have the Main Menu located at the right-sidebar location. It was easier to move the mouse to the right of the screen rather than all the way across to the left, the farthest point away from the vertical scroll control. Early "mice" did not have page-scrolling wheels, so pages had to be scrolled using the on-screen right scroll bar.

Along Comes the Mobile Viewport

When the websites with the left- or right-sidebar location were viewed on mobile devices, the display instantly turned into a wreck. Often times, the Main Menu would actually get pushed to the bottom of the screen. The novel "Hamburger" Menu solved that problem, but the issue of "what to do" with the left- and right-sidebar Content, which could be anything that a Module could display.

Bootstrap solved that problem with the flexible page layout where items that were too wide to display horizontally were simply pushed down one row on the layout. Of course, it isn't really all that simple, but you get the idea.

As far as Joomla! was concerned, this was a big problem. The solution was easy to implement - eliminate the sidebar "Module Positions." This gave birth to those nice long, scroll-forever, vertical pages. They looked great on mobile devices but were a scroll-forever-horror on desktop or wide-screen devices. These type of webpage layouts lend themselves well to the "Mobile First" design concepts.

Website pages now began to be developed using "rows" with embedded "columns" that would have automatic "break points" based on the width of the device's screen. Then, the Joomla! "Modules" that were/are being used were changed into "Content Blocks" and other type layouts. All that worked just fine. Great Templates could be created.

After that, the idea of individual "Pages" came about. Not only that, the creation, layout and use of the one-page layouts was handed off to the Administrator to design and configure. This same technique started being applied to not only single website pages, but to entire Templates as well. Administrators now have full control over all aspects of page/screen design, layout and even Content.

Today, the concept of the "sidebar" layout for Templates is pretty much history, although there are many options available in that area. For example, a website can be created with "sidebar" layouts for wide-screen devices. Thanks to Bootstrap and the third-party "Frameworks," as the screen size gets smaller, the layouts automatically change in a predetermined way. Thus, the current methodology for website page/screen layouts is to optimize the views for large screen sizes to smaller devices using the "Mobile First" concepts. Webpages are designed in reverse, starting with the small-screen device view and upwards from there, utilizing Bootstrap's horizontal "break points" and the "Framework" modifications.

To carry further, for any given "Page Layout" created by some Page Builders, four versions of the "page" can be created, one for each different group of devices, based on their screen width.

Difference Between Template and Page Builders

The "Site Templates" are designed and coded so that they control the layout and display every page/screen on a website. When a Menu Link Item action is executed, the same "Site Template" displays, but with different Content and possibly, different Modules in the "Module Positions." The "Site Template" layout is fixed, and the variables deal with the Content and the display of the Modules. The width of the "Site Template" can be variable to a degree before becoming fully "responsive" to any screen width. The Template has certain "break points," at which time, the wide-screen display changes to a mobile-size, and "breaks" its visual structure.

Many different "Site Templates" can be used on a Joomla! 5 website by associating them with specific Menu Link Items. The display then switches back and forth between "Site Templates" based on which Menu Link Item is clicked, thus giving the traditional "Site Template" website great flexibility and latitude with regard to display design, layout and configuration along with related Modules.

It could be weakly argued that using multiple "Site Templates" is the same as using individual "Pages" to display a website. There are major differences between "Site Templates" and "Pages," as explained earlier. For the time being, consider the use of Templates as being a site-wide application of the style and layout, with Content varying based on the page topic that is selected. The "Site Template" remains the same, the Content (and Modules), change.

A Joomla! "Site Template" normally includes "Module Positions" into which any default-installed Modules, or added-on Third-Party Module Extensions can be placed. If there is no "Module Position" coded-into and/or identified on a "Site Template" page, a Module cannot be assigned. Of course, Modules may be added into Articles, but that's not the same as place them into "Module Positions."

"Site Templates" also may, or may not, contain those "sidebars" as mentioned previously. However, the "sidebars" are likely to be configured in such a way as they only show properly on large-screen website displays. The use of "sidebars" is becoming less and less, in favor of more Bootstrap managed layouts as found in "Page Builders."

Template Builders

At this point in time, there are only three "Site Template" Builders that will create "Site Templates" compatible with Joomla! 5 and can be installed as an Extension. These "Site Templates" are automatically applied to each page on the website when a Menu Link Item action is executed. These, by brand name, are (in no order of preference):

1. **Themler** (successor to *Artisteer*, calls itself a "Template Designer")
2. **Template Toaster** (calls itself a "Website Maker")
3. **NicePage** (calls itself a "Website Builder")
4. **LineLab** (lists the software as a "Template Builder")

Each of these "Site Template" Builders has its own unique advantages. The learning curve for each is somewhat steep (if you have no experience with Templates). This is because of all the different menus, Content insertion options, and the configuration details for each which must be set by the Administrator.

Each also has its own way of creating "Templates" and has many control elements that configure the layout, structure, Content and all aspects of the "visual" part. There are many controls that set the "CSS" parameters of every single part of the Template. It is helpful to have an understanding of "CSS" and how it generally applies.

One of the great features of these programs is that the Content can be added as the Template is being constructed. When it is exported and then installed into Joomla! 5, the Template can take the Content with it, which can then be edited. The Administrator has the options: 1) exporting the created "Site Template" with or without the Content that was created, and 2) export the "Site Template with or without the Template Builder program with which to edit same.

If you have any experience with Templates, all of these programs should generate excitement at the possibility of creating you own, highly customized Templates. The Extensions/Programs are fun to use. They allow the Administrator to experiment with layouts and designs, even previewing them on different screen width devices for testing purposes.

If the Administrator has any Template experience, creating custom "Site Templates" using these programs can be a relatively uncomplicated project to undertake. An advantage of these programs is that the Administrator can "play 'n learn" by experimentation and modification of the elements of the Template. While learning how to create a Template, the Administrator can also hone skills in Template design and the application of the built-in "CSS" configurations.

Explore the Template Builders

Which Template Builder to use? That's a great question and one that can only be answered AFTER some research and exploration. For some Administrators, this can be uncharted territory, so gathering information and knowledge about the products is important.

Each of the Template Builders has a website, they are listed below.

1. **Themler**   https://themler.io/
2. **Template Toaster** https://templatetoaster.com/
3. **NicePage**   https://nicepage.com/
4. **LineLab**   https://www.linelab.org/

It is suggested that you visit each website, read everything about the product, view any of their videos and, by all means, if they have a "demo" or "free build" access to use the product, DO IT! Accumulating knowledge about the workings of Template Builders will be helpful, even if you do not use one.

When reviewing a Template Builder, the best thing to do it to look into every control menu of the program. Look at everything under each menu, which will help to enhance your knowledge of what the controls do and the settings that can be configured. Try and test everything. You can't break the program. Nothing can go wrong if you mess something up.

When experimenting with the Template Builders, work on the projects from a "Mobile First" viewpoint, and use the resize buttons in the menus to look at the layouts as they would appear on different screen-width devices. Each of the Template Builders has this viewing option, which is a very helpful tool.

It may take a while to get familiar with each Template Builder, but the time spent will be well worth the effort.

Joomla! 5: Boots on the Ground, Extended Edition, Volume 3, "Template Builders," will be Published with more information and detailed tutorials about each of the Joomla! 5 Template Builder Extensions: Themler, Template Toaster, NicePage and LineLab. This book will be an excellent detailed reference manual for the Template Extensions, along with the Developer's tutorials and links to videos that can be accessed on the respective Developer's product websites.

Page Builders

These are Joomla! 5 Extensions that "build pages," using the features of Bootstrap 5 and the third-party Developer "Frameworks," both working in conjunction with the core program. These Extensions build individual webpages, which can also include embedded Content. Page Builders do not create individual Articles in the traditional Joomla! method *per se*. They create "pages" or "Sections" of Content, which consists of a wide array of "content types," in many combinations of styles and layouts. Some use the term "blocks" for different parts of the layout.

Page Builders are actually fun to work with – at least those that are set up to be both functional and user-friendly. The construction of the pages/screens can be performed on a top-down basis. After that, Content can be added at any location by simply inserting it at the desired spot. The rest of the "page" automatically adjusts itself to accommodate the new Content insertion.

Of importance when using "Page Builders," is their ability to allow the Administrator to create website pages using the "Mobile First" strategies. Every piece of Content that is added, and every section, row, column and block thereof can be "previewed" and tested on each device screen width while the design is being perfected.

How a "Page Builder" uses Joomla! 5 Articles is rather simple. Content Items can be inserted into any location on the webpage being constructed. One of these Content Item choices is "Article," referring to a Joomla! Article. Thus, an existing Article can be placed into the page layout. It can be edited in the normal Article Workspace when Published.

Bootstrap's Role

Bootstrap plays a major role in the use of "Page Builders" by providing the layout footprint and variables. The third-party "Framework" adds more features to the layouts along with a User interface that allows Content creation and layout manipulation to be performed using easy drag 'n drop methodology.

Bootstrap 5 makes the Joomla! 5 platform operate using advanced techniques. It also allows third-party Developers to integrate their "Frameworks" into the Joomla! 5

platform. They too take advantage of Bootstrap 5 in both the operation and output generated by their Extensions.

In addition to all that, Page Builder Developers have also created "themed" and preconfigured Page Builder layouts (sometimes referred to as their "templates"). These are top-to-bottom layouts whereby all an Administrator need do is add their specific Content and/or replace photos or images. Page Builders function about the same way as the online, cloud-based website builders such as: *SquareSpace, Wix* and others. The difference being that Page Builders are Extensions installed into the Joomla! 5 platform while the online services are accessed via their access-controlled website platform, Extensions are installed within the Joomla! 5 package and are directly integrated.

Content Assets are Plentiful

Another great thing about Page Builders is their inclusion of thousands of variations of "blocks" of Content. These extensive libraries of "blocks" can give the Administrator near unlimited assets and options for layouts and Content presentation. Some of the Page Builders have ready made "sections" that contain "blocks" of layouts.

The unique part is that the "sections" or "blocks" can be changed, modified or customized by the Administrator in every way possible through configuration controls and settings. When a "section" or "block" is placed on the layout, it can be further edited and modified be the Administrator. Such things like the font, font-size, font-color, background color, physical layout and dozens of other settings can be instantly changed.

Page Builders don't skimp on add-ons either. The possibilities are unlimited when the "add-ons" are included with the "sections" and "blocks." Additionally, most of them have "on/off" controls on which of these parts will be displayed on which devices based on their screen size.

Page Builders also make use of pre-designed "templates," which apply only to single "pages" and not an entire website, although then can be used in a similar manner. In any case, it is really a matter of terminology.

Page Builders build individual "pages." That's the bottom line. If you want several pages, you will need to duplicate or build each one separately. How this is done, in practice, is another thing.

After being installed, there are three ways by which Page Builders interact with Joomla! 5, as described below:

As a Component	This type is installed as a Component and operates as a "mini application" running within Joomla! 5. The Component is accessed, and "pages" can begin to be created, then assigned to the Menu Link Items. They can be edited and updated at any time.
As an Article Add-on	With this type, which may also be a Component, the access point is primarily within the individual Article Workspace. When editing, a "Use ..." button is clicked and it switches over from the default

	Article Editor Workspace to a "Page Builder" workspace wherein the layout and Content editing takes place.
As an Online Service	When this type of Component is used, the Workspace is connected directly to an online resource. When the layouts are created and changes made, they are saved within Joomla! 5's structure. The Workspace is separate from Joomla! 5. However, the layout on the website is changed and updated based on the actions taken using the online editor. The two connect to each other for creating and editing Page layouts. In short, layouts are created and/or changed on the Developer's website and then inserted into the working website location.

Naming can be Confusing

Page Builders sometimes uses a naming convention that typically associates with traditional Templates. In fact, some of the parts of the Content of Page Builders are frequently called Templates. Do not mistake them with Joomla! 5 "Site Templates." The Page Builder "templates" refer to the Extensions internal pre-made layouts that fit into their platform. The end-product of a Page Builder may be called a "template," but it is not the same as the Joomla! 5 Template. There is a difference, and this can cause some confusion. Be aware of the differences between the two.

A "Page" is a layout that is displayed for only one webpage. A Menu Link Item connects to the webpage, and each has its own. A Template is a single layout that is used site-wide.

Templates appear by default and the layout is the same on each page, with variations based on use of Modules and Module Positions. Templates are automatically set to be used for each webpage, unless any additional Templates are added, then manually set to display when a certain Menu Link Item is elected.

Page Builder Extensions Available

There are many Page Builders available, as a quick internet search will readily show. Searching for "page builders Joomla" will result in pages that have links directly to Developers websites. There are also "best" listings where all of the Extensions are listed on one website. Some of these "best" lists are outdated and may not contain all of the available Page Builder Extensions. They may also list *Wordpress* Page Builders, which obviously will not work on Joomla! 5 websites.

Here is a list of some of the results listed alphabetically. Some may, or may not, be compatible with Joomla! 5, so due diligence is required to make that determination A simple web search by Extension name will take you to the Developer's website:

1. Azura Joomla Page Builder
2. Blox Page Builder
3. Content Builder
4. Geek Landing Page Builder
5. JA Builder
6. JD Builder
7. Joomla Website Builder Gridbox
8. Page Builder CK
9. Quix Page Builder
10. RS Page Builder
11. SP Page Builder
12. T4 Page Builder
13. YOO theme Page Builder

If any Page Builder Extension/Service has been missed or omitted, our apologies. Contact the Author to advise of the omission.

It is advisable to double-check each Page Builder Extension for Joomla! 5 compatibility and the purchasing options.

Joomla! 5: Boots on the Ground, Extended Edition, Volume 4, "Page Builders," will be devoted to individual reviews and detailed operational information about each of the Joomla! 5 Page Builder Extensions available at the time of Publishing. This will be a single volume that is devoted strictly to Page Builders. *Volume 3*, as previously noted, will address only the use of *"Template Builders."*

Live Demos

Most of the Page Builders have online demonstrations of their products. These will allow you to actually build or make changes to an existing layout. Be sure to "try" each Page Builder before making the commitment to use one. Ensure the Page Builder will create the layouts that are needed for your website. Also, make sure that you are comfortable with the method by which the Page Builder operates to create and manage the Content and layouts. Some can be very easy to use, others not so much.

Similar to buying an automobile, it is advisable to "test drive" the Page Builder before making the purchase decision. Also, please note that more than one Page Builder Extension can be installed and used. This will allow greater flexibility if needed for heavily customized screen layouts. Separate webpages can be created by different Page Builders if desired. All that is needed is to connect the "page" created by the Page Builder to a Menu Link Item to open the screen.

Page Builders are usually built upon a third-party "Framework," and more than one "Framework" can be installed by the Administrator. In fact, when adding a Page Builder Extension, the "Framework" required is usually installed at the same time.

Wordpress or Joomla!

When researching "Page Builders," always check to make sure they are compatible with Joomla! 5. There are several "builders" exclusively for the *Wordpress* platform, and they will not work with Joomla! 5.

However, many "Page Builders" come in two versions: Joomla! 5 and *Wordpress.* Choose the correct version when acquiring the Extension. Also, with "Template Builders," they too can export to *Wordpress* in addition to Joomla! 5. Chose the correct output format when exporting the "Site Template."

Another consideration is that some of the Template Builders create Templates, then give the Administrator the choice of platform during the export process.

Basic vs. Pro Versions

This was mentioned in previous Chapters, but it is worth repeating again because there are "issues" the Administrator should be aware of with Template and Page Builders.

It is possible that some of the Extensions for creating Templates and Page Layouts are available "free." There are also some that have a "Basic" version that is available at a very low cost. These are limited-feature versions of the Extension.

However, to get the full-featured, everything-included version, an upgrade to the "Pro" edition might be required. This may come at an additional cost.

Developers have the right to sell their products in this manner. It is our objective here is to simply bring this to the attention of the Administrator. In fact, it is suggested when the option is available, review the differences between the "Basic" and "Pro" versions of the Extension carefully before purchasing.

Experience has shown that occasionally, the "Pro" version has features that are not needed and the "Basic" version is fine. On some Extensions, it has worked the opposite way. The "Basic" version was feature-lacking, and the "Pro" version included the features that were essential.

The combination and possibilities of how each Template or Page Builder is offered for sale are near endless. This is why the Administrator should be diligent in making acquisition decisions to ensure the Extension will meet the requirements of the website content. Making the right choice will put assets in the hands of the Administrator that will greatly enhance the website.

Templates/Pages "Built With"

Here's a new wrinkle with Templates and Page Builders. Templates and Page Builders are available with "layouts" that are pre-designed and ready-to-use on the website following a standard Extension install. These are often "themed" based on different businesses and industries. The content of the "themed" versions contains elements that are specifically relevant to a certain business type or industry.

These "templates" are built by the Developers using one type of Template or Page Builder or another. When installed, along with the companion Extensions, the template or page can be modified using the specific "builder" Extension. This is a good feature. A pre-built theme or Template is installed that can he modified by a "builder" Extension.

When acquiring the builder-specific Templates or Pages, it really isn't a bad idea to also acquire the Extension/Framework upon which it was built. This gives the Administrator the ability to change, modify and update the layouts. This way, the layout is pre-built for the Administrator, and then, the Administrator has the ability to use the "builder" Extension to make modifications to suite the specific needs of the website design and layout.

Keep in mind that a "themed" Page Builder for an automobile repair company can, in fact, be modified to work with any other type of business. All that need be done is the replacement of photos, headings and Content text. In other words, any "themed" layout for one type of business can be converted to any other business operation. If you "like" one layout, nothing stops the Administrator from using the same one for any other "type" of business.

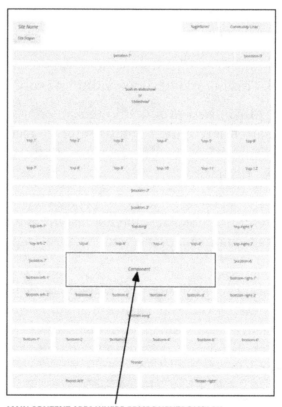

MAIN CONTENT AREA WHERE COMPONENTS DISPLAY
All other locations show on the layout are Module Positions

Figure 19-3
(Source: *energizethemes.com*)

Typical Template Builder Layouts

Joomla! 5 "Site Templates" typically follow the layout scheme of Modules in Rows above and below a Content Area, along with those to the right and left of it. Also, there are "Module Positions" coded within the Content Area that are enclosed above and below it, as shown in Figure 19-3, which is a complex Template that contains a great number of Module Positions.

While not all "Site Templates" may have such large numbers of "Module Position," this is representative of the many options that might be included within the layout.

Typical Page Builder Layouts

Page Builder layouts differ greatly from the typical Site Template layout in that there are no "sidebars," nor is there a fixed location on the page for the Content Area (Component) to display.

The standard layout scheme for Page Builders consists of a "Container," which defines the outer perimeter of the "webpage" itself, and this "Container" is responsive in that its width changes based on the screen width of the viewing device.

Within the "Container" are "Rows" which are horizontal from left to right edges of the "Container." The next part varies between Developers, and each type of Page Builder functions slightly different from this point forward.

Once a "Row" has been added, just about any type of Content can be inserted, and in many different formats – depending upon the Developer's preferences. For example, "Columns" may be added into a "Row," then individual Content Items can be inserted into the "Columns," which do not exceed twelve, which is controlled using Bootstrap 5.

Such Content Items as Articles, Modules, Elements, Blocks, Sections, Tables and more can be added into the "Columns" to create different layout configurations. This is what makes the use of Page Builders such powerful tools for creating website pages. Of course, each Developer gives these different names, so there is a "learning curve" with each one to figure out which is which.

Using a "Page Builder" is simply a matter of "construction," whereby Content is built from the outside in. This established the outside parameters of the layout. Then, the Content is further built from top to bottom. After the vertical Content structure has been established, more Content can be added between the existing Content areas, which makes Page Builders, allowing changes to be made at any time.

Figure 19-4 shows a small section of a Page Builder layout from the Extension by joomlashack.org. Note the rows and the columns, and what is contained within them. Then on the left side, the elements that can be inserted. Of course, not all are shown, but this illustrates how the Page Builder constructs the webpages. The "Content Items," in this instance, are called: "Particles." This, and other "Page Builders," will be covered in greater detail, with more information on how their webpages are constructed can be found in *Joomla! 5: Boots on the Ground, Extended Edition, Volume 4.*

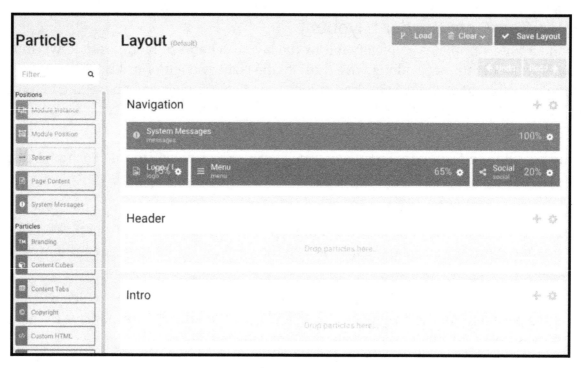

Figure 19-4
(Source: *joomlashack.org*)

It is easy enough to note the similarity between a Template Layout and a Page Builder Layout. The only exception between the two is the "sidebars" and how they function when using a "fluid layout." Keep in mind, that a Template is automatically applied globally to the Content. On the other hand, a Page Builder output is a screen-by-screen display, where each consists of different "webpage." When using Page Builders, the "webpages" may be duplicated and each modified to create the desired layout. This requires a lot of work, especially if the changes are extensive.

Screen Width, "Show" or "Don't Show"

Bootstrap 5 operates under the principle of "break points" which are pixel widths at which point the screen display experiences a "forced" change in layout. This is one of the main advantages of Bootstrap. As screens get smaller in width (or wider), the "break points" kick in and the display rearranges itself.

Along with this unique feature, is a "Show" or "Don't Show" option for the various Content Elements added to the webpage. What happens is this: when an Element of any type is added, most Template and Page Builders have the ability to select a "Show" or "Don't Show" configuration option for the Element.

This option is based on selecting any one of the four "break point" screen widths, and instructing the Template or Page Layout to invoke whichever display option having been set, *re:* "Show" or "Don't Show." This is usually a toggle icon showing the selected Container **[A]** to display on different screen widths **[B]**, as shown in Figure 19-5 below.

Figure 19-5

It doesn't take much of an imagination to figure out the many advantages of making the smaller screen size Content displays less complicated than those of the wider screens. Such items as large graphic headers or banners, which may look great on wider screens, but take up vertical space on the smaller devices, can be eliminated completely on any one of the four "break point" screen width choices.

This feature is yet another marked advantage the Administrator has when creating custom screens and layouts. The ability to control what Content Item or Element "Shows" or "Does not Show" is a valuable feature. Typically, the default setting is to "Show" on all screens. The choice to "Not Show" is performed by clicking on the desired screen-size icon button.

Enjoy the Experience

One takeaway from using both Template and Page Builders is the enjoyment of use. If you have a creative streak, these Extensions (or software), allow the Administrator to create outstanding layouts and configurations.

Using these Extensions can be fun. They are, for the most part, very easy to use once you understand the "construction" methods used. Most are similar, but some do have their own processes for creating Templates or website pages. What differentiates one from the other is the terminology used to accomplish the same end result.

VISUAL:
Images & Media Manager

The newly revised and modified Media Manager is one of the major new parts of Joomla! 5 website administration, and accommodates the ability to place Images and Media into almost any Content. Images can be included as icons, photos in Articles and Modules, photo albums, photo galleries and even as sliding image displays or image carousals. In fact, some Content-type Extensions also integrate with the Media Manager, or create their own control center for managing images used by the Extension.

Images are icons and photos, or graphics that have been created for insertion into the website Content. Graphics (images), on most websites are typically not considered "Media" within the Content consideration. Those graphics are typically part of the Template being used to display the information on the screen. The "Media Manager" controls the graphics and images that are part of the actual Content of the website. Keep this differential in mind: the static and decorative images are part of the Template, while the Content images/graphics are typically part of the Content Item sourced from the Media Manager.

Aside from photos and created images, "Media" also includes movies or videos, such as those found on YouTube or other sources. They can be included within Content using links but cannot be inserted directly. There are Plugins and Modules that will allow that type of video Content to be included. They cannot, however, be included as links nor be incorporated within the Media Manager storage areas. Use of a video Module will be explained later within this Chapter.

Using the Media Manager

Images such as graphics and photos contained within Content are stored and controlled within the Media Manager. It is not mandatory, when using images or photos, to create any special storage areas in the websites' file structure. There is a default catch-all general folder that collects unassigned graphics and images. This is handled within the Media Manager, in which a hierarchy of "Folders," (*aka* "Categories"), can easily be created to arrange and keep the Media organized. To distinguish the classification, the Media Manager calls these items "Folders."

When the "Sample Data" was installed, several Folders were created within the Media Manager. Those also contain Sub-Folders, within which are the images that appear in some of the Sample Data Articles.

When used, Media is uploaded and placed into the Media Manager, within the Folders. Then, from within a Content Item (Article or Module), the Media is sourced and inserted. Make a note that the same Media or images can be used more than one time within Content. They may also be displayed in different sizes using controls within the image controller in the Content Editor.

When an image is added via a Content Editor, it is uploaded into the Media Manager and, at the same time, may be assigned to an existing or a new Folder. From there, it is "selected" and "inserted" into Content. This will be explained in an Exercise in this Chapter.

Accessing the Media Manager

The Media Manager is accessed via the "Home Dashboard" as show in Figure 20-1:

Refer to Figure 20-1 for the following:

A **B**	Access to all Back-End functions is gained via the "Home Dashboard."
C	The first level of access is via the "Content" section in the left menu. This Menu area must be opened to access the link to the Media Manager.
D	The Media Manager may be accessed from either the left menu, or via the "Site" block, "Media" box. This access point appears automatically as part of the Back-End default screen.
	Execute an action to open the Media Manager by clicking on either of the access links.

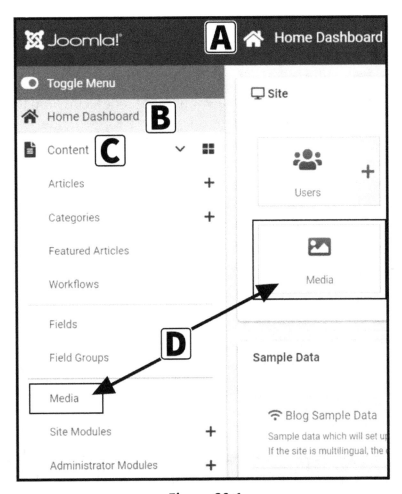

Figure 20-1

Examining the Media Manager

Understanding the different parts of the Media Manager is helpful to be able to use it effectively and efficiently. Once the parts and their function is understood, it will be easier to use and organize the Media used on the website.

Refer to Figure 20-2 for the following:

A	Indicates that the Media Manager is being accessed.
B	List the categories of "Images" that are contained within. These "Categories" are named "Folders" within the Media Manager so as to differentiate them from other methods of Content hierarchy management. When drilling down through the Folders, these also display the path similar to "breadcrumbs" on a website Front-End.
C	There are images that can be uploaded into the Media Manager that do not require assignment to Folders. These are akin to the "uncategorized" classification used in other Content management areas. If an image is in this "non-folder," it/they can be moved into any Folder at any time. Also, images within folders can be moved out,

	or into any other Folder is desired.
D	These are the upper level ("Parent"), Folders for images. Upper level Folders may contain many levels sub-Folders ("Child"), within them.
E	This button allows the creation of a new top level Folder. Only top level Folders can be created here. To create a sub-Folder, open any "Parent" Folder desired, then use the "Create new Folder" button as normal, which will create a new Folder within the Folder that is currently open. Drill down through as many "Parent" or "Child" Folders as necessary to open a destination Folder.
F	The "Upload" button allows the addition of images that are obtained from the local computer. Images that are uploaded are automatically assigned to the currently open Folder. Open the destination Folder BEFORE starting the uploading process. ***Normal functions of "drag & drop" do not work within the Media Manager.***
G	This opens the "Options" that are available for configuration of the types and designation thereof, which may be uploaded into the Media Manager.
H	These icons allow the Images and Folders that display on the screen to be enlarged or reduced by clicking on them, repeatedly if necessary.
I	This button changes the display from graphic to "list view," and back again, which is helpful if there are many images within the Folder.

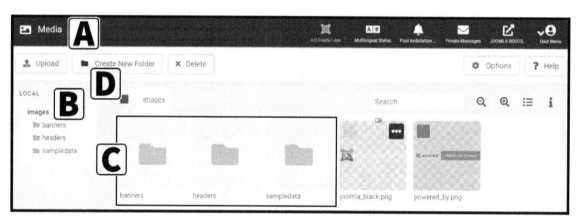

Figure 20-2

EXERCISE 20-1: CREATING A NEW FOLDER IN THE MEDIA MANAGER

Objective: This Exercise will demonstrate how create a new "Parent" Folder within the Media Manager.

Step 1		If not already there, Access the "Home Dashboard" as the Administrator.
Step 2	**A**	Open the "Media Manager" either in the Content Menu in the left, or click on the "Media Manager" in the "Site" Block. Either one will open the "Media Manager."

Step 3	B C	To get to the "top level" of the Folder structure in the Media Manager, click on the "Images" heading in the left column. Only three "top level" Folders should be listed.
Step 4	D	To create a "top level" Folder, click on the "Create New Folder" button in the top menu. This will open a pop up window.

Refer to Figure 20-3 for the following:

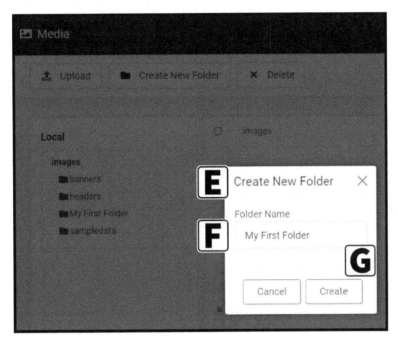

Figure 20-3

Step 5	E F	In the "Create New Folder" popup, for the "Folder Name," enter: "My First Folder" (without quotes).
Step 6	G	Execute a "Create" action by clicking the "Create" button.
Step 7		View the Media Folders on the "top level" list and confirm that "My First Folder" has been created.

Continuing this process, a "second level" Folder will be created within the "My First Folder" previously created.

Refer to Figure 20-4 for the following:

Step 8	B	Click on the folder icon for "My First Folder." This will open the folder, which should be empty.
Step 9		With the "Parent" Folder open, click on the "Create New Folder" button in the top menu. This will open the popup window again.
Step 10	C	For the "Folder Name," enter: "My Second Folder" (without quotes).

373

Step 11		Execute a "create" action by clicking the "Create" button.
Step 12	C	View the results confirm that "My Second Folder" has been created within the "My First Folder," which was originally empty. This can be easily confirmed by viewing the Folder hierarchy in the left column. Figure 20-3 shows the folders in the Media Manager.

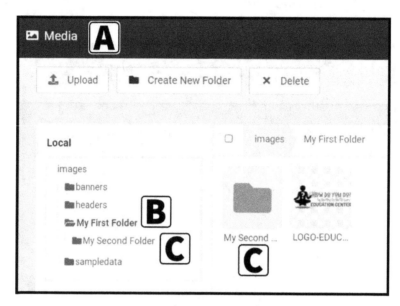

Figure 20-4

The above action can be repeated in a similar manner whenever a Folder is required in the Media Manager.

Methods of Adding Images

Images MUST be in the Media Manager to be able to add them to Content Items. Images should only be added to the Content Item via accessing the Media Manager after the image is uploaded. There are essentially two methods of adding images into the Folders within the Media Manager, as follows:

Method 1	Using the "Upload" feature within the Media Manager.
Method 2	Accessing the Media Manager from within a Content Item to "Upload" and image and "insert" it into the Content.

The next method is possible but not recommended for adding images directly into Content items, as explained:

| Method 3 Should not be used | A "copy & paste" process can be used to add images to Content via it's respective Workspace, but when doing so, it **DOES NOT** add the image to the Media Manager, nor any of the Media Folders. The inherent problem in using this method is that the source image, if derived from another website as a link to "the image," or from a local |

source, may be removed or "Unpublished," thus breaking the link. The image would then no longer appear on the Content Item on the instant website. While it is possible to "copy & paste" images into Content, it is **NOT** a recommended method to be used.

Credit Where Credit is Due

If you are sourcing images from outside sources, it is a wise practice to credit the source of the images. Not doing so could be problemsome if the source entity has protections and/or copyrights on the image.

EXERCISE 20-2: UPLOADING AN IMAGE INTO A SELECTED FOLDER

Objective: The goal of this Exercise is to guide the Administrator through the process of uploading an image into a previously created Folder using the Media Manager itself to do so.

Step 1	A	On the "Home Dashboard," go to: "Content > Media," to open the Media Manager.
Step 2	B	Click on the "My First Folder" image to open it. This will display the sub-Folders within.
Step 3	C	Click on the "My Second Folder" image to open it. This Folder should be empty. Once the Folder is open, an image file may be uploaded into that Folder.

Refer to Figure 20-5 for the following:

Step 4	D	At the top left, click on the "Upload" button.

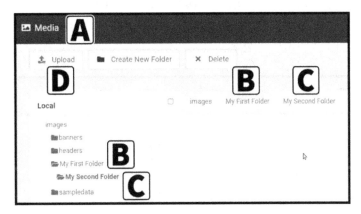

Figure 20-5

Step 5	Access any location on your computer that contains images and select one and double-click on it. An instantaneous action of the file uploading into the Folder will take place when the image is selected.
Step 6	An "Item uploaded" "Success Message" will display upon completion. Clear the message by clicking on the **"X"** to the right side.
Step 7	Upon completion, the image will display along with its title or file name. The image is now available to be inserted into any Content Item that will accept images in layouts.
Step 8	Move up one Folder to the "My First Folder."
Step 9	At the top left, click on the "Upload" button.
Step 10	Access any location on your computer that contains images and select one and double-click on it. An instantaneous action of the file uploading into the Folder will take place.
Step 11	An "Item uploaded" "Success Message" will display upon completion. Clear the message by clicking on the **"X"** to the right side.
Step 12	Upon completion, the image will display along with its title or file name. The image is now available to be inserted into any Content Item that will accept images in layouts.
Step 13	The "My First Folder" should now contain a sub-Folder and an image. The sub-Folder ("My Second Folder"), should also contain an image.

Note there is no "saving action" to be executed to upload image files.

Image Sizes

When images are uploaded, they are uploaded in their native file sizes. Very large images, when inserted into a Content Item, will likely need to be resized to fit. This resizing of images is explained later in this Chapter. Information about any image can be found by selecting the image, then clicking on the **"i"** at the right of the Folder/Image display area. Folder information may be found in the same way.

If you have already installed the JCE Editor, skip this part.

Installing the JCE Editor

The default Article or Content Editor leaves a few things to be desired. It is adequate for most purposes. However, we suggest installing the "Free" or "Paid" version of the Joomla! 5 Extension: "JCE Editor." To have full control over images and text within a Content Item, the "JCE Editor" has many advantages over the default Editor, especially in the management of media and images. Therefore, it is recommended that the "JCE Editor" be installed, as follows:

EXERCISE 20-3: INSTALLING THE "FREE" JCE EDITOR

Objective: This Exercise will guide the Administrator through the process of using the "Install from Web" procedure to add the "JCE Editor" to the website and to make it the "default" Editor for all Content Items.

Step 1	From the "Home Dashboard," open the "System" link.
Step 2	In the "Install" Block, click on "Extensions."
Step 3	Choose the "Install from Web" tab.
Step 4	Find the "JCE" panel and click on the text area of the block. This will open the internal Extension installer.
Step 5	Click on the green "Install" button. The window will scroll up.
Step 6	Click the blue "Install" button at the lower left. This will begin the installing process, which will end with the "Success" message.
Step 7	Go back to the left menu and again access the "System" area.
Step 8	Open the "Global Configuration" in the "Setup" Block.
Step 9	Within the "Site" tab, find the "Default Editor" selector.
Step 10	Within the selector, choose "Editor-JCE" as the default. If the website has many Content Editors, through the "ACL" Permissions System, the individual Editors may use different Editor Extensions. This is useful in many situations to either simplify Content entry, or provide special Editors with unique features.
Step 11	Execute a Save & Close action.

The "JCE Editor" will now be the default Editor that will be in place for creating and editing all Content Items. This will make the management of image parameters a much easier task for the Administrator. Also, within the JCE Editor, there are a number of configuration settings that are accessible much easier than using the "TinyMCE Editor."

Take notice that adding the "JCE Editor" does not eliminate the use of other Editors. In fact, the "TinyMCE Editor" can be assigned to other Editor Roles, and the "JCE Editor" reserved for the Administrator. This is controlled in the Users Permissions.

EXERCISE 20-4: UPLOADING IMAGE WITHIN THE ARTICLE WORKSPACE

Objective: The goal of this Exercise is to upload an image into the Media Manager while within the Article ("Content Item") Workspace. This is not the "copy & paste" method. Instead, this is hard uploading to the Media Manager.

Step 1		Open the "Articles Manager," and then open the "About" Article. There is some brief text in the Article. An image will be inserted after the text.
Step 2		Go to the end of the last line of text, place the cursor, and execute an ENTER action to create a new line.
Step 3		With the text cursor in place, go to the bottom of the "JCE Editor" Workspace. The buttons at this location are a replication of the "CMS Content" drop down in the TinyMCE Editor, which has been replaced by the JCE Editor.
Step 4		Select "Media" in the menu bar at the bottom.
Step 5		Open "My First Folder," then open "My Second Folder."

At this point, an existing image may be selected to be inserted, or another image can be added using the "Upload" feature as used in previous Exercises.

Step 6		At the top left, click on the "Upload" button.
Step 7		Access any location on your computer that contains images and select one and double-click on it. An instantaneous action of the file uploading into the Folder will take place.
Step 8		An "Item uploaded" "Success Message" will display upon completion and the thumbnail of the image will display within "My Second Folder."
Step 9		Upon completion, the image will display along with its title or file name. The image is now available to be inserted into any Content Item that will accept images in layouts.
Step 10		The "My Second Folder" should now contain two images.

Refer to Figure 20-6 for the following:

| **Step 11** | **A** | Select the uploaded image and click on it, which will open a larger window showing the image. |
| **Step 12** | **B** | When the next popup displays, click the "No Description" tick box. By doing so, no "Alt" title for the image is required. Leave the other settings at default or blank. |

Figure 20-6

Step 13	C	Click again on the "Insert Image" button at the bottom right. The images will load into the Article layout. The image will insert at the default pixel size of the uploaded image, which will likely be too large.
Step 14		Execute a Save action.
Step 15		Make the Article a "Featured Article" by changing the setting for the Article in the right column.
Step 16		Go to the Front-End, and click on the "Home " Menu Link Item in the Main Menu. The "About" Article will open and display at the bottom of the screen after selecting the "2" value in the bottom page navigation block.
Step 16		When "About" is viewed, the image display in its original size, and if these is a high-resolution image, it can be quite large. Likely, too large, for all practical purposes.
Step 17		Back in the Article Workspace, click on the image in the Article to select it. The boxes at the corners will allow the image to be manually resized. Make the image smaller by selecting the bottom right box and scaling the image down. This resizes it, but isn't a accurate method of doing so. Note there is a size indicator that displays as the image corner is moved to the left.

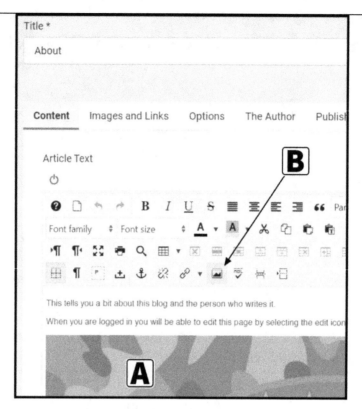

Figure 20-7

Refer to Figure 20-8 for the following:

Step 18	A B	Select the image, if not already selected, the click on the "image" icon in the Menu, located in the approximate middle of the bottom row of icons in the Menu. Notice that the "Width" and "Height" is indicated when the panel opens, along with the fields and controls to change information about the image.

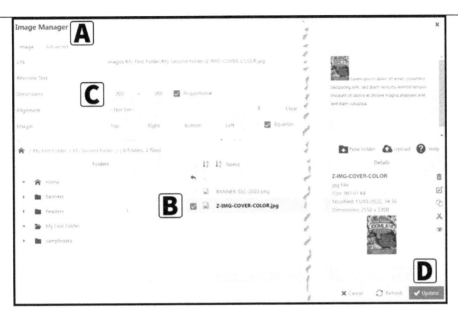

Figure 20-8

Refer to Figure 20-7 for the following:

Step 19	**C**	Change the "Width" of the image to 300. When doing so, note that the "Height" changes proportionately. The "Equalize" tick box to the right, when selected indicates that the image will resize properly when one dimension is changed, the other will also resize proportionately.
Step 20	**D**	Click the "Update" button at the bottom right of the window.
Step 21		The image automatically resizes its width and height automatically and proportionately because that option was selected by default.
Step 22		Execute a Save & Close action.
Step 23		Go to the Front-End and refresh the screen. The image is now reduced to 300 pixels and proportional width.

When the "JCE Editor" was installed, it also included the "JCE File Manager," and this was added to the "Home Dashboard" under the "3rd Party" block. When clicking on the link in the block, the "Media File Manager" opens. This allows images to be uploaded and managed without accessing the Media under the "Content" Menu or via the "Media" block in the "Site" Panel, which can be discretionarily removed by the Administrator.

Images and Text Wrapping

Quite often, it is desired to have text next to and/or wrap around images and to control the "white space" between the image and the text. This alignment can be performed within the "JCE Article Editor." The Exercise below will demonstrate how this is accomplished.

EXERCISE 20-5: POSITIONING AND SETTING IMAGE PARAMETERS

Objective: The positioning, text wrapping and image parameters will be demonstrated in this Exercise.

Step 1		Open the "Articles Manager," and then open the "About" Article. There is some brief text in the Article. An image will be inserted after the text.
Step 2		Go to the end of the last line of text, which is above the photo image.
Step 3		Enter a full paragraph of text. Any text will suffice. Make the paragraph about 10 lines or more longer.
Step 4		Execute a Save action.
Step 5		Select the photo image by right clicking on it, and then delete it from the Article.
Step 6		Execute a Save action.
Step 7		Place the text cursor at the beginning of the inserted paragraph, then click the "Media" button at the bottom of the Workspace to open the new "JCE Image Manager." Make note that the "JCE Image Manager" shows all of the Folders from the Media Manager. Additional configuration fields are also displayed. There are two tabs: "Image" and "Advanced." The "Image" tab is opened automatically by default.
Step 8		Select any image from the "My First Folder."
Step 9		Execute the "Insert Media" action using the button at the bottom right of the panel.
Step 10		Click on the image in the Article.

Refer to Figure 20-9 for the following:

Step 11	A B	Click on the "image" icon in the Editor button row. This will open a screen with configurable parameters for the image.
Step 6		Change the image width to "300" to reduce or enlarge the size.
Step 7	C	In the choices in the "Alignment" selector directly above the size fields, select "Right." This selects the position of the image in relationship to the text.
Step 8		Execute an "Update" action using the blue button at the bottom right of the panel.
Step 9		In the Article Workspace, the image is now shifted to the right and the text is positioned to the left side. However, the text is touching, or is visually too close to the image. Some "padding" or a "margin" is needed in the left side of the image to correct this.

| Step 10 | | Execute a Save action. |

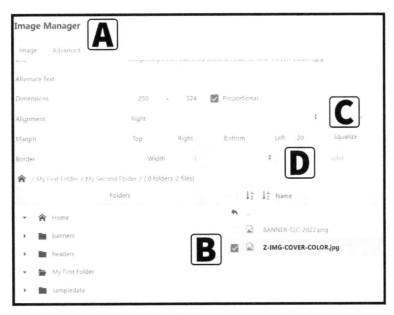

Figure 20-9

Step 10	A	Click on the image and then access the image icon in the Menu bar again to open the Image Managers panel.
Step 11	B	The image that is selected is highlighted on the list.
Step 12		In the "Margin" controls, uncheck "Equalize" to deselect it.
Step 13		In the "Left" value box, enter "20" (without quotes).
Step 14		Execute an "Update" action using the button at the bottom right.
Ste[15		View the results. If there is any text "under" the image, go back to the previous panel and add "10" to the "Bottom" margin field and execute "Update."
Step 16		When the Article Editor opens, execute a Save action.
Step 17		Go to the website Front-End, refresh the screen.

Refer to Figure 20-10 for the following:

| Step 18 | | Notice now the text has been moved away from the left and bottom side of the image. This is something that should be configured for every image placed in any Content Area. The "padding" around the sides of images is an important setting to move the text away from the image for optimum appearance. Of course, the "padding" around specific edges depends upon that actual alignment of the image. |

Step 19	Reopen the "JCE Image Manager," then the "Advanced" tab.
Step 20	Notice that the "Style" can be edited and/or entered manually. This field replicates the settings from the "Image" tab section.
Step 21	Note the "Classes" field. This is where a "CSS" setting can be applied for predetermined layouts. For example, two separate "CSS Classes" can be created for right or left text clearances based on the location of the image.

Proficient use of the "JCE Image Manager" will allow the Administrator to create Content layouts that are pleasing to the eye and arrange Content properly and with consistency. It is suggested that you experiment with image alignment and the "margins" or "padding" around the edges of the images for best visual appearance. Also, bear in mind that images, if very large on the desktop, are usually reduced to the screen-width of the mobile device on which the Content is being viewed.

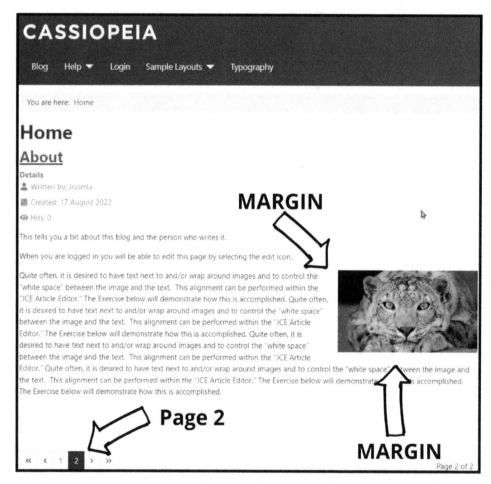

Figure 20-10

Types of Images Allowed

Before actually uploading images into the Media Manager on a live website, a review of the types of image files (or image formats), are allowed to be used and how this is controlled. The file types are controlled within the "Options" for the Joomla! 5 Media Manager, not the "JCE Media Manager."

By reviewing the "Options," you can identify which are allowed. It is also possible to add any particular file types or formats that might want to be used, thus allowing them to be included in website Content Items.

The "most commonly used" file types and formats are included in the "Options" by default. However, in the event another type is needed, add them to the respective fields and execute a saving action. The appropriate "field" is the "Allowed Extensions" and the "Legal Image Extensions (File Types)" and the "Legal Audio Extensions (File Types)" are set in other fields.

Note also that the "Legal Document Extensions (File Types)," may also be designated if the file type is not listed. Simply add the file extension in the appropriate fields and the system will parse those files accordingly. Also, because sometimes file extensions are in either upper or lower case characters, both should be listed as "allowed" file types, *re:* "pdf" and "PDF."

In addition to "allowing" certain file types, by removing any from the identification fields, the Administrator may also "restrict" the use of those that might be designated. Use this technique sparingly and make a record of which have been "restricted." This is probably a wise action if operating a blogging style website with many contributors of Content.

Graphic/Image File Formats

If not familiar with computer graphics and the file formats, the following information may be helpful. There are many different types of file formats for images, each having different uses and applications.

bmp	This is a original Microsoft format for saving uncompressed image data, commonly used to store photos. These files do not resize well without loss of clarity. They tend to get blurry or grainy in appearance.
gif	These are image files saved in a "lossless" format, thus the image's clarity is not degraded. Commonly used for website images such as navigation buttons, icons without color limitations.
heic, heif	Apple's "High Efficiency Image Format" is exclusively used to store image on the Apple IOS devices. It creates high quality files in smaller file sizes. Images in this format should not be installed on any Joomla! website. Convert them to more conventional formats before use.
ico,	These are icons used to identify files and folders, but used more typically as the icon that appears in the browser's title tab, quite often the website's

icons	owner logo or some other miniature graphic.
jpg, jpeg	Supports millions of colors, but has a "lossy" compression while reducing the size of the file. The "losses" are not noticeable. However, like "bmp" above, resizing creates a blurring of the image. The images may look grainy if enlarged to greater sizes.
mp3	An audio file that reduces the file size using "lossy" compression.
mp4	This is an MPEG-4 video file format used for downloading and streaming videos from the internet.
m4a, mp4a	These file formats are typically used to store podcasts, audio books and songs. One type stores audio only, the other both audio and video content within the file.
mov	This is an Apple Quick Time Movie format and the most common video file format, which supports high quality videos.
mpeg	This is a standardized video file format often used when sharing video files over the internet.
odg	This is a native file format created by the "Draw" program, an editing application for logos and illustrations.
odp	Similar to "odg" above, this is a presentation file format created by "Impress."
ogg	An open-source audio file that is very similar to "mp3" formats.
odt	This is an open-source format similar to Microsoft Word documents.
png	A "Portable Network Graphic" is commonly used for web graphics, digital photos and images with transparent backgrounds. It is compressed in a "lossless" format.
ppt pptx	A Microsoft presentation file format created in Microsoft "PowerPoint," or similar program.
svg	A "scalable vector graphic [as compared to bitmap]," that can be scaled by sizes based on the size of the container and is used for web, mobile and print graphics. The "scalable" is the key to this format which allows for manual and automatic resizing of the image.
webm	This is an open-source file format for storing audio and video data in compressed, industry-standard formats.

For more detailed information about each of the above file formats, we suggest that the website: FileInfo.com is used as a reference.

The most common file formats used on websites are: jpeg, gif and png. Of course, others may be used but those three are the ones more typically used for icons, images and photos. The jpeg format at 300 dpi resolution is commonly used for commercial printing purposes.

Sizing Graphics/Image Displays

On website pages, graphics should be sized to fit layouts and that are pleasing to the eye. Large images that require the user to scroll the screen in any direction are not suggested. Images should fit the screen.

Typically, graphics and images are sized using pixels or percentages. They may also be sized relative to "em" and "rem" values of the font settings of the Style Sheet. This sizing is usually a multiple of the "em" or "rem" values proportional to the font-size as designated in the Style Sheet.

Responsive Sizing of Images

Another sizing setting is to use Bootstrap 5 to set the graphic/image as "responsive." This means that the image [or it's container], will be reduced or enlarged automatically depending upon the screen width of the device. The graphic/image is typically set to 100% size, then the "responsive" setting controls the width based on the Bootstrap 5 screen width. Easy enough. No guessing is required to determined "perfect size" for the image.

Displaying Document Formats

Current versions of website browsers can display native document type formats also, such as: pdf, ppt, docx and others. No Joomla! 5 Extensions need to be installed to do so.

When the document file type is opened by clicking a link, the browser understands the file format, and automatically converts the display or opens the program required for viewing.

Some special Extensions are needed, for example, to display a YouTube Video within the website screen. They are available for download via the "JED."

Using "Lazy Loading" Images

There is an option within Joomla! 5 to "lazy load" images. This setting is applied to each individual image on a selective basis via the Media Manager.

The "Lazy Loading" feature delays the loading of graphics/images until the website page actually needs the image to display it. In the past, there was a practice of loading all the images with the "home" screen. This caused some websites to take a long time to complete loading.

This feature reduces and conserves both server and client browser resources by delaying the loading of some images, such as photo galleries, etc. An example is a long scrolling page. Images are not displayed until the User scrolls the browser window [desktop or mobile], to the point where the image is to be displayed, at which time, the image is downloaded. With the newer, higher speeds at which both desktops and mobile devices operate, the slight delay is barely noticeable.

You may experience the "Lazy Loading" of images on the long, one-page websites where images are pulled in from the sides, or fade in, or some other animation is used. The image is not "triggered" to appear until the active browser window is in the location wherein the image is set to display.

The opposite of "Lazy Loading" is "Eager Loading," and you can guess by its name what happens. As soon as a website page with image coding is loaded, ALL of the images will load "eagerly" or immediately. The needed image resources are pulled into the layout immediately. This is the exact opposite to the method by which images are "lazy loaded."

On websites that contain few or limited images, this configuration setting does not matter. On websites containing an abundance of graphics/images, "Lazy Loading" might be the better choice to ensure optimum user browsing experiences.

The setting to use, or not use, "Lazy Loading" is typically found on the screen that is open when the image is selected in the Content Editor, and is configured using a "tick box" to invoke, or shut off, the selection.

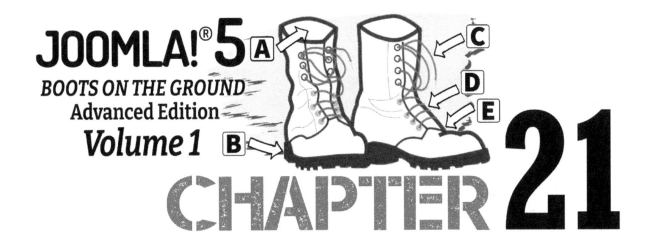

NAVIGATION:
Menu Systems

On Joomla! 5 websites, "navigation," the process of viewing website Content, is accomplished through a system of "Menus" and "Menu Link Items." There is a built-in system for creating Menus, placing Menu Modules on webpages and then adding Menu Link Items to access Content. This Chapter's goal is to provide information to build a foundation of knowledge about the processes of creating website navigation schemes.

The manner in which Menus are configured, positioned and visually controlled is via the "CSS" that is within the Template being used for the individual screen display. As you already know, several Templates can be used on a website, thus there are different Menu configurations that apply.

Menu Link Items cannot be created unless there is a Menu into which it can be assigned. Basically, a Menu is created, and then Menu Link Items are created within it. That's pretty much the basic concept of the Menu methodology on a Joomla! 5 website.

The next part of the Menu System is the actual display of a Menu that is visible on the website itself. This is accomplished by creating a "Menu Module," then placing it into one of the pre-determined "Module Positions" on the webpage Template(s). While the Menu itself may exist, it does not function unless there is a "Published" Menu Module type visible on the webpage, or webpages, depending on the website design.

This Chapter addresses the actions required to create Menus, Menu Link Items, creating the Menu Module and then "Publishing" of a Menu Module on a webpage, along with the "conditions" under which it displays.

You CAN Get There from Here

Creating Menus and Menu Link Items may seem like somewhat of a backward process. The Menu or Menu Link Item is created after Content has been first created. The Content can be Articles, or different Category configurations along with Content that is generated from Components. In short, the Content must first exist before a Menu Link Item can be created to open/view the item.

Here are the sequential steps for creating a Menu Link Item to Content:

Action 1	If Content is to come from Articles, create the Categories and then create/write the Articles and assign them to their respective Categories. Then create a Menu Link Item to the Article, or the other Category display options.
Action 2	If the Content is coming from a Component, configure the Component as needed. If, for example, it is a Contacts Directory, create the Contact Categories and add Contacts to them as needed, then create a Menu Link Item to them.
Action 3	Create a Menu in the Menu Manager, which also automatically creates an action button to "Add a Module for this Menu" in the "Linked Modules" column.
Action 4	Create the Menu Module using the automatic process.
Action 5	Complete the configuration of the new Menu Module by assigning it to a "Module Position" on the currently used Template.
Action 6	Create Menu Link Items within the Menu that links to open Content Items such as: Articles, Category Lists or Components. Connecting the Menu Link Item to the "target content item" is the last step.

When the above actions are completed, there will be a Menu in a "Module Position" on the Front-End view of the website. Not all of them are needed, only those that apply to the type of Content the Menu Link Item targets.

At this point, let's move directly into the Menu creation process and create a new Menu for the website.

Difference Between Templates

When performing any of the Exercises that follow, keep in mind that the default built-in Joomla! 5 Menu System is being used. No additional Extensions need to be installed to create Menus. However, keep in mind that the look and appearance of the Menu [Module] will vary greatly between Templates. Additionally, if an Extension is added that is specifically a Menu feature, regardless of the Template, the Menu Extension will likely have controls that apply only to the Menus created using that Extension.

Third-party Templates or Menu features will likely be built upon "Frameworks" that the various developers use. This means that the Menu Systems might be considerably different, with an array of configuration controls, which have been added into their Extension. These are actually more favorable to use on website that contain a considerable amount of Content versus smaller websites.

In short, if the Template controls the Menu system, then there are limitations. But, if a Menu Extension is added to the website, the configuration "Options" will likely be many with enhanced features. Some "Menu" Extensions are actually Components consisting of a Menu Module, or multiple Menu Modules.

Repeated Information & Exercises

Within this Chapter, there will be both repeated information along with repeated, but different, Exercises regarding Menus. Chapter 7, "Fast Track Double Time Start," contained some of these Exercise, along with the Chapters on "Categories" and "Articles." However, because understanding the "Navigation Methods" in Joomla! 5 is so important, many of the Exercises are worth repeating here. As the website Administrator, mastering Content Navigation is important and vital, particularly when dealing with website that have considerable Content.

Adding and Using the Menu System

The best way to learn how to use the Menu System is to create a Menu and an associated Menu Module which is assigned to one of the Template's Module Positions. Once those two steps are completed, Menu Link Items may be added to complete the navigation to access Content Items or any type..

EXERCISE 21-1: CREATING A MENU AND MENU MODULE

Objective: This Exercise will guide you through the process of creating a Menu and its Menu Module, assigning it to the Template "Module Position" This was already explained in Chapter 7, "Fast Track Double Time Start," and in Exercises in other previous Chapters.

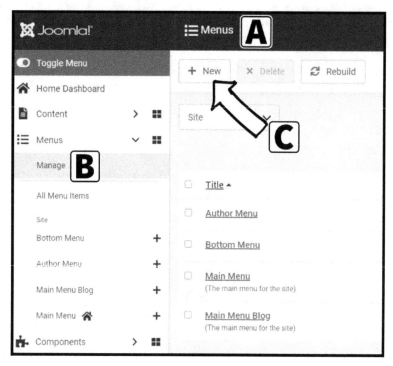

Figure 21-1

Refer to Figure 21-1 for the following:

Step 1	A	In the "Home Dashboard," click on "Menus" in the left Menu and then click on "Manage" to open the Manager.
	B	
Step 2	C	Click on the **"+ New"** button at the top of the screen to open the "Menu: Add" Workspace.

Figure 21-2

Refer to Figure 21-2 for the following:

Step 3	D	The "Menus: Add" Workspace should be open at this point.
Step 4	E	In the "Title" block, enter: "MY NEW MENU" (without quotes).
Step 5	F	For the "Unique Name," enter: "My New Menu" (without quotes). Actually, this step can be eliminated insomuch as the system will automatically create the "Unique Name" based on the "Title."
Step 6	G	Execute a "Save & Close" action, which will return the screen to the Menu Manager.

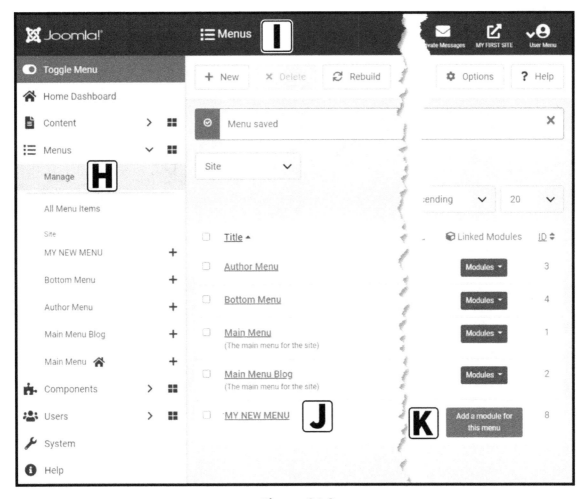

Figure 21-3

Refer to Figure 21-3 for the following:

	H I	In the "Menus Manager," take the following actions.
Step 8	J	Find the "MY NEW MENU" item on the Menus list.
Step 9	K	Click on the "Add a module for this menu" to create the Menu Module for assignment to a Template "Module Position" This is located to the far right of the items information line on the list.

Figure 21-4

Refer to Figure 21-4 for the following:

Step 10	L	The "Add a module for this menu" modal window should be open.
Step 11	M	Enter "MY NEW MENU MODULE" in the Title box.
Step 12	N	In the "Select Menu" drop down, select "MY NEW MENU."
Step 13	O	In the "Position" selector, select "sidebar-right."
Step 14	P	Select "Published" in the Status field if it is not already selected.
Step 15	Q	Execute the Save & Close action.

Unique Names are Auto-Generated

In some Exercise, instructions included entries into the "Unique Name" data field. In most items, this name is automatically generated based on the "Title" field text. In some types of Workspaces, it will be necessary to fill in the "Unique Name" or other data into the field. When the systems requests that, perform the task. Otherwise, the "Alias" or "Unique Name" may be created automatically.

Menu Not Showing on the Front-End

At this point, if you access the website Front-End and refresh the screen, even though the "MY NEW MENU" was "Published" into the "sidebar-right" position, it is not displaying. Why does it not display?

If you recall, mention has been previously made that "empty" Categories, "empty" Menus and so on, will not display unless they have Content within them.

So, a Category will not display unless there is an Article within it, or unless there is an over-ride made to force the system to "display empty Categories."

Likewise with Menus. If there is no Content [Menu Link Item], within a Menu, it will not display on the Front-End. But here's the wrinkle: *There is no over-ride to apply*, thus making it a mandatory requirement for a Menu Module to have at least one Menu Link Item assigned to it. An empty Menu Module simply will not display without Menu Link Items that go to Content targets being added AND Published.

Joomla! 5 has this "thing" about displaying Modules, and even Categories, that are empty. The Menu was created, along with the Menu Module. But there has not been a Menu Link Item added to the Menu to connect to some type of Content. Thus, the "empty" Module does not display. The next Exercise will resolve this and display the Menu with a Menu Link Item to some Content.

EXERCISE 21-2: ADDING AN ARTICLE MENU LINK ITEM TO A MENU

Objective: This Exercise will create a Menu Link Item directly to an Article in the newly created Menu so it will display on the Front-End using the Menu Module created previously in Exercise 21-1.

Figure 21-5

Refer to Figure 21-5 for the following:

Step 1	Q	In the "Home Dashboard," click on "Menus" in the left Menu, which opens the "Modules (Site) Manager. Then click on "MY NEW MENU" to open the Manager.
Step 2	R	The "MY NEW MENU" Manager screen should open and there should be "No Matching Results" indicating there are no Menu Link Items in the Menu.
Step 3	S T	Click on the **"+New"** button at the top of the screen. The "Menus: New Item" screen should open. The **"+"** next to the Menu name in the left column accomplishes the same thing. Click on either one.

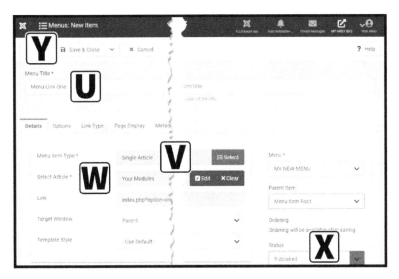

Figure 21-6

Refer to Figure 21-6 for the following:

Step 7	U	In the "Menu Title" field, enter: "Menu Link One" (without quotes).
Step 8	V	For the "Menu Item Type," select: "Articles > Single Article."
Step 9	W	In the "Select Article" dropdown, select the "Your Templates" Article.
Step 10	X	Select "Published" in the Status field if it is not already selected.
Step 11	Y	Execute a "Save & Close" action.
Step 12		Go to the website Front-End, refresh the browser screen. The "MY NEW MENU MODULE" and Menu Link Item just created should display in the right column position of "sidebar-right."
Step 13		Test the link "Menu Link One" to the "Your Templates" Article.
Step 14		This should open the "Your Templates" Article in the Main Content Area.

Other Menu Link Items

In the above Exercises, where a Menu, Menu Module and a Menu Link Item was created, it targeted a single Article. This is the most common method to connect to a single Article, but there are several different options. A couple of these were accomplished in Chapter 7, "Fast Track Double Time Start." However, because there are certain knowledge points that should be explained further, several Exercises will be repeated to demonstrate:

- Adding a Menu Link Item to Display a Category Blog.
- Setting the Category Blog Article Layout & Ordering
- Adding a Menu Link Item to Display a List of Categories.

397

- Adding a Menu Link Item to Display a List of All Categories.
- Adding a Menu Link item to Display Featured Articles.
- Conditional Display of Menu Modules or other Modules

Displaying a Single Category

As already explained, Articles must be assigned to Categories. Also, there may be many "Parent" Categories, along with many "Child" or Sub-Categories underneath the "Parent." One of the "Options" to display the Content with Categories is to create a Menu Link Item directly to it, the Category. When the Menu Link Item is executed, the Category displays, showing its Content. It is often desired to display only the Articles, or Content Items within a single Category.

Why List a Category of Articles?

Here's the goal – there are a dozen or so Articles within a Category and you want website visitors to be able to access them conveniently. There are two choices on the way to do this, which are:

Choice 1	Make a Menu with Menu Link Items to every Article in the Category. This will require: 1) the creation of a dedicated Menu, 2) the creation and placement of a Menu Module into one of the Template's Module Positions then, 3) create a Menu Link Item to every single Article, yes every Article!
	There are so many things wrong with this choice, it would take a lot of space to explain it, but just the complexity and time to accomplish is enough of a deterrent to NOT do it this way.
Choice 2	This choice involves creating a Menu Link Item in any existing Menu, or create a new one. What will be done here is to create a single Menu Link item to a "List of Articles within a Category." When the link is clicked, the Category with all, or a restricted number, of Articles with active links to them will appear in the Main Content Area. One Menu Link Item, one click, one display. The website visitor then can view and/or scroll the list and pick the Articles to read based on: 1) the Article Name, or 2) if the Category is a Blog-type, by the "teaser text" under the Article. What you then have is two click access to the Articles, but only one click to get to the List of Articles.

Types of Category Displays

There are three types of Category Displays, as follows:

Category Blog	A Category Blog is simple a list of Articles, configured into a "blogging" format. Recall that only a Category Blog layout for Articles can contain the "Read More" feature. The Article display is limited to the text BEFORE the "Read More" break insert within the body text of the Article.

Note on the Category Blog Article Layouts	The layout of the display of the Articles in a Category Blog format can be arranged in several ways. EXERCISE 12-4, "Category Blog Article Layout/Ordering" provided guidance on how layouts are created.
Category List	This displays a conventional list of Articles within a single Category, be it a "Parent" or a "Child," or at any other level in the Category hierarchy. This means that a List of Articles in a "Sub-Sub-Category" can be displayed by itself. This applies to every Category, regardless of their location within the hierarchy. Creating a Menu Link Item to a Category List was covered in Chapter 7, Exercise 7-6.
List of Categories	This choice will display a List of every Category on the website. Every Category, whether it be a "Parent" or a "Child," will be listed. There is an Option setting that also displays the number of Articles within the Category, individually.

In the Exercise that follows, Choice 2 from above will be the method employed to create a Menu Link Item of the "Category Blog" type.

EXERCISE 21-3: ADDING A CATEGORY BLOG MENU LINK ITEM

Objective: The objective of this Exercise is to demonstrate how the Content of a single Category (Articles), can be displayed in the main Content Area when a designated Menu Link Item is triggered. The existing "MY NEW MENU MODULE" will be used for the actions within this Exercise. This Menu should display on the right side of the screen. One Menu Link Item to a single Article already exists within this Menu.

Step 1		In the "Home Dashboard," click on "Menus" in the left Menu, which opens the "Menu Modules Manager. Then click on "MY NEW MENU MODULE" to open the Manager for that Menu.
Step 2	A	In the left menu, on the MY NEW MENU line, click on the **"+"** icon to open the "Menus: New Item" Workspace.

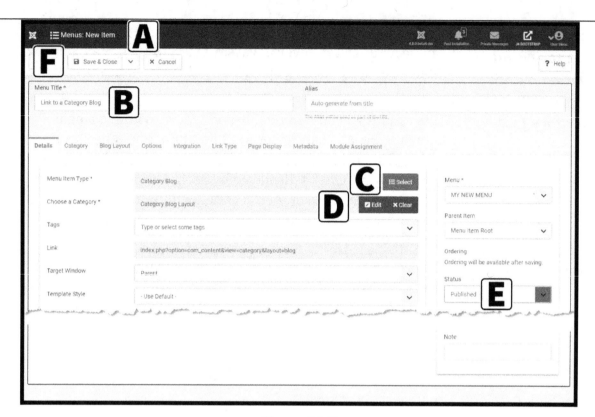

Figure 21-7

Refer to Figure 21-7 for the following:

Step 3	B	For the Title, enter: "Link to a Category Blog" (without quotes).
Step 4	C	Within the "Details" tab, for the "Menu Item Type," open "Articles," then select "Category Blog."
Step 5	D	The "Choose a Category" selection should be: "Category Blog Layout." Scroll down the list to find this Category.
Step 6	E	Make sure the "Status" is set to Published.
Step 7	F	Execute a Save & Close action.
Step 8		Go to the website Front-End and refresh the screen.
Step 9		The "Link to a Category Blog" Menu Link Item should appear in "MY NEW MENU."
Step 10		Open the target for "Link to a Category Blog." Previously, only one Article was assigned to the "Category Blog Layout" Category, so the "Read More Article" should be the only one to display in the Main Content Area.

Remember this Point

If you wish to display a single Article in which you have inserted a "Read More" feature, or if you have a Category that has many Articles within it that have the feature included, then the "Category Blog" Menu Link Item can be chosen to display a collection of Articles.

Very, Very Important Note About "Read More"

The "Read More" feature does not display in association with any other Menu Link Item. The Menu Link Item MUST be of the "Category Blog" type. Additionally, the "Read More" feature MUST be enabled in the "Global Options" for Articles. Remember this when the "Read More" feature is desired in Articles.

Modifying the Blog Display Layout

If every Category Blog layout were the same, websites would have a very boring appearance. Also, because Blog Articles need to be prioritized in terms of current Content, along with access to older Articles, another type of layout is required. Joomla! 5 has these designations with respect to Category Blog Articles. Refer to Figure 21-7 for a graphic layout of the Category Blog display.

Leading Articles	These are the first, or "leading," Articles that appear in a Category Blog Layout. The most important of which is their number, which can be anything from "0" to a higher number. If set to "0," the "Leading Articles" do not display and the layout defaults to "Intro Articles." Leading Articles may be set to display from 1 to 4 Columns. The amount to Article text displayed for "Leading Articles" is set by the "Read More" settings within the Articles themselves.
Intro Articles	Next in order of layout, IF there are "Leading Articles" and their value is set from "1" to any high number. "Intro Articles" may be set to multiple columns, along with the number to be displayed. The amount to Article text displayed for "Intro Articles" is set by the "Read More" settings within the Articles themselves.
Links to Articles	After the number of "Leading" and "Intro" Articles have been set, if there are any additional Articles within the Category Blog selected, access to them is limited to a link directly to the Articles. There is not "intro" text, no "Read More" break, nothing – no text whatsoever.

Other considerations when determining how the Articles are displayed in the Category Blog layout, such as:

Category Order	If a "Top Level" Category is targeting by the Menu Link Item, and contains "child" or "Sub-Categories," the actual order of how the Categories are displayed may be set using a drop down selector in the "Blog Layout" tab for the Menu Link Item.
Article Order	Within the Categories of a Category Blog, the Articles may also be set to any number of display configurations via a dropdown selector. This selector is under the "Blog Layout" tab for the Menu Link Item.

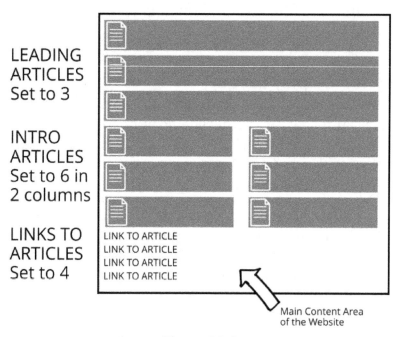

LEADING ARTICLES Set to 3

INTRO ARTICLES Set to 6 in 2 columns

LINKS TO ARTICLES Set to 4

LINK TO ARTICLE
LINK TO ARTICLE
LINK TO ARTICLE
LINK TO ARTICLE

Main Content Area of the Website

Figure 21-8

What are "CSS Classes"

"Classes" are elements of Cascading Style Sheets ("CSS") whereby the "class" can be assigned to Content Items which then take on the characteristics of the "Class." In other words, the "Class," applies and the results are a pre-coded visual display.

A Note About CSS

In "CSS" parlance, a "class" is a code that applies, and can be applied, to one or more "elements" that display on a webpage. On the other hand, an "ID" for a "CSS-coded" element may only appear once on its respective screen. It may appear on "each screen" but not more than one time. Keep this in mind if you begin to dabble in "CSS" on Joomla! 5 webpages.

Setting the Intro Column Layouts

As stated earlier, the "Intro Articles" may be set to display in multiple columns along with the number of Articles to be displayed. Unfortunately, Joomla! 5 does not have a simple 1-2-3 setting for the Number of Columns for Leading Articles. It does, however, have a numerical choice for the Number (#) of Intro Articles. The following Exercise will demonstrate how Multiple Column Layouts for "Intro Articles" are set.

Before proceeding, there needs to be a sufficient number of Articles in the "Category Blog" Category need to be created, which is simple. Ten (10) Articles are needed.

Open the "Read More" Article, then perform a "Save as Copy" action repeated nine times, continue Exercise 21-3 as follows:

Step 11	Open the "Read More" Article.
Step 12	Perform a "Save as Copy" action. Note that the Article Title and Alias now have a (2) suffix, which designates it as a different Article.
Step 13	Perform a Save Action. This locks in Article (2).
Step 14	Perform a Save as Copy action. Note that the Article Title and Alias now have a (3) suffix, which designates it as a different Article.
Step 15	Perform a Save as Copy Action. This locks in Article (3).
Step 16	Keep repeating these task steps until there are *ten (10) Articles* within the Category Blog Layout Category.
Step 17	When completed, there should be 10 Articles. Each Article should have a number suffix – this helps identify them in the layouts.

Here are the pre-configured "CSS classes" that may be applied to "Intro Article" settings to configure the layout:

Step 18	To make it easier to see what is going on when applying the "classes," rename the "Read More Article" to "Read More Article (1)," and its Alias "read-more-article-1.
Step 19	Execute a Save & Close action.
Step 20	Go to the Front-End, refresh the screen, and note now that there are ten "Leading Articles" on display. Let's reduce that number to two.
Step 21	On the "Home Dashboard," exit the Article Manager and open the Menu Manager.
Step 22	Access "My New Menu" and the "Link to Category Blog" Menu Link Item by opening it to the Workspace.
Step 23	Under the "Blog Layout" tab, access the "# Leading Articles" field and enter the number "2" (without quotes). "Leading Articles" are those that stack one

	above the other and expand, by default, to the full-width of the Content Area.
Step 24	In the "# Into Articles" field, enter: "4" (without quotes).
Step 25	In the "# Columns" field, enter: "2" (without quotes).
	The settings in the remaining fields do not need to be changed.
Step 26	Execute a Save Action.
Step 27	Go to the Front-End, refresh the screen, and note now that there are only 2 "Leading Articles" displaying. This is the traditional manner of displaying "Leading Articles," but not the limitation.

With the exception of the number of Leading Articles, compare the resulting layout that was created above with the graphic in Figure 21-8. The layout should be similar.

Priority of Settings for the Category Blog Layout

Because there are "Global Options" that dictate the appearance of webpage or screen element layouts, this is the top level controlling feature. In this case, the settings within the "Blog/Featured Layouts" tab are the top level of settings that control the visual aspects. Once these are set, they apply to every set of Articles that are displayed using the "Articles > Category Blog" layout selection.

It is possible to over-ride the "Global Options" for a single instance to a "Category Blog" layout by modifying the Menu Link Item that opens the display. The "Global Options" can remain set "as is" yet the layout can be altered through modification of the Menu Link Item associated with it. The over-ride settings are found under the "Blog Layout" tab of the Menu Link Item that triggers the screen display.

Any changes made under that tab will modify the layout, but ONLY that particular one. "Global Options" still control all others unless there is an over-ride at the Menu Link Item level.

Classes that apply to Category Blog Layouts

"Blog Layouts" are limited to 4 columns. If no "Blog Class" is specified, the Leading Article display is the full width of the Main Content Area. Otherwise, they are as specified in the available "Blog Classes," of which there are two applications:

Blog Class (Leading Articles)	This "Blog Class CSS," when inserting into the "Leading Article Class" field, applies ONLY to the "Leading Articles."
Article Class (Intro Articles)	This "Blog Class CSS," when inserting into the "Article Class" field, applies ONLY to the "Intro Articles."

It should be pointed out that the actual count of "Leading Articles" should at least equal the number of Columns designated for the layout. In other words, if the "Leading Article Class" specifies a 3-column layout, the "# of Leading Articles" should also be 3 or more.

CSS Classes for Intro Articles

First, the "CSS Class" for "Intro Articles" can be set within the "Global Options," just the same as the "Leading Articles" may be preset. The "CSS Class" for the "Intro Article" can be set to a different value using the same over-ride as the "Leading Articles." The "CSS Classes" that apply to "Leading Articles" can be applied to "Intro Articles."

More information about over-rides can be found in Chapter 44, "Custom & Alternative Layouts," and Chapter 47. "Library of Overrides." Both of these Chapters provide detail instructions and examples of using "CSS Classes" to modify layouts, either Globally or on a per-Content Item basis and are found in *Joomla! 5: Boots on the Ground, Advance Edition, Volume 2.*

Article Details

It is advisable to consider removing all or some of the "Details" of the Articles for a clean, leaner visual appearance of the Blog layout. Perhaps the most relevant to keep would be the "Published" Date entry. Of course, this depends on the specifications for the design and layout of the website Content, but usually, the information in the "Details" area are typically not needed. Useful, yes. Needed, no.

Using Customized Headings

When the "Category Blog Menu Link Item" and related Content display is used, it opens several areas of customization. Some of these same features apply to other types of layouts invoked by different types of Menu Link Items. However, that is not a steadfast rule, so don't make that assumption.

The following a three customizations for the "Page Heading" that can be applied to a Category Blog Layout:

Category Title	This is the name of the Category that is being displayed. There is no override or alternate Category Title feature. The only Option is to display it or not. This Title is generated automatically, coming from the Category's Workspace Category Title field.
Page Heading	A Page Heading can be added. It will appear at the very top of the Content Area. If the Category Title is set to "show," both will display, with the Category Title below the Page Heading. The Page Heading is created in the Menu Link Item Workspace, under the "Page Display" tab.

Page Sub-Heading	A secondary, or "Sub-Heading" can also be added to the screen, and it will appear below the Page Heading. However, both the Category Title and Page Sub-Heading cannot be used at the same time. If using a Page Sub-Heading, the Category Title MUST be set to "Hide," otherwise an undesirable display will result. These settings are found under the "Category" tab in the Menu Link Item Workspace.
Combinations of Customized Titles	Below are the combinations of customized Title that can be used. Of course, each Title can be set to be the only one displayed, but it is the combination of Titles that offer the greatest customization possibilities:

Page Heading over the Category Title	Page Heading over the Page Sub-Heading

The vertical order as shown is how the Titles or Headings will appear on the screen.

Category Title and Page Sub-Heading cannot be used together.

Ordering of Blog Item Categories & Articles

In a typical "blogging" Publishing situation, Articles are typically listed as "last posted, first displayed." This applies across the board for Leading Articles, Intro Articles and Article Links. However, there might be times when this might not be desired.

One of the reasons the Articles within the Category Blog were numbered is to allow the Administrator to experiment with different layout "Options" and overrides and see the results.

For example, assume that Blog Articles are frequently edited or updated. The Authors would want the modified or updated Articles to "rise to the top" so-to-speak as they are changed. To do that, the "ordering" option within the Menu Link Item must be changed, as follows:

Category Ordering

If the "Global Options" for a "Category Blog" is set to show a "Parent" and "Child" Categories, then this setting can be invoked to change the "order" of how they are displayed. First, without changing anything, the "default" setting for displaying of Categories within a "Blog format" is the "Category Order." This means that the "order" in which the Categories are arranged in their respective Category Manager is how they will display under the "default" conditions.

For manual overrides, there are four possible "ordering" "Options" for Categories, as follows:

Default: Use Global (Category Order)	This is the "default" setting and can be changed within the "Options" for Categories & Articles. These are the "Global Options" frequently referred to in this book.
No Order	This will likely display the Categories in somewhat of a "random" or "un-ordered" manner.
Title Alphabetical	This overrides the "default" and "orders" ALL Articles by their Alphabetical Title, A to Z.
Title Reverse Alphabetical	This overrides the "default" and "orders" ALL Articles by their Alphabetical Title, Z to A.
Category Order	In the event the "default" or Global "Options" is set to any other condition, this selection allows the change as explained above. The "default" might be "Title Alpha," and then can be changed to "Category Order."

Article Ordering

Similar to Category Ordering defined above, the Articles within them can also be re-arranged to other layouts based on different parameters. There is also a "default" setting that controls the "ordering" initially, and this too is set in the "Options" for Categories & Articles, thus becoming the "Global Option" for the "ordering" of the Articles in a Blog Layout Format.

In addition to the "default" or "Global Options" setting for Articles, there are twelve (12) other setting that may be invoked as overrides, as follows:

Default: Use Global (Use Recent First)	This is the "default" setting and can be changed within the "Options" for Categories & Articles. By "Most Recent," the reference is by "Published" date.
Feature Articles Order	If the Category is the "Featured Articles," this sets the order of appearance the same way Articles are ordered within the "Featured Articles" Category.
Most Recent First	By the most recent "Published Date," this ordering applies. It does not matter if the field is "Published" or not.
Oldest First	By the most recent, in reverse order "Published Date," this ordering applies.
Title Alphabetical	This is a straight "Title Alpha" listing for the Articles.
Title Reverse Alphabetical	This is a reverse of the "Title Alpha" listing for the Articles.
Author Alphabetical	If there are many Authors, listing the Articles by the

	Authors name might be desired. This isn't a wise choice if there are only one or two Administrators that create/write Content Articles.
Author Reverse Alphabetical	This reverses the order by Author names.
Most Hits	"Hits" are when the Content Item is accessed and is counted by the system regardless if they are shown in the "Details" section of the Article layout or not. As with all other possible "Details," they do not need to be displayed. The "Hits" are recorded in the background.
Least Hits	This is the reverse order from "Most Hits" and displays the Articles based on the least number of times it/they have been accessed.
Random Order	At any given point during access, this will display the Articles in somewhat of a "random" or "un-ordered" manner, similar to shuffling playing cards.
Article Order	This displays the Articles within their respective Categories in the "order" in which they are arranged on this Category List.
Article Reverse Order	This displays the Articles within their respective Categories in opposite "order" in which they are arranged.

In summary, Categories and Articles can be displayed in almost any manner desired to suit the type of layout and the presentation of the Content. However, the format most often used is "Most Recent," or the most recent Content Item "Published" is the first displayed, or displayed at the top of the order.

Publish and Unpublish Options

If Content Items ("Articles") within the Categories are set to a future "Publish" date, or a date to "Unpublish" the Article, they will appear or be removed from the Blog layout. This means that Articles can be written to be "Published" at a later date and they will automatically appear at the top of the Content Item listings. Likewise, when the Articles are set to "Unpublished" at a certain date, they will no longer appear within the layouts.

EXERCISE 21-4: DISPLAY A CATEGORY OF ARTICLES

Objective: The objective of this Exercise is to demonstrate how a Category of Articles can be displayed. This displays a list of the Articles within a single Category. It will also, selectively, display the Sub-Categories within it if there are any. The display of Sub-Categories can be configured.

Step 1		In the "Home Dashboard," click on "Menus" in the left Menu, which opens the "Modules (Site) Manager. Then click on "My New Menu to open the Manager.
Step 2	A	In the left menu, on the "My New Menu" line, click on the **"+"** icon to open the "Menus: New Item" Workspace.

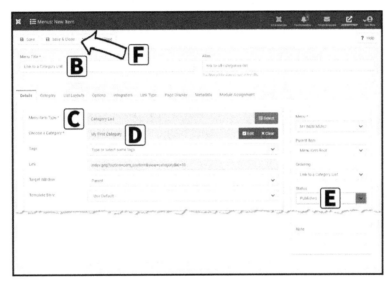

Figure 21-9

Refer to Figure 21-9 for the following:

Step 3	B	For the Title, enter: "Link to Category List" (without quotes).
Step 4	C	Within the "Details" tab, for the "Menu Item Type," open Articles, then select "Category List."
Step 5	D	Then, in the "Choose a Category" select: "My First Category."
Step 6	E	Make sure the "Status" is set to "Published."
Step 7	F	Execute a Save & Close action.
Step 8		Go to the website Front-End and refresh the screen.
Step 9		The "Link to a Category List" Menu Link Item should appear in "My New Menu."

What is now being displayed is: 1) a list of all Articles within the selected Category, and 2) all the Sub-Categories ("Child") that are within, or underneath that Category. There is a setting within the Menu Link Item's Category tab, to disable the display of Sub-Categories or control how they are displayed.

Category Display with No Articles Displayed

Another type of display that is often used is to simply display a "List of All Categories," without Articles included. This means that every Category on the website will be directly accessible from the results of the use of this Menu Link Item, as illustrated in the following exercise.

Category & Article Options

There are many different configurations for the display of Categories and Articles. Chapter 43, "Global "Options" & Settings," in *Joomla! 5: Boots on the Ground, Advance Edition, Volume 2,* will explain the Options, some of which will be demonstrated also in Exercises that follow in this book.

EXERCISE 21-5: DISPLAY A LIST OF ALL CATEGORIES

Objective: The objective of this Exercise is to demonstrate the method used to display a list of all the Categories, including their Sub-Categories, which have been created as part of the Content organization hierarchy.

Step 1		In the "Home Dashboard," click on "Menus" in the left Menu, which opens the "Modules (Site) Manager. Then click on "My New Menu" to open the Manager.
Step 2	A	In the left menu, on the "My New Menu" line, click on the **"+"** icon to open the "Menus: New Item" Workspace.

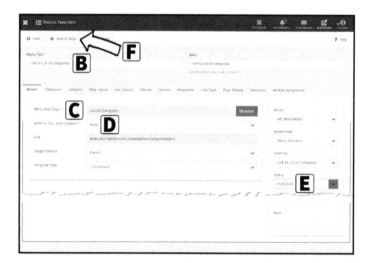

Figure 21-10

Refer to Figure 21-10 for the following:

Step 3	B	For the Title, enter: "Link to List of Categories" (without quotes).
Step 4	C	Within the "Details" tab, for the "Menu Item Type," open "Articles," then select "List All Categories in an Article Category Tree."
Step 5	D	Then, in the "Choose a Category" select: "Root." This means that the "List of Categories" will start at the very "top level" of the Category hierarchy structure.
Step 6	E	Make sure the "Status" is set to "Published."
Step 7	F	Execute a Save & Close action.
Step 8		Go to the website Front-End and refresh the screen.
Step 9		The "Link to List of Categories" Menu Link Item should appear in "My New Menu."
Step 10		The Front-End should display at brief list of Categories. Those that are displayed are the "Top Level" Categories within the "Root," or highest level of Categories. If you have completed all the previous exercises, four named Categories should display in addition to "Uncategorized." The "Article Count" should display next to each Category Title.
Step 11		Adjacent, to the far right, of the "Blog" Category, there will be a **"+"** icon/button. Click on it. This opens the "Blog" Category and lists all of the Sub-Categories within it. This is the indicator that there is a Sub-Category within the "Parent" Category.
Step 12		Note that when the Blog Category is opened, "My First Category" also has the **"+"** icon/button located at the far right. Click on it. This opens "My First Category" and lists all the Sub-Categories within it, which should be three. If not, check the "Global Options" for "Categories," and make sure that "Empty Categories" is set to "Show."
Step 13		With the "Blog" and "My First Category" lists fully expanded, all of the Categories previously created on the website are listed.
Step 14		Clicking the **"−"** icon/button will collapse the expanded list for the respective Category.

EXERCISE 21-6: MENU LINK ITEM TO ACCESS A COMPONENT

Objective: The objective of this Exercise is to demonstrate how to access a Component, in this case, the "Search" Component. It is possible that the website you Administer may have many specialized Components installed, they would likely be access in the same manner as described in this Exercise.

Step 1		In the "Home Dashboard," click on "Menus" in the left Menu. Then click on "My New Menu" to open the Manager.
Step 2		At this point, there are two ways to create a "new" Menu Link Item: (1) Clicking the **"+"** next to "My New Menu" in the left area. (2) In the "My New Menu" Workspace, click on the **"+ New"** button at the top of the screen. Both actions will open the "New Menu Link Item" Workspace.

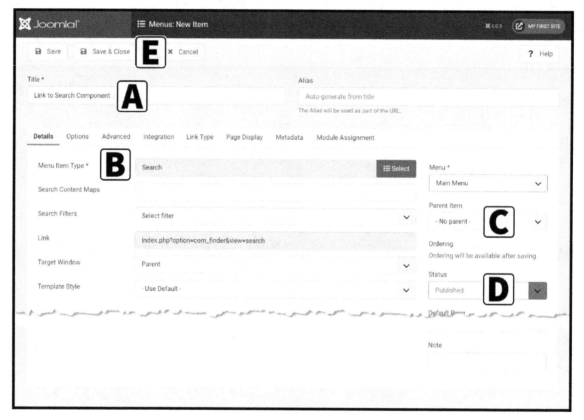

Figure 21-11

Refer to Figure 21-11 for the following:

Step 3	**A**	For the "Menu Title," enter: "Search Component Link" (without quotes).
Step 4	**B**	For the "Menu Item Type," open "Smart Search," then select the "Search" option.
Step 5	**C**	Make sure the "Parent Item" is set to "No Parent."
Step 6	**D**	Make sure the "Status" is "Published."
Step 7		There are no settings within the tabs that need changing. The "default" configuration is sufficient.

Step 8	E	Execute a Save & Close action.
Step 9		Access the website Front-End and refresh the screen.
Step 10		Click on the "Search Component Link" in the "My New Menu" Menu. This will open the "Search Component" in the Main Content Area with the "Advanced Search" button. Use of this Component will be thoroughly discussed in Chapter 30, "Component: Smart Search."

Any Component, or any sub-feature of a Component, can be accessed using the same technique as described in the Exercise above. Let's say, for example, that you wish to open something within the "Contacts" Component. This Component has the following individual parts, each of which may have a Menu Link Item target to open it:

- Create Contact
- Featured Contacts
- List All Contact Categories
- List Contacts in a Category
- Single Contact

Within the "Contacts" Component, it is possible that five (5) Menu Link Items can be created to access the distinct parts, depending upon the desired result.

Of course, remember that both "Categories" and "Contacts" within the Component *MUST* have Content Items. Categories *MUST* exist. Then Contacts *MUST* be created in the Categories in order for the Menu Link Item to display anything. The "show empty" "Options" could be used to override this.

Menus are the Key Elements

No Content, other than that which is set to display on the Front-Page of the website, can be accessed without being connected to a Menu via a Menu Link Item via one method or another. Yes, Articles can be accessed from a Category List view, but the "List View" was trigged to display by a Menu Link Item.

When administering Content on a Joomla! 5 website, thought should be given to the planned Menu structures. Be wary of too many Menus as well as Menus that contain too many Menu Link Items. Find a balance of Menus which will access Content with being "too many" of either instance. Classification of Menus by their subjective "link targets" is usually the best approach to figuring this out.

Vertical or Horizontal Layouts

One of the frequently asked questions in the Joomla! Forum deals with vertical and/or horizontal menu layouts. If those posting the question would have just looked at the Menu Modules, most of their questions would be immediately answered.

In the default layout, the only Menu that is visible is on the right, within a "sidebar"-right Module Position. The Menu Link Items are stacked one above each other and, if there are sub-Menus, they expand below the Menu Link Item Parent. This type of Menu works just fine for layouts that utilize "sidebar" locations

When the Sample Data was installed in Chapter 7, it automatically created a horizontal Menu layout at the top of the screen, directly below the banner. This established one fact. That both vertical and horizontal layouts can be used and used at the same time.

The direction of the Menu layout is dependent upon the Menu Module applied and the "CSS" code that applies. Plus, of course, and Bootstrap "CSS" that is also programmed into the Template.

Extensions for Menus

Sometimes abandoning the default Menu System works better for managing access to Content. There are many, many Menu Extensions available for Joomla! 5, and if not at this present time, there will be before too long.

These Menu Extensions allow the Administrator to take the navigation scheme to a higher level by inserting Menus that are configured to both look good and function well.

When opportunity allows, explore the possibilities available.

NAVIGATION:
Menu Option Settings

Unlike most of the other "Options" that associate with Components and Content Items on the Joomla! 5 platform, the ones that apply specifically to Menus are rather sparse. This is somewhat surprising, but then there is a rational reason for the lack of "Options."

Every Menu Link Item has an abundance of individual configurations that can be applied on a one-off basis, so global options need not be applied. In fact, global options could likely render the configuration of Menu Link Item choices useless.

These settings, which are not "Options," but applied specifically to each single Menu Link Item individually, after only those Content Items to which they are connected. "Global Options" would therefore render this ability inert.

One of the strengths of Menu Link Items is their ability to have many different configuration options to each one individually vs. global controls. Websites and layouts can be made more interesting through the use of micro-settings for Content Items vs. macro-settings that apply globally which, of course, the Global "Options" for Menus would do.

Configuring the Menu Module "Options"
Within the Menu "Options," there are few choices that can be made with respect to global configurations, with those being:

TAB: *PAGE DISPLAY* – limited to three settings

 a) **Browser Page Title** – in the browser's location tab.

 b) **Show Page Heading** – on the Content Item screen.

 c) **Page Class** – requires additional "CSS" coding.

TAB: *PERMISSIONS* – sets permissions for every Joomla! 5 User Group

Page Display Options

As with all parts of Joomla! 5, the Menus have "Options," although in this case, they are minimal, with not many "Options" to configure. There are no "Options" that can be set for Menus or Menu Link Items that apply to only the Back-End Menus, although they do have various settings for each Menu Link Item.

Within the Page Display Options, only the following are available:

Browser Page Title	Any entry here will be displayed in the Browser's Tab.
Show Page Heading toggled "ON"	If an alternate Heading for the Content Item is desired, a new Heading can be inserted which then will display on the Content Item Page/Screen vs. the name of the Menu Link Item. Normally, the name of the Menu Link Item would display, but and text entered will simply replace the Menu Link Item name with the entered text.
Page Class	Each Joomla! 5 webpage may have a different appearance based on the "Page Class" that is applied using "CSS" settings. This lets the Administrator add a custom "CSS" to individual pages/screens. If you are not familiar with "CSS" and "Page Class Suffixes," it is best not to attempt to make changes in this regard.

Setting Menu Permissions

Under the "Permissions Tab," each Joomla! 5 User Group can have their respective "Permissions" set to different values as needed. By default, the "Super User" has been granted full permissions, while all other have been denied, with a few of them inherited from their "Parent" item.

How is this used?

An example of the use of "Permissions" is to "Allow" a Content Item Author to "Create," while allowing a Content Item Editor the "Permissions" to both "Create" and "Edit" a specific Content Item associated with a Menu Link Item.

Any combination of "Permissions" may be set based on the implied actions allowed by Users within the various User Groups.

Of course, unless there is a hierarchy of Content Item Authors, Editors, Reviewers and/or Publishers, there is no need to configure these settings to something other than their defaults. But know that they can be modified as needed by the application of Content Item management.

Review Chapter 21, "NAVIGATION: Menu Systems"

If there are uncertainties about how "Options" work and the setting that may be applied on the individual Menu Link Item, please refer back to Chapter 21.

USERS:
Managing Users

When someone visits a website, they initially show up as "Guests," with no privileges other than to "look around" at Content the Administrator has designated for the viewing level of "Public." In Joomla! 5 "ACL" jargon, this is simply "viewing access."

Most all websites have their Content set to the "Public" viewing level, and the "Guests" are free to click around and view the Content. In short, "Guests" have "Public" viewing privileges.

However, if the Content, or some of the Content is intended to have restricted viewing requirements, then another level of "viewing access" must be granted. This usually requires "Guests" to "register" by creating a User Account, usually consisting of a username, password, email address and other identifying information. Sometimes the User Account is called a User Profile.

The website Content that has been restricted to "Registered," is not viewable by the "Guests," because they have not created a User Account. They are not considered as "Registered Users" for Content viewing access purposes. They have no "Permissions" to access anything the Content Items designated for "Public" viewing.

Only those "Guests" who have "registered" and created an access account may view the "restricted" Content, with viewable permissions for "Registered Users" only. These website visitors are no longer classified as "Guests," but "Registered Users" with respect to their "viewing access" permissions. There are other levels of access, and these will be discussed later.

The Main Differences

Before diving deep into the process of managing Users "viewing privileges" or the "actions permissions," an understanding of how Users interact with the Joomla! 5 website is needed.

Without getting into Users that "register" on the website to create a "User Account," it should be noted that on most websites, such registration process is not generally required to view Content. However, some websites allow "partial viewing," and to view the complete Content item, they must "log in," which requires them to "register" and create an account, etc. This changes their "Status" as a User.

The Content on a Joomla! 5 website, in order to be viewed by all "Guests," is typically set to a "viewing permission" of "Public." Joomla! 5 has this level of viewing as a default sub-Group that inherits the privileges of the "Public" Group.

The "Guests" which access the "Public" Content on the website do not need to have their "viewing" or "actions" permissions configured. Why? Because they visit the website to look around or find specific information. This "public-facing" information is therefore easily accessible. The Access Control List ("ACL") for this is "Public," thus allowing any website visitor (the "Guest"), to view the Content.

There is no distinct difference between a website "Guest" or a website "Visitor," insomuch as both have access to the same "public-facing" website Content.

Figure 23-1 shows the default User Groups and their order within the hierarchy. The indented User Group typically "inherits" the permissions of its direct "Parent" Group.

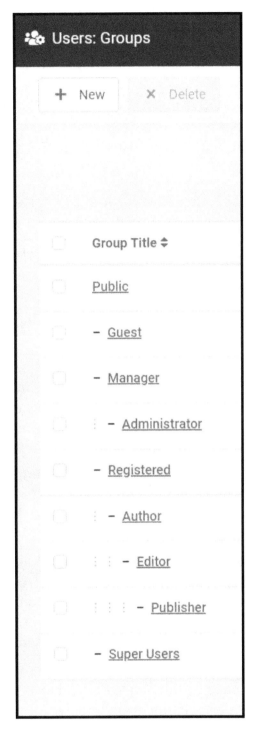

Figure 23-1

Of course, each of the individual User Groups has their own set of permissions, which will be discussed in Chapter 24, "USERS: Controlling Access, Actions & Permissions.

The "Public" & "Guest" Group

Let's consider how to use the "Public" and "Guest" access levels for different actions. The "Public" Group is typically used when the Administrator desires Content to display to all website Users whether they are logged in or not. The "Guest" Group may, as described above, only view Content when NOT logged in using a "Registered" account. The two usually have the same levels of "viewing permissions," but the "Guest" Group might have some different permissions variations configured under certain circumstances.

Protocols That Apply

The Access Control features of Joomla! 5 are bound by a series of dynamic protocols, which are descriptors of how User Groups may be used, as described below:

Protocol 1	The "Guests" can view any Content that is set to the "Public" Access Level.
Protocol 2	To access restricted Content, a website User must "Register" and create a User Account on the website, thus becoming a "Registered User" within the hierarchy.
Protocol 3	Any existing User Group may be designated as the "New User Registration Group." This is the User Group into which Users can be assigned upon registration. However, "Registered" is the Group typically used. This is not a steadfast rule. Any existing User Group may be designated as the default upon registration.
Protocol 4	A "Registered User" may access both the "Public" and the "Registered Group" levels of Content classification. Nothing restricts that level of User from viewing the "Public" Content and then after login, the otherwise designated "Restricted" Content.
Protocol 5	To be assigned to any other Access Group, website Users need to be within the "Registered Group," which requires their access to be started with a formal login process. If they are not a member of the "Registered Group," they cannot be assigned to any other because, in all reality, they simply do not exist as Users in the system.
Protocol 6	"Registered Users" may be assigned to any other level(s) of Group Access, controlled by the Access Control List ("ACL"). The Administrator must make these assignments manually.
Protocol 7	No User, regardless of their Groups, may access the Administrator Back-End unless they are granted access via a Group that is called "Special." This can be in addition to any other assigned Group. This is a very unique access permission that should be used carefully and with definite restrictions in place to prevent the "Special User" from accessing website configuration controls. Limitations on "which areas" of the Back-End a "Special User" may access, or be prevented from

	accessing. The "ACL" is used to assign or limit access permissions.
Protocol 8	There is no limit to the number of User Groups into which any User may be assigned. By default, the "Super User" is automatically assigned to all of them, even when/if a new User Group is created.
Protocol 9	Content may be configured to display under conditions so that it appears ONLY when a User is **NOT** logged into the website.
Protocol 10	Content may be configured to display under conditions so that it appears **ONLY** when a User **IS** logged into the website. This is not limited to Articles. Modules may also be so configured. This was covered in Chapter 12, "CONTENT: Modules."
Protocol 11	A "Guest User" can, via the website "ACL," be assigned to any other Group for "viewing" purposes, creating a situation where "Guests" may view certain Content, but that logged in Users "may not" see the Content. The Content Items are set to "Guest" Access and thus, the "view" allowed is only for the Group of website visitors. The "Public" Content Item setting allows all website visitors to view them, while "Guest" may have certain access limitations and "Registered" very specific access permissions.

As has been shown, the "ACL" features of Joomla! 5 are robust and powerful. This feature allows the creation of websites that can create a full range of "granted" and "limited" privileges, both for "viewing" and for "actions," which encompass creating, editing and modifying Content.

The "viewing" and "actions" part of "ACL" are covered in Chapter 24, "USERS: Controlling Access, Actions & Permissions."

"ACL" isn't Boring, it is Exciting

If you are the Administrator of a small website, "ACL" might be a boring and non-relevant subject. However, if you are tasked with Administration duties for a large website with many Content Authors with different approval levels before the Content is Published, you will delight in the brilliance of "ACL." Also, prescribed "Workflows" might be in effect which absolutely requires a high degree of "ACL" implementation if the intent is to create a "Workflow" that is customized.

Many instances of Content and how it is created and who can view it can be configured, it would take many pages to described them all individually. No attempt will be done to do so in this Chapter.

See Chapter 32, "ADMIN: Workflows," in *Joomla! 5: Boots on the Ground, Advance Edition, Volume 2*, for more information.

Creating Website Users

There are two ways to add, or "register" Users on a Joomla! 5 website: Manual Registration or Self-Registration. The first way is that the registration is performed by the Administrator, in the other method, the Users register themselves.

Manual Registration

Sometimes it is more convenient for the Administrator to affect the Registration of Users. This happens frequently on websites where the "Public" or "Guests" can view all of the Content, which is authored internally. The "Authors" can be entered manually by the Administrator and granted "ACL" privileges that have been pre-determined. This might include Permissions for Users to access the Back-End without having full Administrator privileges. They can also be restricted to certain areas of Content Management with certain conditions applying to their level of access. The "ACL" controls all of these configuration settings. This is a usual case when websites have a limited number of Users with authorship and/or editing and Publishing permissions.

Self-Registration

By this method, Users access a Registration Form on the website Front-End, complete the Form Fields and submit the form. In most instances, an email message is sent to the User as a confirmation. A link in the email targets a screen on the website which "confirms" the User as being legitimate and not a spamming effort.

After this, the User may log into the website and access whichever Content has been designated as "Registered" in the Access selection field for "Registered" Users. This is in addition to still being able to view all "Public" Content.

The method, confirming email and specific access configuration settings can be set by the Administrator and is discussed below.

The User Manager

Within the Administrator Back-End, there is a collection of features that allow the management of all website Users with the ability to set "permissions" relative to "viewing" or "actions" that can take place.

The User Manager has the following control areas:

Manage	This section allows the Administrator to edit and/or modify any User information. It is also the location at which the Administrator may manually create a User. This performed by executing a **"New"** action, then completing the necessary User information and other settings on the User Manager screen.
Groups	These were identified earlier and are the "default" User Groups that are added during install and when the "Sample Data" was added. The Group Manager allows the Administrator to add a "New" Group to the hierarchy that can be a "Parent" or "Child" Group.

Access Levels	This controls the "viewing" permissions of the User Groups and shows only the "Parent" Groups. The permissions assigned to these Groups are typically inherited by their "Child" Groups.
Fields	These are Fields that may be added to the Registration Form. There are 15 Field Formats that can be used as part of the User's Form and User's Profile.
Field Groups	The New User Registration Form may contain additional information Fields that may be structured into "Groups of Fields" if required.
User Notes	The Administrator, if desired, may enter private notes about any User in any Group. Often used to establish a record of reasons for a suspension or other action take with respect to the User.
User Note Categories	Similar to Field Groups, User Notes can be classified into Categories as needed.
Privacy	This section deals with "Registered Users" sending a Privacy Request Message to the Administrator who then configures the User's account with respect to private information, "cookies" and the Joomla! 5 core information collection during User "sessions."
User Actions Log	This is a running log of the "actions" taken by individual Users, recording them in a time sequence accessible by the Administrator only.
Mass Mail Users	In the event a notification of a website action should be sent to all Users, this feature provides that function. The email message can be sent to "ALL" Users, or to and individual User Group.
Messaging	This is a Private Messaging System within Joomla! 5 that allows Users to send messages internally to the Administrator or *vice versa*. It is not capable of sending messages between Users.

Adding New User Manually

As previously mentioned, User may be added manually by the Administrator, or through the use of the Joomla! 5 User Registration method. Manually adding users is fine for small website that may have only a few Users that are permitted to add, edit or otherwise manage Content.

EXERCISE 23-1: ADDING USERS MANUALLY

Objective: This Exercise will demonstrator procedures to follow for creating a "Registered User" manually. This task is limited to the "Super User."

Step 1	If not already there, log into the Administrator Back-End and access the "Home Dashboard."

Step 2	A	The "Users Manager" may be accessed in the "Site" section on the main screen and accessing the "Users" block. The **"+"** sign can be clicked to go directly to the "Users: New" Manager screen.

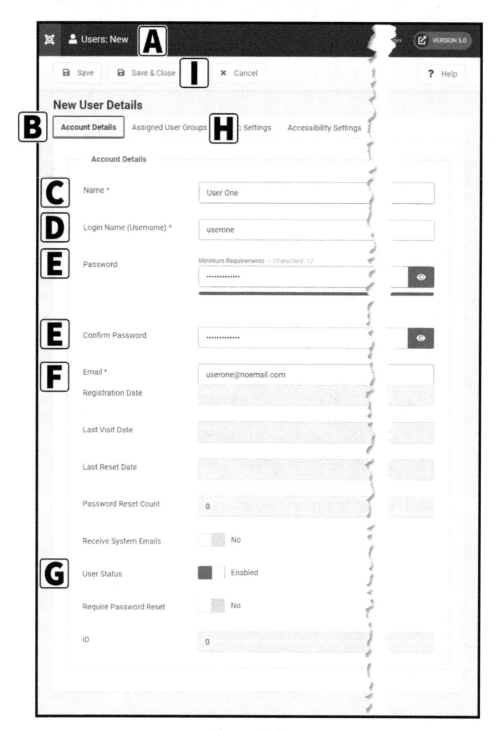

Figure 23-2

Refer to Figure 23-2 for the following:

Step 3	B	Under the "Account Details" tab, enter all the relevant information to create the New User.
Step 4	C	In the "Name" field, enter: "User One" (without quotes).
Step 5	D	In the "Login Name (Username)" field, enter: "userone" (without quotes).
Step 6	E	Enter a "Password" and the "Confirming Password" of your choice.
Step 7	F	For the email, enter: "userone@noemail.com" (without quotes).
Step 8	G	The "User Status" should be set to the "Enabled" state.
Step 9	H	Open the "Assigned User Groups" Tab.
Step 10		Select "Registered" as the assigned group for this User.
Step 11	I	Execute a Save & Close action.

The New User should now appear on the Users List and an email message will have been sent to the New User advising them of the account creation, but only if the "Receive System Emails" was toggled to "Yes."

Make a note that the User's password is included in the email. The password need not be sent, but on manual creation, the User must know what it is.

Blocking Users

Sometimes, usually for website rule violations, it is necessary to "block" a User from accessing restricted Content. This Administrator action is conducted within the User Manager.

When the List of Users is displayed, seek the targeted User and then, under the "Enabled" column, toggle the green icon ("Block"), to the **"X"** icon which indicates the account is in a "Disabled" state.

When an "action" has been taken regarding any User, a "User Note" should be added to the system to make a record of the Administrator's actions and the specific reasons for restricting this User's access permissions.

To undo the action, simply reverse the procedure by clicking on the **"X"** in the "Enabled" column.

Configuring Registration Methods

First, the configuration of the Registration Methods does not comprise the complete spectrum of "ACL" on the website. The configuration discussed herein applies mainly to the "management" of Users and not the actual assignment of advanced or complex "ACL" permissions. This is covered in the previously mentioned Chapter 24, "USERS: Access, Actions & Permissions."

The "User Options" will not be discussed in this Chapter. This topic is extensively covered in Chapter 25, "USERS: Option Settings," where they are discussed with practical applications.

Default Settings

If, as the website Administrator, you want a "plain vanilla" Registration System, with email confirmation, and permissions that allow access to any Content that is designated for "Registered" Users, then there is nothing to do. The default configuration of the website, including the Registration System, is set up to do exactly that. However, the first decision that must be made is whether to have a Registration System invoked and active on the website, or not.

If all website Content is to be available to all visitors, or "Guests," there is no need to establish the Registration System. With one action by the Administrator, the system can be turned off, or disabled, as follows:

Step 1		In the "Home Dashboard," click on "Users" in the left Menu and then click on "Manage" to open the Manager.
Step 2	A	At the top right of the Manager, click on the "Options" button. When the screen opens, the "User Options" tab will automatically open. If not, open it.

Figure 23-3

Refer to Figure 23-3 for the following:

Step 3	**B**	Within the "User Options" tab, there is a selector entitled: "Allow User Registration."
Step 4	**C**	The choice for this configuration is "Yes" or "No," with the results of the selection being obvious. The Default Setting is "No."
Step 5	**C**	Change the setting to "Yes." This setting is required for the examples and explanations in this and the next two Chapters.
		There are other choices available on this same screen. Look them over to become familiar with the configuration settings. Set them as desired, or that might apply, to the User Management requirement of your website. These settings may be changed at any time.
Step 6	**D**	Execute a Save action. Remain in the "User Options" tab area.

Disable the Login Module

If no registration system is to be implemented, make sure that the Module designated as the "Login Form" has the "Status" of "Unpublished." This can be performed on the List of Modules screen or by opening the Module Workspace and changing the "Status" to "Unpublished." There is no need to display a "Login Form" on the Front-End if there is no "registration system" in use, although it can remain but the link to "create a new account" will not display.

As noted, the other default settings included the following:

- The "Default User Group" is "Registered" – meaning that all Content restricted to "Registered" Users is accessible upon registration and confirmation. All other non-restricted Content is also accessible.

- The "Guest User Group" is named "Guest" – meaning that all Content NOT restricted to "Registered" Users is accessible, or that Content granted "Public" access is viewable.

- The new Registered User "password" may be included in the email activation message. It isn't wise to do this, but that option is possible.

- New User Account Activation is set to Administrator – which means that after Registration, the Administrator must individually "activate" each new User. This can be changed to Self-Activation, which means the User will receive an email with an "activation link" included. The Administrator would be "hands off" for this method of User registration.

- Send Email to Administrators – lets the Administrator know, by email notification, when a User has registered. On website with many User Registration actions, this can inundate the Administrator's email, so this "Option" likely should not be used unless absolutely necessary.

Additional Configuration Settings

Overall, there are seven tabs in the "Options" settings for Users. The default settings for these "Options" can remain. However, the User Registration methods and protocols can be customized using more advanced configuration settings found, in addition to the "User Options" tab, also under these topical Tabs:

- Email Domain Options
- Password Options
- Multifactor Authentication
- User Notes History
- Mass Mail Users
- Integration
- Permissions

Refer to Chapter 25, "USERS: Options Settings," for a comprehensive discussion of the "Options" available under User Management and Registration.

Customizing the Registration Page

To create a more comprehensive New User Registration Page, it is necessary to enable and invoke a number of settings that involve the User Profile information. Joomla! 5 has a number of pre-set information fields which can be added to the Registration Form.

Warning! Too Many Fields

People are not welcoming of exhaustive Registration pages on websites, especially if they are viewing the website on a mobile device. Before invoking the use of the pre-set or any custom information fields, consider this from the User-facing side. If you, personally, do not want to put in a lot of information when registering, don't expect website visitors to fill our extensive forms when doing so. Be prudent with the use of many information fields in the form. Do you "really" need to know or store this information?

Invoking the Pre-Set Fields

First, the Registration Page, and the associated information fields, are controlled by a Plugin called "User-Profile." This Plugin can be Enabled or Disabled, with the latter being the default.

Second, there are a number of pre-set information fields that can be set to "Optional, "Required" or "Disabled." This allows for some rationale use of the form to collect New User information.

When "Enabled," the information fields appear below the basic registration form area on the screen when "Create an account" action is executed within the Login Module.

EXERCISE 23-2: INVOKING A "REQUIRED" FIELD

Objective: This Exercise demonstrates is how to access the User-Profile Plugin, which creates the additional information fields on the Registration screen. It also illustrates how an individual field may be "required" when the form is submitted.

Step 1	In the "Home Dashboard," open the "Plugins" Manager.
Step 2	In the search box, enter: "Profile" (without the quotes). The result should be the display of a Plugin List with "User-Profile" listed.
Step 3	Click on the "User-Profile" Plugin to open it.

If any of the User Fields are intended for use, the Plugin must be "Enabled."

Step 4	There are two duplicate sections of Form Fields. One is for the User Profile for Registration. The other for the Administrator User Forms.
Step 5	Change the "Phone" Form Field to: "Required." Do so for both the "User Profile" and the "Administrator" Form.
Step 6	Set the "Status" to "Enabled."
Step 7	Execute a Save action.
Step 8	Go to the website Front-End an execute the "Create an account" action using the link in the "Login Form." View the resulting screen display.
Step 9	Notice that ALL Form Fields are displaying because they are all set to the "Optional" choice, except "Phone," which was set to "Required" and is indicated by the asterisk (*).
Step 10	Go to the Back-End and "Disable" the "User-Profile" Plugin. The additional Form Fields will not be used in further Exercises.
Step 11	Execute a Save & Close action.

It is obvious that some work is required to configure the "User-Profile" Form Fields to meet individual website User information needs. Let a standard rule guide the use of these fields: if they are not highly important, do not implement their use.

431

Be Aware of GDPR Requirements

Most all countries in the EU have stringent User information privacy requirements. In the US, these laws are not so stringent. Regardless of location, User information should be kept secure. This is reason enough to NOT collect unnecessary information. Also, you must issue a privacy policy statement .

Redirecting Users

Another very useful feature is the redirection of "logged in" Users to a designated website page or screen. Upon logging in, this action can be triggered. In addition, when a User "logs out" of the website, they are, or can be, redirected to another designated website page or screen.

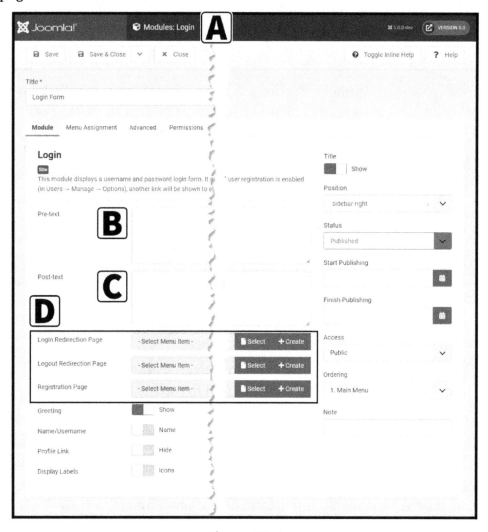

Figure 23-4

Also, if a custom "Registration Page" has been created, when the "Create an account" action is initiated, the User will be redirected to that page to complete the registration action. This allows the full customization of the page to suit the requirements of the website Administrator or organization's requirements.

Redirection Options

There are three "redirect" possibilities within the Registration and Log In, Log Out system. Refer to Figure 23-4 **[D]** above.:

Redirect on Registration	This opens a special, custom designed website page whereby the User is immediately directed as the first page/screen viewed after executing a "Register" action.
Redirect on Log In	When a "Registered User" logs into the website, they can be redirected to a designated custom webpage.
Redirect on Log Out	Upon logging out of the website access, the User can be redirected to a different designated custom webpage.

There can be many beneficial uses for the "Redirects" that are associated with the registration and logging actions by Users.

Login Module Added Text

The registration and login actions take place via a Login Module that is displayed on the website Front-End. This Module has certain configuration settings, two of which are the "Pre-text" and "Post-text."

Pre-Text & Post-Text

Within the "Login Form Module **[A]**," there is an option to enter a text message above and below the login fields. These text areas can include instructions to Users or other helpful information to enhance their registration experience. These text fields are on the Login Form Manager screen, as show in Figure 23-4 **[B] [C]**.

If utilized, these are text messages that will always be displayed above and below the login fields and can be any message desired, but only text.

Use of the above & below text fields is optional. Simply leave the text fields blank if nothing is to be displayed.

As with any other Module, the Login Module can be located in any "Module Position" that is available as part of the current Template. Sometimes, the login is horizontally displayed at the top of the screen. Other times, it is a vertical presentation in a Template Sidebar location. There is no steadfast rule as to which location should be used.

The Login Module should be on the website "Home Screen," but it can be a Module that is conditionally displayed when a specific Menu Link Item associated with it is activated. This configuration option was discussed in Chapter 12, "CONTENT: Modules."

Added Text, Horizontal Location

It is suggested that the above & below text fields NOT be used if the Login Module is in the horizontal format in the top banner area, insomuch as it may cause increased vertical space and may disrupt the visual appearance of the location in which the Module is located.

Managing User Groups

User Groups were previously identified. The Joomla! 5 "ACL" is not limited to just those Groups. Additional User Groups may be added with respective "viewing" and/or "action" permissions.

An example of this would be within an organization that frequently Publishes Articles and uses a "Workflow" to process them through the Author, Editor, Publisher phases. Let's assume that a "Legal" review is needed after the Editor review but before the Publisher may take action. Therefore, a "Legal" User Group can be created and given the necessary permissions.

The "Legal Group" should be a "Registered User," at the same permission levels as an "Editor Group" member and inherit "Permissions" from the "Editor Group." Here is how that is accomplished.

EXERCISE 23-4: CREATING A NEW USER GROUP

Objective: The purpose of this Exercise is to demonstrate how a new User Group is created, made a sub-group under another, thus inheriting the permissions of the "Parent Group."

Step 1	In the "Home Dashboard," Left Menu, open the "Users" Manager.
Step 2	Open the "Groups" Workspace.
Step 3	Open the "Users: New Group" by clicking **"New"** at the top.
Step 4	For the "Group Title," enter: "Legal Review" (without the quotes).
Step 5	Select the "Group Parent" to be: "Editor."
Step 6	Execute a Save action.
Step 7	Next, to ensure that the "Publisher" cannot take action until AFTER "Legal" has approved the Content Item, open the "Publisher Group."
Step 8	Execute a Save action. "Permissions" are now automatically inherited.
Step 9	The "Publisher" should now be under "Legal Review" on the list.
Step 10	This has now set up the conditions to create a "Workflow" that moves the Content Item through "Legal" before "Publishing."

To add additional User Groups, follow the instructions above as needed. The "Workflows" process is covered in *Joomla! 5: Boots on the Ground, Advance Edition, Volume 2,* Chapter 32, "ADMIN: Workflows."

Login Form Reminders & Resets

Forgot your "Username?" Forgot your "Password?" Both of these issues can be resolved with utility features within the "Login Module." Both features have a Menu Link Item within the Login Module that, when executed, initiates an assistance screen for follow-through.

The User should enter the requested information and then "Submit" the form for processing by the Joomla! platform.

The User will receive email messages with a solution for the respective issue in short order. This is a rather simple, straight forward solution to both issues.

Using Multiple Templates & Languages

For each User, if they will be logging into the website Back-End, may be assigned a distinctly different "admin" Template. In addition, if multiple languages have been added for use on the website, both the "Backend Language" and "Frontend Language" may be set according to requirements.

This is accomplished under the "Users > Manage" Menu on the "Home Dashboard," then by opening the respective User's account. Once open, the Template and "Language" settings can be configured under the "Basic Settings" Tab.

In addition, the type of "Editor" the User may use (if more than one Editor Extension is installed), may be assigned to the User. Also, if their "Time Zone" is of critical information, that may also be set under the same Tab.

These settings must be manually configured by the "Super User." The individual User cannot invoke these configuration settings themselves.

Add/Edit Content via the Front-End

If a certain User has "editing permissions," how do they create or edit Content without having Back-End access? This is accomplished by Front-End access to the Content Items to be created or modified by an allowed User.

The process is simple. If the User has "editing privileges," then they need only to log into the Front-End of the website. When doing so, the Content Items they are permitted to "edit" will display an "edit icon."

The "editing privileges" are given by adding the User, in addition to their already "Registered Group," to the "Editor Group." This gives the same User two levels of permissions: 1) access to the "Registered Only" content, and 2) ability to "Edit" any Content Item.

When the logged-in User with the above permissions views any Content Item, the "edit icon" displays and by clicking it, a Content Item Editing Workspace opens. The type of

Editor depends upon which Editor has been allowed by the Administrator for this User to utilized to modify Content.

This "Workspace" also allows editing of "The Author" information, set the "Publishing" information, along with the "SEO Metadata" for the Content Item.

Because there are only "Editing Permissions" allowed, setting of the "Publishing" date information, etc. cannot be performed insomuch as it is reserved for the "Publisher." This is a perfect example of the different levels of "User Permissions" and what they cannot, and can, do with respect to modification of Content. If "Publishing" permissions were granted, the User may change the "Featured" status of the Content Item, the "Start" and "Finish" Publishing dates, and the "Access" designation of the Item.

If it is desired for this same User, with the same "Permissions," to access the Content Items via the Back-End, they must access the Back-End, login and perform the tasks. The additional "Permission" the User must be assign to is "Special."

By default, "Special" automatically includes Users that are Authors, Managers and Super Users. The "Publisher Group" can be easily added to "Special," giving them permissions to access and log into the Back-End.

The method of accomplishing this is easy by opening the "Users" area of the left menu of the "Home Dashboard," then opening "Access Levels." The "Special" level can then be opened, revealing the User Group list. By selecting "Publisher" in addition to those already selected, and executing a Save action, the "Publisher" may now log into the Back-End.

Super User Front-End Login Advantages

The access permissions for the "Super User," when logged into the Front-End, is extended beyond editing Content. When the "Super User" accesses the Front-End via a formal login, ALL of the items display may be edited. This includes Articles, Modules, Menus and everything else not mentioned.

Of course, any User that does not have "Super User" privileges, does not have these same access points, being limited to their assigned User Group permissions.

The "Super User" simply makes any edits desired via the Front-End access points, saves the changes, the logs out. This makes for quick edits and modifications when needed.

USERS:
Controlling Access & Permissions

When it comes to controlling access to a Joomla! 5 website, Administrators will find the "Access Control List, ("ACL") to be a very powerful tool. This Joomla! 5 feature contains configuration, controls who can access, create or edit what Content. For example, users in one group may access Content for which permission to do so has been granted. Users in another group may not access this same Content. There are a multitude of groups and access permissions that can be controlled via "ACL," many of which will be explained in this Chapter.

Some aspects and features of "ACL" we touched upon in the previous Chapters. In this Chapter, a more in-depth exploration of the "ACL" will be accomplished with Exercises and discussion.

Small Websites

If you are the Administrator of a personal or small website, "ACL" will probably will not be an issue. You may skip this Chapter for the time being. "ACL" is only relevant when there are a large number of Content Managers who need certain permissions and restrictions as to what Content they may manage, create, edit or change.

The "ACL" features also come into play when using restrictions on certain Content Items, and limiting access to certain User Groups.

If the website is administered only by one or two, or just a few people, then "ACL" can be set up minimally, with no real concern about who accesses what Content insomuch as the administration relationship is likely to be very informal.

The "ACL" Also Applies to Workflows

One important aspect to understand early in the "ACL" learning process is that it is closely linked, and makes possible, the implementation of complex "Workflows," which might be required in larger, complex websites.

A "Workflow" is a process whereby Content passes through different levels of editing, review and Publishing approvals. Each level of a "Workflow" relies on the permissions granted to the individual User Groups within the flow. The "ACL" system is where this all happens.

Larger Websites

If you Administer a larger or corporate website, then "ACL" is probably required. Such being the case, "ACL" is something the website Administrator(s) must master. A good example of the need for "ACL" is a news-type blogging website with many Editors quite possibly all working from remote locations.

The actual Content they can individually access will likely be controlled and limit each to their own blogging topic areas. Sometimes this can be accomplished if a "blogging" Extension is installed and used. Otherwise, it can be administered via the "ACL" feature of Joomla! 5, and this Chapter will explain precisely how to accomplish "ACL" implementation.

Where to Administer User Permissions

Joomla! 5 has a "User Manager" feature which is accessible via the "Home Dashboard > Users" area. The best way to learn how to administer "ACL" is to go through the processes involved. It is necessary to understand the basics involved in "ACL" administration. At first, "ACL" might seem a bit confusing. However, by the end of this Chapter, you will have performed all of the necessary tasks to gain an understanding of how to implement "ACL" configuration on the website if required to do so.

How to Administer ACL

There are several major steps involved which the Administrator must perform to invoke "ACL," as follows:

Action 1	Manually create Users or allow Users to self-register via a User Registration feature. This places Users into the system, so-to-speak. Users become "Registered" after completing the process. This group has "viewing access" to Content that is restricted to the "Registered" User Group. Administrators must manually assign Users to any other User Group within the "ACL" User Group structure.

Action 2	Create User Groups and assign Users to these Groups. The Groups may have different permissions, which are then granted to the Users assigned to them. Users may be assigned to multiple Groups.
Action 3	Set a specific "viewing rights" for individual Groups to view selected Content Items.
Action 4	Set the specific "action permissions" (create, edit, etc.), for the Groups into which the Users are assigned.

Difference Between "Viewing" and "Actions"

Within the "ACL," there are five "top level" User Groups: Public, Guest, Manager, Registered and Super Users (Administrators), as well as Sub-Groups, all of which were created during installation. See Figure 24-1 below, and note the top level and sub-level categories.

One type of permission deals with the "viewing," of Content. In other words, to restrict or grant Users the ability to view any Content. Typically, a "Registered User" automatically allows those Users to view any Content that has been set to have its "Access" set to "Registered."

The "actions" part of "ACL," includes creating, editing, modifying or the ability to change Content Item settings. Every Content Item has a "Permissions" settings and these can be related to the "ACL User Groups."

Basically, "ACL" has "viewing" and "actions" settings that can be applied to all Content Items, which can also be related to User Groups and the permissions added to the Group. This, too, will be discussed later in this Chapter.

Types of User Actions

Within the "ACL" structure, there are seven "User Actions" for which the Administrator may set "permissions." All permissions are always based on the User Group "Public" and the additional permissions proceed from there. Here are the seven options.

Configure	Use can edit their own User Options, which include the actual Editor Workspace used and other User-specific settings. These settings apply individually to the User.
Access the Administrator Interface	User can log into the Administrator Back-End, but cannot do so at the same permission level as the Super-User. They may log in and access only those Components and Content Items that the respective User Group has permission to access. The User must be assigned to the Content Item User Group AND the "Special" User Group is access the Back-End. Otherwise, the Content Item User Group User only has access to the Content via the Front-End.

Create	User may "Create" a Content Item.
Delete	User may "Delete" a Content Item.
Edit	User can "Edit" Content Items.
Edit State	User can change the "Status" of a Content Item such as "Published," "Unpublished" and dates those items may apply.
Edit Own	This is a more restrictive permission in that the User within that User Groups permission level, may only take "actions" on Content Items the individual User has created. While the User Group may access, for example, a specific Category of Articles, the individual User may only take "actions" upon the Articles they, themselves, have created. Thus, many Authors may contribute to a Category of Content, but only take "action" upon the Content they, individually, have created. This prevents others from changing someone else's Content Item without the "permissions" to do so.

Viewing Group Permissions

In order to Administer Groups and their permissions, there must be a mechanism within the Back-End to accomplish this task. This is performed within the User Manager in the Back-End, accessed via the left Menu or the "Users" block within the Site Module. The Exercise below will guide you through the processing of viewing the permissions for any User Group. This is just a "guided tour" of the "ACL's Permissions" feature. Creating User Groups and permissions settings will be covered in another Exercise in this Chapter.

EXERCISE 24-1: VIEWING THE GROUP PERMISSIONS

Objectives: The goal of this Exercise is to provide information on how to view the "permissions" for any existing User Group. No actions will be taken within this Exercise, other than to view and explore the settings and configurations.

Step 1	If not already there, login as the Administrator to access the "Home Dashboard."
Step 2	Open the "User Manager" via the left Menu "Users" link item, or in the "Site" Panel by clicking on the "Users" block.
Step 3	At the top right of the screen, open the "Options" area of view the "ACL" configuration settings.
Step 4	Open the "Permissions" tab. This screen shows all of the existing User Groups and their respective Group Permissions. The first notable display shows that the "Public" Group is "not allowed" to perform any "actions" with respect to Content.

Step 5	Click on the "Super Users" group. Note this top level User has full "action" permissions with regard to all functions. The "Super User" is "allowed" to do everything.
Step 6	Click on the "Author" Group. This User Group only has permissions to "Create" Content.
Step 7	Click on the "Editor" Group. This Group has permission to both "Create" and to "Edit" Content.
Step 8	Click on the "Publisher" Group. This Group has permission to both "Create" and to "Edit" Content. In addition, the User Group also has permission to edit the "State [Status]" of the Content Items accessible to that User Group.
Step 9	Open one of the drop downs in the "Select New Setting" column. For each of these there are three choices: "Inherited, Denied or Allowed." The default setting is "Inherited," which means the permissions are derived for the User Group "above" it – assuming that it is a "Child" of a "Parent" User Group.

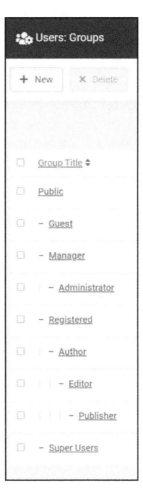

Figure 24-1

Inherited, Denied & Allowed

By the obviousness of their names, the Permission Levels function in three manners. Permissions are either "inherited" from their "Parent" if it is a "Child" User Group. Or, just the opposite, the ability to take "actions" is implicitly "Denied." The opposite is that the "actions" are fully granted, or "Allowed."

Any of these "actions" can be applied selectively for each User Group. This is why the "ACL" is so powerful. It allows the Administrator to grant or deny any User within any User Group access or the ability to take "actions" on any Content Item.

Again, if there is only one Administrator for the website that creates and manages all Content, "ACL" can be ignored. However, if the website has multiple Content Authors, Editors or Publishers, then "ACL" becomes a very important feature to implement and master.

Access Levels

The "default" User Group into which Users are assigned when they complete the Registration Process is: "Registered." This means the approved User is allowed to access ("view"), Content Items where "Access" has been set to "Registered." The connection between the User Group and the Viewing Access permissions are obvious in this case.

The most important aspect of using "ACL" and providing Users with Content "Viewing" or "Action" permissions is that the Administrator must manually make the assignment. A User becomes a member of the "Registered User Group" when the go through the process to become a "Registered Member." After registering, assignment to any other User Group for that User must be performed by the Administrator.

Registered or Another Group as the Default

The "Registered" User Group does not need to be the "default" group upon registration. Within the Joomla! 5 "ACL," there is the option to designate any existing User Group as the "default." The Administrator can create a custom User Group, then designate that group as the "default" when anyone uses the registration process. Only one User Group can be so-designated. Users cannot register into two User Groups via the registration system. The additional User Group assignments must be made manually by the Administrator.

There are Login Form Module Extensions that can be configured to allow Users to register onto the website with selective or multiple User Group assignments. Visit the Joomla! JED for more information about these type of Extensions.

Understanding the "ACL" Rules

If the Administrator has a good understanding of "ACL" permissions and assignments, managing a website with many Authors or Editors can be easily managed. Again, a set of "Rules" cover the "ACL" as listed below:

Rule 1	If a registration system is used, by default, Users are automatically assigned to the "Registered" Group, typically involving verification of their email address. This is the "automatic" registration process.
	If desired, the Administrator may manually add Users, whether an automatic registration method is used or not. The automatic method can be shut off with NO User Registration and performed only manually be the Administrator.
Rule 2	To access restricted Content, Users must be assigned to the "Registered User Group." This Group can only log into the Front-End of the website. In addition to "Public" Content, these Users may also view the Content that as the "Status" of "Registered."
Rule 3	To log into the Back-End of the website, Users MUST also be assigned to the "Special" Users Group, in addition to any other User Group into which they have permissions. Regardless of the "ACL" settings for the User Group or the individual User, unless the User is also given "Special" permissions, they will not be able to access the Back-End.
Rule 4	In addition to having "Special" access to the Back-End, which allows them access to all Content Items, including Components. However, these can be restricted to be accessed by designated User Groups, of which the User must also be assigned. This means there are actually two levels of "ACL" control, giving the system more flexibility on which Users access which Content for "actions" beyond simply "viewing" the Content.
Rule 5	Permissions for a User Group or Sub-Group are automatically "inherited" from their "Parent" Group.
Rule 6	This is important! The "Parent" must have permissions that the "Child" can inherit. Settings in a Sub- or "Child" Group cannot override the settings of the "Parent" Group. If any setting in the "Parent" is set to "denied," it cannot be set to "allowed" in a "Child" Group.

Configuration of the "ACL"

Initially, the "ACL" configuration process might be a bit confusing, but if you follow a systematic approach to setting up the Groups, Access Levels and Permissions for Users, you will master the technique in no time.

Here are the five steps involved in setting up an "ACL" configuration. There will be an Exercise for each involved step later in the Chapter.

Step 1	Create a User Group.
Step 2	Set the global "viewing" access for the User Group.

Step 3	Set the global "actions" permissions for the User Group.
Step 4	Assign an existing User to the User Group.
Step 5	Set the permissions at the Component or Content Item level.

The following Exercises will address and demonstrate each step of the "ACL" management process, so follow the steps in the Exercises exactly as outlined.

EXERCISE: 24-2: CREATING A USER GROUP

Objective: This Exercise will illustrate how a User Group is created. Two User Groups will be created that will be used in subsequent Exercises. This is pretty simple stuff, so there are no screenshots.

Step 1	In the "Home Dashboard," click on "Users" in the left Menu and then click on "Manage" to open the Manager.

Refer to Figure 24-2 for the following:

Step 2	In the left Menu, click on the "Groups" link item. This opens the list display of the User Groups.
Step 3	Click the **"+ New"** button at the top of the screen.
Step 4	On the "Users: New Group" window, in the "Group Title" field, enter "Group A" (without quotes). Leave the "Group Parent" as "Public."
Step 5	Execute a Save & New action.
Step 6	In the "Group Title" field, enter "Group B" (without quotes). Leave the "Group Parent" as "Public." **[C]**
Step 7	Execute a Save & Close Action.
Step 8	The two User Groups should appear at either the top or the bottom of the list, depending upon the "ordering options" in effect.

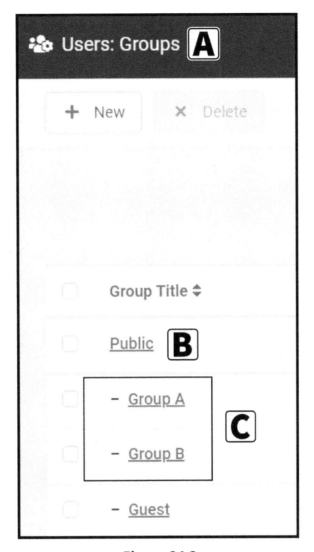

Figure 24-2

EXERCISE: 24-3: DEFINING VIEWING ACCESS LEVELS

Objective: This Exercise illustrates how the "viewing" permissions are set for a User Group, which gives the User Group the permissions necessary to view what then need to view.

Step 1	Access the "Home Dashboard" in the Back-End.
Step 2	In the Site Panel, click on "Users" to open the Manager.
Step 3	In the left Menu, click on the "Access Levels" link item
Step 4	This opens the "Users: New Viewing Access Levels" list **[A]**. Note here that "Group A" and "Group B" are not yet noted – no "viewing" assignments having been made within any of the existing the Groups.
Step 5	Open the "Special" level.

Step 6	Access the "User Groups with Viewing Access" Tab.
Step 6	Select both "Group A" and "Group B" tick boxes.
Step 7	Execute a Save & Close action. On the resulting display, look in the column to the right of "Special," the assigned User Groups will be listed, which now show "Group A" and "Group B" as included **[B]**.
Step 8	Open the "Registered" Group to open it.
Step 9	Select "Group A" and "Group B" tick boxes.
Step 10	Execute a Save & Close action. On the resulting display, look in the column to the right of "Registered" and the assigned User Groups will be listed, which now show "Group A" and "Group B" as included **[B]**.

Refer to Figure 24-3 for the above results:

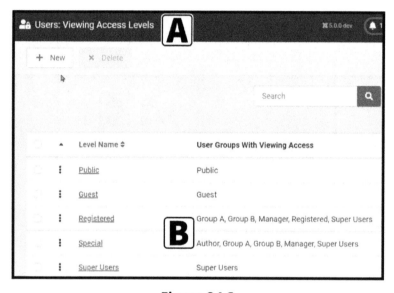

Figure 24-3

At this point, the "viewing" access for User "Group A," and User "Group B" have been granted for the Back-End ("Special"), and the restricted Content ("Registered") on the Front-End.

The next set of steps is to set the "action" permissions for a User Group.

EXERCISE 24-4: SETTING ACTION PERMISSIONS FOR A GROUP

Objective: This Exercise demonstrates how "action" permissions are established for User Groups, which determines what User Groups can do when granted access to Components or Content Items.

Step 1	In the "Home Dashboard," left menu, click on "System" to open the Manager.
Step 2	Click on the "Global Configuration" link to open the Manager.
Step 3	Open the "Permissions" tab located to the right. Notice that both the "viewing" and "actions" permissions are shown and may be modified using the respective drop down selection fields.
Step 4	Click on the "Group A" name, which will open the "permissions" for this User Group.
Step 5	Change the following "permissions" to "Allowed:" ■ Site Login ■ Administrator Login ■ Offline Access ■ Access Administration Interface
Step 6	Execute a Save & Close Action.
Step 7	Click on the "Group B" name, which will open the "permissions" for this User Group.
Step 8	Change the following "permissions" to "Allowed:" ■ Site Login ■ Administrator Login ■ Offline Access ■ Access Administration Interface
Step 9	Execute a Save & Close Action.
Step 10	Go back to "System > Global Configuration > Permissions" and check to make sure the four selected "permissions" for both "Group A" and "Group B" have been changed to "Allowed."

Administrator Login vs. Access Administrative Interface

There were two "admin" settings where "permissions" were set to "Allowed" that deal with Back-End access, and here is what happens for each:

Administrator Login – if the User Group is also assigned to the "Special Group," Users will be able to access the Back-End and manage Components and Content Items. Should the "permissions" be set to "Not Allowed," they will be able to "view" everything but will not be able to take "actions" with regard to any Component or Content Item.

Access Administration Interface – this allows Users in a Group to access the entire Back-End, with the exception of the website's Global Configuration. This is reserved for only those Users that have been designated at "Super Users."

More –This is important! Users MUST have "Special" User Group "permissions" to log into the Back-End.

EXERCISE 24-5: CREATING USERS AND ASSIGNING THEM TO GROUPS

Objective: This exercise creates two Users who will be assigned to a User Group and subsequently given permission of access the Admin Back-End.

Step 1	If not already there, open the "Home Dashboard" display.
Step 2	Open the "Users" Menu, then "Manage" in the left Menu.
Step 3	Create a new User by clicking on **"New"** at the top.
Step 4	Create a User with the following information:

Name	Test User 1
Login Name	testuser1
Password	-enter an easy password-
Confirm Password	-confirm the easy password-
Email	noemail1@noemail.com

Step 5	Scroll down and "Enable" the User.
	Under the "Assigned User Group" Tab, assign this User to "Group A."
Step 6	Execute a Save & New action. Another user will be created.
Step 7	Create a second User with the following information:

Name	Test User 2
Login Name	testuser2
Password	-enter an easy password-
Confirm Password	-confirm the easy password-
Email	noemail2@noemail.com

Step 8	Scroll down and "Enable" the User.
	Under the "Assigned User Group" Tab, assign this User to "Group B."
Step 9	Execute a Save & Close action.
Step 10	Both Users should be on the User list and have the "Registered" permissions User Group designated because this was specified when the User was created.
Step 11	Log out of the Back-End at the Administrator.

| Step 12 | Log into the Back-End as "testuser1" or "testuser2." |

If you access any of the Content Managers in the Back-End, they will open for viewing. However, there will be no buttons visible for "editing" or "modifying" any of the Content. This is because, up to this point, only "viewing" access has been granted to these User Groups. Remember that each user was assigned to a different User Group. The Groups do not have any "action" permissions granted to them – yet! They have "viewing" permissions, but no "action" permissions.

Granting Action Permissions

Now that new User Groups have been created, and Users included into the Group, the "actions" permissions can be created. Because the website only had one User, the "Super User" Administrator, the Exercises would not be correctly functional. This is why two new Users needed to be added to the website. Anyway, the Groups and Users have now been created and the final "ACL" settings can be completed.

Components and Content Items

The "ACL" settings for "actions" apply to two Content Items, the first being Components. The second are Article Content Items. Each has their own "ACL" configurations, which is why Joomla! 5 "ACL" is so powerful. "ACL" can be managed to give the Administrator outstanding control over who and how Content, whether it is a Component or a single Content item, can be assigned.

Recall that while Components may generate Content, there is a difference between the two. Content itself is generally considered to be Categories and Articles. Components are the mini-applications that run inside Joomla! 5 and can generate a wide range of Content (within it), that can be used on the website and displayed via a Menu Link Item action.

EXERCISE 24-6: SETTING PERMISSIONS FOR A COMPONENT

Objective: This Exercise sets the necessary "action" permissions for Users within "Group A" to manage the Contacts Component. After the Exercise is completed, "Group A" Users will be able to do the following within the Contact Manager:

- Access the Components Manager Area.

- Create Contact Categories.

- Create Contacts and Assign them to Categories.

- Delete Contacts.

- Edit Contacts.

- Edit the "Status" of Contacts.

| Step 1 | If not already there, login as the "Super User" Administrator and access the "Home Dashboard." |

Step 2	In the left Menu, open the "System > Global Configuration > Contacts Manager."
Step 3	Open the "Permissions" tab for the "Contacts Component." If not visible, collapse the left menu using the "Toggle Menu" button at the top of that area. Sometimes far right Tabs are hidden due to the width of the monitor screen.
Step 4	When the "Permissions" tab opens, click on "Group A" on the list. The only "Allowed" action was the one enabled in a previous Exercise.
Step 5	Change ALL settings to "Allowed," EXCEPT these two: "Configure "ACL" & Options," and "Configure Options Only." These two "permissions" should be managed only by the "Super User" Administrator.
Step 6	Execute a Save & Close action.
Step 7	The "permissions" for "Group A" within the Contacts Component have now been set.
Step 8	Log out of the Back-End as the Administrator.
Step 9	Log into the Back-End as "testuser1."
Step 10	In the left Menu, open the Components > Contacts > Categories Manager. When the Manager opens, note that the **"+ New"** button at the top now displays – it did not appear before the "permissions" were changed.
Step 11	Go back to the left Menu and open the Components > Banner > Banners Manager. Note that the **"+ New"** button does not display. This is because no "permissions" were granted for "Group A" Users to perform any "actions" within the Banners Component as was performed for the Contacts Component.
Step 12	Log out as "testuser1" and log back into the Back-End as the Administrator.

No "action steps" were included in the above Exercise to create any Contact Categories or individual Contacts. This is pretty much a straight-forward process that an actual Exercise isn't necessary. See Chapter 27, "COMPONENT: Contacts" for information and instructions about creating and managing Contacts.

Controlling Individual Content Item Access

In the previous exercise, only "viewing" was allowed with "actions" NOT allowed. This was changed with "Group A" Users being "Allowed" to do almost everything with respect to the "Contacts Component."

These permissions can be implemented at both "global" and "item-specific" Content. Note that, with the permissions, "Edit" allowed the User to actually modify all of the Content

450

Items in the "Contact Manager." The "Edit Own" setting would limit modifications to only those items the User has self-created. There is a distinct difference.

Exercise 24-7 will guide you through the "User Permissions" for Content Items such as: Categories and Articles. This implementation will allow for fine-tuning the User Permissions in large organizations that have many Authors and Editors who need to have access limited to only those items which pertain to them.

EXERCISE 24-7: SETTING PERMISSIONS FOR A CONTACT ITEM

Objective: This Exercise sets the necessary "action" permissions for Users within "Group B" to manage individual Content Items, which are Categories and Articles.

Step 1	If not already there, login as the "Super User" Administrator and access the "Home Dashboard."
Step 2	In the left Menu, open the "System > Global Configuration > Articles Manager."
Step 3	Open the "Permissions" tab for the Articles Component. If not visible, collapse the left menu using the "Toggle Menu" button at the top of that area. Sometimes far right Tabs are hidden due to the width of the monitor screen.
Step 4	When the "Permissions" tab opens, click on "Group B" on the list. The only "Allowed" action was the one enabled in a previous Exercise.
Step 5	Change the following settings to "Allowed," leaving all others "as is:" "Create," "Delete," "Edit Own" and "Edit Custom Field Value."
Step 6	Execute a Save & Close Action.
Step 7	Log out of the Back-End as the Administrator.
Step 8	Log into the Back-End as "testuser2."
Step 9	Open the "Articles Manager" either from the "Home Dashboard" or in the Left Menu. The "List of Articles" will display. Make note that none of the Articles can be opened by "testuser2," because of the "permissions" previously configured which limits "testuser2" to only be able to "edit own."
Step 10	Create an Article by clicking the **"+ New"** button at the top of the screen.
Step 11	Name the new Article: "Group B Article" (without the quotes).
Step 12	Enter some random text in the "Article Text" field.
Step 13	Execute a Save & Close Action.
Step 14	On the resulting Article List, note now that the "Group B Article" is the only one that is accessible to "testuser2."
Step 15	Log out of the Back-End.

Step 16	Log into the Back-End as "testuser1."
Step 17	Open the Articles Manager to display the List of Articles.
Step 18	Note that the "testuser2" created Article is not accessible by "testuser1," nor are all the others. This is mutually controlled by the "Edit Own" requirement within the "Users Permissions."
Step 19	Log out of the Back-End, and log in again as the Administrator.
Step 20	If you access the List of Articles as the "Super User," you will find that you have full permissions to modify anything with respect to the "Group B Article." Go ahead and open the Article and in the "Workflow" selector, choose "Publish."
Step 21	Execute a Save and Close action.

This is how an individual Content Item has its "actions" restricted to only the User who created it. It becomes obviously apparent of the benefits of setting "User Group" Permissions within large organization to help control not only "who can view what," but also "who can or cannot edit Content Items other than their own."

Global vs. Item Level Permissions

There are two general methods of managing "permissions," which are: "Globally" or by "Individual" Content Items themselves.

Deny or Grant Privileges Globally

If "permissions" are allowed for a Group at the "Global" level, all Components and Content Items are accessible by the Users in the Group – and the "actions" are globally applied. That means, in order to deny any "actions," the denials are set separately for each Component or Content Item. This can be tedious. The "Global" setting may be called *"grant-all, override-many"* method of accomplishing "permission" limitations.

Deny or Grant Privileges Individually

If the other methods are employed, as demonstrated in previous Exercises, the "permissions" for the User Group must be granted in the affirmative, which is likely the easier (and more secure) route. This is called the *"deny-all, override few"* method. This way, Users may "also" be assigned to the Group, which will control the "permissions" they might have for any Content overall.

Through the use of well-planned "User Groups" and then "User" assignments to those Groups, a controlled set of "viewing" and "action" permissions can be configured throughout the Joomla! 5 Content environment.

Super User Controls All Permissions

Without exception, the "Super User," or Administrator, has the full and total "permission" authority to override any of the "viewing" or "action" permissions for any applicable Component or Content Item. This kind of upper-level controls allows the Administrator to maintain full control of the Components and Content Items, regardless of any subordinate settings. The Administrator can simply change the settings and configure anything in the Back-end.

If you are manager of a small website with only one or two Administrators, you won't likely need to be concerned about "ACL." However, using these "ACL" techniques on large corporate websites is a highly important factor in maintaining control of who can "view" and take "actions" on Content.

Extensions for Managing "ACL"

For Joomla! 3, there were several excellent Extensions available that assist the Administrator in managing and maintaining "ACL" for Content and Users, and User Groups.

It is suggested, if you manage a large website with many Content contributors, you may want to explore the use of a specialized "ACL" Extension to make it easier on your part to make rapid configuration changes to "ACL."

It is likely that the previous Joomla! 3 "ACL" Extensions have been, or will be, upgraded for use with Joomla! 5. If you operate a large website with many Users with Authors, Editors, Reviewers and Publishers, you will find that using an Extension to manage "ACL" would be an excellent choice.

The Administrator's "ACL" tasks could be greatly simplified through the use of an appropriate "ACL Manager Extension," and you are encouraged to explore them.

USERS:
Option Settings

In previous Chapters, the "Options" for the Content Areas or functional parts of a Joomla! 5 website have been described. The "Users" area is no exception.

The "Options" generally are ways to more define, control or expand how a part of the website functions. These are important configuration settings. The volunteer developers that work on the Joomla! 5 code programmed some great features into all areas, which are enclosed within groups of "Options" that can be configured in their respective areas.

If you access almost every other part of the website Back-End and open the "Options" Tab, there are an abundance of configuration settings that may be invoked globally to enhance the website's operations. The "Users" area also has configuration settings that perform important functions when invoked.

Option Settings Apply Globally
When setting the "Options" in the "Users Manager," keep in mind that these are applied "globally" across the website. Settings relative to registration, initial access and others apply to every User that completes the Registration Process, no exceptions.

Other than "Assigned User Group" selections, there are no Administrator overrides than can be applied once a User is created. The "Options" cannot be changed on a User-by-User basis.

User Options in Detail

In past Chapters, the "Options" for the Content Areas or functional parts of a Joomla! 5 website have been described. The "Users" management configuration is no exception.

The "Options" are ways to more define, control or expand how a specific part of the website functions. These are important settings. The volunteer developers that work on the Joomla! 5 code programmed some great features into all areas, and the "Users Options" is a prime example of their brilliant work.

If you go to almost every other part of the website Back-End and open the "Options" tab, there are an abundance of configuration settings that may be invoked to further enhance the website's operations. The "Users" area also has configuration settings that perform important functions when activated.

ACCESSING USER OPTIONS

The "Options" for "Users" are accessed via the Back-End by opening any of the "User" areas and the choosing "Options" at the top right of the screen. Therein are eight tabbed configuration areas, as follows:

User Options	These are the most important configuration settings for the website. The mechanics of User Registration and access is established in this area.
Email Domain Options	This allows the Administrator to set "rules" that can be applied to domains to restrict access. It simply can be used to restrict certain domain sourced Users from registering to access the website.
Password Options	The requirements for passwords can be set in this area, thus allowing the Administrator to ensure that the passwords Users enter are as secure as possible.
Multifactor Authentication	Multifactor Authentication is developing into a "must have" feature on websites. This option allows the implementation and configuration of the "MFA" feature, as it is typically called.
User Notes History	This allows the website to store "User History" of items being edited within certain Content on the website.
Mass Mail Users	When "Mass Emails" are sent to Users, this set of configurations can be used to place global information into the email's subject line and body.
Integration	This permits the inclusion of any "Custom Fields" that may be created to be used with the User Registration Form.
Permissions	All User Groups and their Permissions as apply to the Users Section can be set here.

Option Configurations in Detail

Access the "User Options" via the "Home Dashboard" and access the "Users > Manage" link in the Left Menu. Then, at the top right, select the "Options" button to open them.

The following will explain what each of the configuration settings do, or what performance results, when changed or implemented.

Tab: User Options

Allow User Registration	This setting determines whether Users may actually "register" on the website, or not.
New User Registration Group	This designates which User Group is the default Group into which Registered Users are assigned. This User Group's "Permissions" also affect possible actions. A Custom Group may be created and designated the default Group if desired.
Guest User Group	The "Guests" or visitors to the website are automatically part of this User Group.
Send Password	Upon Registration, new Users receive an email and this options allows the Users "Password" to optionally be included in the email. This is helpful if the Administrator creates the User and assigns a password at the same time.
New Account User Activation	New Users must be activated, and this can be "self" or "Administrator" activation. The "Self-Activations" requires the User to respond by clicking a link within the email sent by the system. Otherwise, the Administrator must personally activate each Registered User's account.
Send Mail to Administrators	If the Administrator should receive an email when a new User registers, that choice is made here.
Captcha	"Captcha" is a security feature used during website logins. A "Plugin" must be activated before the "Captcha" feature is included in the login.
Frontend User Parameters	When a User logs into the Front-End, if this option is invoked, the information about the User is displayed on the Front-End after login.
Frontend Language	If multiple Languages are used on a website, this designates which is the default for the main screen.
Change Username	This setting Allows, or does not allow, a User to change their initially selected Username. This is generally not an advisable feature to invoke given the confusion that might result. However, if the Administrator created the account with a generic "User Name,"

	the User may then change it to something other, based on personal preference.

Tab: Email Domain Options

This is where "rules" can be established to "Disallow" Users to Register on the website "if" they come from certain domain, such as certain countries or certain types of domain names. By default, all domains can be used to create a User Account on the website.

The configuration settings are invoked by creating "Rules" that govern the domains.

There are two important settings: 1) the domain name identification and, 2) the option to "Disallow" that domain. Here is an example that prohibits any emails used during Registration that come from "*.rabbit.com" domain names:

Set the Domain	To prevent ALL emails from "@rabbit," the Domain can be set to: [*.rabbit.com] (without the brackets). See the instruction notes on the configuration workspace. The * is a permissible wildcard for designating domains. In this case, the * indicates "ALL" emails within the ".rabbit.com" domain.
	Individual email addresses may also be disallowed by simply listing them and setting the Rule.
Set the Disallow	Once the email address has been set, simply toggle the "Disallow" setting.
Save	When the settings are added, select "Save" to continue adding more domain restrictions or "Save & Close" to complete the actions and exit.

Tab: Password Options

This is an important set of configurations because they apply to the actual passwords that Users enter when registering on the website. For security, a combination of letters, uppercase, number and symbols should be used. Here are the settings that may be configured:

Maximum Reset Count	This sets the number of times that a Password may be reset by a User within a time period, as set below.
Reset Time (hours)	This limits the time period for Password resets.
Minimum Characters	Sets the minimum number of characters in a Password.
Minimum Numbers	Sets the minimum number of integers in a Password.
Minimum Symbols	Sets the minimum number of symbols that must be included a Password.

Minimum Upper Case	Sets the minimum number of Upper Case characters.
Minimum Lower Case	Sets the minimum number of Lower Case characters.

Tab: Multi-Factor Authentication ("MFA")

Using this feature, a "secondary secure code" must be typically entered into an entry field within 30-seconds of displaying on the screen. The Google Authenticator App and a mobile device to produce that code. When triggered by Joomla! 5, the Google Authenticator App will send a code to the mobile device, which must then be input on the website screen within a fixed time period.

There are two multi-factor authenticator services available: Google Authenticator and YubiKey. Both Plugin Extensions come with the default Joomla! 5 installation. You must activate one or the other in order to use the services.

Additionally, a Google or YubiKey account must be established and configured to use either service. Once you have permissions and the configuration information to use either service, the Joomla! 5 options settings must be set by the Administrator, as follows:

Allowed Front-End Module Positions	Designates the location of the Front-End Module Positions that can be used to display MFA.
Show Title in Front-End	Sets the Title Display on the Front-End.
Allow Back-End Module Positions	Allows the user of designated Back-End Module Positions.
Disable Multi-Factor Authentication	Multi-Factor Authentication can be selectively disabled for specified User Groups.
Enforce Multi-Factor Authentication	Multi-Factor Authentication can be selectively enabled for specified User Groups.
Front-End Template Style	If multiple Templates are used, or have been created for use, one may be designated for use in relationship with MFA.
Multi-Factor Authentication after Silent Login	Toggles Silent Login "Yes" or "No."
Silent Login Authentication Response Types	Allows the type of responses that can be generated by the Administrator upon Silent Login use, re: "cookies" or "password-less," etc.
Onboard New Users	Toggles Onboarding New Users to "Yes" or "No."

Custom Redirection URL	Indicates the custom webpage the User will be directed to upon entering MFA code.

Multifactor Authentication implementation on a Joomla! 5 website is not an easy task. It requires some knowledge about their use and some skill, and patience, to configure and implement.

Complete information about this type of login security can be found at Chapter 51, "ADMIN: Multi-Factor Authentication," in *Joomla! 5, Boots on the Ground, Advance Edition, Volume 2.*

Tab: User Notes History

The "Versions" feature is a new addition to the Joomla! 5 website. In short, it simply records the "history" of notes made by the Administrator on the User Account. This often is used when the administrator must make notes on a User's Account relative to misconduct or something along the lines of suspensions, etc.

Enable Versions	This choice toggles the feature "Yes" or "No."
Maximum Versions	The number of "notes events" is set here numerically.

Tab: Mass Mail Users

The Administrator can send or broadcast emails to all Users registered on the website. These settings integrate with that email system to do the following:

Subject Prefix	A "prefix" can be automatically added to the Subject Line of the email that is being sent to all Users.
Mailbody Suffix	This allows a "signature" block, or any text, to be added at the end of the email that will be sent under "mass mailing" conditions.

This feature does not allow sending of emails to individual Users on a selective basis. The feature is only used to send every User on the website an email. This is useful to notify website Users that the websites might be taken offline for maintenance, or for any other topic that all Users should be aware of, or be notified of an action that is going to take place.

Tab: Integration

Within the "Users" sections, it is possible to add "Custom Fields" to the "New User Registration Form." The default Registration Form only requires a Name, a Username, a Password and an Email Address.

There are some pre-configured information fields that can be made part of the Registration Form. They can be invoked on an individual information field basis.

However, most Users do not want to fill out lengthy forms to simply "register" as a User on a website, so caution is advised before implementing this feature.

Also, be mindful of "GDPR" and other privacy requirements and national laws, especially in the UK and EU counties. If the information is not absolutely necessary within the objectives of the website, don't add them to the Registration Form.

Custom Fields may be created using any one of the seventeen possible Form Fields that can be created for inclusion onto the Registration Form.

Edit Custom Fields	Invoking this setting to "Yes," allows the creation and use of Custom Fields within the User Registration Form.

Tab: Permissions

Every "User Group" may have "Permissions" set within the "User Options." Open the "Permissions" tab and click through several of the Groups. Notice that the "Super User" has full permissions, while some of the others have limited permissions for certain "actions." These can be changed as needed, but the default configuration settings are typically adequate for most websites.

Always keeping in mind that permissions can be set regarding "viewing" of Content and the "actions" that a User may perform on Content. Both can be selectively applied to User Groups and Content Items.

Setting Content Item Access

Content Items, such as Articles, may have their "access permissions" set to different configurations. By default, and without "Workflows" activated, the Content Items are automatically set to "Public" access for viewing purposes.

The "Status" of the Content Items can be set to: "Published, Unpublished, Archived or Trashed." By default, the settings are "Published" for viewing, and "Public" for whom that viewing permission is allowed.

To change the "viewing permissions" for a Content Item, with the respective Workspace open, the "Access" setting in the right configuration column can be changed to: "Public, Guest, Registered, Special and Super User." For any designation other than Public or Guest, Users must Login to view the Content Item. This also implies that the Users have an account that has either been manually created by the Administrator, or self-created by the User.

Types of Permissions

Within Joomla! 5, each individual User Group can have two different levels of User Permissions set. They are:

Viewing Permissions Who can "see" what on the Front-End.	These are permissions that can be set that relate to only the ability to "view" Content Items, which can be set to "Public/Guest" or to "Registered" or any other User Group that may have been created for which "viewing" permissions are required. Created User Groups must have their permissions, regardless of which, set within the "Options" Permissions Tab section. Unless specified, created users are automatically under the "Public" viewing group and their permissions are inherited.
Action Permissions Who can "do" what with Content Items.	"Action Permissions" are for things that a logged in User can "do" with a Content Item, such as: create, edit, edit status and field values. These settings are configured in the User "Options" area, under the "Permissions" Tab.

EXERCISE 25-1: SETTING CONTENT ITEM VIEWING PERMISSIONS

Objective: This Exercise will demonstrate how to change the User "viewing permissions" for a Content Item Type, which will be an Article. The application of the same techniques will also apply to any other Content Item Type.

Step 1	If not already there, access the Administrator's Back-End.
Step 2	Open the "Home Dashboard." to display the access areas.
Step 3	Either in the Left Menu, or the Menu Panels on the main screen area, open the "Articles" section. The same area can be accessed in the "Site" Block on the main screen.
Step 4	Open the Article entitled: "Typography." It is opened on the Front-end via a link in the top Menu which was added when "Sample Data" was installed via an Exercise in Chapter 7.
Step 5	With "Typography" opened, while accessing the "Content" Tab, go to the Menu at the right of the screen.
Step 6	In the "Status" selector, select: "Registered."
Step 7	Execute a Save & Close action.
Step 8	Following this action, the "Access" column on the list should indicate: "Registered."
Step 9	Go to the website Front-End. Refresh the browser window to clear its cache.
Step 10	Click on the "Typography" Menu Link Item in the top Menu.
Step 11	The result should be a message indicating that you (the "Guest" User), does not have permission to view this Content Item.

Step 12	Click on the "Home" button in the "Main Menu" in the right column.
Step 13	Log into the Front-End as the Super User.
Step 14	Click on the "Typography" Menu Link Item in the top Menu.
Step 15	The "Typography" Article will/should now open because you, as the Administrator, have the prerequisite permissions to view the item.
Step 16	Execute a "Log Out" in the right side Login Form.
Step 17	The "no permissions" message should display because the screen has now revered back to "Public/Guest Only" viewing permissions.
Step 18	Leave the "Typography" Article set with "Registered" viewing permissions. It will be used again later in this Chapter.

Controlling User Viewing Access

When a User account is created, using the default settings, it is automatically assigned to the "Registered" User Group, thus automatically "inheriting" all the permissions allowed for that Group. The new User inherits all of its permissions automatically.

By accessing the "System > Global Configuration," and opening the "Permissions" Tab, every User Group is listed. By clicking on the User Group Name, the settings of the "Permissions" is displayed.

It is at this admin location where the "Permissions" for each User Group may be modified as required by website objectives. Simply change the setting of the User Group in the drop down and executing a saving action.

As new User Groups are added, they will appear on the "Permissions List," and may have their "viewing" and/or "action" permissions configured as desired.

An Example of Permission Use

Here's the scenario:

The website Publishes information by Topic Expert Authors and the Users have subscribed to view ONLY the Content created by Authors in certain "topics."

First, the Author Group is needed with permissions to create Content Items only within a certain Category of Articles. The Author has "action" permissions limited to creating Articles in the single Category.

Second, the User Group is granted limited permissions to "view" ONLY the Content Items in the Category from the above Author. They do not have any "action" permission. Their interaction is limited only to "viewing."

In addition, when the Users initially Register, they can be directly assigned to the specified User Group. This won't work beyond one User Group, so use caution when implementing the new User Group default assignment.

Of course, they are Extensions that perform these tasks and organize the Content accordingly, but the above example allows the Administrator to configure both the "actions" and "viewing" rights of Users.

Some of the User/Permission Extensions that are available, or will likely be available for Joomla! 5, have many advanced features and configuration options that allow for some highly creating integration of "permissions" into the new "Workflows" schemes, and more.

COMPONENT:
Banners

The best description of a Component is they are "mini-programs" or "mini-applications" that run within the Joomla! 5 core platform. Each Component is a small application that performs certain specific and specialized functions and helps to manage and generate Content.

In addition, more Components can be installed as Extensions and there are hundreds upon hundreds available in the "JED." In fact, the "JCE Editor" that was previously installed, is a Component and it installed within the Component structure.

To obtain a third-party Component, simply go to the "JED" and search for one that will meet your needs. When there are multiple Components that might meet your requirements, it is suggested that you look at each Component thoroughly, especially if payment is required to obtain it. Many Component Developers have a "demo" version online so explore them using that method also.

Make absolutely certain that any chosen Extension is marked "**J!5**," otherwise if it is not, attempting to install the Extension may "break" the website beyond the point of recovery.

Understanding the Banner Component

Joomla! 5 provides a Banner management mechanism. These are not the "Site" Banners that appear at the top of the page. This Component manages advertising style Banners whereby clients may advertise on the website by displaying promotional Banners. The Administrator locates these Adverts in available "Module Position" on the Templates being used.

As a practical reality, the Banner Component isn't used very frequently. But when it is used, it can be a semi-effective way of placing ad panels on the website. If you don't use the advertising Banners for external clients, the Banner Component can be used to manage Banners to promote or showcase some of the items on the website. It can be used as an internal promotional advert panel management Component.

Similar Banner displays can be created by just using Custom Modules, which were discussed in Chapter 12, "CONTENT: Modules." The difference between using the standard Module is the Banner Component has the ability to track any visitor views and/or click-throughs when the Banner is accessed. Standard Modules do not have the "click-tracking" ability.

How Banners are Organized

In previous Chapters, the organization of Content was discussed whereby Content is normally organized into Categories. The Banner Component follows this same Content management plan.

When creating Categories, remember they are Component-specific. This means the Banner Categories will not show up on Category Lists for other Components or Content Categories in general. The Categories applied to Banners reside only within the Banner Component and are only viewed on the Banner List views.

Using the Banner Manager

There is only one way to access the Banner Component which is via the "Home Dashboard" Menu under the Components link. When accessing Components, there are also dropdown sub-Menus that will allow direct connection to specific Managers or Workspaces within the Components.

When the **[A]** "Home Dashboard" is open, and the **[B]** "Components" Menu is accessed, the **[C]** "Banner Manager" Menu is displayed, showing the **[D]** sub-Menus for the Component, as shown in Figure 26-1.

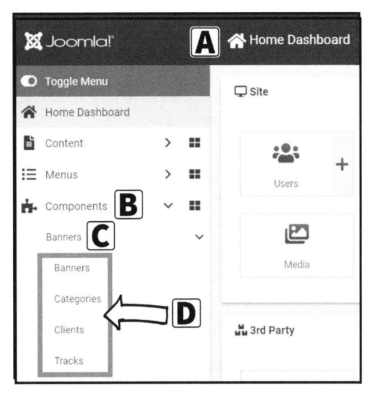

Figure 26-1

Banners	This Workspace manages the individual Banners that may displayed on the website.
Categories	Banners may be sorted by Categories, and this section is used to create and otherwise manage them, not regular Article Categories, or Categories in other Components.
Clients	Clients are "advertisers," and they can be managed as a revenue source for the website. The methodology is performed manually by the Administrator. In this respect, the Component is very clumsy given that Extensions are available that allow more use of integrated actions by the Advertiser and not relying totally on the Administrator to perform most functions.
Tracks	This is where settings are configured for "tracking" the number of times the Banners have been viewed along with the number of "click-throughs" that result.

During the installation of Joomla! 5, the Component was installed but no sample Categories or Banners were included.

Always Create Categories

Note that Categories should always be created first. Throughout Joomla! 5, a Content Item, such as an Article, Banner, Contact, and so on, cannot be created unless there is a Category to contain it. However, most Content areas have an automatic catch-all Category named "Uncategorized," which can be used to temporarily assign content. This would be fine for websites with limited content. On websites with a lot of Content, Categories should be used [created], to help keep Content orderly and easier to manage.

Banners have one Category that other Components do not include, it is the "Clients Category." The Banner Component is intended to allow "outsiders" to post advertising panels [Modules] on the website. The "Clients Category" allows those Banners to be assigned, not only into Content Categories, but to individual advertisers as well.

Banner Viewing Activity

Advertisers always want information about the response rate of advertising panels they display on the website. The Banner Component allows the tracking of website visitor's viewing activity with regard to Banners. Joomla! 5's Banner Component calls these functions "Tracks." These will be discussed more later in this Chapter.

Who Creates What

In this Component, the burden of "creation" is on the Administrator's shoulders. The Category, Client and Banner must be created by the Administrator. This is not an advertising manager system whereby the Client, or Advertiser, creates and manages their own Banners. This is not the case for the Banner Component. The Administrator is tasked with creating and managing every aspect of Banners.

Yes, the Banner Manager does meet initial expectations but lacks considerable operational functions, which are obvious when attempting to use the Component. The best description that can be applied to the Banner Manager is "awkward" because there are too many steps involved. However, on a small scale, the Banner Component might be sufficient.

In any case, it is good to know how the Component is managed.

Creating a Banner Category

Before creating Banners, Categories are required. This allows a wide range of topical Categories to be created, into which Advertisers may place, or classify, their advertising panels [Modules].

EXERCISE 26-1: CREATING BANNER CATEGORIES

Objective: The goal of this Exercise is to create two Categories into which Banners will be added in following Exercises.

Step 1	If not already there, login as the Administrator to access the "Home Dashboard."
Step 2	Open the Component Manager via the left Menu and select the "Banners" link then open the Banner "Category" Manager. Note also there is no direct access to this Manager via the "Home Dashboard" Content Panels. The Category titled: "Uncategorized" should already exist within the Component's Category List.
Step 3	Click the **"+ New"** button at the top of the screen. This will open the "Banners: New Category" Workspace.
Step 4	In the Title Field, enter: "Home Screen" (without quotes).
Step 5	This should be a "Parent" Category so the "Parent" field should be set to "-No parent-"
Step 6	The Status of the Category should be "Published."
Step 7	No other setting changes are required; the default settings are sufficient.
Step 8	Execute a Save & Close action.
Step 9	Click the **"+ New"** button at the top of the screen. This will reopen the "Banners: New Category" Workspace.
Step 10	In the Title Field, enter: "Search Screen" (without quotes).
Step 11	This should be a "Parent" Category so the "Parent" field should be set to "-No parent-".
Step 12	The Status of the Category should be "Published."
Step 13	Execute a Save & Close action.

Step 14	Three Categories should now display on the "Banners: Categories" Manager screen:
	  ▪ Uncategorized
	  ▪ Home Screen
	  ▪ Search Screen

Creating a Client ("Advertiser")

In addition to the Category requirement, there should also be Clients ["Advertisers"] created.

EXERCISE 26-2: CREATING A CLIENT (ADVERTISER)

Objective: The goal of this exercise is to create two Clients ("Advertisers") within the Banner Component. Clients will use the "Custom" type Banners.

Step 1	If not already there, login as the Administrator to access the "Home Dashboard."
Step 2	Open the Component Manager via the left Menu and select the "Clients" link to open the Banner Client Manager. Note also there is no direct access to this Manager via the "Home Dashboard" Content Panels.
Step 3	Click the **"+ New"** button at the top of the screen. This will open the "Banners: New Client" Workspace.
Step 4	In the "Name" field, enter: "Client/Advertiser A" (without quotes).
Step 5	In the "Contact Name" field, enter: "Contact A" (without quotes).
Step 6	Make sure the Client Status is "Published."
Step 7	Set "Track Impressions" to "Yes."
Step 8	Set "Track Clicks" to "Yes."
Step 9	Execute a Save & Close Action
Step 10	The result should show "Client/Advertiser A" on the "Banners: Clients" list.
Step 11	Click the **"+ New"** button at the top of the screen. This will open the "Banners: New Client" Workspace.
Step 12	In the "Name" field, enter: "Client/Advertiser B" (without quotes).
Step 13	In the "Contact Name" field, enter: "Contact B" (without quotes).
Step 14	Make sure the Client Status is "Published."
Step 15	Set "Track Impressions" to "Yes."
Step 16	Set "Track Clicks" to "Yes."
Step 17	Execute a Save & Close Action
Step 18	The result should show "Client/Advertiser A and B" on the "Banners: Clients" list.

Impressions & Clicks Explained

This significant features between "Impressions" and "Clicks" is explained as follows:

Impressions	This records the number of times a Banner has been displayed on a webpage. In other words, when the screen containing the Banner is opened in a website visitor's browser. This is simple the recordation of a "view."
Clicks	Banners generally have links to a Client's domain, or other URL location. This function records how many times the Banner was actually "clicked" to go to the Client's target destination. This is generally referred to as a: "Click Thru."

Creating Banners

Now that Banner Categories have been created, along with Clients, the actual Banners themselves may be created and assigned into them. Banners can be created by using two types of options:

Option 1	*Image* – uses the built-in image feature to add a graphic or photo into the Banner Workspace.
Option 2	*Custom* – allows the use of "Custom Code" to be displayed, which could be text or other content.

In addition to the types of Banner that may be created, there are three groups of management functions that control the display, as follows:

Details	This is where the actual Content of the Banner is inserted using either the "Image" or "Custom" options.
Banner Details	Here is where the information relative to the Advertiser and the duration of their display, as purchased, and impressions
Publishing	Under this tab, the Publishing start/stop dates can be set, along with some Metadata.

Creating an "Image" Banner

An "Image Banner" simply displays a graphic or photo within it, and may have an active "Click URL" which will take the User to another website location. At this time, the link may only open in the same browser window and cannot open a new one. Bear that in mind when using the "Image" type of Banner.

EXERCISE 26-3: CREATING AN IMAGE BANNER

Objective: The goal of this exercise is to create a Banner that is formatted as an "Image Banner" type.

Step 1	If not already there, login as the Administrator to access the "Home Dashboard."
Step 2	Open the Banners Component Manager via the left Menu and select the "Banner" link, then "Banners" to open the Banner Manager. Note again, there is no direct access to this Manager via the "Home Dashboard" Content Panels.
Step 3	Click the **"+ New"** button at the top of the screen. This will open the "Banners: New" Workspace.
Step 4	In the "Name" field, enter: "BANNER ONE" (without quotes).
Step 5	In the "Category" field to the right, select: "Home Screen" as the Category choice.
Step 6	In the "Image" field, click on the "Select" button.
Step 7	When the Media Manager opens, go to: "Banners" and select the "white.png" image, which will then display in the image window. This is a Joomla! logo image.
Step 8	Within the "Width" field, select or enter "100%."
Step 9	In the "Description" field, enter: "This is BANNER ONE." (without quotes).
Step 10	Ensure the "Status" of the Banner is "Published."
Step 11	Execute a Save action.
Step 12	Open the "Banner Details" tab.
Step 13	In the "Client" field, select: "Client/Advertiser A."
Step 14	Set "Track Impressions" to "Yes."
Step 15	Set "Track Clicks" to "Yes."
Step 16	Execute a Save & Close action.
NOTE	Any Banner can be configured with time-specific dates & times to "Start Publishing" and to "Finish Publishing." This will allow the automatic control when the Banner begins to display and when it ends, all within the configuration of the Banner Module created to display it.

The "Image" Banner has now been created and is ready to be set up for display. This involves the creation of a "Banner Module," and performing the necessary steps to connect the Module to the Banner, then designate a "Module Position" on the webpage, wherein the Banner will be displayed.

EXERCISE 26-4: CREATING A MODULE TO DISPLAY IMAGE BANNER

Objective: The goal of this exercise is to create a Module, assign it to a Template's "Module Position" on the webpage, and connect an "Image" Banner to it.

Step 1	If not already there, login as the Administrator to access the "Home Dashboard."
Step 2	In the Site panel, click on "Modules" or click on the **"+."** icon in the Modules block.
Step 3	Choose the "Banners" Module and click on **"+."** This will open a new Banner Workspace.
Step 4	In the "Title" field, enter: "BANNER ONE MODULE" (without quotes).
Step 5	In the "Client" selector, choose: "Client/Advertiser A" from the Banner Clients selections.
Step 6	In the "Category" selector, choose: "Home Screen" from among the Banner Category selections. An interesting feature here is that the Banners, if multiple, may be sourced from multiple Banner Categories.
Step 7	In the "Header Text" field, enter: "HEADER TEXT FROM MODULE ONE" (without quotes).
Step 8	In the "Footer Text" field, enter: "FOOTER TEXT FROM MODULE ONE" (without quotes).
Step 9	Assign the Module to the "sidebar-right" location.
Step 10	Make sure the "Status" is set to "Published."
Step 11	Open the "Menu Assignment" tab.
Step 12	For the "Module Assignment," select: "Only on the pages selected" from among the choices.
Step 13	Below that, execute a "None" selection action.
Step 14	Scroll down the list and tick the box next to "Home" in the "Main Menu." This simply relates the "Home Screen" Category for quick reference/selection purpose. The intent is to display this Banner ONLY on the website "Home" screen.
Step 15	Execute a Save & Close action.

Step 16	Go to the Front-End and refresh the browser window.
Step 17	If not on the "Home" screen, click "Home" in the Main Menu.
Step 18	In the right column, the "BANNER ONE MODULE" should display with the "Support Joomla" graphic with text above and below it.
Step 19	Click on any other Menu Link Item(s).
Step 20	Note the "BANNER ONE MODULE" no longer appears. This because it is assigned to display ONLY when the "Home" screen is displaying in the browser window. The "Menu Assignment" can be used to display the Module on many pages in many different types of display choice combinations.

The "Image" Banner has now been created, along with the companion Banner Module, which is required to place the Banner display on the webpage.

Creating a "Custom Banner"

The "Custom Banner" is more advanced than the "Image" Banner. This type of Banner can target a URL and open the destination in a new browser window. The "Image" Banner does not have that capability; thus the "Custom Banner" fills the void. It is, however, more complicated to create and implement.

EXERCISE 26-5: CREATING A CUSTOM BANNER

Objective: The goal of this exercise is to create a Banner that is formatted as a "Custom Banner" type. This is a more complicated type of Banner to create and actually requires some knowledge of "html" coding, although this type of Module may also have an image added to it, along with text.

Step 1	If not already there, login as the Administrator to access the "Home Dashboard."
Step 2	Open the Component Manager via the left Menu and select the "Banner" link to open the Banner Manager. Note again, there is no direct access to this Manager via the "Home Dashboard" Content Panels.
Step 3	Click the **"+ New"** button at the top of the screen. This will open the "Banners: New" Workspace.
Step 4	Name the Banner: "BANNER TWO MODULE" (without quotes).
Step 5	For "Type," selected "Custom" and in the "Custom Code" field, enter the entire code string below:

```
<a href="{CLICKURL}" target="_blank"><img src=
https://howtodoit.guru/images/website-banner.png ></a>
```

Step 6	In the "Click URL" field, enter: "http://howtodoit.guru" (without quotes). The {CLICKURL} above calls this action from within the Joomla! 5 code structure.
Step 7	In the "Description" field, enter: "This is BANNER TWO" (without quotes).
Step 8	Set the "Status" to "Published."
Step 9	Assign the Banner to "Category" named "Search Screen." This is simply for organizational reasons.
Step 10	Open the "Banner Details" tab.
Step 11	THIS IS IMPORTANT! In the "Client" selector, choose: "Client/Advertiser B." If no advertiser is chosen, the Banner will not display.
Step 12	Set "Track Impressions" to "Yes."
Step 13	Set "Track Clicks" to "Yes."
Step 14	Execute a Save & Close action.

The "Custom Banner" has now been created. And, as with the "Image Banner," a Module must be created and configured to display the Banner somewhere on the webpage and controlled by the "Menu Assignment" choices that are available.

EXERCISE 26-6: MODULE TO DISPLAY THE CUSTOM BANNER

Objective: The goal of this exercise is to create a Module, assign it to a position on the webpage, and associate a "Custom" Banner to it.

Step 1	If not already there, login as the Administrator to access the "Home Dashboard."
Step 2	In the Site panel, click on "Modules" or click on the "+" icon in the Modules block.
Step 3	Choose the "Banners" Module and click on "Select." This will open a new Banner Workspace.
Step 4	In the "Title" field, enter: "BANNER TWO MODULE" (without quotes).
Step 5	In the "Category" selector, choose: "Search Screen" from among the Banner Category selections. An interesting feature here is that the Banners, if multiple, may be sourced from multiple Banner Categories.
Step 6	Make sure the "Status" is set to "Published."

Step 7	In the "Client" selector, choose: "Client/Advertiser B" from the Banner Clients selections.
Step 8	Assign the Module to the "sidebar-right" location.
Step 9	Execute a Save action. It is wise to frequently "save" Content as it is created to prevent the loss of entries.
Step 10	Open the "Menu Assignment" tab.
Step 11	For the "Module Assignment," select: "Only on the pages selected" from among the choices.
Step 12	Below that, execute a "None" selection action.
Step 13	Scroll down the list and tick the box next to "Typography" Link in the "Main Menu Blog." The intent is to display this Banner ONLY on the website screen when this specific Menu Link Item is executed.
Step 14	Execute a Save & Close action.
Step 15	Go to the Front-End and refresh the browser window.
Step 16	If not on the "Home" screen, click "Home" in the Main Menu at the top of the screen.
Step 18	In the right column, click on the "Typography" Link within the "Main Menu Blog" Blog top Menu. The "How To Do It?" graphic should display. The "no access" message will appear because the access was changed from "Public" to "Registered" in a previous Exercise.
Step 19	View the right side of the displayed page and the linked graphic should display in the "sidebar-right" Module Position.
Step 20	Click on any other Menu Link Item(s).
Step 21	Note the "BANNER TWO MODULE" does not appear. This because it is assigned to display ONLY when the "Typography" Menu Link Item in the top Menu is clicked. If desired, the "Menu Assignment" can be used to display the Module on many pages in many different combinations of display choices.

The "Custom" Banner has now been created, along with the companion Banner Module, which is required to place the Banner display on the webpage.

What About the Tracks?

If you have clicked on any of the graphics within the Banner Modules that were added above, the action was recorded by the Banner Component. If you have not clicked on them, do so now, a couple of times on each one.

Then, go to the "Home Dashboard > Components > Banners" and execute the "Tracks" link. The page that displays will indicate how many times the graphic link in the Modules have been clicked.

There isn't much information on the "Banners: Tracks" screen, but it does let the Administrator know that actions on the Banners have taken place. Its value is limited because the same person can click on the adverts multiple times and each is recorded. This a false recordation for value analysis purposes.

Monetizing the Website Using Banners

The Banner Manager has the capabilities for the Administrator to "sell" Banners, or Advertisings Panels, which in the UK are called "Adverts." The problem with the Joomla! 5 Banner Manager Components is that it is 100% task intensive, including the processing of payments, advert location on the webpage and more.

Additionally, it is very clumsy, there are many settings that need to be tied together to display and Adverts for the given time period the Clients ("Advertiser") desired. There are too many tasks involved in which the Administrator and the Client must be directly involved with, which makes the work effort more difficult.

Additionally, all payment transactions between the Advertisers and the Administrator must be handled manually or via email. We all know the risks of sending credit card payment information via email, so this makes the use of the Banner Components an unsuitable consideration.

In truth, if you have a website that advertisers might want to place adverts, you are better off installing a Third-Party Component that will give the Administrator full management of everything, and allows Advertisers the ability to self-manage, including making payments. The small fee for the Advertising Component, in both the short- and long-term, will be well worth the expense.

About "This" Banner Manager's Usefulness

Banner Managers on websites can be useful. It gives website "owners" a way of generating a revenue stream by promoting items on the website. However, "this" Banner Manager falls far short of making that an easily accomplished task. For one thing, it is way, way too clumsy to manage. Secondly, Advertisers cannot directly post, delete, access or control their respective adverts. Thirdly, this Component, declared as a "Banner Manager," is way too clumsy in all respects.

This Component,– in the beginning of version Joomla! 3 – should have been put on trial for its life, convicted of many inadequacies, and removed from the platform. It requires too much "hands on" involvement by the website Administrator.

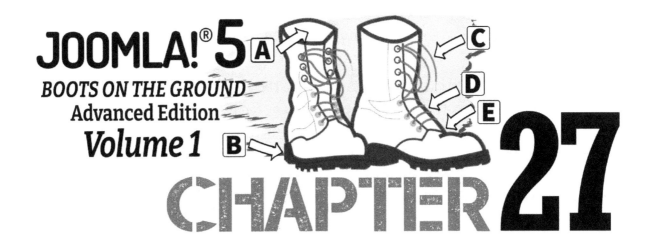

COMPONENT:
Contacts

There are two scenarios that can apply to the use of the Contact Component on a Joomla! 5 website.

If the website does NOT require the need for website visitors to send emails to employees or corporate Contacts, skip this Chapter and come back to it on a rainy day.

If the website content structure DOES requires a complex listing of business Contacts associated with the website in a company that requires a more robust method of contacting everyone important via an email form, then this Chapter will provide guidance for setting up the email contact mechanisms.

The Contacts Component operates in such a way whereby Categories of Contacts are created with individual Contact information added. Then, some method of displaying the Contacts to website visitors/guests is needed. The Contacts Manager is dramatically much easier to use than the Banner Manager, and certainly serves a more useful function on the website. Also, there are many more "Options" that can be invoked within the Contact Managers.

This Chapter addresses the Contacts Manager's management in such a way that the Administrator can quickly grasp the basics and understand the repetitive tasks that are involved.

The Contacts Manager is a powerful and useful Component that may be used in different ways. This Chapter will provide information on how to implement, configure and make functional all aspects of the Component.

Understanding the Contacts Component

The Contacts Component allows the creation of forms to send emails to designated "Contacts" on any organization's website. It can also be used to create a special Contact Form to send messages to the website Administrator.

The Contact Manager Component can be used to create either simple or complex forms for website visitors to send emails to various company staff, if it is on a corporate style website.

In addition to the many default form fields that may be used, custom fields may also be created. The custom fields can fine-tune the information that will be either displayed to website visitors, or in the email sent to the form's recipient.

To access a form, a Menu Link Item can be created that opens an individual form.

Because Contacts can be created within named Categories, re: "Sales, Marketing, Accounting, etc.," and Contacts assigned within them, Menu Link Items can be created that opens "Categories" of Contacts vs. an individual one. If the organization is large, the categorization of the Contacts is a greatly beneficial feature, especially if the website is being used strictly as an internal resource.

The creation and administration of Contact Forms is rather fundamental and very easy to learn. Once the decision is made as to which Contact Form Fields to use, or the custom fields to add, creation of the form is easily accomplished via the Form Manager – and each individual Contact has its own Form Manager.

Explore the Contacts Manager to familiarize yourself with the screens and the various configurations that may be created. When creating a Contact Profile or a Contact Form, you should review the Form Fields that are available before undertaking the tasks of creating Custom Form Fields for either display, or for information transmission.

How Contacts are Organized

By now, as explained in previous Chapters, Content on a Joomla! 5 website is typically first organized into Categories. The Contacts Manager is no exception. The reason for all this "categorization" is that is allows large amounts of Content, in this case Contacts, to be organized for set up in logical display formats and easy accessed.

If you, as the Administrator, are only going to list yourself as a "Contact," that's easy enough to do. But if you are going to list many, many Contacts, the task is a bit more complicated but very doable if you follow and repeat the instructions in this Chapter and use a little "organizational imagination" to create the structure for the Contacts Categories and the individual Contacts.

Complex Undertaking

The creation of a highly customized Contacts system is complex. There are many settings involved and elements that need configuration. In fact, there is even an "Option Manager" specifically for the Contacts Component, wherein global settings may be pre-configured for implementation within the Component. This makes setting up the Contacts much easier by using "preset" configurations.

Of course, by now you should also know that whenever there are "Options" for any part of Joomla! 5's Content, there is complexity involved and decisions to be made on the "how's" of the configuration. And trust us, the management of the Contacts Component is going to have a learning curve that is somewhat steep. But as we have done in previous Chapters, all of this complexity will be broken down into understandable discussions and practical Exercises.

Let's start with the main element of the Contacts Manager, which are defined and discussed below.

Contact Manager Elements

There are four main elements of the Contacts Manager, one of which drills down into many more configuration settings ("Options"). But first, the essential elements should be explained, as follows:

Contacts	Once everything is set up and configured, this is where all the individual Contacts are added. The details on the use of this element is discussed later in this Chapter.
Categories	Categories, in this Component, refers to the Categories that are created for exclusive use of the Contacts Component. They do not show up on any other "Lists of Categories" in any other part of the Back-End. Categories may also contain "Child," or Sub-Categories, thus the ability to create a hierarchy of Contact Categories for even more detailed structure.
Fields	Fields are simply additional bits of information that can be added to a Contacts listing, which is separate from, or in addition to, those that are available in the default Contacts Component configuration. This is where a bit of information about the individual Contact can be included that might be deemed essential, but are not one of the pre-configured Fields. The Fields Options are discussed below.
Field Groups	These are Groups of Fields, which also be considered as "Categories" of Fields, just named differently to avoid confusion with Contacts Categories. There are three types of Field Groups: *Contact, Mail, Category*. Each can be set up, configured and applied separately, giving wide latitude in expanding the Contact Manager for use with large companies. It allows for a comprehensive method of classifying

	the Fields into applicable Field Groups (categories), in each of the three groupings.
Options	This is where the presets are configured, or where the default configuration for each Contacts Category, Contact, Field Group or Field can be modified. There are eight areas of settings that can be implemented. These will also be discussed below.

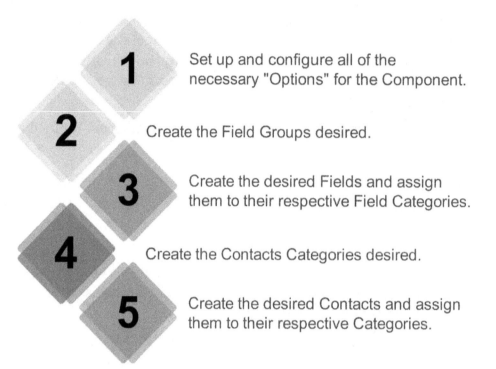

1. Set up and configure all of the necessary "Options" for the Component.

2. Create the Field Groups desired.

3. Create the desired Fields and assign them to their respective Field Categories.

4. Create the Contacts Categories desired.

5. Create the desired Contacts and assign them to their respective Categories.

Figure 27-1

The Working Order

When setting up the elements of the Contacts Manager, it is strongly suggested the "creation flow" shown below be followed. However, it is also strongly suggested that the Administrator have a written game plan to follow for these creation actions. It is much easier to configure this Component if you have these actions reduced to a written plan first. Figure 27-1 demonstrates five steps involved.

Of course, if the website does not need any custom Fields, neither the Field Groups or the Fields need to be created and/or configured.

Once these actions are completed, the Contacts can be included for access via the website's Front-End, which is a different process all onto itself and will be described in a separate Exercise later in this Chapter.

Setting Up the Options

While it may appear that this process is backwards, be assured – at least for the Contacts Component – setting up the Options is the first series of actions that should be completed in setting up the Contact Manager.

Within the Contacts Component Options, there are eight areas of setting that can be configured. These are described below. During some of the Exercises dealing with the Forms and Contacts, some of these setting will be changed. This will be a quasi-learn-as-you-go process. But first what to these configuration areas include?

Contact	Here is where the actual "Fields" of information to be displayed are designated for an individual Contact. Most of the "Fields" can be toggled to the Hide or Show configuration. There are several other choices. All settings can be overridden by the Contact or Menu Link Item that triggers the Contact display.
Icons	Six custom Icons can be set for display on the individual Contact listing. The settings can be icon, text or none. The latter are configured automatically, while the icons need to be created and uploaded in this configuration area.
Category	This configures the Categories and Sub-Categories and their display in general. There are more choices available for a single Category than for the Sub-Categories. This applies to the individual Category display trigged by a Menu Link item.
Categories	This configures the Categories and Sub-Categories and their display in general. They apply when a Menu Link Item is triggered directly to a Sub-Category of Contacts.
List Layouts	When viewing "lists" of Categories and/or Contacts, certain information can be displayed in the columns of the display. They can be selected or de-selected here. They may also be overridden in the Menu Link Item that triggers viewing access.
Form	This is where the settings are located that apply to the actual Contact Form. These settings are global to the Contacts Manager, but can be overridden in the Contact settings or in the Menu Link Item, which can override many other settings.
Integration	Settings here can be set to determine how the Contact Component will integrate with other Extensions, such as: RSS Feed Link, Routing and Custom Fields.
Permissions	This will allow the Administrator to hand off some of the permissions to change settings within the Component to the Users in the defined User Groups. A specific User Group can be created and Users assigned to it to allow certain types of changes in the Contacts Component.

Each Contact also has its own "Options Settings," which can be configured with the Contact's Workspace open and viewing the individual Tabs. These Tabs are described at the end of this Chapter.

Setting up the Field Groups

Step two in the configuration process for the Contacts Category is setting up Field Groups, or "categorization" to collect and consolidate different custom Fields.

The actions needed to set up a Field Group are simple. Give the Field Group a "Title" [something related to the Contacts], and an optional "Description."

Contact, Email & Category Options

In the "Contacts: Field Groups" Workspace, there is a dropdown selector. By changing this selector, the Field Groups being created can be assigned into three classifications: *Contact, Email and Category*. By selecting one of the options, the Field Group is thus assigned to it.

Select the Correct Option

When adding Fields from within Field Groups, make sure that the correct "Option" is selected in the dropdown field. The default is for the "Contact," so make sure that is where the Field should apply. If not, select the applicable "Option" and add the field. Check this each time because when closed, the field selector returns to the default.

Contact Option

This allows the addition of Fields from within Field Groups to be added ONLY to the Contact listing or display. While there are already many default fields within the Contact display, more can be added. This is for the display of the Contact information only.

Email Option

The addition of Fields can be accomplished on the Email Form that is used to send to Contacts. This can be very selective with regard into which Contact the Form will be emailed by the system.

Category Option

Categories within the Contact Component may also have Fields from Field Groups added to them. This will allow for the expansion of the Options that can be applied through the Category Option.

Field Groups

As has been previously explained, "Field Groups" are simply "Categories" in the applicable manner which they are used. It is worth noting that the "Field Groups" within the Contact Category are NOT the same as the "Field Groups" for the Fields that may be applied to Articles. They are also separate from the "Field Groups" within the Users Manager.

However, the "Field Groups" in the Contacts Manager apply for use with each of the "Options" as noted above.

It is important to keep in mind that the "Field Groups" from the "Content" Manager are distinct and different from those within the "Contacts" Manager. Each has its own set of "Field Groups" that can be created and applied within their respective Components.

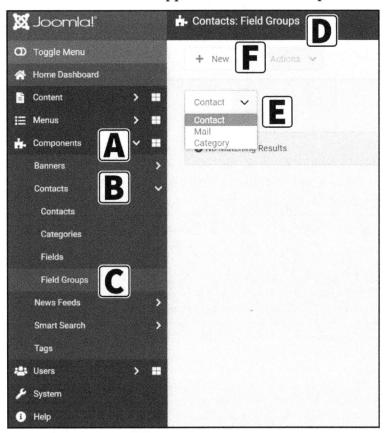

Figure 27-2

EXERCISE 27-1: CREATING CONTACTS FIELD GROUPS

Objective: The objective of this Exercise is to demonstrate the creation of "Field Groups," and to create two such groups into each of the three group option locations to be used in later Exercises.

Step 1		If not already there, login as the Administrator to access the "Home Dashboard."

Refer to Figure 27-2 for the following:

Step 2	A	Open the "Component Manager" via the left Menu and select the "Contacts" link to open the "Contacts Manager." There is no direct access to this Manager via the "Home Dashboard" Content Panels.
	B	

| Step 3 | C
D
E | Click on the "Field Groups" link item, which will open the Field Groups Manager. There is a dropdown field that includes: *Contact*, *Email* and *Category* choices. These are explained below. Create the first Field Groups within the "Contact" group. |
| Step 4 | F | Click the **"+ New"** button at the top of the screen. This will open the "Contacts: New Field Group" Workspace. |

In a "real life" scenario, the "FG-1" naming would likely to be something more descriptive and conventionally named on a working website.

Step 5		In the Title Field, enter: "Contact FG-1" (without quotes).
Step 6		Execute a Save & New action – this is the only choice other than Save & Close. Another Field Group is going to be created.
Step 7		In the Title Field, enter: "Contact FG-2" (without quotes).
Step 8		Execute a Save & Close action, resulting in a list display of the Field Groups that were created. The "success" message will display at the top. Close the message panel.
Step 9		Click the **"+ New"** button at the top of the screen. This will open the "Contacts: New Field Group" Workspace.
Step 10		Select the "Mail" option in the dropdown.
Step 11		In the Title Field, enter: "Mail FG-1" (without quotes).
Step 12		Execute a Save & New action – this is the only choice other than Save & Close.
Step 13		In the Title Field, enter: "Mail FG-2" (without quotes).
		Execute a Save & Close action.
Step 14		Click the **"+ New"** button at the top of the screen. This will open the "Contacts: New Field Group" Workspace.
Step 15		Change the dropdown choice to: "Category."
Step 16		In the Title Field, enter: "Category FG-1" (without quotes).
Step 17		Execute a Save & New action – this is the only choice other than Save & Close.
Step 18		In the Title Field, enter: "Category FG-2" (without quotes).
Step 19		Execute a Save & Close action.

At this point, there should be two Field Groups within each of the Categories in the dropdown: *Contacts, Mail, Category* – all of which apply exclusively only to the

"Contacts Component." This is important to keep in mind. These Categories and Field Groups no appear or apply to any other type of Content Item.

Setting up the Contacts Categories

Categories are established in the Contact Manager so that individual Contacts can be assigned to them. This isn't for just convenient classification, but to create an efficient and effective way for website visitors to contact personnel within the corporate structure.

For purposes of demonstration, three Contact Categories will be set up, assuming that the company or corporation has these divisions: *"Accounting, Human Resources and Marketing."* Once these Contact Categories have been created, the contact form to key people within those divisions can be created and assigned to their respective Contact Categories.

EXERCISE 27-2: CREATING CONTACT CATEGORIES

Objective: The objective of this Exercise is to demonstrate the creation of "Contact Categories" and make them available for the assignment of Contacts within them.

Step 1	If not already there, login as the Administrator to access the "Home Dashboard."
Step 2	In the left Menu, access: Components > Contacts > Categories to open the Contact: Category Manager.
Step 3	Click the **"+ New"** button at the top of the screen. This will open a Contact Category Workspace.
Step 4	In the "Title" field, enter: "ACCOUNTING DEPARTMENT" (without quotes).
Step 5	Execute a Save and New action.
Step 6	In the "Title" field, enter: "HUMAN RESOURCES DEPARTMENT" (without quotes).
Step 7	Execute a Save and New action.
Step 8	In the "Title" field, enter: "MARKETING DEPARTMENT" (without quotes).
Step 9	Execute a Save and Close action.

Refer to Figure 27-3 for the results of the above:

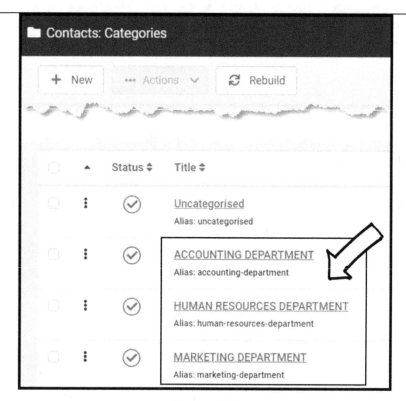

Figure 27-3

The resulting Contact Category list should display four Categories as shown in Figure 27-3. "Uncategorized" is a default Category that is automatically added in the Joomla! 5 installation process.

Creating the Contact & Email Fields

Now that the "Field Groups" and "Contact Categories" have been created, "Fields" may now be added to each of them. The purpose of adding "Fields" is to fine-tune and customize how much information is listed for Contacts, and which "Fields" are assigned to which Contact Categories.

A complete Chapter is devoted to Custom Fields can be found in *Joomla! 5: Boots on the Ground, Advance Edition, Volume 2*, Chapter 37, "ADMIN: Custom Fields." At this time, the Types of Fields will be listed with a short description. There are 17 different Fields that can be used, so the referenced Chapter 37 will describe them all in greater use details.. *Volume 2* has more advance Chapter topics, which is why they are included there with greater detail.

TYPE OF FIELD AVAILABLE	DESCRIPTION
Calendar	Displays a text box for the entry of a date, with a pop-up Calendar date picker.
Checkboxes	A checkbox can be created for selection actions. Several checkboxes may be included.
Color	Displays an input box for a hex color along with a Color picker utility.
Editor	Shows a list of the Editors available on the website.
Integer	Shows a list of Integers available to choose from a low to high value.
List	Makes a Custom List available from a drop-down list of entries.
List of Images	Makes a Custom List of Images available from a drop-down list of entries.
List of Menu Items	Makes a Custom List available from a drop-down list of the existing Menu Link Items on the website.
Media	Opens a modal window access to the website's Media Manager for uploading of Images.
Radio	Provides a "this one only" choice in a group of buttons from which to make item choices.
Subform	[Formerly "Repeatable Form"]. This allows a sub-group of fields that can be duplicated many times such as selecting an "image" and then adding a "caption."
SQL	Shows a list of entries to be allowed for running a query to a MySQL Joomla! 5 database.
Text	A simple text field for entry of one line data.
Text Area	A text field for entry of multi-line text or data such as paragraphs, etc.
URL	Text input field for a website URL entry.
User	From a modal pop-up, ability to select a User from among the list displayed.
User Groups	Drop down field to display a list of the User Groups available on the website.

489

Configuring the Options

Configuring the "Options" can be somewhat of a mind altering event because there are so many decisions and actions that must be taken with the different configuration settings. But this is okay, because most of the decisions are pretty much intuitive anyway. Yet, the "Options" need to be configured in a manner that is relative to the desires of the end display of Contacts on the website, which by the way, all happens using Menu Link Items within Menus.

Below are the configuration tabs within the Contacts Component "Options:"

Menu Link Items can Over-Ride

The global settings described below may be changed or configured for each Menu Link Item to change how the Contact is displayed. This allows for global settings, along with Category or Individual Contact display changes.

TAB: Contact

Most of these settings are pretty obvious, especially when looking at the form fields to be displayed, or not, on the Contact's information screen. Review all of the selection options to help give you a better understanding of their use and function.

TAB: Icons

Allows the Administrator to add icons or text in association with different form fields. This adds some graphic or text elements to each field.

TAB: Category

This section deals with the individual Category into which a Contact has been assigned and how they can be configured to display on the Front-End. These are global settings for ALL Contacts.

TAB: Categories

This section deals with multiple Categories if "Parent" and/or "Child" Categories are used within the Contact Manager.

TAB: List Layouts

This sets the default layout for "Lists" as they might display for an individual Contact.

TAB: Form

Certain security matters are handled within this Tab section, which helps insure that the Contact forms are not misused when display on the website.

TAB: Integration

These selectors deal with "RSS Feeds," URLs and use of the Custom Fields.

TAB: Permissions

Here is where the "Permissions" can be set for each User Group as they might apply to the use of the Contact Component, in particular the ability to create and/or modify any of the Contact information or settings.

Again, it is suggested that you spend time reviewing all of the global configuration "Option" available for the Contacts Component. Of course, if you have a small website, this Component will likely not be used. On the other hand, on a large corporate-style website, many Contacts might be listed with each having a different display configuration.

Creating Individual Contacts

Unless otherwise configured, Contacts are added manually by the website's Administrator, or any other user that has the "Permissions" to "Create" a Contact. In general practice, creating a Contact might be administratively be exclusively delegated to the Human Resources or Personnel Department. A User Group and Users can be assigned to perform the task, provided they have the proper permissions. An Exercise later in this Chapter will guide you through this process.

Regardless of which individual creates a Contact, they should all follow these procedures:

EXERCISE 27-3: CREATE CONTACTS MENU

Objective: This Exercise will guide you through the process of creating a "Contacts Menu" to be displayed on the right side of the website screen, then assigned to the "Home" Menu Link Item as a "display = yes" trigger, then the addition of all the Menu Link Items within the Menu as similar triggers.

The process used here will be: "Menu First, Module Second."

Step 1	If not already there, login as the Administrator to access the "Home Dashboard."
Step 2	Open the Menu Manager via the left Menu and select the "Manage" link to open the website's List of Menus. There is no direct access to this Manager via the "Home Dashboard" Content Panels.
Step 3	At the top left, click **"+New"** button at the top left of the screen.
Step 4	If not open, open the "Menu Details" Tab.
Step 5	Enter "Contacts Menu" (without quotes), in the "Title" and "Unique Name" fields.
Step 6	Execute a Save & Close action. The List of Menus will again display. The "Contacts Menu" should appear on the List.

The Menu has now been created but still needs an associated "Menu Module" to be assigned to a "Module Position" on the Template. In this case, it will be the "sidebar-right" Module Position.

Step 7	In the "Linked Modules" column of the Menus List, click on the "Add a Module for this Menu" button.
Step 8	In the "Title" field, enter: "Contacts Menu," which will easily show that it is associated with the Menu of the same name.
Step 9	If not open, open the "Module" Tab section.
Step 10	In the "Select menu" field, select: "Contacts Menu."
Step 11	In the "Positions" field, choose the "sidebar-right" Module Position. This is likely to be near the bottom of the list, so scroll down.
Step 12	Make sure the "Status" is set to "Published"
Step 13	Open the "Menu Assignment" Tab section and make sure the "Module Assignment" is set to: "On all pages."
Step 14	Execute a Save & Close action at the bottom right of the panel.

Everything with respect to a Menu and its associated Menu Module placed in a Template "Module Position" is now set. Individual Contacts may now be added.

The Contacts Menu choices also have their own additional "Options Settings," which can be configured with the Contacts Menu Link Item's Workspace open and viewing the individual Tabs. These Tabs are described at the end of this Chapter.

Using Contact Categories

As with most other Joomla! 5 Components, the individual items can be assigned to "Categories." This helps with the organization and management of large numbers of items within the Component.

For demonstration purposes, three "Contacts Categories" will be created: "ACCOUNTING DEPARTMENT, HUMAN RESOURCES DEPARTMENT and MARKETING DEPARTMENT." The following Exercise will guide you through the process.

Creating Contacts

During the above Exercise, the "Contact Categories" were created that will be used in demonstrating not only how to create Contacts, but also using the different options for the Menu Link Items to access individual Contacts or Lists of Contacts, depending on how they are/will be used on the website.

Enter Info or Leave Blank

When creating Contacts and including information fields, if any data is entered into a field, it will display in the "Contact View" on the website Front-End. If the pre-set information field is not to be used, simply leave the field blank when adding the Contact. Blank = no display.

EXERCISE 27-4: CREATING CONTACT ENTRIES

Objective: This Exercise will demonstrate how to create Contacts and assign them to a previously created Contact Categories.

Step 1		If not already there, login as the Administrator to access the "Home Dashboard."
Step 2		Open the Component Manager via the left Menu and select the "Contacts" link to open the Contacts Manager. There is no direct access to this Manager via the "Home Dashboard" Content Panels.
Step 3		In the Contacts Manager Menu, select: "Contacts," which will open the "Contacts Lists," which will be blank, with no entries at this point.
Step 4		At the top left, click **"+New"** or in the middle of the screen, click "Add your first Contact" button. This opens the "Contacts: New" Workspace.
Step 5		If not opened by default, click on the "New Contact" Tab. This is the tabbed section where most of the Contact information will be entered.
Step 6		In the "Name" field, enter: "Arthur Johnson" (without quotes).
Step 7		In the "Position" field, enter: "Accounts Receivable Manager" (without quotes).
Step 8		In the right column, set the "Category" to: "ACCOUNTING DEPARTMENT."
Step 9		In the right column, toggle "Featured" to the "Yes" which will also display a green "affirmative" color block.
Step 10		In all of the other fields under the "New Contact" Tab, enter information into any of the fields desired. Only those fields that contain any content entries will display.
Step 11		In the right column, set the "Category" to: "Accounting."
Step 12		Execute a Save & New action. This will open a new, blank Workspace to add a new Contact.
Step 13		In the "Name" field, enter: "Don Menendez" (without quotes).

Step 14	In the "Position" field, enter: "Accounts Payable Records" (without quotes).
Step 15	In the right column, set the "Category" to: "Accounting."
Step 16	In the right column, toggle "Featured" to the "Yes" which will also display a green "affirmative" color block.
Step 17	In all of the other fields under the "New Contact" Tab, enter information into any of the fields desired. Only those fields that contain any content entries will display.
Step 18	In the right column, set the "Category" to: "ACCOUNTING DEPARTMENT."
Step 19	Execute a Save & New action. This will open a new, blank Workspace to add a new Contact.
Step 20	In the "Name" field, enter: "Edward English" (without quotes).
Step 21	In the "Position" field, enter: "Accounts Payable Admin" (without quotes).
Step 22	In the right column, set the "Category" to: "ACCOUNTING DEPARTMENT."
Step 23	In the right column, toggle "Featured" to the "Yes" which will also display a green "affirmative" color block.
Step 24	In all of the other fields under the "New Contact" Tab, enter information into any of the fields desired. Only those fields that contain any content entries will display.
Step 25	In the right column, set the "Category" to: "Accounting."
Step 26	Execute a Save & New action. This will open a new, blank Workspace to add a new Contact.
Step 27	In the "Name" field, enter: "Bob Anderson" (without quotes).
Step 28	In the "Position" field, enter: "Personnel Manager" (without quotes).
Step 29	In the right column, set the "Category" to: "HUMAN RESOURCES DEPARTMENT."
Step 30	In the right column, toggle "Featured" to the "Yes" which will also display a green "affirmative" color block.
Step 31	In all of the other fields under the "New Contact" Tab, enter information into any of the fields desired. Only those fields that contain any content entries will display.

Step 32		Execute a Save & New action. This will open a new, blank Workspace to add a new Contact.
Step 33		In the "Name" field, enter: "Charles Barcode" (without quotes).
Step 34		In the "Position" field, enter: "Company Sales Manager" (without quotes).
Step 35		In the right column, set the "Category" to: "MARKETING DEPARTMENT."
Step 36		In the right column, toggle "Featured" to the "Yes" which will also display a green "affirmative" color block.
Step 37		In all of the other fields under the "New Contact" Tab, enter information into any of the fields desired. Only those fields that contain any content entries will display.
Step 38		Execute a Save & Close action. No additional Contacts will be added in this Exercise.

There are now three Categories of Contacts set up and there are five Contacts added into them. Three into "Accounting" and one each into "Human Resources" and "Marketing." These will be used in different Exercises that will create Menu Link Items that will open displays of information as follows:

Single Contact	Displays a single Contact's information.
Single Contact Category	Displays a list of all of the Contact's that have been assigned to a single Contact Category. The Category is selected from a List of Contact Categories.
Category Tree Display	This selection results in a complete "tree display" of all of the Categories and/or Sub-Categories that have been created within the Category Manager.
Featured Contacts	Shows only those Contacts that have been set to "Featured = Yes" on the individual Contact Workspace screen.
Create a Contact	This is a Front-End feature whereby a logged in Registered User can create a Contact.

Creating Contact Menu Link Items

As noted above, there are four types of Menu Link Items that can be created to display information within the Contact Manager in different ways. There is also a feature that will allow properly authorized Users to create a Contact, or modify a listing, after logging into the website Front-End. Perform the following Exercises to learn how to accomplish each task.

Single Contact Menu Link Item

EXERCISE 27-5: CREATING SINGLE CONTACT DISPLAY LINK

Objective: This Exercise will demonstrate how to create a Menu Link Item that will display a Single Contact's information on the website Front-End.

Step 1	If not already there, login as the Administrator to access the "Home Dashboard."
Step 2	In the left Menu, open the "Menus" section.
Step 3	With the "Menus" section list displayed, click on the "Contacts Menu" that was created in a previous Exercise. This opens the administrator screen "Menus: Items (Contacts Menu)."
Step 4	Click on the **"+New"** button at the top of the screen.
Step 5	When the "Menus: New Item" Workspace opens, enter "Personnel Manager" in the Title field.
Step 6	For the "Menu Item Type," select: "Contacts > Single Contact."
Step 7	In the "Select Contact" field drop down, select: "Bob Anderson."
Step 8	In the right column, ensure that "Contacts Menu" is selected in the "Menu" field.
Step 9	The "Status" field should be set to "Published."
Step 10	All other fields should remain in their default state.
Step 11	Execute a Save & Close action.
Step 12	Go to the website Front-End and refresh the browser window.
Step 13	Go to the "Contacts Menu."
Step 14	Execute the "Personnel Manager" Menu Link Item action.
Step 15	The resulting display will/should be the Contact Information for "Bob Anderson," which was previously created.

If the display is correct, proceed to the next Exercise. If not, review the Contact's information page and perform the creation steps again, including those within this Exercise.

Contact Category Menu Link Item
EXERCISE 27-6: CREATING CONTACTS IN A CATEGORY LINK

Objective: This Exercise will demonstrate how to create a Menu Link Item that will display a list of Contact's from within a single, selected Contact Category.

Step 1		If not already there, login as the Administrator to access the "Home Dashboard."
Step 2		In the left Menu, open the "Menus" section.
Step 3		With the "Menus" section list displayed, click on the "Contacts Menu" that was created in a previous Exercise. This opens the administrator screen "Menus: Items (Contacts Menu)."
Step 4		Click on the **"+New"** button at the top of the screen.
Step 5		In the "Title" field, enter, in ALL CAPS: "ACCOUNTING DEPARTMENT" (without quotes).
Step 6		For the "Menu Item Type," select: "System Links > Separator," which will create an entry into the Menu, but it does not have an active link to any target page/screen.
Step 7		Execute a Save New action.
Step 8		Click on the **"+New"** button at the top of the screen.
Step 9		In the "Title" field, enter, in ALL CAPS: "HUMAN RESOURCES DEPARTMENT" (without quotes).
Step 10		For the "Menu Item Type," select: "System Links > Separator," which will create an entry into the Menu, but it does not have an active link to any target page/screen.
Step 11		Execute a Save & New action.
Step 12		Click on the **"+New"** button at the top of the screen.
Step 13		In the "Title" field, enter, in ALL CAPS: "MARKETING DEPARTMENT" (without quotes).
Step 14		For the "Menu Item Type," select: "System Links > Separator," which will create an entry into the Menu, but it does not have an active link to any target page/screen.
Step 15		Execute a Save & Close action.
Step 16		The "Contacts Menu" list administrator screen should be open.
Step 17		Click on the **"+New"** button at the top of the screen.

Step 18	In the "Title" field, enter: "Accounts Payable Manager" (without quotes).
Step 19	For the "Menu Item Type," select: "Contacts > Single Contact."
Step 20	Select "Arthur Johnson" for the "Select Contact" field choice.
Step 21	In the right column, for "Parent Item," select: "ACCOUNTING DEPARTMENT" (without quotes).
Step 22	The "Status" should be: "Published."
Step 23	No other changes need to be made in any field under any of the other Tabs, which will be displayed below.
Step 24	Execute a Save & New action. A "New Menu Link Item" Workspace screen will open.
Step 25	In the "Title" field, enter: "Accounts Payable Administrator" (without quotes).
Step 26	For the "Menu Item Type," select: "Contacts > Single Contact."
Step 27	Select "Don Menendez" for the "Select Contact" field choice.
Step 28	In the right column, for "Parent Item," select: "ACCOUNTING DEPARTMENT" (without quotes).
Step 29	The "Status" should be: "Published."
Step 30	No other changes need to be made in any field under any of the other Tabs, which will be displayed below.
Step 31	Execute a Save & New action. A "New Menu Link Item" Workspace screen will open.
Step 32	In the "Title" field, enter: "Accounts Payable Admin" (without quotes).
Step 33	For the "Menu Item Type," select: "Contacts > Single Contact."
Step 34	Select "Edward English" for the "Select Contact" field choice.
Step 35	In the right column, for "Parent Item," select: "ACCOUNTING DEPARTMENT" (without quotes).
Step 36	The "Status" should be: "Published."
Step 37	No other changes need to be made in any field under any of the other Tabs, which will be displayed below.
Step 38	Execute a Save & New action. A "New Menu Link Item" Workspace screen will open.

Step 39		In the "Title" field, enter: "Personnel Manager" (without quotes).
Step 40		For the "Menu Item Type," select: "Contacts > Single Contact."
Step 41		Select "Bob Anderson" for the "Select Contact" field choice.
Step 42		In the right column, for "Parent Item," select: "HUMAN RESOURCES DEPARTMENT" (without quotes).
Step 43		The "Status" should be: "Published."
Step 44		No other changes need to be made in any field under any of the other Tabs, which will be displayed below.
Step 45		Execute a Save & New action. A "New Menu Link Item" Workspace screen will open.
Step 46		In the "Title" field, enter: "Company Sales Manager" (without quotes).
Step 47		For the "Menu Item Type," select: "Contacts > Single Contact."
Step 48		Select "Charles Barcode" for the "Select Contact" field choice.
Step 49		In the right column, for "Parent Item," select: "MARKETING DEPARTMENT" (without quotes).
Step 50		The "Status" should be: "Published."
Step 51		No other changes need to be made in any field under any of the other Tabs, which will be displayed below.
Step 52		Execute a Save & New action.

Creating the three "Separators" above will provide non-link "Headings" within the "Contacts Menu," under which, other "active links" can be displayed. Next, in this Exercise, three Menu Link Items will be added for each of the ACCOUNTING personnel and displayed as sub-items under the ACCOUNTING DEPARTMENT "Separator" heading. The two other departments each have a single Contact link. See Figure 27-4.

Contacts Menu

Personnel Manager

ACCOUNTING DEPARTMENT

  Accounts Payable Manager

  Accounts Payable Computers

  Accounts Payable Administrator

HUMAN RESOURCES DEPARTMENT

  Personnel Manager

MARKETING DEPARTMENT

  Company Sales Manager

Figure 27-4

Contact Category Tree Menu Link Item
EXERCISE 27-7: CREATING CONTACT CATEGORY TREE LINK

Objective: This Exercise will demonstrate how to create a Menu Link Item that will display, in a Category Tree format comprised of a list of all of the Categories, and Sub-Categories, for all Contact Categories.

Step 1	If not already there, login as the Administrator to access the "Home Dashboard."
Step 2	In the left Menu, open the "Menus" section.
Step 3	With the "Menus" section list displayed, click on the "Contacts Menu" that was created in a previous Exercise. This opens the administrator screen "Menus: Items (Contacts Menu)."
Step 4	Click on the **"+New"** button at the top of the screen.
Step 5	In the "Title" field, enter, in ALL CAPS: "CATEGORY TREE MENU" (without quotes).
Step 6	For the "Menu Item Type," select: "Contacts > List All Categories in a Contact Category Tree."
Step 7	The "Top Level Category" choice should be: "Root."
Step 8	In the right column, the "Status" should be: "Published."
Step 9	Execute a Save & Close Action

Step 10	Go to the website Front-End and click on the "CATEGORY TREE MENU" item within the "Contacts Menu."
Step 11	The resulting display should show a list of the three "Contacts Categories" along with a count of Contacts within the Categories.
Step 12	Click on the "Accounting" link, which will open a list of Contacts within that Category, along with some basic information from their individual profiles.

Designating "Featured" Contacts
EXERCISE 27-8: CREATING "FEATURED CONTACTS" LISTING

Objective: This Exercise will demonstrate how to create a Menu Link Item that will display a list of all of the Contacts that have been designated as "Featured" within the Contact Manager. This is similar to the "Featured Articles" function.

During creation of the individual Contacts, each was, or should have, been designated as a "Featured Contact" within their profile via a toggle button in the right column.

Step 1	If not already there, login as the Administrator to access the "Home Dashboard."
Step 2	In the left Menu, open the "Menus" section.
Step 3	With the "Menus" section list displayed, click on the "Contacts Menu" that was created in a previous Exercise. This opens the administrator screen "Menus: Items (Contacts Menu)."
Step 4	Click on the **"+New"** button at the top of the screen.
Step 5	In the "Title" field, enter, in ALL CAPS: "FEATURED CONTACT LINK" (without quotes).
Step 6	For the "Menu Item Type," select: "Featured Contacts."
Step 7	In the right column, the "Status" should be: "Published."
Step 8	Execute a Save & Close Action
Step 9	Go to the website Front-End and click on the "FEATURED CONTACT LINKS" item within the "Contacts Menu."
Step 10	The resulting display should be listing in table format of all of the Contacts that have been designated as "Featured," along with some minimal information about their function in the organization. The items in the list may be set selectively to "not show" if desired.

Creating Contacts Entries via the Front-End

Within larger organizations, rather than the website Administrator being inundated with numerous requests to add, correct or otherwise modify a Contact, it is simpler to have departments perform this task.

This is done by creating a User Group account with "Registered" permissions so they can log into the website Front-End. When they do so, the "Create New Contact" Menu Link Item will display, and when clicked, the User will be able to create, or modify, a Contact.

Creating this User Group requires that certain "Permissions" must be set within the "Contacts" Component. This is important to limit access to only certain "actions" that are managed via "Permissions," so as to prevent the User Group's Users from making any other modifications.

EXERCISE 27-9: CREATING CONTACT EDITOR USER GROUPS

Objective: This Exercise will demonstrate how to create a User Group that will have "Permissions" to create and/or modify Contacts. Any of the website's Registered Users may be manually assigned to the permitted User Group by the website Administrator.

Creating the Contact Editor User Group

Step 1	If not already there, login as the Administrator to access the "Home Dashboard."
Step 2	In the left Menu, access: "Users > Groups." This will open the screen that lists all of the User Groups that have been added during installation, during inclusion of "Sample Data" and User Groups created in previous Exercises.
Step 3	Click on the **"+New"** button at the top of the screen.
Step 4	Create a "Group Title" named: "Contacts Editor" (without quotes).
Step 5	The "Group Parent" setting should be: "Registered."
Step 6	Execute a Save & Close action.

The next phase of this Exercise is to grant the necessary "Permissions" to the "Contacts Editor" User Group. This is performed within the User Group Manager, as follows:

Step 7	In the left Menu of the "Home Dashboard," open the "System" section.
Step 8	In the "Setup" block, open the "Global Configuration" area.
Step 9	With the "Global Configuration" open, which also displays the "Component" list, click on the "Contacts" link.

Step 10		If not open, click on the "Permissions" Tab.
Step 11		Click on the "Contacts Editor" User Group name.
Step 12		Grant "Allowed Permissions" for the following actions: • Create • Delete • Edit • Edit State • Edit Custom Field Value
Step 13		Execute a Save & Close action.

Creating a New Contact via the Front-End

This new User needs to have a way of accessing the "Contacts Manager" without accessing the Back-end. This can be accomplished by creating a Menu Link Item in the Contacts Menu that specifically allows that action to take place.

EXERCISE 27-10: CREATE A CONTACT VIA THE FRONT-END

Objective: This Exercise will demonstrate how a Menu Link Item is added to the website Front-End so that a designated User in a designated User Group can access the Contact's Manager.

Step 1	If not already there, login as the Administrator to access the "Home Dashboard."
Ste[2	In the left Menu, access: "Menus > Contacts Menu."
Step 3	Click on the **"+New"** button at the top of the screen.
Step 4	In the "Title" field, enter: "CREATE A CONTACT - Login Required" (without quotes).
Step 5	For the "Menu Item Type," select: "System > Separator."
Step 6	The "Status" should be: "Published."
Step 7	No other setting need to be changed from the default.
Step 8	Execute a Save & Close action.
Step 9	Click on the **"+New"** button at the top of the screen.
Step 10	In the "Title" field, enter: "CREATE A CONTACT" (without quotes).
Step 11	For the "Menu Item Type," select: "Contacts > Create Contact."
Step 12	Set the "Access" value to: "Registered."

Step 13	The "Status" should be: "Published."
Step 14	Execute a Save & Close action.
Step 15	In the "Contacts Menu," only the "CREATE A CONTACT - Login Required" should be visible.

Because more than one User may be given "Permissions" to create or modify a Contact listing, the "Edit Own" should not be in the "Allowed" configuration. If it were, no other Users would be allowed to modify any Contact created by another User. Be aware that this would restrict the functional use of this task.

Assigning a User as a Contacts Editor

Step 16	In the left Menu of the "Home Dashboard," open: "Users > Manage," to display a list of all the users on the website.
Step 17	Open "Test User 1" by clicking on the "User name" link.
Step 18	Open the "Assigned User Group" Tab.
Step 19	Below the "Registered" Group click on the box to select the "Contacts Editor" as one of the User's permitted User Groups.
Step 20	Execute a Save & Close action.
Step 21	Go to the website Front-End.
Step 22	Click on the "CREATE A CONTACT" link in the Contacts Menu.
Step 23	Access to the desired target will fail because you are not logged into the Front-End as an allowed "Register User > Contacts Editor."
Step 24	Log into the Front-End as "testuser1" using the password you created when creating that User.
Step 25	Go back to the "Contacts Menu" and click on "CREATE A CONTACT" Menu Link Item again.
Step 26	This time, the "New Contact" creation form will open. Thereby a new Contact can be created.

The above summarized is how a "new" Contact is created. What about "editing" an existing Contact. This is easily accomplished.

Step 27	You should still be logged in as "testuser1." If not, do so again on the Front-end.
Step 28	Once logged in, open the "FEATURED CONTACT LINKS" in the "Contacts Menu."

Step 29		Click on any of the names that display on the resulting list. This will open their Contact profile.
Step 30		At the top right of the Contact's profile window, there is a small button/link displaying "Edit." Click on it. That action opens the Contact's profile, which may now be edited.
Step 31		Perform the required edits, then execute "Save" at the bottom portion of the screen.

If desired, any User within the "Registered Group" can be assigned to the "Contact Editor Group" and will be able to perform all permitted actions with respect to any Contact via a Front-End login.

Fixing Contact Menu Display

The Contacts Menu is a Module assigned to a Module Position. To ensure its continual visibility, it is necessary to set the Module's display so that it will be visible when any Menu Link Item within the Contacts Menu is clicked.

This is accomplished by completing the following Exercise.

EXERCISE 27-11: DISPLAY MENU WITH ALL LINKS

Objective: This Exercise will demonstrate how to create a User Group that will have "Permissions" to create and/or modify Contacts. Any of the website's Registered Users may be manually assigned to the permitted User Group by the website Administrator.

Step 1		If not already there, login as the Administrator to access the "Home Dashboard."
Step 2		On the "Home Dashboard" main screen, click on the "Modules" link in the "Site block." A list of all the Modules on the website will display.
Step 3		Open the "Contacts Menu" Module.
Step 4		In the Workspace, open the "Menu Assignment" Tab.
Step 5		The Module Assignment should be "on all pages."
Step 6		Execute a Save & Close action.
Step 7		Go to the website Front-End and refresh the browser window.
Step 8		Click on each of the Menu Link Items in the "Contacts Menu" to ensure that the Menu remains in view following each click.

CONTACTS MENU LINK ITEM TYPES

In addition to the Contacts "Global Options" and the individual Contact "Options" that are invoked as overrides, the Menu Link Item for the type of Contact listing also has some important settings.

Details	Selects the Menu Item Type and the Contact or Contacts Category.
List Layouts	Configures how the Contacts List is displayed on the Front-End for Categories. This makes each "List" Display a customizable feature for each Menu Link Item that displays any type of Category List. In most cases, not all of the information fields need be displayed, so this feature allows the non-desired fields to "not display" by selection.
Form	This Tab contains setting relative to the display of the Contact's Form, for the Contact(s) that are included within the display. Each Contacts Menu Link Item can be set differently as needed.
Mail Options	Controls how the email is handled when the Contact Form is submitted. Most of the settings purpose are obvious as to their purpose.
Link Types	Allows configuration of the Contact's Link settings.
Page Display	A unique display can be created/configured for the Page for this Contact or Contact List. Again, this is another way to highly customize the Front-End display.
Metadata	Metadata can be entered to allow search engines to gather information.
Module Assignment	This table display indicates which Modules on the website are associated with the Contacts Menu Link Item that is being inspected.

COMPONENT:
Multilingual Associations

The internet has created an international community. It is very often desirable to communicate with website visitors in something other than your own native "Language" upon which your website has been built. In Joomla! 5. This can be accomplished by the use of "Multilingual Associations," which is just another way of saying "different Languages."

Previously, Joomla! websites that wanted multiple Languages simply had to install a Google Translate Extension. This added country "Language" flags on the site and when clicked, the site was translated into the selected Language.

Back then, translations were problematic. For instance: the phrase *"the horse goes in front of the cart"* could be translated into *"the horse before the cart put."* Even worse, *"your sister looks like a farm animal"* could easily have resulted from an incorrect transliteration. These types of "Language" errors could easily offend people from other countries who observe a different syntax and word meanings.

Over the past twenty-plus years, instant online translations have been dramatically improved with very good results. This makes the new Joomla! 5 "Multilingual Associations" set up a way to "perfectly" translate existing Content into the target Language.

Not Using Languages?

If you are not using multiple Languages, skip this Chapter and come back to it if needed. Otherwise, continue without getting involved with implementing "Language" functions that are not needed.

Terminology Change

Using the term "Multilingual" is somewhat clumsy, so we are going to take some authorship liberty and refer to this function as: "Multi-Language" within this Chapter. It is intended to mean the same.

Multi-Language Overview

Other than the actual "Titles" and "Textual Content" that the Administrator creates manually when creating content, there are predetermined "text strings" that generate fixed terms or words that are displayed on the website. Joomla! 5 has a long and extensive list of "strings" that each Component or part of the website that is called when Menu Link Items have been clicked, or an action executed. There are literally thousands of "strings" on the website that control all of the "fixed text" that is generated. The "fluid text" is content that is entered onto the website in the form of titles, content, messages, notes and other displayable text.

Here is an example of a "strings" with the accompanying text, which applies to the "Read more" text that can be applied to Categories and Articles:

MOD_ARTICLES_CATEGORY_READ_MORE="Read more: "

MOD_ARTICLES_CATEGORY_READ_MORE_TITLE="Read More ... "

MOD_ARTICLES_CATEGORY_REGISTER_TO_READ_MORE="Register to read more "

The first part of these are the actual code "strings" which generate the text as indicated.

So, the process of creating the "Language" text for the website is to first identify the "strings" on the website, then configure the "associations."

Also worth noting is that any Extension that is installed onto the website may also have "Language Strings" that are included. These are installed within the Joomla! 5 "Languages" folder. They are accessible for editing if desired.

Language Application Concepts

Using the built-in "Language" management system every additional "Language" being applied on the website actually requires "parallel content" in every Language. Two additional Languages would be required to have two parallel definitions for "strings." If five additional Languages, there must be five parallel definitions, and so on.

With hundreds of "strings," there will be the need for hundreds of parallel definitions for EACH Language. Yes, for EACH!

Now the question is: "How does the Administrator perform the tasks necessary to add new "Language" strings?"

Joomla! 5 has "Language Packs" that contain translations of all of the "fixed terms" that will display on either the Back-End or Front-End of the website. An example are the terms Articles, Categories, Modules, admin text, table headings, or other similar static texts. These are standard terms or descriptions that are common throughout. There is a "Language Pack" for every "Language" that translates the common terms used in Joomla! 5. The Administrator need not create any of them. The "Language Packs" simply need to be installed and/or activated to be available.

WARNING!
DO NOT ATTEMPT TO INSTALL MULTILINGUAL DATA

In Chapter 7, "Fast Track Double Time Start" the "Sample Data" was installed. Once this is done, the "Multilingual Sample Data" cannot be installed with, or "over the top," of the previous data. Do not attempt to do so. It is not necessary for any of the following Exercises.

Default "Language" Packs

During the initial actions that took place during the Joomla! 5 installation process, a number of "Language Packs" were also installed – but not "enabled." Only one "Language" was enabled, based on the choice of "Language" made during install, which was "English – United Kingdom," which works well for initial purpose for most English-speaking countries.

Must be Individually Installed

If any additional Languages are desired, even though the "Language Packs" were installed, they were simply put into a website folder from where they can be actually "added" into the website.

EXERCISE 28-1: INSTALLING "LANGUAGE" FILES

Objective: This Exercise will demonstrate how to "add to the website," any of the Languages made available during the initial installation process.

Step 1		If not already there, login as the Administration to access the "Home Dashboard."
Step 2		In the left Menu, open the "System" area.
Step 3		In the "Install" block, click on the Languages link. This will display all of the files within the "Language Library" that can be, or have been, installed.
Step 4		To view the entire three page list, select "All" in the quantity box at the top right of the screen.

Step 5	To "Install" any "Language" into the website, scroll to the desired Language.
Step 6	Select "English, USA" by clicking on the "Install" button.
Step 7	When completed, a "Success" message will display. Close the message display.
Step 8	Scroll down and select "German" and click on the "Install" button.
Step 9	When completed, a "Success" message will display. Close the message display.
Step 10	Scroll down and select "Spanish" and click on the "Install" button.
Step 11	When completed, a "Success" message will display. Close the message display.

The "Language" Managers

Now that three additional Languages have been "added," in addition to the default "English UK" version, the Languages can be controlled within the "Manage" panel on the "Home Dashboard."

There are three Managers that apply to "Languages," as follows:

Languages	This displays the list of every "Language" that is available to be used on the website. The list also indicates other information about the Languages, including which "Language" is the "Default" for the website. See the Exercise below to perform this task.
Content Languages	This list displays those Languages and their "Status," along with other general information. At this point, only one (the default), "Language" should be "enabled," as indicated by the green "checkmark" in the "Status" column. If not "enabled," the Languages will not be available for use.
Language Overrides	This feature allows "Language Overrides" to be created for any existing "Language String" for any "Language" that has been installed. There is a dropdown near the top of the screen to make the appropriate selection.

Set the Default Language

When using Multiple Languages on the website, at one of those that have been installed from the "Language File Library" should be designated as the "default" for the entire Website. At this point, English UK, English US, German and Spanish have been installed. Let's set the "default" to English US.

EXERCISE 28-2: SETTING THE DEFAULT LANGUAGE

Objective: This Exercise will demonstrate how to designate a specific installed "Language" as the "Default Language" for the website.

Step 1	If not already there, login as the Administrator to access the "Home Dashboard."
Step 2	In the left Menu, open the "System" area.
Step 3	In the "Manage" block, click on the "Languages Link." This will display all of the files within the "Language Library" that are installed.
Step 4	Under the "Default" column, all Languages, except one, will have a grey circle indicating they are "not" the "default" Language.
Step 5	The "default" "Language" has an orange star icon in the column.
Step 6	To change to "English US," click on the grey icon in the "Default" column, which will change its Status to "Default."
Step 7	A "Success" message will display. Read the message text. Then close the message panel.

The condition of the website now has the "English US" as the "default" "Language" for all Users except those, upon "Registration," have chosen any other "Language" to be "their" default.

Enable the Installed Languages

In order to actually use the installed Languages, they must be actually added to the website. At this point, they were simply "installed" and their files made ready for use. They have not yet, individually (except the default), been completely "Enabled" for use. This is a simple process, as follows:

EXERCISE 28-3: ENABLE INSTALLED LANGUAGES

Objective: This Exercise will demonstrate how to enable any one, or more, of the available Languages so they can be used on the website.

Step 1	If not already there, login as the Administrator to access the "Home Dashboard."
Step 2	In the left Menu, open the "System" area.

Step 3	In the "Manage" block, click on the "Content Languages" link. This will display all of the Languages that have been installed.
Step 4	At this point, under the "Status" column, three Languages should be "greyed out," and one should display the green checkmark icon.

There are two methods of "Enabling" the Languages, one of which is to simply click on the grey **"X"** icon in the "Status" column. This will automatically "Publish" the Language. The alternative "group method" will be used next.

Step 5	At the top of the first column, click on the checkbox. All of the Languages will then be selected.
Step 6	Unselect the Language(s) that are already installed. This leaves three Languages to be installed.
Step 7	Execute the "Publish" link within the "Action" button near the top of the screen.
Step 8	The "Success" Message will display. Close it.
Step 9	The "Install Languages" button will take you to the List of available Languages to install additional if desired. No additional Languages are to be installed at this time.
Step 10	The result is that all Languages have a "Published Status."

Create a Simple "Language" Override

Every item of text that displays on the Joomla! 5 website consists of two parts:

Language Constant	This is a fixed string of words that can be placed into any file that will display the same exact text on the screen in the designated location.
Text	This field is the actual "text" that will display when the "Language Constant" is invoked by a screen display action.

EXERCISE 28-4: "LANGUAGE" OVERRIDES

Objective: This Exercise will demonstrate how the "Languages: Edit Override" can be used to modify a text display. This will be a simple demonstration to provide instruction on how an "override" can be accomplished. It will be "undone" at the end of the Exercise.

Step 1	If not already there, login as the Administration to access the "Home Dashboard."
Step 2	In the left Menu, open the "System" area.

| **Step 3** | In the "Manage" block, click on the "Language Overrides" link. This will display all of the "overrides" that have already been created, but in this case, the list should be empty. |
| **Step 4** | Click on the **"+New"** button at the top of the screen. |

At the top of the screen there is a heading that displays: "Languages: Edit Override," which is simply the name of this screen display.

Step 4	Copy the name and paste "Languages: Edit Override" (without the quotes), into the "Search Text" field at the lower right of the screen.
Step 5	Execute the "Search" action. The button may need to be clicked again to display the "Search Results.
Step 6	Click on the text in the Search Results box. This action will populate the "Language Constant" and the "Text" fields in the "Create a New Override" area to the left.
Step 7	Change the "Text" to read: "My Languages: Edit Override" (without the quotes).
Step 8	Execute a Save action.
Step 9	The "Success" message will display. Close it.
Step 10	View the "Page Heading" which now has been changed. The "Language Constant" string, wherever it displays on the webpages will have the "My" word in the "Text" display.
Step 11	Edit the "Text" again by removing the "My" text previously added.
Step 12	Execute a Save action.
Step 13	The "Success" message will display again. Close it.
Step 14	Verify that the "Page Heading" has been changed.
Step 15	Execute a Save & Close action.
Step 16	Notice now that the override is now displayed on the resulting List.

Because no change was actually maintained, it makes sense to remove the override from the List.

Step 17	Select the override by clicking on the box in the first column.
Step 18	In the top Menu, execute a "Delete" action.
Step 19	A popup window will open asking for conformation of the action.
Step 20	Click "OK" in the popup window.

Step 21	The "Success" Message will display indicating the override has been deleted.

Language Manager Options

As you know by now, just about every Component or part of Joomla! 5 has some sort of an "Option" group that may be configured. In the case of the "Languages: Options," the only configuration that is permitted are changes to the "Permissions" for the individual "User Groups."

If needed, change any "Permissions" as may be required to meet the objectives of the website Content management.

Language Packs Cannot be Uninstalled

The "Language Packs" themselves cannot be deleted in the same way that Modules or other Extensions are removed or "uninstalled" from the website. The "System > Content Languages > Languages" New/Edit" screen should be accessed and the "Status" of the Languages to be "uninstalled" should be changed from "Published" to "Unpublished." That designation actually is a "used" and "not used" choice.

Using Multi-Language Extensions

Joomla! 5 has been programmed to accept and invoke Extensions that can be used to perform certain tasks and modifications with respect to Languages, which can supersede the default Languages.

The Manual "Language" Switcher

Joomla! 5 has the capabilities of creating many different Languages and invoking them for almost all Content Items. This is performed by use of "Language Packs" and different install/configuration settings.

The processes involved in using different Languages on the website have their share of complications. It also involves having an individual "Language" version for each piece of Content, making the possibility for an incredibly large website.

If you would like to explore how the Manual "Language" Switcher works, install another instance of Joomla! 5 and then install the "Multilingual Sample Data." Do not install the standard "Sample Data." The two do not work together.

Once the "Multilingual Sample Data" is installed, explore the Articles, Menus and the "Language Switcher Module" in the Back-End and Front-End. You will see the many different Articles that were created, etc.

Because the "manual" method of implementing is so complicated, it is suggested that an alternative method be explored. This is described next.

Install the "GTranslate" Extension

To save yourself a lot of time and effort, it is suggested that a highly functional "Translation Extension" be installed and it's use implemented. One such Extension that has been successfully used for years on Joomla! websites is "GTranslate."

"GTranslate" uses the horsepower of Google Translate for 103 Languages and is statistically used by 99% of all internet users, or approximately 500 million daily.

An Extension has been available since 2006, well-maintained and has been upgraded to work with Joomla! 5.

What is GTranslate?

Google's Translation API Basic uses Google's neural machine translation technology to instantly translate texts into more than one hundred Languages. Translation API Advanced offers the same fast, dynamic results you get with Basic and additional customization features. Customization matters for domain- and context-specific terms or phrases, and formatted document translation.

As you can see, GTranslate performs instant translations on-the-fly, along with the ability to make customizations, which is the function of "Language Overrides" within the Joomla! 5 context. When the GTranslate Extension is installed, it takes over the translations functions. Then, when "overrides" are created, they take precedence over the Extensions "Language" display.

Download & Install the Extension

The Joomla Extension Directory ("JED") lists the "GTranslate" Extension as being available for both J!3 and J!4. However, when attempting to download it, there is no J!4 "free" version available from the Developer's download links. We believe that is simply an oversight on their part. The version for "GTranslate" Joomla! 5 IS available but a different installer method must be used, as discussed below – the "Install from Web" feature.

Using "Install from Web" Feature

Joomla! 5 has four different ways of adding Extensions to the website:

- Upload Package File
- Install from Folder
- Install from URL
- Install from Web

The "GTranslate Extension" should be installed using the latter method. Follow the steps in the Exercise below to affect the process.

EXERCISE 28-5: USING "INSTALL FROM WEB" FEATURE

Objective: This Exercise demonstrates how an Extension can be installed by using the "Install from Web" feature of the installer package. This involves connecting to the Developer's website download location, which will automatically begin the process of adding the Extension to the website.

Step 1	If not already there, login as the Administration to access the "Home Dashboard."
Step 2	In the left Menu, click on: "System."
Step 3	In the "Install" Panel, click on: "Extensions." This will open the screen with the install method choices.
Step 4	Click on the "Install from Web" tab, which opens a set of "JED" Extension listings that conform with the Joomla! rules for updating and upgrading Extensions, thus allowing the to appear here.
Step 5	In the "Search" field, enter: "GTranslate" (without the quotes).
Step 6	Click in the lower portion of the "GTranslate" product graphic.
Step 7	On the next screen, the "Install" button must be clicked at both locations; at the top, then again at the bottom, which starts the installing actions.
Step 8	When completed, the "Success" Message will display, along with a block of text, suggesting an upgrade to a paid version. The "free version" has limitations, and the features are expanded with the "paid" version. The "free" version is adequate for use at this time.
Step 9	Clear the "Success" Message block by clicking on the **"X"** at the right.
Step 10	The "GTranslate" Extension has now been installed and is ready for use. No other actions are required.

The "GTranslate" does not use the Joomla! 5 "Language Packs" as a resource. "GTranslate" is an online service that uses the internet by reaching out to the Google "Language" Library to make the translations that appear on the website.

The Extension responds to the "Language" display choice on the website, then reaches out to its own "Language" database and makes the translation, sending it back to the website instantly – or pretty close to instantly. The change usually takes place during a very fast screen refresh.

Implementing the Translation Feature

The "GTranslate" Extension only establishes the connection between the website and the Google Translation Library. Any actual implementation must be accomplished through the use of a dedicated "Language switching" Module, but NOT the default "Language Switcher."

When the "GTranslate" Extension was installed, the process also installed a dedicated "GTranslate" Module. This is different from the "Manual "Language" Switcher" Module discussed previously. It is a Module that is managed exactly the same as any other. It can be positioned anywhere on the webpage and take advantage of the "Menu Assignment" options, along with some other internal Module features.

Adding the GTranslate Action Module

Using the "GTranslate" Extension is much easier than creating a copy of every Content Item is a desired "Language" and configuring the website to display them properly. Using this Extension is very, very easy, and it explained below.

EXERCISE 28-6: ADDING THE "GTRANSLATE" MODULE

Objective: This procedure will demonstrate how to add the specialized "GTranslate Module" to the "sidebar-right" "Module Position" on the Front-End of the website.

Step 1		If not already there, login as the Administration to access the "Home Dashboard."
Step 2		On the "Site" Panel, click on the "Modules" block. This will open the list of Modules currently installed on the website.
Step 3		Click on the **"+New"** button at the top of the screen.
Step 4		Scroll the screen until you see the "GTranslate" Module and then click on the main image.
Step 5		In the "Title" field, enter: "GTranslate Module" (without the quotes).
Step 6		In the "Position" field, at the right, select: "sidebar-right."
Step 7		In the "Look" field, select: "Nice dropdown with flags" as the type of display option. Note which other options are also available.
Step 8		Execute a Save action.
Step 9		Go to the website Front-End and verify the "GTranslate Module" is located in the "sidebar-right" location. The Module Title should be displayed, along with a
Step 10		The display and list of "Languages" is configured within the Module's Admin Workspace.
Step 11		Return to the Module Workspace in the Back-End.

Step 12	At the top right of the screen, click on: "Toggle Inline Help." This will put "help texts" with some elements in the Workspace.
Step 13	Scroll down the screen and note the various settings and the Languages that are active and how they might be displayed.
Step 14	Experiment with the different "Look" settings, making changes, then executing a Save action followed by accessing the Front-End, refreshing the browser window, and viewing how the "GTranslate Module" is displaying the selected "Look."
Step 15	When completed, select: "Nice dropdown with flags" as the type of display option which should remain as the default, so execute a Save action.
Step 16	Review all of the different configuration settings that may be applied in the Module's Workspace.
Step 17	It is suggested that only the Languages necessary be selected to be included in the Front-End access point.
Step 18	When completed, execute a Save & Close action.

Switching Front-End "Language" Choices

With the "GTranslate Module" located on the Front-End, website Users can switch to any of the available Languages by simply making the selection from the list of those displayed in the dropdown.

When a choice is changed, the website does a quick refresh and pulls in the appropriate translation of fixed ("Static") elements, along with those within Content Items such as: Categories, Articles and other Content Items what contain custom-created texts. Everything that is not a "Static" text item, is translated quickly and automatically by the Google Translation Service.

This is why use of the Extension is so much easier to use versus installing various "Languages," and then creating Content Items in each one selected, and so on.

Users Choice of Language

Here's an interesting asset of the Multi-Language feature. Each individual website visitor, or Registered User, may choose their own "Language" to be displayed. If the website is based on English-US, and Spanish and German is available, the Users may select any one of them for themselves.

This makes the website highly functional for visitors from locations that speak a "Language" other than the one selected as the default. The "choice flag" or dropdown selector can be used to make the selection.

However, this does not apply when the "GTranslate Extension" is used because the User can instantly choose their "Language of choice" immediately. There is no need to set a "Default Language" for themselves.

We have no vested interest.

In this Chapter, we are using the Joomla! 5 Extension entitled: "GT Translate." It was installed "via the web" and not from the Extension download on their website – the J! 4 version link was not visible there, so an alternate download method was executed successful. We do not have a vested interest with regard to this translation Extension. This is a free Extension made for use with Joomla! 5.

Using Other Translation Services

There are other Translation Services that can be used with not only a Joomla! 5 website, but others as well. There is one thing you should know, however. Most of these are: 1) not tightly integrated with Joomla! 5, and 2) they typically require payment for use.

If you must use a "Language Service," we suggest that you research all of them and select the best one that will serve selected Languages onto your website, and they do so within a budget you can control. Be cognizant of "use fees" or "subscriptions" and other charges that may apply.

JOOMLA!®5 Ⓐ
BOOTS ON THE GROUND
Advanced Edition
Volume 1 Ⓑ
CHAPTER 29
Ⓒ Ⓓ Ⓔ

COMPONENT:
News Feeds

When websites started becoming popular, they used to offer their Content out for syndication. The method allowed other websites to display Content from others. This became a frequently used method for a small, bare Content website, to load up on Content and make them look interesting. These novelty "RSS" feeds were a nuisance because it cluttered up website screens, especially on websites that were managed by beginners with not much knowledge of website construction.

The method used to syndicate Content was via Really Simple Syndication ("RSS"). The syndicated Content was output in a certain format and an "RSS" interpreter of that format was located on the re-displaying website. This made it quite easy for websites to capture and display the third-party Content that was generated in a compatible "RSS" format.

At the syndicated website, the information could be displayed automatically via "Home" page settings and configurations, or via Menu Link Items. For example: an "RSS" feed could be included in a Module that is assigned to a "Module Position" Then, the Module can be set to display when certain Menu Link Items are triggers, "Home" being an example. The Module would be set to be displayed on the "Home" screen and so forth.

Syndication of Content from other websites comprised the majority of Content displayed on a large number of websites. When the internet was still in its infancy, it was considered "cool" to have all sorts of stories and Articles on websites that, in fact, actually had no meaning other than to replicate Content pulled in via "RSS." That fad eventually faded away as more of the informational websites stopped generating outbound "RSS" feeds altogether, and the internet was/is better for it.

Today, because websites are more protective of their Content, "RSS" feeds are decreasing in both use and popularity. However, "RSS" type feeds are being heavily used by commercial online stores and selling websites to syndicate their Content to other websites under "affiliate" auspices with other websites for a commission on the sales of any products.

Of course, another use of "RSS" feeds ends up being those nuisance adverts that appear all over website pages and popup as pages are scrolled. There is a good side to "RSS" feeds, and also some unbelievably bad uses that make a visual mess out of the websites that pull in the feeds. Of course, "cookies" play a significant role in which type of ads get dumped off into your browser, so "RSS" should not carry the full burden of the blame of them.

In some form "Cookies" have generally replaced "RSS" for dumping Content, often unwanted, onto website browsers, but that is fodder for another Chapter. In the case of "RSS" feeds, the Content display is voluntary on the part of the website administrator. The "Cookies," on the other hand, are "force-fed" and involuntary displays of Content (in most situations).

What does RSS Mean?

The term "RSS" means "Really Simply Syndication." Which is where a website puts out its content in a format that allows other sites to display it, and thus the "syndication" becomes rather simple. The "RSS" feeds gather the linked feeds, update them in real time and display them in a designated location on a hosting website.

Using News Feeds

The big question is: "How does a website use 'News Feeds' and why?"

The answer to this question is simple. All that is needed is a "News Feed Reader" and a desire to Publish someone else's Content on a Joomla! 5 website. It really isn't very complicated in that regard.

However, using "News Feeds" can get complicated because there is an abundance of "News Feed" generators, which are utilities that make Content on a website available to other websites. An Administrator cannot just yank content down from any website. The sharing-website must Publish their content via an "RSS."

One great thing about "News Feeds" is that they can be updated in real time. If your website re-publishes a feed from another site, and they update it, that update is automatically made to the Content on the hosting site. Why? Because all the hosting website is doing is providing a live link to the transmitting website.

How Does a Website Read Newsfeeds

The "RSS" "News Feeds" from a source website are generally created in a specific format This is a standardized format that generates Content by a program called a "Feedburner." Then, on the other end, a "Feedburner" Reader converts these feeds to something that can be displayed on a webpage.

The default Joomla! 5 News Feed Component has this built-in News Feed Reader that is compatible with "Feedburner." It is actually a simple "aggregator," or collector of information from "RSS" feeds. The "aggregators" check websites on every page load to determine and display updated content. This saves website visitors from going to each website to check each "newsy" content. The "RSS Aggregator" does the checking and converts the connected content to the format needed for the viewing website.

How are "News Feeds" Organized

For effective administration, "News Feeds" should be arranged in Categories (like what's new?). After that, the "RSS" feed links are assigned to their respective Categories.

Will use the Joomla RSS Feeds

In the examples and Exercises in this Chapter, the "RSS News Feeds" available on the joomla.org website will be used. Here are the Categories of "RSS News Feeds" available from that source.

The "RSS News Feeds" used will be: "Joomla! News Feeds" and "Joomla! Community." There are others, but these two will be sufficient for demonstration purposes.

The joomla.org website uses the "Feedburner" to generate the "RSS News Feeds" for the content shared by the website.

Creating News Feed Categories

As is almost everything else in Joomla! 5, Content Items are generally assigned to named Categories, or if not, at least to a Category entitled: "uncategorized." The "News Feeds" Component is no exception to this general rule.

EXERCISE 29-1: CREATING NEWS FEED CATEGORIES

Objective: The objective of this Exercise is to demonstrate how to create Categories within the "New Feeds" Component.

Step 1		If not already there, login as the Administrator to access the "Home Dashboard."
Step 2	A	Open the Components Manager via the left Menu and select the "News Feeds" link to open the "News Feeds" Manager. Note also there is no direct access to this Manager via the "Home Dashboard" Content Panels

| Step 3 | B C | Click on the "News Feeds > Categories" link item, which will open the "News Feeds" Manager. Note there is the default Category of "uncategorized." |

Refer to Figure 29-1 for the following:

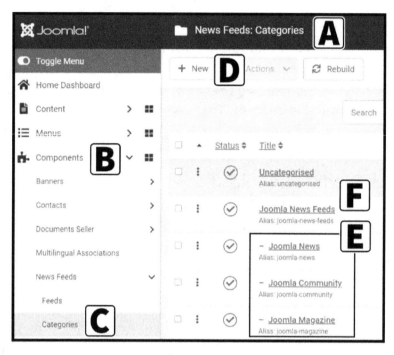

Figure 29-1

Step 4	D	Click the **"+ New"** button at the top of the "News Feeds" Manager screen. This will open the "News Feeds: New Workspace."
Step 5		For the Tag Title, enter: "Joomla News Feeds" (without quotes). This will be the "top level" Category for the three that will be created below.
Step 6		Execute a Save & New Action.
Step 7	D	Click the **"+ New"** button at the top of the "News Feeds" Manager screen. This will open the "News Feeds: New Workspace."
Step 8	E	For the Tag Title, enter: "Joomla News" (without quotes).
Step 9	F	Assign the Category in the right Menu to the "Parent" named "Joomla News Feeds."
Step 10		Execute a Save & New Action.
Step 11	D	Click the **"+ New"** button at the top of the "News Feeds" Manager screen. This will open the "News Feeds: New Workspace."
Step 12	E	For the Tag Title, enter: "Joomla Community" (without quotes).

Step 13	F	Assign the Category in the right Menu to the "Parent" named "Joomla News Feeds."
Step 14		Execute a Save & New Action.
Step 15	D	Click the **"+ New"** button at the top of the "News Feeds" Manager screen. This will open the "News Feeds: New Workspace."
Step 16	E	For the Tag Title, enter: "Joomla Magazine" (without quotes).
Step 17	F	Assign the Category in the right Menu to the "Parent" named "Joomla News Feeds."
Step 18		Execute a Save & Close Action.

The results of the above actions should display a list of four "News Feeds" Categories.

Now that the News Feed Categories have been created, the actual News Feed links from the source website can be added to them.

What's Next?

Before moving forward, please go to the website link below:

https://www.joomla.org/rss-news-feeds.html

The "RSS News Feeds" in the following Categories will be added to their respective Categories created above:

Joomla News	**4 News Feeds**
Joomla Community	**2 News Feeds**
Joomla Magazine	**1 News Feeds**

EXERCISE 29-2: CREATING NEWS FEED ITEMS

Objective: The goal of this Exercise is to create the "RSS News Feed" items from the hosting website and assign them to their respective Categories, replicating how they are configured on the joomla.org website.

Step 1		If not already there, login as the Administrator to access the "Home Dashboard."
Step 2		Open the Components Manager via the left Menu and select the "News Feeds" link to open the "News Feeds" Manager. Note also there is no direct access to this Manager via the "Home Dashboard" Content Panels
Step 3		Open the "News Feeds" Manager using the Menu Link Item in the Components area.

Step 4	Filter the list using the "Filter" feature and within the "Category" selector, select: "Joomla News" as the choice. Four "News Feeds" will be created in this Category.

From this point forward, "News Feed" links will be copied from the Joomla.org website from this link:

https://www.joomla.org/rss.html

Step 5	Click the **"+ New"** button at the top of the "News Feeds" Manager screen. This will open the "News Feeds: New" Workspace. This will automatically place every "News Feed" that is created into the Category that has been selected in the previous "Filter" instructions.
Step 6	Title the feed: "Joomla Announcements" (without quotes).
Step 7	Copy the first "Announcements" link from the Joomla website location above.
Step 8	Paste the link into the "Link" field for the feed item.
Step 9	Execute a Save & New action.
Step 10	Title the feed: "Joomla Announcements" (without quotes).
Step 11	Copy the "Joomla Announcements" link from the Joomla website location above.
Step 12	Paste the link into the "Link" field for the feed item.
Step 13	Execute a Save & New action.
Step 14	Title the feed: "Joomla Security Announcements" (without quotes).
Step 15	Copy the "Joomla Announcements" link from the Joomla website location above.
Step 16	Paste the link into the "Link" field for the feed item.
Step 17	Execute a Save & New action.
Step 18	Title the feed: "Joomla Latest Extensions" (without quotes).
Step 19	Copy the "Joomla Extensions News" link from the Joomla website location above.
Step 20	Paste the link into the "Link" field for the feed item.
Step 21	Execute a Save & New action.
Step 22	Title the feed: "Joomla Documentation Wiki" (without quotes).
Step 23	Copy the "Joomla Documentation Wiki" link from the Joomla website location above.

Step 24	Paste the link into the "Link" field for the feed item.
Step 25	Execute a Save & Close action.

Change the Filter the list using the "Filter" feature and within the "Category" selector, select: "Joomla Community" as the choice. Two "News Feeds" will be created in this Category.

Step 26	Click the **"+ New"** button at the top of the "News Feeds" Manager screen. This will open the "News Feeds: New" Workspace. This will automatically place every "News Feed" that is created into the Category that has been selected in the previous "Filter" instructions.
Step 27	Title the feed: "Joomla Community Blog" (without quotes).
Step 28	Copy the "Community Blog" link from the Joomla website location above.
Step 29	Paste the link into the "Link" field for the feed item.
Step 30	Execute a Save & New action.
Step 31	Title the feed: "Joomla Leadership" (without quotes).
Step 32	Copy the "Leadership Blog" link from the Joomla website location above.
Step 33	Paste the link into the "Link" field for the feed item.
Step 35	Execute a Save & Close action.

Change the Filter the list using the "Filter" feature and within the "Category" selector, select: "Joomla Magazine" as the choice. One "News Feeds" will be created in this Category.

Step 36	Click the **"+ New"** button at the top of the "News Feeds" Manager screen. This will open the "News Feeds: New" Workspace. This will automatically place every "News Feed" that is created into the Category that has been selected in the previous "Filter" instructions.
Step 37	Title the feed: "Joomla Magazine Issues" (without quotes).
Step 38	Copy the "Latest Issue" link from the Joomla website location above.
Step 39	Paste the link into the "Link" field for the feed item.
Step 40	Execute a Save & Close action.

At this point, three "News Feeds" Categories have been created and each have been populated with individual "News Feeds" that are "feedburner" links from the joomla.org website.

What needs to happen now, as with all other website Content, a Menu Link Item is needed to activate the screen display.

Creating News Feed Menu Link Items

The native Joomla! 5 "News Feeds" Component is configured to allow the display of "RSS" "News Feeds" in three ways:

Single News Feed	Selectively displays a single News Feed from an "RSS" source.
List News Feeds in a Category	If "News Feeds" are assigned to multiple Categories, a list of all the "News Feeds" in one Category can be displayed.
List all News Feed Categories	This is used when there are many "News Feed" Categories, they may all be displayed and access to each one can get made via drill-down into the individual Categories.

In the following Exercises, three Menu Link Items will be created. One will open an individual "News Feed," which will be the Joomla! Announcements "RSS News Feed."

The second will create a Menu Link Item that will display a single "RSS" "News Feeds" Category by displaying "ALL" of the "News Feeds" assigned to it.

The third will create a Menu Link Item to show "ALL" of the "News Feeds" Categories, allowing a "drill down" to the "News Feeds" that were created and assigned to the separate Categories.

EXERCISE 29-3: CREATE MENU LINK ITEM TO SINGLE NEWS FEED

Objective: This Exercise is to create a Menu Link Item to a single, individual "RSS News Feed" from the joomla.org website. The feed will be for the Joomla! Announcements.

Step 1		If not already there, login as the Administrator to access the "Home Dashboard."
Step 2		Open the "Menus > Main Menu Blog" Menu.
Step 3		Click the **"+ New"** Button at the top of the screen. This opens a New Menu Link Item screen to create a Menu Link Item in the Main Menu Blog Menu.
Step 4		For the title, enter: "JOOMLA One News Feed" (without quotes).
Step 5		For the Menu Item Type, select: "Newsfeeds > Single News Feed."
Step 6		In the Feed field, select: "Joomla Announcement." This will pull in the "RSS Joomla Announcement" feed that is periodically updated by the organization. The source of the URL for the feed is in the previously created Categories and the Feeds assigned to them.
Step 7		Execute a Save action.

Step 8	Go to the website Front-End and refresh the screen.
Step 9	In the "Main Menu Blog" Menu block, select the "JOOMLA One News Feed." The result should be the display for the most recent Announcements from the hosting (source) website.

On point to note here is that the website Administrator has absolutely no control of what the content of the News Feed consists of. It is simply a re-showing of the same content that is displayed on the hosting (source) website. The content and layout is replicated exactly on the website.

EXERCISE 29-4: CREATE MENU LINK ITEM TO SINGLE NEWS FEED CATEGORY

Objective: A Menu Link Item that will display a single Category of "News Feeds" will be created in the Main Menu Blog Menu.

Step 1	If not already there, login as the Administrator to access the "Home Dashboard."
Step 2	Open the "Menus > Main Menu Blog" Menu.
Step 3	Click the **"+ New"** Button at the top of the screen. This opens a New Menu Link Item screen to create a Menu Link Item in the Main Menu Blog Menu.
Step 4	For the title, enter: "JOOMLA Single Category Feeds" (without quotes).
Step 5	For the Menu Item Type, select: "Newsfeeds in a Category."
Step 6	In the Category field, select: "Joomla Community." This will pull in the "RSS Joomla Community" feed that is periodically updated by the organization. The source of the URL for the feed is in the previously created Categories and the Feeds assigned to them.
Step 7	Open the "List Layouts" tab.
Step 8	For the "Feed Links" change the selection to "Hide" from the "Use Global (show)" setting. This setting can be set to "Hide" in the "News Fields: Options," within the "List Layouts" by setting the "Field Links" to "Hide." The Global setting with then "Hide" all of the field link URLs.
Step 9	Execute a Save action.
Step 10	Go to the website Front-End and refresh the screen.
Step 11	In the "Main Menu Blog" Menu block, select the "JOOMLA One News Feed." The result should be the display for the most recent Announcements from the hosting (source) website.

EXERCISE 29-5: CREATE MENU LINK ITEM TO LIST OF NEWS FEED CATEGORIES

Objective: A Menu Link Item that will display a list of all of the Categories in a "Parent Category." In this case, the "Parent" (or "Top Level"), will be "Joomla News Feeds."

Step 1		If not already there, login as the Administrator to access the "Home Dashboard."
Step 2		Open the "Menus > Main Menu Blog" Menu.
Step 3		Click the **"+ New"** Button at the top of the screen. This opens a New Menu Link Item screen to create a Menu Link Item in the Main Menu Blog Menu.
Step 4		For the title, enter: "JOOMLA News Feeds" (without quotes).
Step 5		For the Menu Item Type, select: "List All News Feed Categories."
Step 6		In the Select a Top Level Category field, select: "Joomla News Feeds." This will display ALL of the Categories that were previously assigned into the "Top Level" or "Parent" Category.
Step 7		Open the "List Layouts" tab.
Step 8		For the "Feed Links" change the selection to "Hide" from the "Use Global (show)" setting.
Step 9		Execute a Save & Close action.
Step 10		Go to the website Front-End and refresh the screen.
Step 11		In the "Main Menu Blog" Menu block, select the "JOOMLA News Feeds." The result should be the display for the three "Child" Categories previous established from the hosting (source) website.

News Feeds Not Permanent

Very often, "News Feeds" "break," that is: they either no longer work, or the screen display isn't working correctly. There is nothing that a website Administrator can do to fix this. It is an issue on the hosting (source) website. Be aware of this should an "RSS" News Feed "break" or fail to display correctly. Feed sources also change and/or modify their feed content, which will also alter the display on your current website.

News Feeds in Modules

In some instances, websites displaying "Newsfeeds" do not want them to appear in the main content area of the screen. Quite often, the feeds are displayed in side panels and are limited to the number of "feed items" they display. On Joomla! 5 websites, this is accomplished using a "Feed Display" Module. The default Joomla! 5 installation has such a Module type available for that use.

The Module is placed into a "Module Position" on the website, connected to certain Menu Link Items for display purposes, and contains a link to a single "News Feed." Additionally, the Module has parameter settings for the display of the feeds, as will be illustrated in the Exercise below.

EXERCISE 29-6: CREATING A NEWS FEED MODULE

Objective: It is the objective of this Exercise to demonstrate how to create and implement the use of the "News Feed" Module on a website.

Step 1	Determine "where" on the website the Module should appear and identify the "Module Position" by name. In this example, "sidebar-right" in the default Template will be used and display only when the "Blog" Menu Link Item in the "Main Menu Blog" is selected.
Step 2	If not already there, login as the Administrator to access the "Home Dashboard."
Step 3	In the "Site" block, click on the **"+"** icon, to access the list of available Modules.
Step 4	Find the "Feed Display" Module and click on "Select," which will open the Module Workspace.
Step 5	For the "Title," enter: "CNN News Feed" (without quotes).
Step 6	For the New Feed, enter the following URL, which is from the CNN cable channel: http://rss.cnn.com/rss/cnn_topstories.rss
Step 7	In the right column, assign the Module to the "Sidebar-right" Module Position.
Step 8	Under the "Menu Assignment" tab, configure the settings to: "Only on the pages selected."
Step 9	Select the "None" option button to clear the list.
Step 10	Select the "Blog" Menu Link Item in the "Main Menu Blog" Menu.
Step 11	Execute a Save action.
Step 12	Go to the website Front-End and refresh the screen.

| Step 13 | | Click on the "Blog" Menu Link Item in the "Main Menu Blog" Menu. |

The resulting display should be a Module at the bottom of the "Sidebar-right" location. View it to confirm. Return to the Back-End and configure the Module settings as follows:

Step 14		Under the "Module" tab, set the "Feed Description" to "Hide."
Step 15		Change the "Word Count" to "20."
Step 16		Execute a Save Action.
Step 17		Go to the website Front-End and refresh the screen.
Step 18		Click on the "Blog" Menu Link Item in the "Main Menu Blog" Menu.

Notice now that the content of the Module has been visually reduced by removing some of the feed content and limiting the number of words display. The full feed may be read my simply clicking on the content text.

Multiple RSS News Feeds

To place multiple "RSS News Feeds" on a website, repeat the above "Feed Module" creation steps and enter the "RSS Feed" desired to be displayed.

The location and Menu Link Item association can be different for each "Feed Module" that is added to the website.

Can Get Crowded

If there are too many "News Feeds" all over the website, the main message of the website can easily get lost among the clutter. Don't overdo "RSS" feeds and use only those that add informational value to the website. "RSS" feeds should not be used as "filler text" just because there is no relevant Content to Publish.

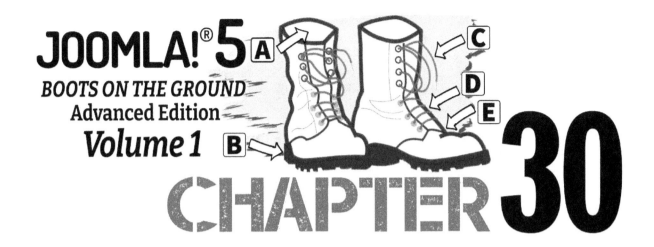

JOOMLA!® 5 Ⓐ
BOOTS ON THE GROUND
Advanced Edition
Volume 1 Ⓑ
CHAPTER 30

COMPONENT:
Smart Search

In previous versions of Joomla!, the "Search" and "Smart Search" features were included as separate Components. In Joomla! 5, only "Smart Search" has been included. The regular "Search" feature was removed in favor of the use of "Smart Search" as the primary Searching Component.

The "Smart Search" Component allows the entire Content of a website to be thoroughly "indexed" for information. Rather than searching through every Content item individually, which can take a long time on every Search, the website is completely "indexed" making any "search actions" quicker.

On an "indexed" website, any searching action performed will be accomplished faster because the "search" looks at the "index" and not each individual Content Item in detail. This speeds things up considerably.

Is a Search Feature Really Needed
On small websites, a search feature probably isn't needed. But on larger, content laden websites, having a search feature that functions to quickly provide results of searches. Smart Search offers a solution towards that goal.

What's Needed for Smart Search

There are several things that are required to operate an effective "Smart Search" feature on a Joomla! 5 website, such as:

Action 1	*Indexed Content* – this can be done any time that more content is added to the website.
Action 2	Create a **Smart Search Module** – this is how website visitors will affect a searching action.
Action 3	*Position the Module* on the webpage – this provides the Administrator discretion on "where" and on "which" pages/screens the Smart Search Module will display.

Creating the Index

Before making a website live, or accessible to visitors, it is suggested that a complete "index" action be performed as outline in the following Exercise.

EXERCISE 30-1: INDEXING THE WEBSITE

Objective: The goal of this Exercise is to demonstrate how to "index" a website.

Step 1	If not already there, login as the Administrator to access the "Home Dashboard."
Step 2	Open "Components > Smart Search > Index," to open the "Smart Search: Indexed Content" list display, which may or may not be empty.
Step 3	If the list is populated, "Select All" Items. This is the tick box to the left of the "Status" column heading.
Step 4	Then, in the top button row, select: "Clear Index." The system will begin clearing all of the previous indexes. When completed, several messages will display to that effect.
Step 5	In the top button row, select "Index" to start a new indexing action. The "Indexer Running" message box will display.

DO NOT DO ANYTHING TO THE SCREENS WHILE THE INDEXER IS RUNNING. DO NOT CLOSE ANY WINDOWS AT THIS POINT UNTIL THE INDEXING IS COMPLETED.

Step 6	When completed, the list will display all of the "indexed" Content Items. Review them for familiarization.
Step 7	If desired, individual Content Items may be "Unpublished" from the Indexed List.

Step 8	To find out the results of the indexing action, and what has been indexed and where within the content, the "Content Maps" feature of the Smart Search Component can be used.

EXERCISE 30-2: VIEWING THE CONTENT MAPS

Objective: This Exercise demonstrates how to access and view the Content Map, which is generated each time an "indexing" action is performed in the "Smart Search" Component.

Step 1	If not already there, login as the Administrator to access the "Home Dashboard."
Step 2	Open "Components > Smart Search > Content Maps," to open the "Smart Search: Content Maps" list display.

What is displayed is every "indexed" item on the website and the number of pieces of "indexed content" that has resulted within each.

Step 3	Click on any of the buttons under the "Published Index Content" column heading to view the items that have been marked by the "indexing" action.

This displays the "items" that have been "indexed" under the key heading that was selected.

Step 4	The only "action" that can be implemented on the individual item shown is to "Unpublish" it.

Smart Search Options

As with most all other Joomla! 5 Components and other settings, the "Smart Search" Component also has "Options" which can be configured to provide certain expected results. By now, you should have noticed a "pattern" with Joomla! 5 Components and other features. They have both direct control configuration settings AND the "Options," which generally apply globally to all the Content within it.

It is a good idea, always, to check, review and configure the "Options" for any Component or Content Area to ensure that when created, the Content displays according to plan.

For the "Smart Search" Component, here are the "Options" that can be applied:

Note here that you must open at least one part of the Component to make the "Options" button visible on the screen.

There are three "Options" for the "Smart Search" Component:

Smart Search	The settings under the "Smart Search" tab is used to configure certain User Options with regard to the actual process of search for indexed Content.

Index	This is where the settings and configuration of the actual "indexing" action and results can be set.
Permissions	This is where User Groups may be granted "Permissions" to perform certain actions within the Component.

It is suggested that all of the 'Options" setting remain set at the "default" level unless there is a compelling reason to alter them. The need to change the configuration settings may become apparent over time, at which point, changes can be applied and evaluated for effectiveness.

Getting Smart Search Statistics

When an "indexing" action is completed, all of the Content Items have been scanned and added to their respective Content definitions, re: Article, Category, etc.

To find out the exact "count" of "indexed" items following an "indexing" action, the "Statistics" button at the top of the screen will open a display window with that information.

A summary of the total items and lines with the attributes in the branches is defined. Along with that information, the actual breakdown of the "Count" is displayed.

Content Mapping & Results

After "indexing," the result is "Content Mapping" where the information is presented about each "Mapping Group" that is involved. Once that information is displayed, the Administrator can "drill-down" to find specific items that are within which "Map Group" following the "indexing" action, as follows, which are the "Content Map Groups:"

This particular "Filtering" action applies when the "Smart Search Index" is selected within the Component.

In addition to the "Content Map Groups," the same information can be accessed by the actual "Type of Content," based on the standard Content on the website, such as:

Article	Shows a list of all indexed Articles.
Category	Shows a list of all indexed Categories.
Contact	Lists all Contacts found during the indexing action.
News Feed	All News Feeds on the website are listed.
Tag	If "Tags" are used, the listing of them will be displayed.

Within the "Content Map," the actual detailed items resulting from the "indexing" action can be individually or further connected to the "Type of" Filter above. In the "Filter" dropdown, this information is displayed in a "tree format," showing all of the indexed items under the "Map Group."

Author	Lists every Author of Content on the website.
Category	Provides a list of every Category on the website.
Country	Displays the list of applicable Countries for Content.
Language	Indicates the Languages indexed by Content.
Region	If "Regions" are used anywhere in the website, they will be displayed here; generally from within the Contact Manager entries, but not limited to only that type of Content.
Type	This refers back to the Filters above, which does not work in combination when this "Content Map" item is selected.

The only alteration that can be performed on any of the Content Type items is to either "Publish" or "Unpublish" it.

Filters Used in Combination

If some advanced work needs to be performed on the "Content Map," the filters may be used in combination. The "Type of Content" can be matched with the "Content Map" elements.

For example, "Articles" can be displayed when parsed against the "Content Map" option choice of a specific Author. Of course, any combination may be applied based on specific needs to make determinations on classifications.

This combination filtering is especially handy if the Administrator wants to find out which "Articles" and within which "Category" from an "indexed" viewpoint. Yes, the same information can be obtained through filtering of the "Articles" Content List. But, that result will not show whether a certain Content Item has been "indexed" or not.

Preset Filters for Searching

Within the "Smart Search" Component is the ability to preset the "Filters" that might be frequently used to determine "indexing" results.

When creating a "Filter," the choices are to select by: Type, or Author, or Category, or Region or Country in any combination. Multiple different "Filters" can be created based on specific selection of the available "index" Content on the website.

If this information is needed frequently, the Administrator should create as many "Filters" as needed to facilitate the Back-End searching actions.

Under the "Options" tab, more filtering parameters may be set relative to the "dating" settings for the actual "Publishing" of the Content Items, and then the valid term of the 'Filter Timeline."

Use the Help Screens

If there are confusing items within the "Filter" creation process, use the "Help" screens for more information.

Front-End Smart Search

To make the website "searchable" via the Front-End, it is necessary to create a Menu Link Item that connects to the "Smart Search" Component.

The choice for using the "Smart Search" Component is limited to only on selectable type, that is: "Search." This places a pre-configured searching Module display into the main Content Area of the website.

EXERCISE 30-3: CREATING A SEARCH MENU LINK ITEM

Objective: This Exercise demonstrates the method by which a Menu Link Item is created to "Search" the website.

Step 1	If not already there, login as the Administrator to access the "Home Dashboard."
Step 2	Open the "Menus" and then the "My Search Module."
Step 3	Click the **"+New"** button at the top of the screen.
Step 4	In the "Menu Title" field, enter: "Search Component Link" (without quotes).
Step 5	For the "Menu item Type," select: "Smart Search," then "Search."

No other settings need to be changed. The default settings are sufficient for the operation of the general "Search" function, but can be modified as needed for more complex searching operations.

Step 7	Execute a Save & Close action.
Step 8	Go to the website Front-End and refresh the screen.
Step 9	In the "My Search Module," select the "Search Component Link."
Step 10	At this point, any search term may be entered. Experiment with a couple of terms and view the results.
Step 11	Click on the "Advanced Search" choice within the searching area.
Step 12	There are instructions on how to enter search terms, which are word combination filtering actions.
Step 13	There are also "Type" search options displayed as drop-down filters. These correspond to the Filters on the Component in the Back-End.
Step 14	When using the "Type" filtering choice, you MUST ALSO enter a "Search

Step 15	Term."
Step 16	The details results are displayed in the Main Content Area.

Another Way to Search

The above Exercise discussed accessing the "Smart Search" feature through the use of a Menu Link Item, assigned within an existing Menu. This is an easy way of doing it which displays the search screen within the Main Content Area of the website.

There is another way to activate a "Smart Search" feature and that is by way of placing a "Smart Search Module" into a "Module Position" on the active Template being used. Joomla! 5 has a default "Smart Search" Module available for that function.

Here is how this task's action is accomplished:

EXERCISE 30-4: CREATING A SMART SEARCH MODULE

Objective: This Exercise demonstrates how to create a "Smart Search" Module and assigned it to a "Module Position" on the Template(s) in use.

Step 1	If not already there, login as the Administrator to access the "Home Dashboard."
Step 2	In the "Site Panel > Modules," click on the "**+**" button to create a new Module.
Step 3	Scroll down and "Select" the "Smart Search" Module. That action will open the Module's Workspace.
Step 4	For the Module "Title," enter: "Smart Search Module" (without quotes).
Step 5	Assign the Module to "Position" of "main-top."
Step 7	No other default settings need be changed.
Step 8	Execute a Save & Close action.
Step 9	Go to the website "Front-End" and refresh the screen.
Step 10	The "Smart Search" Module should appear in the Main Content Area.
Step 11	In the search box, enter: "Books" (without quotes).
Step 12	The result should be the display of three Articles, assuming that all of the previous Exercises in this book have been completed to create the content.

Smart Search Extensions

At present, the Joomla! Extensions Directory ("JED") has a number of customizable search Modules available, but only for Version 3. However, it is reasonable to assume that these same, or similar, Modules will be available to operate on the new Joomla! 5 version.

When researching these Extensions or Modules, make absolutely sure they are Joomla! 5 compatible.

Use the Smart Search Wisely

Let's face it, not every Joomla! 5 website needs a searching feature. Simple, topical or small business websites typically do not have sufficient content to require User searches.

Make the decision on the "need" for a Smart Search feature implementation based on the volume and depth of the Content and an analysis of whether it is actually needed on the website.

JOOMLA!® 5 Ⓐ
BOOTS ON THE GROUND
Advanced Edition
Volume 1 Ⓑ
CHAPTER **31**

COMPONENT:
Tags

One of the features of Joomla! 5 is the "Tags Component," which offers website Administrators the opportunity to classify Content using a method that is separate from both the Category and Fields features.

As a refresh, just about every type of Content must be assigned to a Category, within some sort of categorization hierarchy. Fields and Field Groups may also be used for certain types of categorization.

"Tagging" breaks away from the formal method of categorization by allowing Content Items to be "tagged" with one or more words, which may then be used to search for, retrieve and display the Content, based on the "tag" word(s).

One thing about "Tags" is that it allows the creating of a display of Content Items which all have the common "Tag" that is requested with a Menu Link Item. These can be from any and all Categories. But remember, "Tags" are distinctly separated from Categories. Please do not confuse "Categories" with "Tags."

The best way to think about "Tags" is that they are a "comparative indexing" system rather than a "classification" or "categorization" process.

As the website Administrator, you can think of Categories as being somewhat linear in nature – they have shape and structure and must be ordered in a certain way. "Tags," on the other hand, allow a different way of grouping common Content Items based on a freeform or *"ad hoc"* naming relationship.

The bottom line for tags is that they allow Content to be organized and allow website visitors to find information with the commonality of a "Tag" word. Searching for the "Tag" results in a display of all the Content that shares the same "Tag" word.

If you recall the rule that a Content Item [Articles], may be assigned to only one Category. The "Tags" do just the opposite in that the Content Items that may use the same "Tag" word is unlimited across the entire Content hierarchy.

So, in short, "Tags" are nothing more than a label that is attached to a Content Item for the purpose of "indexing" them by common terms or terminology.

Understanding the "Tags" Component

This Component allows the website Administrator and Content Authors to add "Tag" information to their Content.

Through use of "Tags," the Content Items may be "tagged" with one or more words which then allow them to be searched for, and retrieved, based on the "tag word." Thus, the Content similarly "tagged" can then be displayed, regardless of their primary Category assignments.

Do not misunderstand, "Tagging" is not a substitute for good Content hierarchy management through Categories. The conventional methods allow more paths to access and presentation of different layouts of Content Items. The "Tagging" process, while it does retrieve via second assignment methods, is strictly limited to one resulting display. "Tagging" is best use to connect the commonality of "Content Subjects" within Content Items, for access via the "Tag Search" actions.

Category assignment can be thought of in a linear nature, whereby Categories are either "Parents" or "Child of Parents" or "Children of Children," and so on. However, "Tags" when assigned to Content Items actually pull the Content together in a parallel nature, gathering it from multiple Category hierarchies through the use of single "Tag Search" terms.

Sample Data Included "Tags"

Initially, when the "Sample Data" was installed as instructed in Chapter 7, "Fast Track Double Time Start," Categories and Articles assigned therein were added to the website.

Included within this Content creation were four pre-configured "Tags" as follows: *"Millions, Worldwide, Love, Joomla 4."* When Articles with the assigned "Tags" are viewed, the "Tag" name buttons will appear below the "Sample Data" Articles when viewed on the Front-End.

How are "Tags" Created

Website "Tags" are created within the "Tags Manager" which is accessed via the "Home Dashboard > Components Menu > Tags" link. "Tags" only require a name and, optionally, a description.

Tags may have "Child Tags" in a fashion similar to standard Categories.

Modules Cannot Be Tagged

Only Content Items that can be assigned to "Categories" can be "Tagged." Knowing this, and knowing that Modules are not assigned to any hierarchy, common logic will tell you that Modules cannot be assigned "Tags" of any type. Keep this in mind when creating the "Tagging" structure for a website.

Tagging Requirements

To effectively use "Tags" on a Joomla! 5 website, there are several basic requirements to keep in mind, as follows:

Requirement 1	The "Tags" must exist. "Tags" cannot be assigned to Content unless the "Tag" is already in existence. Thus, a pre-determination of the "Tags" to be applied should be made and entered into the "Tag Library" in the Back-End. When typed into the "Tag" field in a Content Item, the text is a "search trigger," and is automatically saved within the "Tags List" when the **[Enter]** action is executed after the "Tag" is added.
Requirement 2	Content must also exist. These are typically Articles. However, Categories, News Feeds, and Contacts are also candidates for the addition of "Tags" to them. For the most part, if there is any kind of a Content Item, it can be tagged from the "Tag Library." A special field exists on the Content Items Workspace to select and add a "Tag(s)." The "Tag" is made a feature when the **[Enter]** action is executed.
Requirement 3	Similarly tagged Content Items must have some sort of logical relationship with each either. An example is cats and dogs both being animals. Thus, a standard Category of "Animals" could have many Articles that are tagged "cat" or "dog," or both "cat and dog." Thus, the Category is "animals," and the "Tags" are the type of animals within the Category.
Requirement 4	Content Items should be tagged upon their creation, but they may be tagged at any time thereafter. Anytime a new, not previously existing, "Tag" is available and logical to assign, it can be done, but only if the new "Tag" has been created within the "Tag" Library.

Best Practices for Tags

When used properly, "Tags" can be a valuable asset to any website that has an abundance of Content, especially when the Content is interrelated.

When used incorrectly, "Tags" can interfere with Content access and create confusion when too many "Tags" are used in too many pieces of Content.

Here are some define Rules for "tagging" Content Items:

Rule 1	Never use "Tags" as a substitute for assigning Content into Categories. Yes, "Tags" can be used to separate Content that is in one Category, but it is not the best way to keep it formally organized such as can be accomplished via a Category hierarchy.
Rule 2	Plan the use of "Tags" when you plan Content. Determine if "Tags" even fit into the Content needs of the website. If they are not needed, simply don't use them.
Rule 3	Don't "over-tag" Content. Having too many "Tags" assigned to Items, while it might serve some complex cross-navigation needs, they may not serve the purpose of the website. An analogy of eggs might apply here. If you only need one egg, don't scramble all of them.
Rule 4	Make sure the "Tags" are descriptive enough to accurately define the "tag" purpose. Limit the number of words for a "Tag" to the least possible to fit the need. One word is best, two are allowed, but more than that can create a complexity that might not be desired.

How to Implement Tagging

By way of review, Content structure consists of Categories, Items and then a Menu Link Item. This Chapter is focused on using Articles for "tagging" examples.

Articles may be accessed in five ways:

1. Directly from a Menu Link Item.
2. From a Category List.
3. From a List of Categories with a drill down.
4. As a "Featured" Article.
5. From a "Tag," wherever the Tag Name is displayed.

To use "Tags" effectively on a Joomla! 5 website, there are several requirements:

Requirement 1	The "Tags" must exist, either by manual creation in the "Tags Component," or added/created within a Content Item, which will also add the "Tag" to the main listing when added.
Requirement 2	Some sort of Content must also exist. For the purposes of this Chapter, Articles will be assumed, but News Feeds, Categories and

		Contacts can also be "tagging" candidates. For the most part, if it is a Content Item of any type, it can be "tagged."
Requirement 3		The Content Items should have some sort of logical relationship to each other. For example, cats and dogs are both animals. So, a category of Animals could have many Articles that may be "tagged" either as "cat, dog" or both.
Requirement 4		The individual Content Items need to be "tagged" either at the time they are created, or any time thereafter. Once a Content Item has a "Tag" assigned to it, it automatically becomes accessible via the "tag" links that are displayed in the Content Items.

Once all that is accomplished, the "Tags' can reference a Content Item or provide a method of accessing Content Items via Menu Link Item, or the "Tag" link within a Content Item Itself.

An example of this, assuming that ten Articles have the same "Tag," is that when one Article is accessed, clicking on the "Tag" within the Article, will display the remaining nine Articles together with the first. This is a perfect example of "indexing" the Articles by using a common, or same, "Tag" to do so.

Creating Tags

There are essentially two ways to create "Tags" in Content Items, and the Exercises below demonstrate these methods. Remember, the Content Item [Articles in these examples], should and must be assigned to their respective Category or separate Categories.

EXERCISE 31-1: CREATING TAGS IN THE COMPONENT

Objective: This Exercise demonstrates how to create "Tags" by way of the "Tags" Component itself. This involves creating a list of "Tags" one after another, making them available to Content Items.

Step 1		If not already there, login as the Administrator to access the "Home Dashboard."
Step 2	**A**	Open the Components Manager via the left Menu and select the "Tags" link to open the Tags Manager. Note also there is no direct access to this Manager via the "Home Dashboard" Content Panels.
Step 3	**B** **C**	Click on the "Tags" link item, which will open the "Tags Manager."
Step 4	**D**	Click the **"+ New"** button at the top of the "Tags Manager" screen. This will open the "Tags: New" Workspace.
Step 5		For the Tag Title, enter: "Planes" (without quotes).

Step 6	A "Description" may be entered, but it is not necessary unless a definition is needed for clarity.
Step 7	Execute a Save action.
Step 8	Open the "Options" tab and review the contents.
Step 9	Open the "Permissions" tab and review the contents.
Step 10	In the right column, the default settings need not be changed, but check to make sure the "Status" is set to "Published."
Step 11	Execute a Save & New action.
Step 12	For the Tag Title, enter: "Trains" (without quotes).
Step 13	A "Description" may be entered, but it is not necessary unless a definition is needed for clarity.
Step 14	In the right column, the default settings need not be changed, but check to make sure the "Status" is set to "Published."
Step 15	Execute a Save & New action.
Step 16	For the Tag Title, enter: "Autos" (without quotes). Note here that the short form of the term "Automobiles" is being used for brevity.
Step 17	A "Description" may be entered, but it is not necessary unless a definition is needed for clarity.
Step 18	In the right column, the default settings need not be changed, but check to make sure the "Status" is set to "Published."
Step 19	Execute a Save & Close action.

Refer to Figure 31-1 for reference:

	A	Components link.
	B	"Tags" link.
	C	"Tags Workspace" identifier.
	D	Creates a "New Tag."
	E	The "Title" field lists the results of the "Tags" created above.

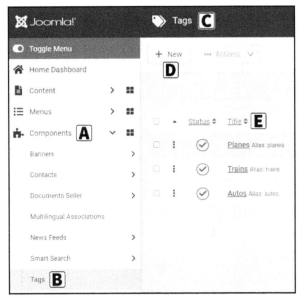

Figure 31-1

The "Tags:" Planes, Trains, Autos have now been created and are automatically available to be used with Content Items.

There is a second way of creating "Tags" for Content Items that is separate, but integrated with, the method described above. The above illustrated the method of creating the "Tags" via a central manager.

The alternative method is to create "Tags" within each, or any individual, Content Item, as follows:

EXERCISE 31-2: CREATING TAGS IN THE CONTENT ITEM

Objective: This Exercise demonstrates how to create "Tags" within a Content Item [Article], which then become part of the Component's list of "Tags" available for use with other Content Items. Although the Article example is being used, the "Tags" function may only be used within these Content Items:

- Featured Articles
- Articles
- Article Categories
- Banner Categories
- Contacts
- Contact Categories
- News Feeds
- News Feed Categories

Step 1		If not already there, login as the Administrator to access the "Home Dashboard."
Step 2	A	Open the Content Manager via the left Menu and select the "Articles" link to open the Article Manager.

Refer to Figure 31-2 for the following:

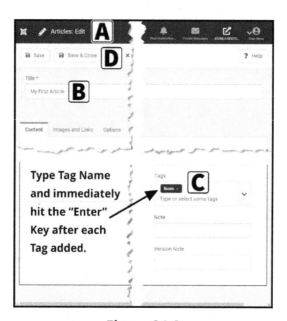

Figure 31-2

Step 3	B	Find the "My First Article" and open it.
Step 4	C	In the right column, put the mouse cursor into the "Tags" field.
Step 5		Enter: "Boats" (without the quotes). *Execute an "Enter" action immediately before doing anything else.* This locks in the "Tag" name and adds it to the "List of Tags" in the "Tags" Component.
Step 6	D	Execute a Save & Close action.

Refer to Figure 31-3 for the following:

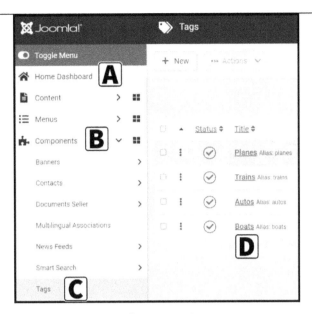

Figure 31-3

Step 7	A B C D	Open the "Components" menu and select "Tags." The list of "Tags" will now display showing that "Boats" has been added to the list.
Step 8		Go to the Front-End, "Home" screen.
Step 9		Scroll down to "My First Article," and notice the "Tag" button for "Boats" is visible and located "above" the Article Content, right below the "Details" info block.
Step 10		Open the Article itself and notice the "Tag" is also visible between the Article Details and the Article Content.

"Tags" are displayed as part of the "Details" Block on the Article.

The location is set either on a "Global Options" basis or on an individual Content Item "Options," if control his handed off to the Content Item in the Menu Link Item. This is accomplished as follows:

Step 11		Go to "Content > Articles" and open the "Options" settings.
Step 12		Under the "Articles" tab, check the "Position of Article Info" setting, which should be set to "Above." This means that ALL "Details" and "Tags" within Articles only, will be displayed "Above" the Article Content/Text. This is the default or controlling setting.
Step 13		Determine which Menu Link Item will open the Article that will have the location of the "Details, Tags" repositioned from "Above" to "Below." In this case, the Menu Link Item is "Home."

Step 14	Go to "Menus > Main Menu > Home" and open the Article. This will open "Home" Menu Link Item, which also controls the "Featured Articles," setting, which is a "Blog Layout."
Step 15	Open the "Options" tab.
Step 16	Locate the "Position of Article Info."
Step 17	Change the selection to "Use Article Settings." This invokes an override of the "Global Options" for Articles and hands off the control of Blog/Featured Layouts to the "Article" itself. Thus creating the ability of override the "Global Settings."
Step 18	Execute a Save & Close action.
Step 19	Go to "Content > Articles" [or "Featured Articles"] and open "My First Article."
Step 20	Under the "Options" tab, locate the "Position of Article Info" selector.
Step 21	Change the setting to "Below," which will then override the "Above" which is the "Global Setting."
Step 22	Execute a Save & Close Action.
Step 23	Go to the website Front-End and refresh the screen.
Step 24	"My First Article" is a "Featured Article" and will display on the List of Articles. Find it on the list.
Step 25	Note now that the "Article Details" and the "Boats Tag" is now below the Article Content/Text. All other Articles have this information "Above" the Article Content/Text.

The above actions have created an issue? What is it?

Because this is a "Featured" Article and the setting was handed off to the "Article Settings" under the conditions that the Article was part of a Blog Configuration, if the Article is opened, the Article Info still remains "Above" rather than "Below."

The Article is actually connected directly to another Menu Link Item, "My Article Link." Because this is NOT a Blog Layout, the "Global Options" continue to control the display.

To resolve that problem, do the following:

Step 26	Go to "Menus > Main Menu > My Article" Link and open the item.
Step 27	Open the "Options" tab.
Step 28	Find the "Position of Article Info" and change the setting to "Below."

Step 29	Execute a Save & Close action.
Step 30	Go to the website Front-End.
Step 31	Open the "My Article Link" to access the Article.
Step 32	Note the "Article Info" is now "Below" the Article Content/Text, which is consistent with the settings changed in the earlier steps.

This dilemma only happens IF an Article has both a direct Menu Link Item to open it, and the Article is also set as a "Featured Article," which is a "Blog" style layout. Make a note of that issue.

If the Article is ONLY opened as part of a non-Blog style layout, the setting is controlled by the Menu Link Item that opens it. There is no "Article Settings" to be applied for a direct menu link to open the "Article," as would be needed if it was part of a "Blog" style layout.

In any case, individual Articles can have the Article Details/Tags configured to display "Above" or "Below" the Article Content/Text through: A) Global Settings, B) Menu Link Item overrides, or C) via a Menu Link Item override handoff to Article setting control, but only IF it is part of a "Blog" layout.

Using the "Split" Selection

The "Split" option breaks the Article Details into two groups. When that option is selected and ALL of the Details have been selected, they are broken, or "split" as follows:

These remain "Above" the Content/ Text of the Article:

- Author
- Parent Category
- Show Category
- Show Associations
- Show Publish Date

When the "Split" is selected, the following automatically "break" to appear "Below" the Content/Text of the Article:

- Created Date
- Modified Date
- Hits
- Tags

Of course, if any one of the Article Details should not appear, regardless of location, simply unselect or "Hide" the item within the Article's "Options" tab in the individual Article Workspace.

The Article Details may also be controlled under the "Global Options" settings under the "Articles" tab.

Tips About Article Details

First, if you are the only Administrator and create all of the Articles and other content, having Article Details showing on every Article isn't a good idea.

If others create Articles and it is necessary to identify them as such, then the Article Details can be useful.

All of the line items that display, or can display, as Article Details have "Global Options" that toggle them on/off.

Chapter 11, "CONTENT: Category & Article Options" discussed all of the "Option" settings in depth.

The configuration settings are accessed via "Content > Articles > Options" under the "Articles" Tab. Simply toggle On/Off those Article Details which are to be displayed Above or Below the Article Content/Text.

For demonstration purposes, the defaults settings for the Article Details are used, which displays a few of the items.

Adding Existing Tags to Articles

At this point, there are four "Tags" that have been created. Three were created manually within the "Tags Component." One was created directly in an Article, which automatically added it to the list of "Tags." These "Tags" are: "Planes, Trains, Autos & Boats."

Now that a list of "Tags" exists, they should be added to Articles so they can be used as an "index" of commonality between them. After all, that is the basic purpose of using "Tags" to begin with. They provide a method of topically "indexing" Articles from any Category into which they are assigned.

In a previous Exercise, a number of "Read More" demonstration Articles were created. In the following Exercise, "Tags" will be assigned to these Articles.

EXERCISE 31-3: ASSIGNING TAGS TO ARTICLES

Objective: The goal of this Exercise is to demonstrate how to assign existing "Tags" to Articles and then use them to create an "index" of Articles that have common "Tag" identification.

The "Read More" series of Articles will be used in the Exercise.

Step 1	Open the Article Manager in "Content >Articles."

Step 2		In the search box, enter (without quotes): "Read More." The results should be a list of ten Articles.
Step 3		Click on the "Title" table heading which will sort the list from lowest to highest.

Refer to Figure 31-4 for the following:

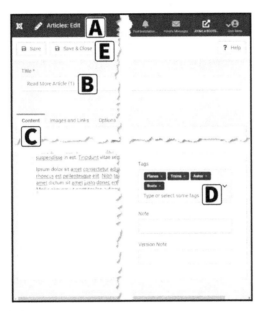

Figure 31-4

The following steps should be repeated for each of the ten "Read More" Articles according to the table that follows the first set of actions.

Step 4	A B	Open the "Read More Article (1)."
Step 5	C	In the right column, scroll down to the "Tags" selection box under the "Content" tab.
Step 6	D	Enter (without quotes) the following: "Planes" (without quotes), *followed immediately with an "Enter" action.*
Step 7	D	Enter (without quotes) the following: "Trains" (without quotes), *followed immediately with an "Enter" action.*
Step 8	D	Enter (without quotes) the following: "Autos" (without quotes), *followed immediately with an "Enter" action.*
Step 9	D	Enter (without quotes) the following: "Boats" (without quotes), *followed immediately with an "Enter" action.*
Step 10	E	Execute a Save & Close action.

Before proceeding, go to the website Front-End and in the "My New Menu Module," click on the "Link to a Category Blog." This will open all of the "Read More" Articles.

Step 11	View the Articles and notice that the four "Tags" now display in the "Read More Article (1)."
Step 12	Click on the "Boats" Tag. Two Articles should display, one having previous "tagged" with "Boats" using the Article to create the "Tag."

Next, following the same steps as outlined above, for the remaining nine "Read More" Articles, open the individual Articles and add the "Tags" as per this schedule:

Article	Planes	Trains	Autos	Boats
Read More (1)	PLANES	TRAINS	AUTOS	BOATS
Read More (2)	PLANES	NO	NO	BOATS
Read More (3)	NO	TRAINS	NO	BOATS
Read More (4)	PLANES	NO	AUTOS	BOATS
Read More (5)	PLANES	TRAINS	AUTOS	NO
Read More (6)	NO	NO	AUTOS	BOATS
Read More (7)	PLANES	TRAINS	NO	NO
Read More (8)	PLANES	NO	NO	NO
Read More (9)	NO	NO	NO	BOATS
Read More (10)	NO	TRAINS	NO	NO

Go to the website Front-End and refresh the browser window.

Each of the Articles now have "Tags" assigned to them as an "index" based on the tag word. Click on some of the "Tag" buttons and view the results. Notice how the Articles are now displayed and sorted by their "Tag" values, yet they are in the same Category, except for the one Article with the "Boats" tag.

Displaying a List of Tags
Now that "Tags" have been created and Articles have been "tagged," a Menu Link Item is needed that will display a list of the "Tags."

EXERCISE 31-4: CREATING LINK TO TAG LIST

Objective: This Exercise will demonstrate how a Menu Link Item can be created to display a "List of Tags."

Step 1	If not already there, login as the Administrator to access the "Home Dashboard."
Step 2	Open the Menus Manager via the left Menu and select the "My New Menu Module" and open it.
Step 3	Click the **"+ New"** button at the top of the "Menus" Manager screen. This will open the "Menus: New" Workspace.
Step 4	For the Menu Title, enter: "Link to Tag List" (without quotes).
Step 5	For Menu Item Type, select: "Tags > List All Tags."
Step 6	No other changes are needed, the default settings are adequate.
Step 7	Execute a Save & Close action.
Step 8	Go to the website Front-End and refresh the screen.
Step 9	In the "My New Menu Module," click on the "Link to Tag List" Menu Link Item.

The screen should now display a list of the names of the "Tags" that have been created.

Click on the "Tag" names and view the results, which should be consistent with those from previous "Tag" views.

Options to Display Tagged Items

The above explained how to create a "Link to Tagged List," which displayed a complete list of all Articles that have been "Tagged."

There are two other Menu Link Items that can be created that display "Tagged" items:

List of Tagged Items	This Menu Link Item displays a list of all of the Content Items that have been "Tagged," and may be inclusive of one to any number of identified "Tags," along with the "what" type of Content Item should be displayed.
Compact List of Tagged Items	Same as above, except the actual display is smaller visually and more compact.

In application, a "List of Tags" can be created for display, along with a choice of two formats for a "List of Tagged Items" that have been configured. The latter allows for the "Tag" names to be included, or excluded, as desired.

Modules for Tag Displays

Additionally, there are two default "Modules" that can be used relative to "Tagged" items. The following describes the function of the Modules:

Tags – Popular	This Modules displays tagged items by their number and can be limited to display those within a certain time period, re: "Last Day" or "Last Week" and other selections. There are several other settings that fine tune the display.
Tags – Similar	The display of "Tags" that are similar to others can be displayed using this Module. The relationship of the "matches" can be configured based on their actual naming.

Extensions to Control Tag Displays

Because of the powerful features and possible use on websites that have large amounts of Content, "Tags" can be used extensively as a way to "index" the Articles. And, because of this, Developers have created and made available a number of Extensions that allow for various displays and uses of the "Tag" system.

Explore them on the Joomla Extensions Directory ("JED") and check if any apply or can be beneficially used on the website your administer.

Reminder - No Substitute for Categories

Don't be tempted! "Tags" are very useful and good to use. But don't use "Tags" as an alternative to good Category structuring of website Content. The best practice is to use both – use Categories to formally organize Content, and use "Tags" to make Content further accessible as if it were assigned to multiple topic-based Categories.

APPENDIX A

The following are the Chapter Titles for *Joomla! 5: Boots on the Ground, Advance Edition, Volume 2:* Some titles may change based on Joomla! 5 modifications.

Chapter 32	ADMIN: Workflows
Chapter 33	CONTENT: Using Form Extensions
Chapter 34	FONTS: Adding & Using Custom Fonts
Chapter 35	ADMIN: Backing-Up a Joomla! 5 Website
Chapter 36	UPDATING: Prior Versions to Joomla! 5
Chapter 37	ADMIN: Custom Fields
Chapter 38	INSTALLING: Using cPanel Server
Chapter 39	INSTALLING: Using the Plesk Server
Chapter 40	INSTALLING: Relocating a Joomla! 5 Instance
Chapter 41	ADMIN: Joomla! 5 Private Messaging Feature
Chapter 42	ADMIN: GDPR & Cookie Topics
Chapter 43	CONTENT: Global Options & Settings
Chapter 44	VISUAL: Custom & Alternative Layouts
Chapter 45	ADMIN: Using "CSS" Classes
Chapter 46	ADMIN: Joomla! 5 Third-Party Frameworks
Chapter 47	ADMIN: Library of Overrides
Chapter 48	SEO: MetaData Guidelines
Chapter 49	SEO: Search Engine Optimization
Chapter 50	VISUAL: Editing & Customizing Email Templates
Chapter 51	ADMIN: Multifactor Authentication Methods
Chapter 52	To be determined.
Chapter 53	VISUAL: Using Page/Screen Footers
Chapter 54	VISUAL: Using Mega Menu Extensions
Chapter 55	VISUAL: Cheat Sheets for "CSS"
Chapter 56	VISUAL: Using Bootstrap 5 Elements
Chapter 57	VISUAL: Hosting Video & Music Files
Chapter 58	VISUAL: Displaying YouTube Videos
Chapter 59	INTERACTION: Connecting to Facebook
Chapter 60	CONTENT: Using Forms to Create Articles